Best Wishes
Jeremy
from
Duncan Pierce
February 1992

Who's Who of
Welsh International Rugby Players

Who's Who of
Welsh International Rugby Players

John M Jenkins, Duncan Pierce, Timothy Auty

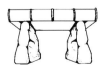

Bridge Books, Wrexham, Clwyd

First published in Great Britain by
BRIDGE BOOKS
61 Park Avenue
Wrexham, Clwyd
LL12 7AW

I Non, Hannah a Sam - J M J
To my family - T A

British Library Cataloguing in Publication Data

Jenkins, John M
Who's who of Welsh international rugby players
I. Title II. Pierce, Duncan
III. Auty, Timothy
796.3330922

ISBN 1 872424 10 4

Printed and bound in Wales by
WBC Ltd
Bridgend

CONTENTS

Some years ago, the internationally famous Welsh author and wit, Gwyn Thomas, claimed that Welsh Rugby Internationals like Gareth Edwards, Barry John, J.P.R., Mervyn and Gerald Davies, marched in spirit alongside the great Celtic Heroes of the past who, it is believed, tried to remove the iron dentures from the mouth of Edward the first in the 13th Century!

He also told of a man in Llanelli who claimed he had cured his shingles by touching the boot of Phil Bennett when that boot was charged with miracles after he had kicked five goals against England!

Having been weaned on catalogues of famous rugby names and wondered at their deeds and having lusted after a rugby ball at a tender age, it came as a shock to me - like being smacked in the face by a wet towel - when I discovered that a current Welsh International did not know the significance of the Gwyn Nicholls Memorial Gate that guards the main entrance to Cardiff Arms Park and that a current England three-quarter had never heard the name Jeff Butterfield.

It became frighteningly clear to me that my generation has been negligent. We have not taken the trouble to tell tales and to hand down the stories and deeds of our rugby folk heroes. Shame on us! It is by telling tales and breathing fire and recording for posterity that makes a Nation a proud one and offers hope to future generations.

We have an obligation to be informed and this volume, listing the names of men who have won the right to wear the distinctive and instantly recognisable red jerseys of Wales on the rugby field, does exactly that.

It is an honours board worthy of our Nation.

INTRODUCTION

On 19 February 1881, James Bevan, born in Australia, captained Wales in their first international. On 2 March 1991, Paul Thorburn, born in Rheindalen, Germany, captained Wales in their four hundredth match - coincidentally, both were educated at Hereford Cathedral School. In the one hundred and ten years that have passed between those two dates, Wales has fielded eight hundred and ninety two players.

In 1888, the first ever tour by a British Isles team visited Australia and New Zealand, followed by a similar tour to South Africa in 1891. To date, one hundred and fifteen Welsh internationals have worn the British Isles jersey in international games in these three countries, a figure which does not take account of those Welsh players who went on the tours but only appeared in the non-international matches.

Tracing details of so many individuals has not been an easy task, especially when one considers the relative shortage of surnames in Wales. A survey of the more common names in this Who's Who clearly illustrates the problem - Jones (60), Davies (53), Evans (43), Williams (43), Thomas (31), Morgan (21). This difficulty has been overcome in most instances but, occasionally, particularly with the very early players, it has not been possible to identify their birth from those of so many others with the same name.

During the Second World War, no caps were awarded for a series of unofficial matches which were played against the Red Cross in 1939-40, the Services from 1941-42 to 1944-45 and the Victory matches in 1945-46.

The split of rugby into Union and League came about because of a demand for payment for working time lost by playing and the first Rugby League (or Northern Union as it was originally known) season started on 7 September 1895. Since that date, one hundred and fifty six Welsh international players have 'gone North' - 17% of the total.

This book chronicles, in alphabetical order, all the players who have represented Wales. Naturally, a number of the entries contain less information than others. This has proved unavoidable owing to a paucity of sources in certain areas.

The entries are arranged as follows:
Surname, christian names.
Place and date of birth, place and date of death (or place birth or death was registered).
Career: listing the educational establishments attended, and the clubs played for.
Position of the player, and the number of appearances, listing the opposing countries and the year when played against. A record of points scored, in the order - try(ies)[t], conversion(s)[con], drop goal(s)[dg]/goal(s) from a mark[gm], penalty goal(s)[pg]. N.B. The goal from a mark existed as a scoring device from the 1890-91 season to the 1977-78 season but has only been executed by three Welsh players: W Bancroft, against Scotland in 1895; H B Winfield, against England in 1904; W C Powell, against England in 1931. Bancroft and Winfield's efforts were worth four points, and Powell's three points.
British Isles and Anglo-Welsh tours.
Brief biography, outlining achievements in other sports; decorations awarded; service record in both World Wars; memoirs, and other writings on rugby; connections with other rugby players, and sportsmen and sportswomen; occupation.

Undoubtedly, readers of this book will discover items of information which they know about a particular player to be missing from his entry. This is inevitable in a work of this nature and the authors would be grateful for any additional information which can be sent to them via the publisher.

John M Jenkins
Duncan Pierce
Timothy Auty

ACKNOWLEDGEMENTS

As authors, we owe a substantial debt to many people who have assisted us with the preparation and research of this book. A few words seem meagre repayment for the gift of long hours and unselfish support without which this volume would have remained trapped among the files on our shelves. If there remain errors, it is in spite of the yeoman efforts of those listed below.

To Cliff Morgan for generously agreeing to write the Foreword and thereby lending some status to our efforts; to John Griffiths, for urging us, in his unassuming way, to produce on the printed page a record of our findings which have been at the back of our minds for many years; to Gareth Davies, for being so insistent, and for his humour; to Jean-Pierre Bodis for lending his rugby knowledge generally; to Robert Gate, the rugby league historian, for his counsel and for passing on data from his collection; to Piers Morgan, for running down information in his outstanding library; to Phil Atkinson, for taking the time to answer our questions in his own inimitable way; to the prolific Tony Lewis (Kenfig Hill), for his great efficiency; to Huw Thomas, Hugh Thomas, Andrew Hignell and David Smith, for falling over themselves to help; to Brian Lile (the great grand nephew of Dai Samuel), at the National Library of Wales, for unaccountably pretending to be delighted by our requests; to Pierre Lafond, for his love for the game; to Gareth Williams, for his readiness to give aid at even the most awkward moments; to Colin Curtis, for his sleuthing; to Rod Chester, for patiently answering all queries; to Gordon Westcott, for digging into the South Wales Police records; to Jeremy Glenn and Basil Bastin, for unearthing material in their respective archives; to Gareth Hughes, for his Scarlet knowledge; to Willow Murray of Dublin, for allowing us to pore through his photograph collection; to Rex King, in Twickenham, for letting us have the freedom of the Rugby Football Union Library; to Keith Clayton, for taking time from his busy schedule to give assistance; to Richard Huws and Gwyn Jenkins for their vigilance; to J B G Thomas, Wayne Thomas and Hubert Price for making available their unique photographic collections and extensive knowledge about rugby football; and to Alister Williams of Bridge Books for his thoroughness, patience, advice and knowing how not to interrupt.

To those former international rugby players who have assisted us we extend our sincere thanks. To the relatives of former players and those with an interest in, and knowledge of the sport, who have generously given us their time and information: the late George Andrews and Mrs Andrews, Tony Ambrosen, Miss Connie Attewell, R W E Barton, Paul Beken, E. Alwyn Benjamin, John Billot, Campbell Black, Elizabeth Boardman, Philip Boys-Stones, Joe Broom, Duncan Brown, Padraig Burgess (Lafayette Photography), Jack Burrell, Brian F. Cartwright, the late Brian Chappin, Lady Clark, W H Clement, G H Cornish, Douglas Crampton, Jo Currie, John A. Dauncey, Eunice Davies, Roger R. Davies, Hilda Deverell, Ted Donovan, E Donovan, T J Edwards, Fred J Ellison, Olwyn Emerson, Howard Evans, Tom Bevan Fielding, Walter Gott, Mrs Nina Gough, Terry Griffiths, David Gronow, S J Gunn, Hywel Gwynfryn, William Hancock, Leslie Harris, Mrs Mabel Hayes, the late Wilf Hill, David James, Dr. C R R Jenkins, Anita Jenkins de Cabral, Horace Jefferies, the late Cliff Jones, Desmond T Jones, Dorothy W. Jones, Ken Jones (Baglan), Peter K. Jones, Richard G Jones, Stanley J P Jones, Tony Jones, Mark Knott, the late V J Law, Durbar Lawrie, Cliff Lewis, Gilbert Lewis, Wayne Lewis, William Lewis, Mrs Valerie Little, Paul A Lovatt, Miss Margaret McCarley and Mrs McCarley, Duncan McDaniel, John McLaren, Adam Machell, Mrs J A Machell, David Makin, Jean Maggs, Nancy Martinez, Robert Mathias, Mrs Dilys Miles, Brian Morgan, the late Mr and Mrs D E Morgan, Glenys Morgan, L Morgan, Professor W H Morris-Jones, John Nichols, Beth Owen, A Ege Parker, Eddie Parker, Peter S V Pegge, Glyn Phillips (Maesteg), R James Pierce, Jennifer Pollock, John R Powell, D P Price (Hon Sec Swansea Cricket & Football Club), Rev D T W Price, Corin W B Purdon, Daniel Quayle, Nick Quayle, Mrs Christine Redmore, D F Rees (Penclawdd), Edward H Rees, Gwyn L C Rees, Mrs Mim Rees, Bill Richards, the late Jack Rhapps Jnr, David Richards, the late Gwyn Richards and Mrs Richards, Eddie Rickard, Gwyn L Saint, Dr Ian Salmon, the late J A Saville, Mr and Mrs F Scrine, Ron Slateford, Winifred Strange, Trevor Tasker, Fiona Thomas, Gwyn D Thomas, Hywel Thomas, J C Thomas, Trevor R Thomas, S. George Thorn, Henry Toulouse, R L Trump, Mrs B R Turnbull, Rene Uzzell, Paul D Wapshott, Owen Ward, Vivienne Weaver, the late Tom Webb, Bryan D White, Barrie Williams, Bryan Williams, Bryn Williams (Newport), the late Bryn Williams (Llanelli), Mrs Gladys Watkins, G. Williams, Miss Gladys Williams, Graham Williams, Shirley Williams, the late Mrs W A Williams, Zena Williams - to all of them, and to so many more, our heartfelt and sincere thanks.

ABBREVIATIONS

AAA: Amateur Athletics Association
AFC: Association Football Club

Bart: Baronet
BBC: British Broadcasting Corporation
BEM: British Empire Medal
Bn: Battalion
BSC: British Steel Corporation

c: circa
CBE: Companion of the Order of the British Empire
CCC: County Cricket Club
CMG: Companion of the Order of St Michael and St George
con: conversion
CVO: Commander of the Royal Victorian Order

DCM: Distinguished Conduct Medal
DD: Doctor of Divinity
DFC: Distinguished Flying Cross
dg: drop goal
DL: Deputy Lieutenant
DSO: Distinguished Service Order

FA: Football Association
FC: Football Club

gm: goal from a mark
GWR: Great Western Railway

HTV: Harlech Television

IB: International Board
ICI: Imperial Chemical Industries
IRFU: Irish Rugby Football Union

JP: Justice of the Peace

KBE: Knight Commander of the Order of the British Empire
KC: King's Counsel
KCB: Knight Commander of the Order of the Bath

Lt: Lieutenant

MBE: Member of the Order of the British Empire
MC: Military Cross
MCC: Marylebone Cricket Club
MM: Military Medal
MOH: Medical Officer of Health
MP: Member of Parliament

NCB: National Coal Board
nr: near

OBE: Officer of the Order of the British Empire
OTC: Officer Training Corps

PC: Privy Councillor
PE: Physical education
pg: penalty goal
POW: Prisoner of War

r: replacement
Rev: Reverend
RFC: Rugby Football Club
RL: Rugby League
RLFC: Rugby League Football Club
RU: Rugby Union

SRU: Scottish Rugby Union

t: try
TD: Territorial Decoration

UAU: Universities Athletics Union

VD: Volunteer Decoration

WRU: Welsh Rugby Union

YMCA: Young Men's Christian Association

Who's Who of
Welsh International Rugby Players

ACKERMAN, Robert Angus
Born Ebbw Vale, 2 March 1961
Career: Christ College, Brecon; Exeter University; St Mary's College Twickenham; Welsh Secondary Schools; Newport; Eastern Suburbs (Australia); Cardiff; London Welsh; Barbarians; Wales B

Wing/centre in 22 matches, against: New Zealand, 1980; England, 1981, 1982, 1984, 1985; Scotland, 1981, 1982, 1983, 1984, 1985; Australia, 1981, 1984; Ireland 1982, 1983, 1984, 1985; France, 1982, 1983, 1984, 1985; Romania, 1983; Fiji, 1985: Scored 1t - 4 points

British Isles 1983 tour New Zealand: 2 caps (1r)

Currently employed in computer sales, Rob Ackerman joined Whitehaven RLFC in April 1986 making his debut against Huddersfield on 13 April, and moved to Leeds RLFC in 1990. His father Doug is on the committee of Newport RFC.

ALEXANDER, Edward Perkins
Born Monknash, 7 August 1863; died Holt, Wiltshire, 26 October 1931
Career: Llandovery College; Cambridge University; Brecon; Wasps; London Welsh; Richmond; Blackheath

Forward in 5 matches, against: Scotland, 1885, 1886; England, 1886,1887; Ireland, 1887

Cambridge Blue (1884-6), E P Alexander was a member of the Jesus College, Cambridge crew which won the Grand Challenge Cup at Henley in 1885. A farmer, local councillor and stalwart Conservative in Wiltshire, he named his farm Glan yr Afon. He also played cricket for the South Wales XI.

ALEXANDER, William
Born Glynneath, 16 July 1874
Career: Ferndale; Glynneath; Llwynypia; Glamorgan Police

Forward in 7 matches, against: Ireland, 1898, 1899, 1901; England, 1898, 1899; Scotland, 1899, 1901

Billy Alexander, a police officer in Glamorgan until he resigned on 16 August 1904, was later employed as an engineer. His cap is in the South Wales Police clubroom at Waterton Cross, Bridgend and his jerseys are in the Llantrisant Rugby Club. His son, Noel Alexander, played for the Metropolitan Police before the Second World War.

ALLEN, Andrew George
Born Newport, 5 April 1967
Career: Croesyceiliog Comprehensive School; Cwmbran; Welsh Youth; Welsh Counties Under 23; Newbridge; Monmouthshire Under 23; Barbarians

Lock in 3 matches, against: France, 1990; England, 1990; Ireland, 1990

ALLEN, Charles Peter PC MP
Born Prestwich, Lancashire, 2 December 1861; died London, 18 September 1930
Career: Rugby School; Oxford University; Manchester

Back in 2 matches, against: England, 1884; Scotland, 1884: Scored 1t - 3 points

Charles was the son of Peter Allen, the manager of the *Manchester Guardian*. He gained his Blue whilst at Oxford University (1881-83), qualified as a barrister and went on to become a newspaper proprietor. Allen holds the unique honour of having scored Wales' first try against England in 1884. During the First World War he served as a Major in the 5th Battalion, The Gloucestershire Regiment. He served as the Liberal MP for Stroud 1900-14, during which time he was created a Privy Councillor. He was later appointed a Deputy Lieutenant for Gloucestershire. In later life he played cricket for Beaumaris.

ANDREWS, Frank
Born c1886; died Leeds, 22 November 1944
Career: Pontypool; Newbridge

Forward in 4 matches, against: South Africa, 1912; England, 1913; Scotland, 1913; Ireland, 1913

Steelworker Frank Andrews joined Hunslet RLFC making his first appearance for them against Salford on 13 September 1913.

ANDREWS, Frederick Graham
Born Swansea, 15 September 1864; died Gower, 2 June 1929
Career: Cheltenham College; Swansea

Forward in 2 matches, against: England, 1884; Scotland, 1884

Frederick Andrews was a chartered engineer who captained the school team at Cheltenham College. He later spent some time living in New Zealand before returning to Wales.

ANDREWS, George Edward
Born Newport, 24 August 1904; died Carshalton, 21 December 1989
Career: Taunton School; St Julian's High School Newport; Newport

Wing in 5 matches, against: England, 1926, 1927; Scotland, 1926; France, 1927; Ireland, 1927: Scored 3t - 9 points

George Andrews scored a try for Newport against New Zealand on 2 October 1924. A dock broker in his father's firm, and later a commercial traveller and a painter and decorator, he joined Leeds RLFC in 1927, making his debut on 6 April. During the Second World War he was a supervisor in a Newport tool setting firm.

ANTHONY, Leslie
Born Rhiwfawr, 21 November 1921
Career: Cwmllynfell; Neath

Prop in 3 matches, against: England, 1948; Scotland, 1948; France, 1948

Les Anthony, a collier and sheet metal worker, joined Oldham RLFC, making his debut on 28 August 1948.

ARNOLD, Paul
Born Morriston, 28 April 1968
Career: Bishop Gore School; Swansea Youth; Swansea; Wales Under 21

Lock/No 8 in 7 matches, against: Namibia, 1990 (2); Barbarians, 1990; England, 1991; Scotland, 1991; Ireland, 1991; France, 1991: Scored 1t - 4 points

Paul Arnold is employed as a builder by the BJ Group of Swansea.

ARNOLD, William Richard
Born Morriston, 7 July 1881; died Morriston, 30 July 1957
Career: Morriston; Llanelli; Swansea; Neath; London Welsh; Glamorgan

Wing in 1 match, against: Scotland, 1903

Willie Arnold was a surveyor/architect. During the 1902-3 season he scored thirty-five tries for Llanelli and at Swansea, a season later, scored a further thirty-two tries. He played in the unbeaten Swansea XV in 1904-5, appeared for Glamorgan against New Zealand in December 1905 and played for Llanelli against South Africa in 1906. A keen all-round sportsman, he served on the committee of Glamorgan CCC and was the first secretary and one of the founders of Morriston Golf Club. He weighed between 8st 7lbs and 9st. His brother Arthur played for the Swansea 2nd XV.

ARTHUR, Charles Suckling
Born 1863, registered in King's Lynn, Norfolk; died Cardiff, 12 December 1925
Career: Queen Elizabeth Grammar School, Carmarthen; Newton College Devon; Carmarthen; Bristol; Cardiff

Back in 3 matches, against: Ireland, 1888; New Zealand Natives, 1888; England, 1891

By profession a solicitor and later a schoolmaster, Charlie Arthur captained Cardiff in 1889-90 and was the secretary of the club from 1892 to 1925. He was one of 3 brothers who played for Cardiff. He was the author of *Cardiff RFC History and Statistics 1876-1906*, which was published c1907.

ARTHUR, Tom
Born Pontypridd, 10 January 1906; died Cardiff, 1 November 1986
Career: Glynneath; Neath; Glamorgan Police

Forward in 18 matches, against: Scotland, 1927, 1929, 1930, 1931, 1933; France, 1927, 1929, 1930, 1931; Ireland, 1927, 1929, 1930, 1931; England, 1929, 1930, 1931, 1933; South Africa, 1931: Scored 4 tries - 12 points.

Tom Arthur was a blacksmith before becoming a police officer in Glamorgan. He was recognised as a hard, vigorous forward and was also a heavyweight boxer of some note, appearing in the British boxing team against the Irish Free State in 1925. He played for Neath and Aberavon against New South Wales in September 1927 and captained Neath in 1931-32. His son, Tom, played for Penarth.

ASHTON, Clifford
Born Cwmavon, 17 December 1932

1. 1881 v England
The first Welsh team.
Back row: W D Phillips, G F Harding, R Mullock (manager), F T Purdon, G Darbishire, E Treharne, R D G Williams.
Middle row: T A Rees, E Peake, J A Bevan (C), B E Girling, B B Mann.
Front row: L Watkins, C H Newman, E J Lewis, R H B Summers.
[*John Griffiths*]

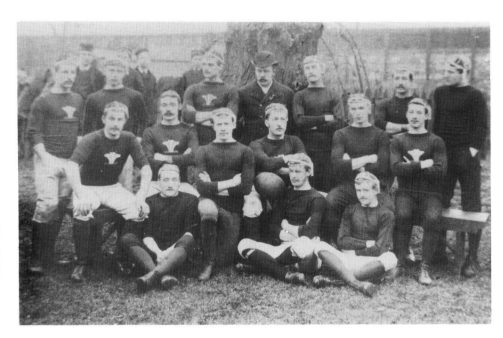

2. 1882 v Ireland
Back row: C H Newman, H C Vincent, G F Harding, R Mullock (umpire), S S Clark, W F Evans, T B Jones.
Middle row: F T Purdon, W D Phillips, T Williams, C P Lewis (C), R Gould, W B Norton.
Front row: T J S Clapp, G L Morris, J Bridie.
[*Wayne Thomas*]

3. 1883 v Scotland
Back row: H S Lyne, J Bridie, F T Purdon, T B Jones, T J S Clapp, G F Harding.
Front row: R Mullock (umpire), G L Morris, W F Evans, C P Lewis (C), A Cattell, W B Norton, C H Newman.
Absent: R Gould.
J Griffin, T H Judson and J A Jones are known to have been in this photograph but cannot be identified.
[*Welsh Folk Museum*]

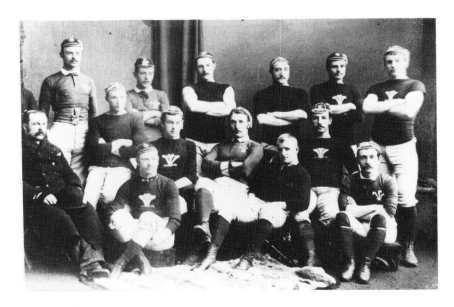

Career: Cwmavon Junior School; Cwmavon; Cardiff; Aberavon; Chepstow
Stand-off in 7 matches, against: England, 1959, 1960; Scotland, 1959, 1960; Ireland, 1959, 1960, 1961: Scored 1t - 3 points

Cliff Ashton had a varied career as a physical training instructor and a steelworker. He captained Aberavon in 1955-57 and also coached Chepstow RFC.

ATTEWELL, Stephen Leonard
Born Newport, 31 December 1895; died Newport, 26 February 1983
Career: Newport Intermediate School; Goldcliff; Pill Harriers; Newport

Forward in 3 matches, against: England, 1921; Scotland, 1921; France, 1921

Len Attewell was a farmer in Nash, Newport.

BADGER, Owen
Born Llanelli, 3 November 1871; died Llanelli, 17 March 1939
Career: Seaside Stars; Llanelli

Centre in 4 matches, against: England, 1895, 1896; Scotland, 1895; Ireland, 1895

Steel shearer Owen Badger, who captained Llanelli in 1896-97, joined Swinton RLFC (making his debut on 4 December 1897) and went on to win two Wales RL caps. He was a trustee of the Royal Alfreds (Friendly Society).

BAKER, Albert Melville
Born Newport, 1885
Career: Newport; Griqualand West

Wing in 3 matches, against: Scotland, 1909, 1910; France, 1909: Scored 4t - 12 points

British Isles 1910 tour South Africa: 1 cap

Engineer Mel Baker, as a member of a back division that were all to become international players, scored the only try for Newport against Australia in December 1908. He scored six tries in twelve appearances for the British Isles team which toured South Africa in 1910 and, while touring the De Beers diamond mine in Kimberley, was offered a job and stayed in South Africa. He played for the Griqualand West team which won the Currie Cup in 1911, for which his reward was a gold medal and a gold model of the Currie Cup. Surprisingly, during a holiday visit to his family in Wales, he made one final guest appearance for Newport in 1922 when he played in a match against the Barbarians, scoring a try twelve years after his previous

appearance.

BAKER, Ambrose
Born 1897, registered in Swansea; died Oldham, 24 November 1976
Career: Neath

Forward in 5 matches, against: Ireland, 1921, 1923; England, 1923; Scotland, 1923; France, 1923: Scored 1t - 3 points

Collier and later licensee, Ambrose Baker joined Oldham RLFC and made his debut against Barrow on 19 January 1924 and won two caps for Wales RL.

BANCROFT, John
Born Swansea, 1879; died Swansea, 7 January 1942
Career: Swansea

Full back in 18 matches, against: England, 1909, 1910, 1911, 1912, 1914; Scotland, 1909, 1910, 1912, 1914; France, 1909, 1910, 1911, 1914; Ireland, 1909, 1910, 1911, 1912, 1913: Scored 38con 4pg - 88 points

Jack, the brother of William Bancroft [qv], was employed, at various times, as a copper worker, groundsman and licensee. He kicked eleven conversions during the 1909 season and a further eight conversions against France in 1910. He also played cricket for Glamorgan from 1908 to 1922. On 13 June 1907, at St Helen's Ground, Swansea, Jack, while batting in a net practice, drove the ball with great force, hitting Harvey Thomas, a member of the Swansea 3rd XI behind the ear. The blow felled Thomas, rendering him unconscious, a state in which he remained for over an hour. Recovering at his home, Thomas' condition worsened and, after again losing consciousness, he died on 16 June.

BANCROFT, William
Born Swansea, 2 March 1871; died Swansea, 3 March 1959
Career: St Helens School; Excelsior; Brynymor; Swansea

Full back in 33 matches, against: Scotland, 1890, 1891, 1892, 1893, 1894, 1895, 1896, 1899, 1900, 1901; England, 1890, 1891, 1892, 1893, 1894, 1895, 1896, 1897, 1898, 1900, 1901; Ireland, 1890, 1891, 1892, 1893, 1894, 1895, 1896, 1898, 1899, 1900, 1901: Scored 20con 1dg 4pg 1gm - 60 points

Billy Bancroft, a cobbler, appeared in thirty-three consecutive international matches, captaining Wales eleven times and Swansea in 1893-4 and from 1896-1901. The brother of Jack Bancroft [qv], he played cricket for South Wales, Glamorgan, and the West of England. Another brother George played for the Swansea 2nd XV.

16

BARLOW, Thomas Marriott
Born Salford, 1864; died Chester, 27 January 1942
Career: Cardiff

Full back in 1 match, against: Ireland, 1884

In addition to his rugby honours, solicitor Tom Barlow gained a considerable reputation as a golfer and was runner up in the Welsh Amateur Golf Championship of 1895, winner in 1900 and runner up 1903. He served as the secretary of the Welsh Golf Federation and played cricket for Glamorgan (1894-97).

BARRELL, Robert John
Born Newtown, Mountain Ash, 1 November 1905; died Sandridge, Hertfordshire, 13 January 1967
Career: Penarth; Cardiff; Glamorgan Police

Forward in 4 matches, against: Scotland, 1929; France, 1929; Ireland, 1929, 1933: Scored 1t - 3 points

Bob Barrell, who captained Penarth in 1935-36, was employed as a coal boy by Powell Dyffryn, then a sawyer before becoming a police officer. He played for Cardiff against New South Wales in December 1927. He was commended for bravery by his Chief Constable following his actions at a serious road accident at Bryncethin in May 1952.

BARTLETT, John Dudley
Born Carmarthen, 6 August 1907; died Hayling Island, 17 January 1967
Career: Llandovery College; Cambridge University; St David's College Lampeter; Welsh Secondary Schools; Carmarthen Quins; Llanelli; London Welsh

Wing in 3 matches, against: Scotland, 1927, 1928; England, 1928: Scored 1t - 3 points

Bartlett was a curate and Royal Navy chaplain

BASSETT, Arthur
Born Kenfig Hill, 28 June 1914
Career: Pyle Council School; Pyle; Kenfig Hill; Neath; Maesteg; Swansea; Aberavon; Cardiff; Glamorgan Police; Derby Police; British Police

Wing in 6 matches, against: Ireland, 1934, 1935; England, 1935, 1938; Scotland, 1935, 1938

Bassett had a varied career as a driller/machinist, police officer, licensee and head of security at Chatsworth House in Derbyshire. He was taught by Clem Lewis [qv] and, after playing a number of games at full back for Kenfig Hill, Maesteg and Neath, he started playing for Glamorgan Police in the 1933-4 season, where he was placed on the wing. He received his first cap after G R R Jones, the original choice, had to withdraw through injury. He scored 99 tries in 101 appearances for Cardiff. Before leaving for the North of England, he was stationed in Cadoxton where the sergeant in charge was John Sullivan, brother of Jim Sullivan who became a legend in the Rugby League game. In January 1939, six years after being approached by the club, Bassett joined Halifax RLFC and in 1948 moved to York RLFC. He gained three Wales RL caps and played in two Great Britain RL Tests in Australia in 1946, scoring a hat-trick in the first Test. He was the brother of J A Bassett [qv].

BASSETT, John Archibald
Born Trebanog, 11 July 1905; died Cardiff, 19 February 1989
Career: Kenfig Hill Council School; Kenfig Hill; Pyle; Penarth; Glamorgan Police; Cardiff; Barbarians

Full back in 15 matches, against: England, 1929, 1930, 1931, 1932; Scotland, 1929, 1930, 1931, 1932; France, 1929, 1931; Ireland, 1929, 1930, 1931, 1932; South Africa, 1931: Scored 10con 3pg - 29 points

British Isles 1930 tour New Zealand: 4 caps, Australia: 1 cap

Jack Bassett was employed as a collier before joining the police force. In addition to his Welsh rugby honours he also appeared in thirteen matches for the British Isles in New Zealand in 1930. He captained Penarth from 1927-32. He was the brother of Arthur Bassett [qv].

BATEMAN, Allan Glen
Born Maesteg, 6 March 1965
Career: Maesteg Comprehensive School; Welsh Youth; Maesteg Celtic; Maesteg; Neath

Centre in 4 matches, against: Scotland, 1990; Ireland, 1990; Namibia, 1990, 1990

Allan Bateman is employed as a scientific officer in a medical laboratory. He joined Warrington RLFC in September 1990, making his debut on 7 October.

BAYLISS, Gwyn
Born Brynmawr, May 1907; died Blaina, 10 March 1976
Career: Brynmawr Grammar School; Brynmawr; Ebbw Vale; Pontypool; Llanelli; Tredegar; London Welsh; Wolverhampton; North Midlands

Full back in 1 match, against: Scotland, 1933

A schoolmaster and journalist, Gwyn Bayliss contributed a lively column to the publication *Welsh Rugby*. He captained Pontypool in the 1934-35 season and played for

4. 1884 v Scotland
Back row: H J Simpson, F L Margrave, W D Phillips.
Middle row: G L Morris, T B Jones, H S Lyne, T J S Clapp, F G Andrews, R Gould.
Front row: C H Newman (C), C P Allen, W H Gwynn, C P Lewis, C G Taylor, W B Norton.
[*Welsh Folk Museum*]

5. 1885 v Scotland
Back row: A Duncan (umpire), E P Alexander, S J Goldsworthy, A F Hill, W H Thomas, T J S Clapp, C G Taylor, D Morgan, R Mullock (WRU official).
Middle row: H M Jordan, L C Thomas, C H Newman (C), J A Gould, F E Hancock, R Gould.
Front row: W H Gwynn, T B Jones.
[*Auty Collection*]

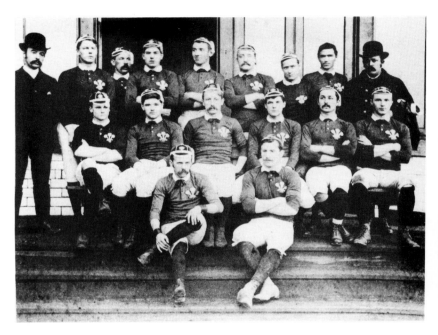

6. 1886 v Scotland
Back row: R Gould, E P Alexander, T J S Clapp, A F Hill, G A Young, C P Lewis, D H Bowen, W A Bowen, D Morgan, C H Newman.
Middle row: A Duncan (umpire), W H Thomas, C G Taylor, F E Hancock (C), J A Gould, W Douglas, A A Mathews, W Wilkins.
Front row: D H Lewis, W J Staddan.
[*Tony Lewis*]

Llanelli against New Zealand in 1935.

BEBB, Dewi Iorwerth Ellis
Born Bangor, 7 August 1938
Career: Friars School, Bangor; Trinity College, Carmarthen; Cardiff Training College; Colwyn Bay; Beaumaris; Royal Navy; United Services, Portsmouth; Swansea; Barbarians

Wing in 34 matches, against: England, 1959, 1960, 1961, 1962, 1963, 1964, 1965, 1967; Scotland, 1959, 1960, 1961, 1962, 1964, 1965, 1967; Ireland, 1959, 1960, 1961, 1962, 1965, 1967; France, 1959, 1960, 1961, 1962, 1963, 1964, 1965, 1966, 1967; South Africa, 1960, 1964; New Zealand, 1963: Scored 11t - 33 points

British Isles 1962 tour South Africa: 2 caps; 1966 Australia: 2 caps, New Zealand: 4 caps

Dewi Bebb appeared in only eight matches for the British Isles in South Africa but, four years later, in New Zealand, he was joint leading try scorer with Mike Gibson. He captained Swansea from 1963-65. He played for Swansea against South Africa in 1960, New Zealand (captain) in 1963 and Australia in 1966. Formerly a teacher at Fairwater, he currently works for HTV.

BECKINGHAM, Geoffrey Thomas
Born Barry, 29 July 1924
Career: Romilly School; Dinas Powys; Barry; Cardiff

Hooker in 3 matches, against: England, 1953; Scotland, 1953; France, 1958

Geoff Beckingham was a municipal gardener before being appointed an area playing fields supervisor for Ogwr Borough Council. He coached Penarth RFC and Barry Plastics RFC after over 300 appearances for Cardiff.

BENNETT, Ivor
Born Aberkenfig, 16 June 1913
Career: Tondu; Bridgend; Aberavon; Glamorgan Police

Forward in 1 match, against: Ireland, 1937

Bennett served as a police officer for many years and, after retiring, was employed as a club steward. He joined Warrington RLFC, scoring a try on his debut on 28 August 1937, and later moved to Bridgend RLFC. During the Second World War he served in the 484th Anti-Aircraft Battery, mainly in Malta. His son-in-law, Malcolm Thomson and his grandson also played for Warrington RLFC.

BENNETT, Percy
Born details unknown

Career: Roath; Cardiff Harlequins

Forward in 4 matches, against: England, 1891; Scotland, 1891, 1892; Ireland, 1892

Contemporary accounts describe Bennett as weighing over 13 stone and standing a little under 6 feet. He is one of two players capped directly from Cardiff Harlequins.

BENNETT, Philip OBE
Born Felinfoel, 24 October 1948
Career: Coleshill Secondary School; Welsh Secondary Schools; Felinfoel Youth; Welsh Youth; Llanelli; Barbarians

Wing/centre/full back/stand-off in 29 matches, against: France, 1969(r), 1970, 1973, 1974, 1976, 1977, 1978, South Africa, 1970 ; Scotland, 1970, 1972(r), 1973, 1974, 1975(r), 1976, 1977, 1978; New Zealand, 1972; England, 1973, 1974, 1976, 1977, 1978; Ireland, 1973, 1974, 1975, 1976, 1977, 1978: Scored 4t 18c 2dg 36pg - 166 points

British Isles 1974 tour South Africa: 4 caps; 1977 New Zealand (captain): 4 caps

Variously employed as a steelworker, sports shop-keeper, brewery representative and television reporter, Phil Bennett was the first Welshman to be capped as reserve. He partnered Gareth Edwards in a record twenty-five appearances for Wales. He captained Llanelli from 1973 to 1979. In South Africa in 1974, Bennett scored 103 points, a valuable contribution to a successful tour. He was also the top scorer for the British Isles team that toured New Zealand in 1977, where he again scored over 100 points. Awarded the OBE in 1978, his autobiography *Everywhere for Wales*, was published in 1984.

BERGIERS, Roy Thomas Edmond
Born Carmarthen, 11 November 1950
Career: Queen Elizabeth Grammar School, Carmarthen; Cardiff Training College; Carmarthen Athletic; Welsh Colleges; Bridgend; Llanelli; Barbarians; Wales B

Centre in 11 matches, against: England, 1972, 1973, 1974; Scotland, 1972, 1973; France, 1972, 1973; New Zealand, 1972; Ireland, 1973, 1975; Australia, 1973: Scored 2t - 8 points

British Isles 1974 tour South Africa

An excellent all-round athlete, Roy Bergiers, who is a school teacher, represented the Welsh AAA junior team in Holland in 1968 and won the Welsh Colleges hurdles and high jump titles on two occasions. He made ten appearances for the 1974 British Isles team in South Africa.

BEVAN, Griffith Wilfred
Born Burry Port, 15 August 1914
Career: Burry Port; Birmingham Welsh; Llanelli; Devonport Services; Royal Navy

Prop in 1 match, against: England, 1947

Steelworker Griff Bevan was a founder member of the Birmingham Welsh RFC and captained Llanelli from 1946-48. He served in the Royal Navy during the Second World War.

BEVAN, James Alfred
Born Caulfield, Victoria, Australia 15 April 1858; died Leytonstone, 3 February 1938
Career: Hereford Cathedral School; Cambridge University; Abergavenny; Newport

Back in 1 match, against: England, 1881

Jim Bevan was orphaned at the age of eight when his parents were drowned while returning to Australia from Wales and the family fortune was lost. Solicitor's articled clerk, clergyman and Cambridge Blue (1877 and 1880), Bevan had the unique distinction of serving as Wales' first captain, against England, at Blackheath in 1881. He was the father of thirteen children and six of his seven sons followed him into the church, one of them becoming the Bishop of East Szechuan (China) in 1940 and is living in Yorkshire in 1991. His church principles were strongly protestant fundamentalist and his grandchildren found him narrow and severe. He was a good cricketer, playing for his college and the Crusaders at Cambridge and, when living in the Bristol area, played against the Grace brothers. Whilst at Cambridge he won his college sprints and the long jump. He was once the holder of the course record at Caistor Golf Club.

BEVAN, John Charles
Born Tylorstown, 28 October 1950
Career: Ferndale Grammar School; Cardiff College; Tylorstown; Cardiff; Barbarians

Wing in 10 matches, against: England, 1971, 1972, 1973; Scotland, 1971, 1972, 1973; Ireland, 1971; France, 1971, 1972; New Zealand, 1972: Scored 5t - 19 points

British Isles 1971 tour Australia, New Zealand: 1 cap

Former physical training instructor and licensee John Bevan is now a schoolmaster at Arnold School, Blackpool. He scored 51 points, from seventeen tries, in thirteen matches for the British Isles in New Zealand. He joined Warrington RLFC in September 1973, appeared six times for the Great Britain RL team and made seventeen appearances for the Wales RL team. He is a qualified lifeguard. His son John Rhys toured Italy in March 1991

with the Welsh Schools Rugby Squad.

BEVAN, John David
Born 12 March 1948, registered in Neath; died Port Talbot, 5 June 1986
Career: Neath Grammar School; St Luke's College, Exeter; Bryncoch; Aberavon; Neath; Barbarians; Devon; Wales B

Stand-off in 4 matches, against: France, 1975; England, 1975; Scotland, 1975; Australia, 1975: Scored 1dg - 3 points

British Isles 1977 tour New Zealand

Schoolmaster John Bevan appeared in eleven matches in New Zealand for the British Isles and was assistant manager for the 1983 Wales B tour to Spain. He coached Aberavon RFC from 1982 to 1985 and played cricket for Neath and Wales. He was the Welsh National team coach from July 1982 until November 1985.

BEVAN, Thomas Sidney
Born Morriston, 2 May 1877; died Swansea, 17 October 1933
Career: Ardwyn Grammar School; Morriston; Swansea; Glamorgan

Forward in 1 match, against: Ireland, 1904

British Isles 1904 tour Australia: 3 caps, New Zealand: 1 cap

Sid Bevan was a metal broker and then a stockbroker. During the First World War, he was commissioned as a 2nd Lieutenant in the 6th Bn the Welch Regiment.

BEYNON, Benjamin
Born Swansea, 14 March 1894; died Swansea 21 May 1969
Career: Manselton; Swansea

Stand-off in 2 matches, against: England, 1920; Scotland, 1920

Employed as a docker and painter and decorator, Ben Beynon played soccer for Waunwen and Swansea Town. He played his first game for the Swans on 28 November 1914 and his last on 17 April 1922. His greatest moment was when he scored the goal that knocked Blackburn Rovers (who finished third in Division One) out of the cup in January 1915 - his only goal in four FA Cup appearances. He scored a hat-trick for Swansea against Norwich in September 1920 at the Vetch Field. He joined Oldham RLFC in September 1922, and won a Challenge Cup medal in 1925. The WRU withheld his international cap after he had accepted professional terms with Swansea

Town in 1920.

BEYNON, George Edward BEM
Born Gower, 1902; died Carshalton, 14 October 1957
Career: Mumbles; Swansea; London Welsh

Forward in 2 matches, against: France, 1925; Ireland, 1925

Eddie Beynon was employed as a railway police officer and was selected to play for an England/Wales Railways XV against an Irish Railways XV in Dublin in February 1930.

BIGGS, Norman Witchell
Born Cardiff, 3 November 1870; died Sakaba, Nigeria 27 February 1908
Career: Cardiff College; Cambridge University; Richmond; London Welsh; Cardiff; Bath; Barbarians; Somerset

Back/wing in 8 matches, against: New Zealand Natives, 1888; Ireland, 1889, 1892, 1893, 1894; England, 1893, 1894; Scotland, 1893: Scored 2t - 4 points

Police officer Norman Biggs was, at 18 years and 1 month, the youngest player to be capped for Wales when he took the field against the New Zealand Natives on 22 December 1888. He captained Cardiff in 1893-94, Bath in 1899-1900 and played in 'friendly' cricket matches for Glamorgan. He served as a private in the Glamorgan Yeomanry during the Boer War and was a Superintendent in the Nigerian Police. He was killed by a poisoned arrow during a native ambush. The son of a brewer in Cardiff and Bath, he was the brother of Selwyn Biggs [qv] and Cecil Biggs, who captained Cardiff in 1904-05. Three other brothers also played for Cardiff.

BIGGS, Selwyn Hanam
Born Cardiff, 1872; died Weston-super-Mare, 12 January 1943
Career: Cardiff; Richmond; London Welsh; Bath; Barbarians; Somerset

Stand-off in 9 matches, against: England, 1895, 1897, 1898; Scotland, 1895, 1896, 1899; Ireland, 1898, 1899, 1900

Solicitor and company director Selwyn Biggs captained Cardiff in 1897-98 and was the brother of Norman Biggs [qv]. He was also an opening bowler for Glamorgan for many seasons and a reasonably good golfer. Badly gassed during the First World War, he was an invalid for the remainder of his life and was unable to pursue his profession.

BIRCH, James
Born St Andrews, Northampton, 30 December 1889; died

Northampton, 17 April 1968
Career: Northampton; Neath; Cardiff; Glamorgan Police

Forward in 2 matches, against: Scotland, 1911; France, 1911

The selection of Englishman Jim Birch, who had only recently moved to live in Wales (he had been a boot and shoe dealer in Northampton), and had played for Northampton at the age of sixteen, was seen as a tit for tat reprisal by the Welsh selectors against their English counterparts who had selected Stanley Williams, a Welshman, to play for England earlier that season. The selection of Williams - one of the major successes in South Africa in 1910 - caused an uproar in rugby circles, but was largely the fault of the Welsh selectors who had denied him his chance for several seasons. He joined the Glamorgan Constabulary in April 1910, played cricket for the Force XI and won both his caps in convincing victories in Inverleith and Paris. He served on the Northampton RFC committee, having returned to the town on retiring.

BIRT, Fred
Born Newport, 10 November 1886; died Beaufort, Monmouthshire, 5 July 1956
Career: Newport; London Welsh; Monmouthshire

Centre/full back in 7 matches, against: England, 1911, 1912, 1913; Scotland, 1911, 1912; Ireland, 1912; South Africa, 1912: Scored 1dg 1pg - 7 points

Education officer Fred Birt scored a drop goal and a conversion for Newport in their 9-3 win over the South Africans in October 1912. He captained Newport in 1919-20. Birt also played bowls for Wales. During the First World War he served with the Royal Engineers.

BISHOP, David Joseph
Born Cardiff, 31 October 1960
Career: St Cadoc's Royal Catholic School; St Illtyd's College; Rhymney Technical College; Old Illtydians; Cardiff Youth; Welsh Youth; Cardiff; Ebbw Vale; Pontypool; Wales B

Scrum half in 1 match, against: Australia, 1984: Scored 1t - 4 points

David Bishop, who was a welder and is now a sales representative, was advised to give up playing rugby after breaking his neck in 1981. A good all-round sportsman, he has boxed for the Welsh amateur team and played baseball for Wales. He was suspended by the Welsh Rugby Union from the end of the 1985-6 season to September 1987 for allegedly punching a player in a Pontypool match against Newbridge. Bishop joined Hull Kingston Rovers RLFC in July 1988 and toured Australia with the Great

Britain RL team in 1990. In 1979, he received the Royal Humane Society Award for rescuing a mother and child from the river Taff.

BISHOP, Edward Hopkin
Born Swansea, 10 October 1864; died Keynsham, 24 February 1919
Career: Llandovery College; Swansea

Back in 1 match, against: Scotland, 1889

Teddy Bishop played in the Llandovery College- Christ College, Brecon match in 1882-83 and for Swansea against the New Zealand Natives on Christmas Eve, 1888.

BLACKMORE, Joseph Henry
Born details unknown; died Aberbeeg, 26 March 1964
Career: Abertillery; Tredegar; Monmouthshire

Forward in 1 match, against: England, 1909

Employed as a collier, Jake Blackmore appeared for Monmouthshire against South Africa in 1906. He played rugby league for Hull Kingston Rovers, having made his debut against Dewsbury on 3 September 1910, and gained two Wales RL caps.

BLACKMORE, Steven Walter
Born Cardiff, 3 March 1962
Career: Fitzalan School Cardiff; Cardiff

Prop in 4 matches, against: Ireland, 1987; Tonga, [1987(r) World Cup]; Canada, [1987 World Cup]; Australia, [1987 World Cup]

Steven Blackmore is a car mechanic.

BLAKE, John
Born Cardiff, c1875; died Cardiff, 15 February 1933
Career: Cardiff

Forward in 9 matches, against: England, 1899, 1900, 1901; Scotland, 1899, 1900, 1901; Ireland, 1899, 1900, 1901

Jere Blake, a coal trimmer, made 125 appearances for Cardiff.

BLAKEMORE, Reginald Edward
Born Newport, 1 September 1924
Career: Newport Saracens, Newport

Prop in 1 match, against: England, 1947

Reg Blakemore was a docker and later became the proprietor of a fish and chip shop. During the Second World War he served in the South Wales Borderers. On 25 September 1947, he made his debut for St Helen's RLFC against the New Zealanders.

BLAND, Alexander Frederick
Born Haverfordwest, 24 November 1866; died Barry, 18 October 1947
Career: Cardiff; London Welsh

Forward in 9 matches, against: England, 1887, 1890; Scotland, 1887, 1888, 1890; Ireland, 1887, 1888, 1890; New Zealand Natives, 1888

Solicitor Alec Bland was one of the biggest men to have played for Wales. He was the secretary to the Cardiff RFC from 1889-92.

BLYTH, William Roger
Born Swansea 2 April 1950
Career: Swansea Grammar School; St Mary's Technical College, Ealing; Swansea; Barbarians; Wales B

Full back/centre in 6 matches, against: England, 1974, 1980; Scotland, 1975 (r), 1980; France, 1980; Ireland, 1980: Scored 1t 1con - 6 points

Roger Blyth, the managing director of the family protective clothing business, is the son of Leonard Blythe [qv] and the nephew of Alun G Thomas [qv]. In 1979-80 he scored 348 points for Swansea, making him the leading scorer in Welsh rugby that season.

BLYTHE, Leonard Grist
(Spelt Blythe on birth registration)
Born Swansea, 20 November 1920
Career: Dynevor School; Gorseinon; Swansea

Flanker in 3 matches, against: South Africa, 1951; England, 1952; Scotland, 1952

Len Blythe served in the Royal Navy during the Second World War and later became a company director. He captained Swansea in 1951-52. He is the father of Roger Blyth [qv] and the brother-in-law of Alun G Thomas [qv].

BOON, Ronald Winston
Born Barry, 11 June 1909
Career: Barry County School; Trinity College, Carmarthen; Dunfermline College of Physical Education; Welsh Schools; Dunfermline; Ayr; Cardiff; Territorial Army; London Welsh; New Brighton; Barbarians

Wing in 12 matches, against: Scotland, 1930, 1931, 1932; France, 1930, 1931; England, 1931, 1932, 1933; Ireland,

7. 1891 v England
Back row: T W Pearson, H Packer, J Hannan, A Duncan (umpire), W R Evans, E V Pegge, P Bennett.
Middle row: D Gwyn, D W Evans, C S` Arthur, W A Bowen (C), R L Thomas, W Bancroft.
Front row: C J Thomas, D P M Lloyd, H M Ingledew.
[*Swansea C & FC*]

8. 1892 v England
Back row: W H Watts, T Deacon, F M Mills, C B Nicholl, T C Graham, J Hannan.
Middle row: T W` Pearson, R M Garrett, W M McCutcheon, J A Gould (C), R L Thomas, W Bancroft, A W Boucher.
Front row: G A Rowles, H P Phillips.
[*Newport Athletic Club*]

9. 1895 v England
Back row: T Williams (touch judge), T H Jackson, F M Mills, T W Pearson, A W Boucher, W J Elsey, S H Biggs.
Middle row: C B Nicholl, J Hannan, W H Watts, J A Gould (C), T C Graham, W Ll Thomas.
Front row: O Badger, W Bancroft, B Davies.
[*Auty Collection*]

1931, 1932, 1933; South Africa, 1931: Scored 4t 2dg - 20 points

A former schoolmaster, Ronnie Boon became an Inspector of Schools. He scored a try for Cardiff against South Africa in 1931. His try and drop-goal against England in 1933 enabled Wales to achieve their first victory at Twickenham. A good, all-round sportsman, he became the Welsh AAA 220 yards champion in 1929 (representing Roath Harriers) and played cricket for Glamorgan and Fifeshire. He was honorary secretary to London Welsh RFC from 1961-9 and was elected president of Barry RFC in 1971. Trinity College Carmarthen granted him an honorary fellowship in July 1990.

BOOTH, Joseph
Born Abergavenny, 1873; died Sedgefield, Durham, 28 April 1958
Career: Pontymister; West Hartlepool; Durham County

Forward in 1 match, against: Ireland, 1898

Joe Booth, who was a coal trimmer, captained Pontymister in 1897-98 and was the first player from a Monmouthshire valley team to be capped. After his international debut at Limerick, he joined West Hartlepool in the autumn of the same year and played for Durham County for five seasons, making nine appearances.

BOOTS, John George
Born Aberbeeg, 2 July 1874; died Newport, 30 December 1928
Career: Aberbeeg; Cross Keys; Newport; Pill Harriers; Blackheath; London Welsh

Forward in 16 matches, against: Ireland, 1898, 1899, 1900, 1901, 1902, 1903; England, 1898, 1900, 1901, 1902, 1903, 1904; Scotland, 1900, 1901, 1902, 1903: Scored 1t - 3 points

George Boots, whose parents came from Oxfordshire, played his first game for Newport on 28 October 1895 and went on to make a total of 365 appearances for the club, captaining them in 1903-04. On 5 April 1919, he captained Pill Harriers against Guy's Hospital. He was banned by the Scottish Union for allegedly signing professional forms but this did not affect his status in Wales. In later years he was an umpire in Minor Counties cricket. He was employed in the insurance business, and was also a councillor in Newport. Several brothers were also first class players.

BOUCHER, Arthur William
Born Gobowen, Shropshire, 29 June 1870; died Dinas Powys, 25 April 1948
Career: Clytha School; Newport; Barbarians

Forward in 13 matches, against: England, 1892, 1893, 1894, 1895, 1896, 1897; Scotland, 1892, 1893, 1895; Ireland, 1892, 1893, 1895, 1896: Scored 1t - 3 points

Arthur Boucher, who was a shipping executive, captained Newport in the 1895-97 and 1898-99 seasons and was the secretary of the club from 1894-99. He was also a vice-president of Dinas Powys RFC. A tall, mobile and fast forward, he often played in the backs. Newport's young player of the year trophy is named after him.

BOWCOTT, Henry Morgan
Born Cardiff, 30 April 1907
Career: Cardiff High School; Cambridge University; Welsh Secondary Schools; Cardiff; London Welsh; Wasps; Barbarians; Middlesex

Centre/stand-off in 8 matches, against: Scotland, 1929, 1931; France, 1929; Ireland, 1929, 1933; England, 1930, 1931, 1933 : Scored 1t - 3 points

British Isles 1930 tour New Zealand: 4 caps, Australia: 1 cap

A former Cambridge Blue (1927-8), Harry Bowcott spent his working career in the civil service. He captained London Welsh in 1934-35 and, after retiring from playing rugby, he took on a number of important administrative posts in the sport including WRU selector (1963-74), WRU president (1974-5) and assistant manager for the Welsh tour to Argentina in 1968. Out of a total of twenty-one matches played by the 1930 British Isles tourists in New Zealand, he appeared in sixteen, scoring six tries. His brother Jackie, a scrum-half, was also a Cambridge Blue (1933-34) and played for Cardiff.

BOWDLER, Frederick Arthur
Born Abercarn, 4 January 1901; died Chepstow, 17 December 1962
Career: Abercarn; Cross Keys

Hooker in 15 matches, against: New South Wales, 1927; England, 1928, 1929, 1930, 1932; Scotland, 1928, 1929, 1932 ; Ireland, 1928, 1929, 1932, 1933; France, 1928, 1929; South Africa, 1931

Lonza Bowdler, a collier at Cwmcarn Colliery, often went directly from the pit to play in a match. He played for Abertillery and Cross Keys against New South Wales in 1927 and South Africa in 1931. He captained Cross Keys in 1928-29.

BOWEN, Bleddyn
Born Trebanos, 16 July 1961
Career: Cwmtawe Comprehensive School; Welsh Secondary Schools; Welsh Youth; South Wales Police;

Swansea; Glamorgan; Barbarians; Wales B

Centre/stand-off in 24 matches, against: Romania, 1983; Scotland, 1984, 1986, 1988, 1989; Ireland, 1984, 1986, 1988, 1989; France, 1984, 1986, 1988; England, 1984, 1986, [1987 World Cup], 1988; Fiji, 1985, 1986; Tonga, 1986; Western Samoa, 1986, 1988; Canada, [1987 World Cup]; New Zealand, [1987 World Cup]; United States, 1987: Scored 5t, 1con, 5pg - 37 points

Former South Wales Police officer Bleddyn Bowen captained Wales in five games and South Wales Police in 1987. He is now a sales representative in the photocopying business.

BOWEN, Clifford Alfred
Born Morriston, 3 January 1875; died Rickmansworth, 30 April 1929
Career: Athenaeum School, Llanelli; Wycliffe College; Llanelli; Plymouth Albion

Wing in 4 matches, against: England, 1896, 1897; Scotland, 1896; Ireland, 1896: Scored 1t - 3 points

Cliff Bowen captained Llanelli in 1895-96. He was also a keen cricketer and played for Carmarthenshire in the Minor Counties Championship. He was employed as a docks official in the Naval Dockyard, Devonport.

BOWEN, David Harry
Born Llanelli, 4 May 1864; died Bynea, 17 August 1913
Career: Normal College, Bangor; Llanelli

Back in 4 matches, against: England, 1882, 1886, 1887; Scotland, 1886

Harry Bowen, who captained Llanelli from 1885-87, spent a lifetime in education and ended his working career as a headmaster. He was a WRU selector, an International Board representative (1908) and refereed the 1905 England v Scotland match. He was also the rugby correspondent for the Cardiff *Evening Express*.

BOWEN, George Einon
Born 1863, registered in Swansea; died Porthcawl, 13 January 1919
Career: Swansea; Llanelli

Half-back/back in 4 matches, against: Scotland, 1887, 1888; Ireland, 1887, 1888

George Bowen was an official at the Ashburnham Tinplate works, Burry Port and served as Mayor of Kidwelly. He also played cricket for Glamorgan.

BOWEN, William
Born Swansea, 6 December 1897
Career: Hafod School; Swansea Schoolboys; Welsh Schoolboys; Baycliffe; Swansea

Stand-off in 6 matches, against: Scotland, 1921, 1922; France, 1921, 1922; England, 1922; Ireland, 1922: Scored 2t - 6 points

Bowen was employed as a railway checker and later as a groundsman. He joined Leeds RLFC in August 1922 scoring a try on his debut on 2 September.

BOWEN, William Arnold
Born 1862, registered in Pembroke; died Swansea, 26 September 1925
Career: Swansea

Forward in 13 matches, against: England, 1886, 1887, 1890, 1891; Scotland, 1886, 1887, 1889, 1890, 1891; Ireland, 1887, 1889, 1890; New Zealand Natives, 1888

Bowen, who captained Swansea from 1889-92 and Wales against England in 1891, was employed as a docker and later a builder.

BRACE, David Onllwyn
Born Gowerton, 16 November 1932
Career: Gowerton Grammar School; University College Cardiff; Oxford University; Welsh Secondary Schools; Gorseinon; Aberavon; Swansea; Newport; Llanelli; Royal Air Force; Combined Services; Barbarians

Scrum-half in 9 matches, against: England, 1956, 1957; Scotland, 1956, 1960; Ireland, 1956, 1960, 1961; France, 1956, 1960: Scored 1t - 3 points

Onllwyn Brace, an Oxford Blue (1955-6), captained Wales in two matches and Llanelli from 1959-61. He was employed by the Steel Company of Wales as an assistant education officer before joining BBC Wales where he became Head of Sport. He was the brother-in-law of the late Gwynne Walters, the international referee.

BRADDOCK, Kenneth James
Born Treowen, 28 August 1938
Career: Greenfield Secondary Modern School; Cwmcarn United; Crumlin; Abertillery; Cross Keys; Newbridge; Newport Borough Police; Monmouth Police; Welsh Police; English Police; British Police

Flanker in 3 matches, against: Australia, 1966; Scotland, 1967; Ireland, 1967

After working for ten years as a collier at Celynen North colliery, Ken Braddock became a police officer and has captained every police side that he has appeared for. He played for Abertillery and Newport against Fiji in September 1964. In his free time he grows exhibition fuschias and is a keen coarse fisherman.

BRADSHAW, Keith
Born Cefn Cribbwr, 7 April 1939
Career: Ogmore Grammar School; Welsh Secondary Schools; Cefn Cribbwr; Tondu; Bridgend; Barbarians

Centre in 9 matches, against: England, 1964, 1966; Scotland, 1964, 1966; Ireland, 1964, 1966; France, 1964, 1966; South Africa, 1964: Scored 1t 6con 7pg - 36 points

Keith Bradshaw, who captained Bridgend in 1964-65, was employed as a draughtsman for the National Coal Board before becoming a schoolmaster. He is the chairman of the selectors at Aberavon RFC. His son Chris has played for Bridgend and Swansea.

BREWER, Trevor John
Born Newport, 16 August 1930
Career: Newport High School; Oxford University; Welsh Secondary Schools; Newport; London Welsh; Gloucester; The Army; Combined Services; Hampshire

Wing in 3 matches, against: England, 1950, 1955; Scotland, 1955: Scored 2t - 6 points

Oxford Blue (1951) Trevor Brewer toured Japan with the university team during September and October 1952 and captained London Welsh in 1956-57. As well as his prowess on the rugby field, he was a good athlete and won the Welsh Secondary Schools AAA senior 220 yards in 1947 and, in the same year, set the Newport High School 100 yards record of 10.1 seconds. He ran for Wales in 1946 and 1947. He is employed by Imperial Chemical Industries as a production services manager.

BRICE, Alfred
Born Weare, Somerset 23 September 1871; died Port Talbot, 28 May 1938
Career: Ogmore Vale; Aberavon; Cardiff; Glamorgan Police; Somerset

Forward in 18 matches, against: England, 1899, 1900, 1901, 1902, 1903, 1904; Scotland, 1899, 1900, 1901, 1902, 1903, 1904; Ireland, 1899, 1900, 1901, 1902, 1903, 1904: Scored 2t 1con - 8 points

A one time collier and police officer, Alfred Brice was suspended for eight months for swearing at the referee in the match against Ireland in 1904. He captained Aberavon from 1900-02 and also played water polo for Port Talbot. He played for Cardiff against South Africa in January 1907. In 1919, he was awarded the certificate of the Royal Life Saving Society for attempting to save a drowning girl. Sporting his Welsh cap he became a well-loved figure, running the line in a number of matches.

BRIDGES, Christopher Jeffrey
Born Beddau, 31 August 1968
Career: Bryncelynnog Comprehensive School, Pontypridd; Beddau Youth; Welsh Youth; Llantwit Fardre; Wales Under 19 and Under 21; Neath

Scrum-half in 6 matches, against: Namibia, 1990 (2); Barbarians, 1990; England, 1991 (r); Ireland, 1991; France, 1991: Scored 1t - 4 points

Chris Bridges works in the construction industry.

BRIDIE, James
Born Scotland, c1857
Career: St Madras College; Greenock Wanderers; Cardiff; Penarth; Newport; Monmouthshire

Half-back in 1 match, against: Ireland, 1882: Scored 1t - 3 points

Little is known of Bridie's background. He moved from Greenock to Cardiff where he was a works manager. He had been chosen to play against Scotland in Edinburgh in 1883 but was apparently withdrawn from the team after it had arrived in Edinburgh because of Scottish objections to his selection to represent Wales and, as a result of this late change, his name appeared as a member of the Welsh team in some newspapers. It appears that in order to effect this change, George Harding moved from forward to half-back and John Griffin was drafted into the pack.

BRITTON, Gordon Richard
Born Risca, 10 September 1939
Career: Pontymister Secondary Modern School; Risca Youth; Pontypool; Newport; Monmouthshire

Centre in 1 match, against: Scotland, 1961

Gordon Britton is a police sergeant in Newport. He represented Monmouthshire AAA in the long jump.

BROUGHTON, Augustus Stephen
Born Llandough, Penarth, 29 April 1904; died Llwynypia, 22 September 1981
Career: Treherbert; Treorchy; Penarth; Glamorgan Police; British Police

Forward in 2 matches, against: New South Wales, 1927; Scotland, 1929

Originally a mortar miller, Gus Broughton became a police

officer and, after retiring from the force, was a security officer. He weighed over 16 stone when he won his Welsh cap. He captained Treorchy in 1927-28 and 1929-30 and also played water polo. His son Russell captained Treorchy in 1966-67.

BROWN, Archie
Born details unknown
Career: Risca; Cross Keys; Newport

Scrum-half in 1 match, against: Ireland, 1921

Formerly an electrician, Archie Brown later became a schoolmaster. He joined Leeds RLFC in 1921, playing his first game on 29 August. He later moved to Dewsbury RLFC.

BROWN, James
Born Cardiff, 22 March 1901; died Gabalfa 30 July 1976
Career: Stacey Road School, Cardiff; Cardiff Romilly; Cardiff

Forward in 1 match, against: Ireland, 1925

Dock worker Jim Brown joined Pontypridd RLFC, making his debut against the New Zealanders on Christmas Day 1926.

BROWN, John Alfred
Born Cardiff, October 1881; died Cardiff, 3 August 1936
Career: St Peter's; Cardiff; Glamorgan

Forward in 7 matches, against: England, 1907, 1908, 1909; Scotland, 1907, 1908; Ireland, 1907; France, 1908: Scored 1t - 3 points

John Alf Brown (who had a Scottish father and an Irish mother) was employed as a coal trimmer and died of pneumoconiosis. He played for Glamorgan against South Africa in October 1906 and for Cardiff against the same opponents in January 1907. His son Duncan played for Cardiff and appeared for Wales in a Service international match against England in 1943.

BROWN, Mark Anthony
Born Newport, 18 December 1958
Career: Fairwater Comprehensive School; Cwmbran; Pontypool; Blaenavon

Flanker in 6 matches, against: Romania, 1983; England, 1986; Scotland, 1986; Fiji, 1986(r); Tonga, 1986; Western Samoa, 1986

Mark Brown captained Pontypool in 1988-89 and is employed as a quantity surveyor.

BRYANT, David John
Born Bridgend, 21 February 1967
Career: Bryntirion Comprehensive School; South Glamorgan Institute; Welsh Schools; Welsh Students; Bridgend; Wales B

Flanker in 8 matches, against: New Zealand, 1988, 1988; Western Samoa, 1988; Romania, 1988; Scotland, 1989; Ireland, 1989; France, 1989; England, 1989

At the time of publication, David Bryant is a student.

BUCHANAN, David Anthony
Born Ystradgynlais, 30 June 1955
Career: Ystradgynlais; Llanelli

Prop in 5 matches, against: Tonga, [1987 World Cup]; England, [1987 World Cup]; New Zealand, [1987 World Cup]; Australia, [1987 World Cup]; Ireland, 1988

Anthony Buchanan was a colliery supervisor before becoming a sales representative. He had played in goal for the Neath and District Soccer League before taking up rugby with Ystradgynlais, where he played at No 8.

BURCHER, David Howard
Born Newport, 26 October 1950
Career: Newport High School; St Luke's College Exeter; Welsh Secondary Schools; Bath; Newport; Cardiff; Barbarians; Eastern Counties; Wales B

Centre in 4 matches, against: Ireland, 1977; France, 1977; England, 1977; Scotland, 1977

British Isles 1977 tour New Zealand: 1 cap

David Burcher, a former school master, appeared in fourteen matches during the 1977 British Isles tour of New Zealand. He was a replacement for Elgan Rees on the Welsh tour of the United States and Canada in May 1980. In October 1980 he played for Cardiff against New Zealand and captained Newport from 1976-78. A Welsh selector, he is currently a building society manager.

BURGESS, Robert Clive
Born Manmoel, 25 November 1950
Career: Glyncoed Secondary Modern School, Ebbw Vale; Croesyceiliog; Ebbw Vale; Breschia (Italy); Wales B

Flanker in 9 matches, against: Ireland, 1977, 1981; France, 1977, 1981, 1982; England, 1977, 1982; Scotland, 1977, 1982: Scored 1t - 4 points

A former merchant seaman, Clive Burgess is now employed as a driver. He is a nephew of Ron Burgess the Welsh soccer international and a cousin to Welsh rugby

10. 1896 v England
Back row: W H Watts, F H Dauncey, F M Mills, C B Nicholl, A W Boucher, S H Ramsay, W Bancroft.
Middle row: E E George, J A Gould (C), H Packer, A M Jenkin (standing).
Front row: D Morgan, C A Bowen, B Davies, O Badger. *[Auty Collection]*

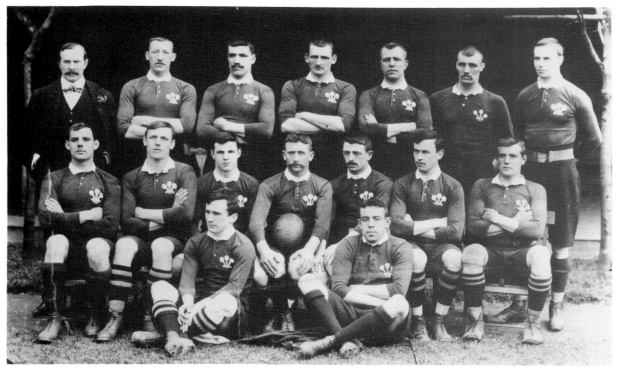

11. 1899 v Ireland
Back row: T Williams (WRU official), A Brice, J Blake, D Hellings, W H Alexander, D J Daniel, E G Nicholls.
Middle row: F H Cornish, J G Boots,W Bancroft (C), H V P Huzzey, R T Skrimshire, J J Hodges.
Front row: G Ll Lloyd, S H Biggs. *[J B G Thomas]*

international Ian Watkins [*qv*].

Tredegar Rifle Club.

BURNETT, Roy
Born Abercarn, 6 October 1926
Career: Abercarn; Newport; Barbarians

Stand-off in 1 match, against: England, 1953

Roy Burnett, who captained Newport in 1952-53, a former schoolmaster is now employed as a steelworks official. Newport fans were unable to understand how Cliff Morgan kept him out of the Welsh team. In later years he made a successful move to the wing position which prolonged his career to 373 appearances from Newport between 1947-59. His brother Doug was killed in the Llandow air crash in 1950.

BURNS, James
Born Cardiff, 22 February 1899; died Cardiff, 1971
Career: Cardiff

Forward in 2 matches, against: France, 1927; Ireland, 1927

Jim Burns appeared for Cardiff against New South Wales in December 1927. A marine engineer who later became a licensee, Burns was a cousin of boxer Jim Driscoll.

BUSH, Percy Frank
Born Cardiff, 23 June 1879; died Cardiff, 19 May 1955
Career: Penygraig; University College Cardiff; Cardiff; London Welsh; Nantes (France); Glamorgan

Stand-off in 8 matches, against: New Zealand, 1905; England, 1906, 1908; South Africa, 1906; Ireland, 1907, 1910; Scotland, 1908, 1910: Scored 2t 1con 3dg - 20 points

British Isles 1904 tour Australia: 3 caps, New Zealand: 1 cap

A former schoolmaster, Percy Bush taught at Wood Street School, Cardiff before becoming a consular official and serving as British vice-consul in Nantes, France. On his departure from France, the French government awarded him the Medaille d'Argent de Gratitude. During the 1904 British Isles tour of New Zealand, he appeared in all five matches and was the team's top scorer. He captained Cardiff in the 1905-07 and 1908-09 seasons. Playing for Nantes against Le Havre in 1910, Percy scored 54 points, made up of ten tries, eight conversions and two drop goals. He also played cricket for Glamorgan and MCC. His brother Fred played in the Cardiff backs before moving to the north of England. In a letter to Percy written in 1908, he expressed that he had a poor opinion of the rugby league game, "it is nothing more than a kick and rush affair". Percy's father James was one of the prime movers of the

BUTLER, Edward Thomas
Born Newport, 8 May 1957
Career: Monmouth School; Cambridge University; Pontypool; Barbarians; Wales B

No 8 in 16 matches, against: France, 1980, 1983, 1984; England, 1980, 1983, 1984; Scotland, 1980, 1982, 1983, 1984; Ireland, 1980, 1982, 1983, 1984; New Zealand, 1980(r); Romania, 1983; Australia, 1984: Scored 2t - 8 points

British Isles 1983 tour (r) New Zealand

Cambridge Blue (1976-8) Eddie Butler is a schoolmaster and rugby pundit. After arriving in New Zealand as one of five replacements, he played in the seventeenth and penultimate match of the British Isles 1983 tour.

CALE, William Raymond
Born Usk, 18 July 1922
Career: Ebbw Vale; Newbridge; Pontypool

Flanker in 7 matches, against: England, 1949, 1950; Scotland, 1949, 1950; Ireland, 1949, 1950; France, 1950: Scored 1t - 3 points

Ray Cale was a greengrocer and is a director of a dairy. In December 1947, he played for Pontypool, Blaenavon and Talywain against the Australians. He failed to be selected for the Australasian tour in 1950 (when by common consent he was regarded as the best back row forward in Europe) because he was apparently too rough for the New Zealanders. He joined St Helen's RLFC in September 1950 and gained four Welsh RL caps.

CARTER, Alun Jonathan
Born 13 December 1964
Career: West Monmouth College; Kelly College Tavistock; Welsh Schools; British Police; Combined Services; Pontypool; Millau (France); Newport; Wales B

Flanker in 2 matches, against: England, 1991; Scotland, 1991

Alun Carter, who captained the Welsh Schools side that went to Canada in 1983, was, for a period, a police officer in the Gwent Constabulary. He toured New Zealand with a Great Britain police side in 1988.

CATTELL, Alfred
Born Cottesmore, Rutland 27 April 1857; died Sheffield, 10 September 1933
Career: Cottesmore School; St Mark's Church of England

College, Chelsea; Oxford University; Llanelli

Forward in 2 matches, against: England, 1882; Scotland, 1883

A headmaster and sometime wholesaler, Alfred Cattell served as Lord Mayor of Sheffield and was the chairman of Sheffield United FC.

CHALLINOR, Cyril
Born Neath, 13 May 1912; died Neath, 29 November 1976
Career: Crynant; Neath

Forward in 1 match, against: England, 1939

Collier Cyril Challinor, the captain of Crynant in 1935-36, was one of five brothers who played for the club.

CLAPP, Thomas John Sercombe
Born Marylebone, 1858
Career: Monmouth School; Blaina; Newport

Forward in 14 matches, against: Ireland, 1882, 1884, 1887, 1888; England, 1883, 1884, 1885, 1887; Scotland, 1883, 1884, 1885, 1886, 1887, 1888: Scored 2t - 6 points

Tom Clapp captained Blaina in 1880-81 and Newport from 1884-86 and Wales three successive times, including the first win over Scotland. He had also captained Abergavenny Cricket Club in 1880. Clapp emigrated to the United States at the end of the 1880s.

CLARE, James Arthur
Born London, 1857; died Cardiff, 4 January 1930
Career: Christ College, Brecon; Cardiff

Back in 1 match, against: England, 1882

James Clare was a merchant seaman and qualified as a channel pilot. According to the records at Christ College, he was employed as a secretary to the Rev J D Williams, headmaster of the school. In the first football match between the College and the town of Brecon, played under the rugby code when the teams were twelve a side, Clare played for the school team. His cap is in the Cardiff RFC museum.

CLARK, Samuel Simmonds TD
Born Weymouth, 1857; died Mumbles, 25 May 1947
Career: Neath

Back/full back in 2 matches, against: Ireland, 1882, 1887

Solicitor Samuel Clark served as an officer in the Territorial Army. He was the secretary of the South Wales Football Union in 1880 and captained Neath from 1885-88. A good all round sportsman, he played cricket for Neath, Chippenham and the MCC, started a soccer team in Neath in 1893 and also played hockey for the town.

CLEAVER, William Benjamin JP
Born Treorchy, 15 September 1921
Career: Pentre School; University College, Cardiff; Treorchy; Pentre; Bridgend; Cardiff; Newbridge; Barbarians

Centre/stand-off/full back in 14 matches, against: England, 1947, 1948, 1950; Scotland, 1947, 1948, 1950; France, 1947, 1948, 1950; Ireland, 1947, 1948, 1949, 1950; Australia, 1947: Scored 1t 1dg - 6 points

British Isles 1950 tour New Zealand: 3 caps, Australia

Mining engineer Billy Cleaver was Deputy Director of Mining for the South Wales Coalfield until his retirement in August 1983. He is the chairman of the Butetown Railway Historical Society and was appointed vice chairman of the Welsh Arts Council and a member of the Arts Council of Great Britain. He played in thirteen matches for the British Isles tourists in New Zealand and in two matches in Australia. He appeared in 141 games for Cardiff from 1945-51.

CLEGG, Barry George
Born Cymmer, 30 October 1951
Career: Cymmer County School; Cwmavon Secondary Modern School; Dyffryn County School; Cwmavon Youth; Cwmavon; Maesteg; Swansea; Neath; Welsh Fire Service; Great Britain Fire Service; Glamorgan; Wales B

Lock in 1 match, against: France, 1979

A former bricklayer, Barry Clegg became an officer in the fire service. He boxed for Glamorgan at schoolboy level and has also represented the fire service at soccer.

CLEMENT, Anthony
Born Morriston, 8 February 1967
Career: Llansamlet Junior School; Morriston Comprehensive School; Welsh Schools; Welsh Youth; Wales Under 20/21; Swansea; Barbarians; Wales B

Centre/full back/stand-off in 11 matches, against: United States, 1987 (r); England, 1988; New Zealand, 1988, 1989; Western Samoa, 1988 (r); Romania, 1988; Scotland, 1990(r), 1991 (r); Ireland, 1990 (r); Namibia, 1990, 1990: Scored 2t - 8 points

British Isles 1989 tour (r) Australia

Tony Clement, who played soccer for Swansea Schools, is now employed as a car leasing executive. He played in two matches for the British Isles in Australia in 1989

CLEMENT, William Harries OBE, MC, TD
Born Llanelli, 9 April 1915
Career: Llanelli County School; Felinfoel; Llanelli

Wing in 6 matches, against: England, 1937, 1938; Scotland, 1937, 1938; Ireland, 1937, 1938: Scored 1t - 3 points

British Isles 1938 tour South Africa

A local government employee, Bill Clement played in six matches for the British tourists in South Africa in 1938 and was captain of Llanelli in 1938-39. He was the WRU secretary from 1956-81. He served as a Major in 4th Bn, The Welch Regiment during the Second World War and was awarded the Military Cross after the 'Battle of the Bulge' in 1944. He received the OBE in the 1981 New Years Honours List, prior to retiring as secretary of the WRU at the end of the centenary season.

COBNER, Terence John
Born Blaenavon, 10 January 1946
Career: West Monmouth Grammar School; Madeley College, Staffordshire; Welsh Secondary Schools; Blaenavon; Pontypool; Walsall; Barbarians; Gwent; Staffordshire; Wales B

Flanker in 19 matches, against: Scotland, 1974, 1975, 1976, 1977, 1978; Ireland, 1974, 1975, 1978; France, 1974, 1975, 1977, 1978; England, 1974, 1975, 1976, 1977, 1978; Australia, 1975, 1978: Scored 2t - 8 points

British Isles 1977 tour New Zealand: 3 caps.

Terry Cobner is a schoolmaster at Oundle School. He appeared for the Wales Under 25 team against Fiji and captained Pontypool for an amazing ten consecutive seasons. In 1970 he played for Midland Counties East against South Africa, and appeared in eleven matches for the 1977 British Isles tourists in New Zealand. He has the great ability of tackling the opposition and emerging with the ball and his only fault was a tendency to drop passes, which may have been caused by indifferent eyesight. He was an influential figure in the 1977 tour of New Zealand and was captain of the Welsh side that toured Australia in 1978. Since retiring from playing he has contributed to the game as a coach to the Welsh XV. His father-in-law serves on the committee of Wigan RLFC.

COLDRICK, Albert Percival
Born Caerleon, 1888; died Wigan, 26 December 1953
Career: Crumlin; Newport; Weston-Super-Mare; Monmouthshire
Forward in 6 matches, against: England, 1911, 1912; Scotland, 1911, 1912; Ireland, 1911; France, 1912

Percy Coldrick, a railway platelayer, joined Wigan RLFC in August 1912 and later played for the Wales (two caps) and the Great Britain RL teams. He (and Gus Merry) asked to be reinstated as amateurs in 1919 but were both refused as they had played RL regularly between 1914-19. His grandson, Graham, is a Wales Under 23 footballer.

COLEMAN, Ernest Owain
Born Newport, 3 November 1917
Career: Newport Juniors, Newport

Prop in 3 matches, against: England, 1949; Scotland, 1949; Ireland, 1949

Ernie Coleman, who was a steelworker, played in a wartime Services international whilst serving in the 1st Bn Monmouthshire Regiment. He played for Newport against Australia in 1947. His brother John played flanker for Newport.

COLES, Fenton Godfrey
Born Blaenavon, 14 September 1937
Career: Blaenavon Secondary School; Blaenavon; Pontypool; Monmouthshire

Wing in 3 matches, against: Scotland, 1960; Ireland, 1960; France, 1960

Fenton Coles was a collier and later, an electrician. He played for Pontypool and Cross Keys against South Africa in November 1960 and was captain of Pontypool in 1964-65. He is a member of the committee at Pontypool.

COLLINS, John Ernest
Born Aberavon, 16 January 1931
Career: St Joseph's School, Aberavon; Cwmgwrach; Aberavon Green Stars; Aberavon; Devonport Services; Royal Navy; Barbarians

Wing in 10 matches, against: Australia, 1958; England, 1958, 1959, 1960; Scotland, 1958, 1959; France, 1958, 1959, 1961; Ireland, 1959: Scored 3t - 9 points

A steelworker and licensee, John Collins spent some years living in Majorca. He represented Port Talbot YMCA and Wales in athletics and won the Welsh AAA 440 yards in 1952. In January 1961 he played for Neath and Aberavon against South Africa.

COLLINS, Richard Graham
Born Cardiff, 2 March 1962
Career: Mostyn School, Cardiff; St Alban's Youth; Pontypridd; Newport; South Wales Police; Cardiff; Johnsville (NZ); Wales B

Flanker in 14 matches, against: England, 1987(r), [1887 World Cup], 1988, 1989; Ireland, 1987, [1987 World Cup], 1988, 1989; New Zealand, [1987 World Cup]; United States, 1987; Scotland, 1988, 1990; France, 1988; Romania, 1988

A police officer in South Wales, Richie Collins has also represented Wales at basketball.

COLLINS, Thomas
Born Mountain Ash, 1897; died Aberdare, 10 October 1958
Career: Mountain Ash

Centre in 1 match, against: Ireland, 1923

Tom Collins was employed as a collier and served in the First World War. On 1 September 1923, he played his first game for Hull RLFC. His son Howard, has been the European Karate Champion.

COOK, Terence
Born 27 June 1927, registered in Pontypridd
Career: New Tredegar Technical College; Pontypool; Cardiff

Wing in 2 matches, against: Scotland, 1949; Ireland, 1949

Terry Cook, an engineering draughtsman, played for Pontypool, Blaenavon and Talywain against Australia in 1947. He joined Halifax RLFC where he scored a try in his debut game on 26 August 1950. He gained four caps for Wales at rugby league.

COPE, William Baron, Bart, KC, JP, DL
Born Roath, 18 August 1870; died St Mellons, 15 July 1946
Career: Mr Shewbrook's Academy; Repton; Cambridge University; Cardiff; Blackheath; Barbarians

Forward in 1 match, against: Scotland, 1896

Barrister and Cambridge Blue (1891), William Cope, who was the son of a colliery owner, practised as a solicitor and was a director of several companies including Albion Colliery and Welsh Navigation. He served as a Major in the Glamorgan Yeomanry during the First World War and was elected to parliament as the member for Llandaff and Barry in 1918, serving the constituency until 1929 when he lost the seat - it was regained for the Conservative Party in 1931 by P M Munro, a Scottish rugby international and Oxford Blue. Cope was created a baronet in the King's Birthday Honours in June 1928 and was appointed Comptroller of the Royal Household in the same year. In 1932, he was appointed High Sheriff of Glamorgan. He was made a Knight of St John, a sub-

prior of the Priory of Wales and a Justice of the Peace. In 1946, he was created Baron Cope of St Mellons (the peerage becoming extinct when he died thirteen months later). Cope also played cricket for Glamorgan.

CORNISH, Frederick Henry
Born Bridgwater, 1876; died Cardiff, 27 April 1940
Career: Bridgwater & Albion; Grangetown Stars; Cardiff

Forward in 4 matches, against: England, 1897, 1898; Ireland, 1898, 1899

A boilermaker by trade, Fred Cornish changed rugby codes and joined Hull RLFC in August 1899. The uncle of Arthur Cornish [qv], he was one of six members of his family who played for Cardiff RFC.

CORNISH, Robert Arthur
Born Cardiff, 30 June 1897; died Cardiff, 29 July 1948
Career: Grangetown Council School; Canton High School; University College, Cardiff; Welsh Schools; Cardiff; Royal Navy

Centre in 10 matches, against: England, 1923, 1924, 1925, 1926; Scotland, 1923, 1925, 1926; France, 1925, 1926; Ireland, 1926: Scored 1t 1dg - 7 points

The headmaster of Lansdowne Road Boys School, Cardiff, Arthur Cornish served in the Royal Navy during the First World War. He was the vice-captain of Cardiff in 1921-22 and captain the following season. He played in the Centenary Match at Rugby School in 1923 and also played soccer for Cardiff Corinthians. He served as chairman of Cardiff in 1945-47 and secretary in 1946-48 and was, until his death, the chairman of the Welsh selectors. He was the nephew of Fred Cornish [qv].

COSLETT, Thomas Kelvin
Born Bynea, 14 January 1942
Career: Welsh Schools; Welsh Youth; Aberavon; Llanelli

Full back in 3 matches, against: England, 1962; Scotland, 1962; France, 1962: Scored 1pg - 3 points

Employed as a steelworker and later a haulage contractor, Kel Coslett 'went North' to join St Helen's RLFC in 1962 where he scored four goals on his debut against Salford on 18 August. He later joined Rochdale Hornets RLFC and was a member of the Wales RL team, winning twelve caps. After retiring from playing, he was appointed coach to the Wales RL team. Coslett won the Lance Todd trophy in 1972.

COWEY, Bernard DSO, OBE, DL
Born Tidworth, Wiltshire, 20 November 1911

12. 1905 v Ireland
Back row: A J Davies (touch judge), W O'Neil, D Jones, A F Harding, H V Watkins, G Travers, W Joseph, W Williams (RFU referee).
Middle row: J F Williams, J J Hodges, R T Gape, W Llewelyn, E G Nicholls, E Morgan.
Front row: R M Owens, G Davies, A W Jones.
Insets: D Rees, W J Trew, R H Jones, C M Pritchard.
[*Mrs C W Jones*]

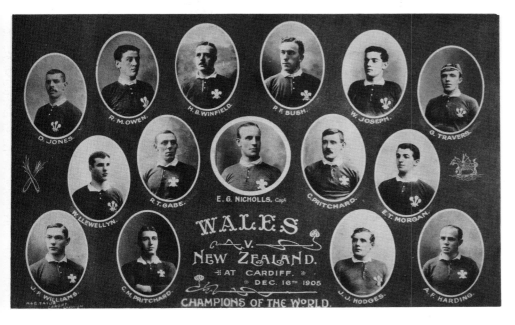

13. 1905 v New Zealand
Top row: D Jones, R M Owens, H B Winfield, P F Bush, W Joseph, G Travers.
Middle row: W Llewelyn, R T Gape, E G Nicholls (C), C C Pritchard, E Morgan.
Bottom row: J F Williams, C M Pritchard, J J Hodges, A F Harding.
[*Auty Collection*]

14. 1906 v Ireland
Back row: T Williams (touch judge), D Westacott, C M Pritchard, G Travers, W Rees (Sec WRU), T Evans, W Joseph.
Middle row: J Powell, E T Morgan, J J Hodges, E G Nicholls (C), R T Gape, H T Maddocks, A F Harding.
Front row: R M Owen, H B Winfield, R A Gibbs.
[*WRU*]

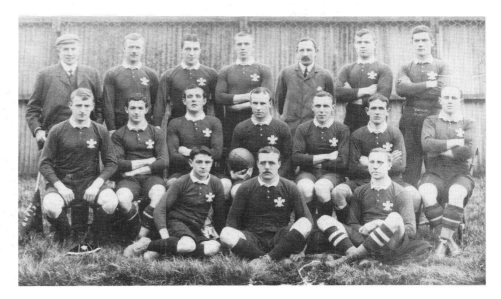

Career: Wellington College; Royal Military College, Sandhurst; Welch Regiment; The Army; Newport; London Welsh; Barbarians; Sussex

Wing in 4 matches, against: England, 1934, 1935; Scotland, 1934; Ireland, 1934: Scored 3t - 9 points

'Bun' Cowey, a regular army officer, had also represented his regiment at athletics. He took command of the 2nd Bn the Welch Regiment in Burma in 1945 and was awarded the Distinguished Service Order for his skillful and determined leadership of the battalion during May of that year. He was the chairman of the Army Rugby Union Referees Society from 1963-73 and was appointed Deputy Lieutenant of Nottinghamshire in 1973.

CRESSWELL, Brian Robert
Born Newport, 9 November 1934
Career: St Julian's High School, Newport; Welsh Schools; Abertillery; Newport Saracens; Newport

Flanker in 4 matches, against: England, 1960; Scotland, 1960; Ireland, 1960; France, 1960: Scored 2t - 6 points

A former steelworker, Brian Cresswell was controversially left out of the Newport team which beat New Zealand in 1963. He is now employed as a sales manager.

CUMMINS, William
Born 20 March 1892
Career: St Peter's Cardiff; Treorchy; Penygraig; Glamorgan Police

Forward in 4 matches, against: England, 1922; Scotland, 1922; Ireland, 1922; France, 1922: Scored 1t - 3 points

Police officer Will Cummins captained Treorchy in 1922-23. He won the Glamorgan Police boxing championship and middleweight boxing championship of Wales in 1914. In an interview with 'Argus' of the *Llanelly Star,* J G Stephens claimed that, during the match against France in 1922, he had scored the try which was officially credited to Cummins.

CUNNINGHAM, Leonard John
Born Port Talbot, 3 January 1931
Career: Aberavon Quins; Aberavon; Cheltenham; Barbarians

Prop in 14 matches, against: England, 1960, 1962, 1964; Scotland, 1960, 1962, 1964; Ireland, 1960, 1962, 1964; France, 1960, 1962, 1964; New Zealand, 1963; South Africa, 1964

Employed as a steelworker then a licensee, Len Cunningham played for Neath Aberavon against New Zealand in 1954. He captained Aberavon in 1958-59 and 1962-63 and now serves on the committee at the club.

DACEY, Malcolm
Born Swansea, 12 July 1960
Career: Cefn Hengoed Comprehensive School, Swansea; Welsh Youth; Bonymaen; Swansea; Cardiff; Barbarians; Wales B

Stand-off in 15 matches, against: England, 1983, 1984; Scotland, 1983, 1984; Ireland, 1983, 1984; France, 1983, 1984, 1987(r); Romania, 1983; Australia, 1984; Fiji, 1986; Tonga, 1986, [1987 World Cup]; Western Samoa, 1986: Scored 1con 3dg 7pg - 32 points

Malcolm Dacey appeared for British Isles(r) against the Rest of the World at Cardiff in 1986 and for the Five Nations against an Overseas XV at Twickenham in the same year. He now plays cricket for Bonymaen and is employed in marketing.

DANIEL, David John
Born Llanelli, 1871; died Llanelli, 30 April 1948
Career: Llanelli; Wortley

Forward in 8 matches, against: Scotland, 1891, 1894; England, 1894, 1898, 1899; Ireland, 1894, 1898, 1899

Employed as a mason and a brewery worker, Daniel was the father of thirteen children, including 'Gipsy' Daniel, the British light-heavyweight boxing champion.

DANIEL, Laurance Thomas David
Born Pontypool, 5 March 1942
Career: Abersychan Grammar School; Caerleon Training College; Blaenavon; Pontypool United; Ebbw Vale; Pontypool; Newport

Wing in 1 match, against: Scotland, 1970: Scored 1t 1con - 5 points

Laurie Daniel, who is a schoolmaster, captained Pontypool from 1967-69. He was one of the few successes on the 1968 Wales tour of Argentina and was unfortunate not to win more caps. In 1971-72, he became Newport's record scorer with 305 points, a total which included thirty tries. He was a member of the Newport side which beat South Africa in 1969. He is a coach to Pontypool United.

DANIELS, Patrick Charles Thomas
Born Cardiff, 15 May 1957
Career: Millfield School; Welsh Youth; Glamorgan Wanderers; Cardiff; Wales B
Centre in 2 matches, against: Australia, 1981; Ireland, 1982

Pat Daniels toured Australia in 1978 with Wales when he played in four games and, in 1980, appeared on the wing in all five matches for Wales B on their tour of the United States and Canada. In October of the same year he played for Cardiff against New Zealand and, one year later, for Wales B against Australia. He is the head of Welsh Smoked Products, a fish curing company.

DARBISHIRE, Godfrey
Born Chorlton, Lancashire, 26 September 1853; died Florida, USA, 29 October 1889
Career: Rugby School; Oxford University; Bangor

Forward in 1 match, against: England, 1881

Godfrey Darbishire, a civil engineer, was a member of the family who developed the granite quarries at Penmaenmawr and Trefor in Caernarfonshire. In addition to his university rugby honours he also rowed for the Balliol College Eight. He later became a Fellow of the Royal Geographical Society and moved to Florida where he had an orange farm and a geographical survey business. His early death was caused by exposure at sea, off Key West.

DAUNCEY, Frederick Herbert
Born Pontypool, 1 December 1871; died Newport, 30 October 1955
Career: Abergavenny Grammar School; Newport

Wing in 3 matches, against: England, 1896; Scotland, 1896; Ireland, 1896

A solicitor, Bert Dauncey captained Newport in 1897-98 and was a member of the Newport side which was unbeaten during the season 1891-92 (for which he received a magnificent gold pocket watch). His sons Bryan and John also played for the club. He also played hockey and lawn tennis for Wales.

DAVEY, Claud
Born Garnant, 14 December 1908
Career: Ystalyfera County School; Swansea University; Welsh Secondary Schools; Cwmgors; Amman United; Swansea; Sale; Aylesbury; Reading; London Welsh; Rosslyn Park; Barbarians; Lancashire; Berkshire

Centre in 23 matches, against: France, 1930, 1931; England, 1931, 1932, 1933, 1934, 1935, 1937, 1938; Scotland, 1931, 1932, 1933, 1934, 1935, 1936; Ireland, 1931, 1932, 1934, 1935, 1937, 1938; South Africa, 1931; New Zealand, 1935: Scored 5t - 15 points

A schoolmaster and electrical engineer, Claud Davey was renowned for his ferocious tackling. In October 931 he scored a try for Swansea against South Africa. He captained the national side on eight occasions and London

Welsh from 1945-47. He is the president of Cwmgors RFC.

DAVID, Richard Jenkin
Born Cardiff, January 1879; died Llandaff, 24 October 1936
Career: Albany Road School, Cardiff; Cathays United; Mackintosh; Cardiff; Bath; Glamorgan

Scrum-half in 1 match, against: Ireland, 1907

Formerly a window cleaner and later the proprietor of the Canton Window Cleaning Company, Dickie David appeared for Cardiff against New Zealand on Boxing Day 1905 and South Africa on 1 January 1907. He joined Wigan RLFC in November 1907.

DAVID, Thomas
Born Pontypridd, 2 April 1948
Career: Hawthorn Secondary Modern School; Pontypridd; Llanelli; Barbarians

Flanker in 4 matches, against: France, 1973, 1976; Australia, 1973; Ireland, 1976

British Isles 1974 tour South Africa

Tommy David began his working life as a fitter and is now a company director. He made nine appearances and scored five tries during the 1974 British Isles tour of South Africa and captained Pontypridd in 1979-80. He joined Cardiff RLFC in August 1981, aged 32 years and 4 months and made two appearances as a member of the Wales RL team.

DAVIDGE, Glyn David
Born Newport, 31 December 1933
Career: Welsh Youth; Newport; Tredegar

No 8/flanker in 9 matches, against: France, 1959, 1960, 1962; Scotland, 1960, 1961; Ireland, 1960, 1961; South Africa, 1960; England, 1961

British Isles 1962 tour(r) South Africa

Glyn Davidge is a fitter and has also been employed as a brewery representative. He made three appearances for the British tourists in South Africa in 1962 and captained Newport in 1962-63. His finest match was for Newport against New Zealand in 1963 when his contribution was immense. He ranks as one of the bravest post-war players.

DAVIES, Abel
Born Narberth, c1861; died 18 June 1914, registered in Llanelli
Career: University College London; London Welsh; United

Hospitals; Llanelli

Wing in 1 match, against: Ireland, 1889

Abel Davies was a Doctor of Medicine.

DAVIES, Adrian
Born Bridgend, 9 February 1969
Career: Pencoed Comprehensive School; Cambridge University; Welsh Schools; Wales U-19; Welsh Uni-versities; Neath; Wales B

Centre in 1 match, against: Barbarians, 1990(r)

At the time of publication, Adrian Davies, a Cambridge Blue (1988-90) is still a student at Cambridge University. He played soccer for Welsh Schools U-15. His brother Graham, a Cambridge Blue in 1988-89, has also played for Neath.

DAVIES, Alun Eirian
Born Carmarthen, 25 March 1956
Career: Stradey Secondary Modern School; Llanelli Grammar School; Welsh Secondary Schools; Llanelli; Wales B

Flanker in 1 match, against: Australia, 1984

Surveyor Alun Davies' only appearance for Wales is unfortunately best remembered as the occasion when Australia gained a push-over try after he had left a scrum on his own line. He made 288 appearances for Llanelli before retiring from the game in 1985, shortly after being a member of the victorious Llanelli team against Cardiff in the 1985 Cup Final.

DAVIES, Benjamin
Born Llanelli, 5 June 1873; died Llanelli, 23 June 1930
Career: Seaside Stars; Llanelli

Half-back in 2 matches, against: England, 1895, 1896

A licensee, Ben Davies, who captained Llanelli in 1894-95 and 1898-99, was the club secretary. He was, at one time, the coach at Llandovery College and wrote articles on rugby for the *Daily Mail* c1905.

DAVIES, Carwyn
Born Llandovery, 17 April 1964
Career: Llandovery School; Llandovery; Llanelli; Wales B

Wing in 4 matches, against: Western Samoa, 1988; Scotland, 1989; Ireland, 1989(r); France, 1989

Carwyn Davies is a farmer in Llandovery.

DAVIES, Cecil Rhys
Born 12 September 1909, registered in Pontypridd; killed in action, 25 December 1941
Career: Cardiff High School; Cardiff High School Old Boys; Cardiff; Bedford; Royal Air Force; London Welsh

Prop in 1 match, against: England, 1934

Cecil Davies joined the peace-time Royal Air Force where he beat George Beamish, the Irish rugby cap, in the final of the 1932 Royal Air Force heavyweight boxing championship. He was a reserve for the Canadian boxing team in the 1932 Olympics. His brother Selby also played for Cardiff.

DAVIES, Charles Lynn
Born Bancyfelin, 30 December 1929
Career: Queen Elizabeth Grammar School, Carmarthen; Trinity College, Carmarthen; Welsh Secondary Schools; Carmarthen Athletic; Blaengarw; Cardiff; Llanelli; Glamorgan Wanderers

Wing in 3 matches, against: England, 1956; Scotland, 1956; Ireland, 1956: Scored 2t - 6 points

A schoolmaster and electrical engineer, 'Cowboy' Davies had won the Welsh Secondary Schools 100 yards in 1947, beating Trevor Brewer [qv] into second place.

DAVIES, Christmas Howard
Born Llanelli, 25 December 1916; died Llanelli, 5 November 1987
Career: Burry Port; Swansea; Llanelli

Full back in 6 matches, against: Scotland, 1939, 1947; Ireland, 1939, 1947; England, 1947

Howard Davies was employed as a steelworker and later worked in a power station in Carmarthen. He played in two Service and two Red Cross internationals and is one of the few internationals to have played either side of the war.

DAVIES, Clifton
Born Kenfig Hill, 12 December 1919; died Bridgend, 28 January 1967
Career: Kenfig Hill Junior School; Kenfig Hill Senior School; Kenfig Hill; Steel Company of Wales; Bridgend; Cardiff; Barbarians

Prop in 16 matches, against: Scotland, 1947, 1948, 1950, 1951; France, 1947, 1948, 1949, 1950; Ireland, 1947, 1948, 1950, 1951; Australia, 1947; England, 1948, 1950, 1951: Scored 1t - 3 points

British Isles 1950 tour New Zealand: 1 cap, Australia

Cliff Davies was a collier. He scored a try for Cardiff in their victory over the 1947-48 Wallabies and was the senior member of the 1950 British Isles team that toured in New Zealand and Australia, appearing in ten games in New Zealand and two in Australia.

DAVIES, Cyril Allan Harvard
Born Ammanford, 21 November 1936
Career: Amman Valley Grammar School; University College, Cardiff; Welsh Secondary Schools; Ammanford; Swansea; Llanelli; Cardiff; Barbarians

Centre in 7 matches, against: Ireland, 1957, 1958; Australia, 1958; England, 1958, 1961; Scotland, 1958; South Africa, 1960

Cyril Davies is an electronics engineer working in the field of computers.

DAVIES, David MC
Born Llanwenog, 3 December 1884; died Hendon, 24 August 1968
Career: St David's College School, Lampeter; St David's College; Oxford University; Bishop's College, Cheshunt; Llanelli; London Welsh

Full back in 1 match, against: England, 1907

A schoolmaster and clergyman, 'Bailey' Davies was an Oxford Blue between 1905 and 1907. Following an assistant mastership at Llandovery College in 1908-09, he was appointed an assistant master at the Merchant Taylors School in 1910 where he served in the Officer Training Corps. He was commissioned as a captain in the Territorial Force and then, during the First World War, a 2nd Lieutenant in the Welsh Guards. On the restoration of peace, he returned to the Merchant Taylors School where he remained until 1946. Ordained in 1926, he was Rector of Sutton and Vicar at Eyeworth, Bedfordshire from 1946 until 1957.

DAVIES, David Brian
Born Weston-super-Mare, 7 July 1941
Career: Llanelli Grammar School; University College, Swansea; Llangennech; Llanelli; Cardiff; Newbridge; Neath; Pentyrch; Newport

Centre in 3 matches, against: Ireland, 1962; England, 1963; Scotland, 1963

Brian Davies, the son of David Idwal Davies [qv], is employed as a lecturer and rugby broadcaster.

DAVIES, David Evans George JP
Born Cardiff, 23 June 1887; died Cardiff, 2 September

1979
Career: Cardiff High School; Llandovery College; University College, London; Cardiff; London Welsh; Middlesex

Wing in 2 matches, against: England, 1912; France, 1912: Scored 2t - 6 points

A solicitor and cinema chain owner, Ewan [sic] Davies built, in 1931, what was the largest cinema in Wales, the Plaza, Swansea. He was the Liberal candidate for Cardiff South in 1924 and Llandaff & Barry in 1929. He is reputed to have been the Welsh 100 yards champion. A landowner in Pembrokeshire, he bred Hereford cattle. The president of the Welsh Youth Rugby Union for many years, he was also honorary solicitor to Cardiff Athletic Club.

DAVIES, David G
Born Treorchy, c1897
Career: Treorchy; Pontypridd; Cardiff; Rugby

Forward in 2 matches, against: England, 1923; Scotland, 1923

Dai Davies was a carpenter.

DAVIES, David Harris
Born Tonna, 27 October 1877; died 30 September 1944
Career: Tonna; Neath; Glamorgan Police; Glamorgan

Forward in 1 match, against: Scotland, 1904

Davies was a police officer in Glamorgan and was later prominent in Welsh rugby administration. He captained Neath in 1902-03.

DAVIES, David Henry
Born Port Talbot, c1894; died Cimla, Neath, 8 May 1979
Career: Sandfields School; Aberavon Quins; Aberavon

Centre in 1 match, against: England, 1924

Hunt Davies, a fitter on the Great Western Railway saw active service and was wounded during the First World War.

DAVIES, David Horace
Born 1898, registered in Bridgend; died Bridgend, 22 September 1967
Career: Bridgend; Cardiff

Centre in 2 matches, against: Ireland, 1921, 1925

Daph Davies, a telephone engineer, was captain of Bridgend in 1925-26 and later chairman. He also played

15. 1907 v Ireland
Back row: unknown official, T Evans, W Dowell, J Brown, W E Rees (Sec WRU), G Travers, J Watts, W Neill, unknown official.
Middle row: J Evans, D P Jones, C M Pritchard, R T Gape (C), H B Winfield, J L Williams, A F Harding.
Front row: P F Bush, R J David.
[*J B G Thomas*]

16. 1908 v Ireland
Back row: A Webb, G Hayward, E J Thomas, T H Evans, W O'Neil, W H Dowell.
Middle row: G Travers, R A Gibbs, W J Trew, H B Winfield (C), R T Gape, J L Williams, J Watts.
Front row: R H Jones, R M Owens.
[*Willow Murray*]

NB This team played in trial match jerseys as the wrong kit had been packed. The same mistake occurred fifty years later at Twickenham.

17. 1911 v England
Back row: J Pugsley, A Webb, W J Perry, A P Coldrick, H Jarman, T H Evans, D J Thomas.
Middle row: W I Morgan, W Spiller, R A Gibbs, W J Trew (C), F Birt, J L Williams.
Front row: J Bancroft, R M Owens.
[*Auty Collection*]

in a Civil Service international. His father Ned captained Bridgend in 1894-95 and 1901-02, while his brother Arthur E Davies captained the same club. Another brother Illtyd also played for Bridgend.

DAVIES, David Idwal
Born 10 November 1915; died Llanelli, 7 July 1990
Career: Llanelli County School; Trinity College, Carmarthen; Hendy; Pontarddulais; Swansea

Centre in 1 match, against: England, 1939

Schoolmaster Idwal Davies was the father of Brian Davies [qv]. In January 1939 he joined Leeds RLFC and won one cap with the Wales RL team. He had to wait until he was fifty-nine before receiving his cap from the WRU.

DAVIES, David John
Born Neath, 20 February 1941; died Dewsbury, 16 April 1969
Career: Maesteg Grammar School; Welsh Secondary Schools; Neath

Flanker in 1 match, against: Ireland, 1962

John Davies, a schoolmaster, joined Leeds RLFC in April 1963. He later moved to Dewsbury RLFC where, tragically he collapsed and died during a match.

DAVIES, David Maldwyn
Born Penygraig, 2 May 1925
Career: Craig yr Eos School, Penygraig; Penygraig; Somerset Police; British Police; Welsh Counties; Somerset; Barbarians

Hooker in 17 matches, against: England, 1950, 1951, 1952, 1954; Scotland, 1950, 1951, 1952; Ireland, 1950, 1951, 1952, 1953; France, 1950, 1951, 1952, 1953; South Africa, 1951; New Zealand, 1953

British Isles 1950 tour New Zealand: 2 caps, Australia: 1 cap

A former collier and police officer, Dai Davies played in eleven matches for the 1950 British tourists in New Zealand and was in competition with Karl Mullen, the tour captain, for a berth in the team. He also played for Western Counties against South Africa in January 1952 and New Zealand in November 1953.

DAVIES, Eiryn Gwyne
Born Aberkenfig, 23 June 1908
Career: Kenfig Hill; Cardiff; Cheltenham; Gloucester

Wing in 3 matches, against: France, 1928; England, 1929;

Scotland, 1930

Gwyn Davies, a furniture manufacturer, made his debut for Wigan RLFC against St Helen's on 11 October 1930. He gained three Wales RL caps, and was a member of the Great Britain side to Australia in 1936. He was a nephew of Johnny Thomas of Wigan RLFC, who scored tries in six successive rugby league tests.

DAVIES, Emlyn Price
Born Port Talbot, 15 January 1922
Career: Maesteg Grammar School; Cymmer; Glyncorrwg; Cwmavon; Aberavon; Swansea; Maesteg; British Railways; Glamorgan

Prop in 2 matches, against: Australia, 1947; Ireland, 1948

Emlyn Davies began his working life as a office boy at Port Talbot Steelworks and ended it as a terminal manager with British Railways. He played stand-off for Glyncorrwg and only began playing in the front row after joining Aberavon. On 25 October 1947, he played for Neath and Aberavon against Australia and captained Aberavon in 1949-50. He has been on the Aberavon RFC committee since 1955. He served in the Home Guard during the Second World War.

DAVIES, Evan
Born Maesteg, c1892; died c1946
Career: Plasnewydd School, Maesteg; Maesteg Rangers; Maesteg; London Welsh; Llanelli; Glamorgan

Full back in 1 match, against: New Zealand Army, 1919

Ianto Davies, a collier, captained Maesteg in 1920-21 and was known as the 'Mighty Modest Matador'. He served in the Royal Field Artillery and the Welch Regiment during the First World War.

DAVIES, George
Born 25 December 1875; died c1942
Career: Llandeilo; Swansea

Centre/full back in 9 matches, against: England, 1900, 1901, 1905; Scotland, 1900, 1901, 1905; Ireland, 1900, 1901, 1905: Scored 1t 4con - 11 points

George Davies was a stonemason.

DAVIES, Glyn
Born Cilfynydd, 24 August 1927; died Bristol, 7 November 1976
Career: Pontypridd Grammar School; Cambridge University; Welsh Secondary Schools; Cilfynydd; Cardiff; Glamorgan Wanderers; Pontypridd; Bristol; The Army;

Barbarians; Yorkshire

Stand-off in 11 matches, against: Scotland, 1947, 1948, 1949, 1951; Australia, 1947; England, 1948, 1949, 1951; France, 1948, 1949; Ireland, 1949

Cambridge Blue (1948-50), Glyn Davies, was a wine merchant. At the end of the Second World War, while still at school, he played in two Victory internationals. He was the brother-in-law of opera singer Sir Geraint Evans.

DAVIES, Harold Joseph
Born Newport, 5 December 1898; died Newport, 29 March 1976
Career: St Julian's High School, Newport; Welsh Schoolboys; Newport

Wing in 1 match, against: Scotland, 1924

British Isles 1924 tour(r) South Africa: 1 cap

Butcher Harold Davies was a fine track athlete. He captained the Welsh Schoolboys against their English counterparts at Leicester in 1913 and appeared in nine matches (scoring seven points) for the 1924 British tourists in South Africa. He captained Newport in 1925-26. During the First World War he served in the London Civil Service Battalion.

DAVIES, Harry Graham
Born Llanelli, 19 April 1899; died Llanidloes, 22 May 1990
Career: Llandovery College; Guy's Hospital; New Dock Stars; Llanelli; London Welsh; Newport; Tredegar

Centre in 3 matches, against: France, 1921, 1925; Ireland, 1921

After practising in Tredegar during the depression, Harry Davies served as the Medical Officer of Health for Llanidloes. He attributed his success on the playing field to his speed.

DAVIES, Haydn John
Born Cowbridge, 21 November 1936
Career: Cowbridge Grammar School; Cambridge University; Welsh Secondary Schools; London Welsh; Aberavon

Centre in 2 matches, against: England, 1959; Scotland, 1959

Haydn Davies played both rugby and cricket for Welsh Schools and for Mill Hill in the Middlesex Sevens. He read law and economics at Cambridge University where he gained a Blue in 1958. He toured South Africa in 1964 as a utility back with the Welsh team and captained

London Welsh in 1964-65. A chartered accountant, he is the financial director of Clive Lewis and Co, surveyors.

DAVIES, Henry Stanley
Born Ystrad, 23 April 1895; died Ystrad, 14 February 1966
Career: Goldsmith's College; Treorchy; Treherbert; Penygraig; Cardiff; Glamorgan

Forward in 1 match, against: Ireland, 1923

Headmaster Stan Davies served in the Cyclist Corps during the First World War. He was a founder member of Ystrad Rhondda RFC and a rugby referee.

DAVIES, Hopkin
Born details unknown
Career: Swansea

Forward in 4 matches, against: Ireland, 1898, 1901; England, 1898; Scotland, 1901

DAVIES, Howell
Born Pyle, 6 June 1959
Career: Kenfig Comprehensive School; Pyle; Bridgend; Glamorgan; Wales B

Full back in 4 matches, against: Scotland, 1984; Ireland, 1984; France, 1984; England, 1984: Scored 1t 4con 9pg - 39 points

Howell Davies, by trade a welder, now coaches Pyle RFC with fellow internationals, John Richardson and Clive Shell. On 26 April 1984, he scored 40 points for Bridgend against Penarth.

DAVIES, Howell John
Born details unknown
Career: Neath

Forward in 2 matches, against: England, 1912; Scotland, 1912

Davies joined Huddersfield RLFC, making his debut on 2 September 1912.

DAVIES, Ivor Thomas
Born Carmarthen, 6 April 1892; died Hampstead, 2 July 1959
Career: Queen Elizabeth Grammar School, Carmarthen; St David's College School, Lampeter; St David's College; Carmarthen Quins; Llanelli; London Welsh

Wing in 3 matches, against: Scotland, 1914; France, 1914; Ireland, 1914: Scored 2t - 6 points

Civil servant Ivor Davies served in the First World War in the 2nd Dragoon Guards (The Queen's Bays) and the Machine Gun Corps.

DAVIES, Jenkin Alban
Born 5 September 1885, registered in Aberaeron; died Los Angeles, USA, 18 July 1976
Career: St John's School, Leatherhead; Llandovery College; Oxford University; Swansea; Cardiff; London Welsh; Llanelli; Glamorgan

Forward in 7 matches, against: Scotland, 1913, 1914; France, 1913, 1914; Ireland, 1913, 1914; England, 1914: Scored 2t - 6 points

A clergyman and schoolmaster, Alban Davies (who failed to get a Blue at Oxford) was the captain of the 'Terrible Eight' against Ireland in 1914. He served as a chaplain, attached to the Royal Field Artillery, in the First World War.

DAVIES, John David
Born Carmarthen, 1 February 1969
Career: Ysgol y Preseli; Crymych; Pembrokeshire Schools; Welsh Youth; Neath; Pembrokeshire; Wales Under 21; Wales B

Prop in 2 matches, against: Ireland, 1991; France, 1991

John Davies is a farmer in Crymych.

DAVIES, John Henry
Born c1897
Career: Steel Company of Wales; Aberavon

Forward in 1 match, against: Ireland, 1923

John Davies was employed as a steelworker and clerk.

DAVIES, Jonathan
Born Trimsaran, 24 October 1962
Career: Gwendraeth Grammar School; Trimsaran Youth; Trimsaran; Neath, Llanelli; Welsh Districts; Barbarians; Wales B

Stand-off in 27 matches, against: England, 1985, 1986, 1987, [1987 World Cup], 1988; Fiji, 1985, 1986; Scotland, 1986, 1987, 1988; Ireland, 1986, 1987, [1987 World Cup], 1988; France, 1986, 1987, 1988; Tonga, 1986, [1987 (r) World Cup]; Western Samoa, 1986, 1988; Canada, [1987 World Cup]; New Zealand, [1987 World Cup], 1988, 1988; Australia, [1987 World Cup]; Romania, 1988 : Scored 5t 13dg - 59 points

Painter, later financial consultant, Jonathan Davies scored

a record thirteen drop goals for Wales. He captained Neath in 1985-87 and joined Widnes RLFC in January 1989. He toured Australia with the 1990 Great Britain RL team. On 26 August 1990, he scored 34 points for Widnes against Whitehaven, thereby equalling the club record of points scored by an individual in one match. In scoring 342 points by the end of the 1990-91 season, he became the club's leading points scorer in one season. He was chosen as the RL First Division 'Player of the Year' in May 1991 and went to play RL in Australia for the Canterbury Bulldogs during the closed season of the same year. He is the brother-in-law of Phil Davies [qv] and the author of *Jonathan: An Autobiography* which was published in 1990.

DAVIES, Leonard Morris
Born Bynea, 29 December 1930; died Morriston, 23 September 1957
Career: Stradey School; Bynea; Llanelli; Kent

Flanker in 3 matches, against: France, 1954; Scotland, 1954; Ireland, 1955

Len Davies, the brother of Terry Davies [qv] was employed on the railways and was later a clerk with an engineering firm.

DAVIES, Leslie
Born Swansea, 13 July 1913; died Swansea, 4 September 1984
Career: Danygraig School; Bonymaen; Swansea

Forward in 2 matches, against: Scotland, 1939; Ireland, 1939

Leslie Davies, who was employed as a wagon repairer, played in two Red Cross internationals. He served on the committee at Swansea.

DAVIES, Lyn
Born Blaengarw, 2 February 1940
Career: Blaengarw; Bridgend Sports; Bridgend; London Welsh; The Army

Wing in 3 matches, against: England, 1966; Scotland, 1966; Ireland, 1966

Colliery worker Lyn Davies used his bulk to smash his way to the line.

DAVIES, Mark
Born Maesteg, 9 July 1958
Career: Maesteg Comprehensive School; Nantyffyllon; Swansea; Wales B

Flanker in 3 matches, against: Australia, 1981; Ireland,

1982; Fiji, 1985

Mark Davies, a physiotherapist at Singleton Hospital, Swansea, was coached at school by J J Williams [qv]. He played for Swansea against New Zealand in 1980, and for Wales B against Australia in 1981. He captained Swansea from 1984-86.

DAVIES, Michael John CMG, OBE, DCM
Born South Africa, 7 October 1918; died Heathfield, Sussex, 8 July 1984
Career: Diocesan College, Cape Town; University of Cape Town; Oxford University; Blackheath; Barbarians

Centre in 2 matches, against: Scotland, 1939; Ireland, 1939: Scored 1t - 3 points

Rhodes Scholar, Mickey Davies, took up a career in the Colonial Service and, in 1940, went off to Tanganyika where he remained until 1947. He was awarded the OBE in 1957. He later became secretary and clerk to the Governors of Imperial College, London, and was awarded an Honorary Fellowship in 1979. He was awarded the Medaille de la Belgique Reconnaissante in 1961 and in the same year was created a CMG. He played in the Varsity match of 1939 for which he gained a wartime Blue. His failure to be selected for Oxford in 1938 astonished critics.

DAVIES, Neville Glyn
Born Cefn Fforest, Monmouthshire, 29 November 1927
Career: Lewis School, Pengam; Bedwellty Grammar School; Cross Keys; Blackheath; London Welsh; Barbarians; Sussex

Flanker in 1 match, against: England, 1955

Glyn Davies, a former language master at schools in the Home Counties and Manchester and later a managing director of the 3M Company, was chosen to appear for Wales against the 1953 All Blacks but was unable to play and his place was taken by Sid Judd. He captained Southern Counties against New Zealand on 31 October 1953. He also played basketball at international level, trialled for the British Olympic team and was the Welsh Universities heavyweight boxing champion.

DAVIES, Nigel Gareth
Born 29 March 1965
Career: Ysgol y Strade, Llanelli; Polytechnic of Wales; Welsh Youth; Welsh Students; Trimsaran; Llanelli; Wales B

Centre in 4 matches, against: New Zealand, 1988; Western Samoa, 1988; Scotland, 1989; Ireland, 1989

Nigel Davies, who was a member of the winning Llanelli

team in the 1991 Welsh Cup final, is employed as a quality engineer in a factory.

DAVIES, Philip Thomas
Born Seven Sisters, 19 October 1963
Career: Llangatwg Comprehensive School; Neath Schools; Welsh Secondary Schools; Seven Sisters; Llanelli; Barbarians; Wales B

No 8/lock/flanker in 27 matches, against: England, 1985, 1986, 1987, 1989, 1990; Fiji, 1985, 1986; Scotland, 1986, 1989, 1990; Ireland, 1986, 1987, 1989, 1991; France, 1986, 1987, 1989, 1990, 1991; Tonga, 1986, [1987 World Cup]; Western Samoa, 1986, 1988; Canada, [1987 World Cup]; New Zealand, [1987 World Cup], 1989; Romania, 1987: Scored 3t - 12 points

A former police officer and financial consultant, Phil Davies is now running a packing company. He is the most capped Llanelli forward, having overtaken the record which was previously held jointly by Norman Gale and Delme Thomas. He captained Llanelli in 1987-90. He is the brother-in-law of Jonathan Davies [qv].

DAVIES, Robin Harvard
Born Battersea, London, 12 January 1934
Career: King's College School, Wimbledon; Oxford University; King's College School Old Boys; London Welsh; Barbarians; Surrey

Flanker in 6 matches, against: Scotland, 1957, 1962; Ireland, 1957; France, 1957; Australia, 1958; England, 1962: Scored 1t - 3 points

Former Blue (1955-7) Robin Davies gained a Doctorate in Chemistry at Oxford. He captained London Welsh in 1959-60 and is now the fixtures secretary for the London club. He is employed in industry.

DAVIES, Terence John
Born Llwynhendy, 24 September 1933
Career: Stradey School; Bynea; Swansea; Llanelli; Devonport Services; Royal Marines; Royal Navy; Barbarians; Devon

Full back in 21 matches, against: England, 1953, 1957, 1958, 1959, 1960, 1961; Scotland, 1953, 1957, 1958, 1959, 1961; Ireland, 1953, 1957, 1959; France, 1953, 1957, 1958, 1959, 1961; Australia, 1958; South Africa, 1960: Scored 7con 12pg - 50 points

British Isles 1959 tour Australia, New Zealand: 2 caps

Terry Davies played for Swansea against South Africa in December 1951. He was the leading points scorer on the New Zealand leg of the 1959 British Isles tour, scoring 72

18. 1911 v Scotland
Back row: T B Schofield (touch judge), G Travers, J Webb, R Thomas, T Evans, J Birch, A P Coldrick, W E Rees (Sec WRU).
Middle row: J Pugsley, W Spiller, R A Gibbs, W J Trew (C), L M Dyke, J L Williams, D J Thomas.
Front row: R M Owen, F W Birt.
[*J B G Thomas*]

19. 1912 v France
Back row: W J Jenkins, G Stephens, J A Merry, A P Coldrick, H Uzzell, L C Trump.
Middle row: D E G Davies, W Spiller, J P Jones, T H Vile (C), R C S Plummer, F J Hawkins, H Hiams.
Front row: W J Martin, H Thomas.
[*Welsh Folk Museum*]

20. 1912 v South Africa
Back row: E Johns (touch judge), B G Hollingdale, F Andrews, R Thomas, J L Morgan, F L Perrett, H W Thomas.
Middle row: H H Wetter, W Spiller, R C S Plummer, T H Vile (C), P L Jones, G Stephens, W P Geen.
Front row: R F Williams, F Birt.
[*Welsh Folk Museum*]

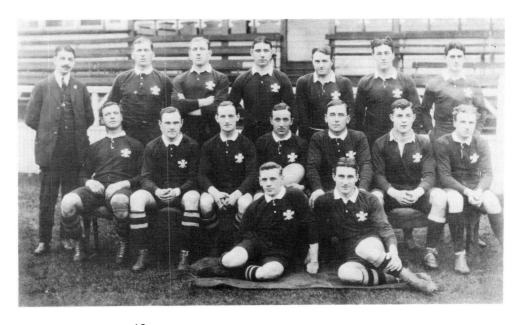

43

points in nine appearances. The brother of Leonard Davies [*qv*], he is the proprietor of a saw mill.

DAVIES, Thomas Gerald Reames
Born Llansaint, 7 February 1945
Career: Queen Elizabeth Grammar School, Carmarthen; Loughborough College; Cambridge University; Welsh Secondary Schools; Kidwelly; Llanelli; Cardiff; London Welsh; Barbarians

Centre/wing in 46 matches, against: Australia, 1966, 1969, 1973, 1978, 1978; Scotland, 1967, 1968, 1969, 1971, 1972, 1973, 1974, 1975, 1976, 1977, 1978; Ireland, 1967, 1969, 1971, 1973, 1975, 1976, 1977, 1978; France, 1967, 1969, 1971, 1972, 1973, 1974, 1975, 1976, 1977; England, 1967, 1968, 1971, 1972, 1973, 1974, 1975, 1976, 1977, 1978; New Zealand, 1969, 1969, 1972: Scored 20t - 72 points

British Isles 1968 tour South Africa: 1 cap; 1971 Australia, New Zealand: 4 caps

Schoolmaster, press correspondent, broadcaster and now Technical Officer at the National Sports Centre of Wales, Cambridge Blue (1968-70) Gerald Davies shares with Gareth Edwards the record of having scored the most tries for Wales. He was capped eleven times at centre, and thirty-five times on the wing. He played in nine matches during the 1962 British tour of South Africa, and ten matches in the 1971 tour of New Zealand. He captained Cardiff from 1975-79 and is the author of *Welsh Rugby Scrapbook*, published in 1983, and *Sidesteps, A Rugby Diary, 1985*, (written with John Morgan), published in 1985.

DAVIES, Thomas Mervyn
Born Swansea, 9 December 1946
Career: Penlan County School; Swansea College of Education; Old Guildfordians; London Welsh; Swansea; Barbarians; Surrey

No 8 in 38 matches, against: Scotland, 1969, 1970, 1971, 1972, 1973, 1974, 1975, 1976; Ireland, 1969, 1970, 1971, 1973, 1974, 1975, 1976; France, 1969, 1970, 1971, 1972, 1973, 1974, 1975, 1976; England, 1969, 1970, 1971, 1972, 1973, 1974, 1975, 1976; New Zealand, 1969 (2), 1972; Aus-tralia, 1969, 1973, 1975; South Africa, 1970: Scored 2t - 7 points

British Isles 1971 tour Australia, New Zealand: 4 caps; 1974 South Africa: 4 caps

A former schoolmaster, now in business, Mervyn Davies made thirteen appearances (scoring three tries) for the 1971 British Isles team in New Zealand. This was followed up, three years later, by five tries in twelve appearances for the British Isles during their tour of South Africa. He captained Wales in his last nine matches and Swansea in

1975-76, but his playing career was cut short by a sudden illness during a match at St Helen's, Swansea. His father played in a Victory international match in 1946. His autobiography, *Number 8*, was published in 1977.

DAVIES, W
Born details unknown
Career: Barry; Cardiff Stars; Cardiff; Glamorgan

Forward in 1 match, against: Scotland, 1896

Often referred to as Barry Davies after his home town.

DAVIES, William
Born Aberavon, 27 December 1890; died Exeter, 18 September 1967
Career: Aberavon Council School; Port Talbot County School; Exeter University; Aberavon; Swansea; Plymouth; Devon Albion; Glamorgan; Devon

Centre in 2 matches, against: Scotland, 1912; Ireland, 1912: Scored 1t - 3 points

Schoolmaster William Davies captained Glamorgan against South Africa in October 1912. He joined Leeds RLFC in March 1913 after being suspended by Wales and Devon for alleged professionalism, and was a member of both the Wales (2 caps) and Great Britain RL teams. He served in the Army during the First World War and played rugby for various unit sides.

DAVIES, William
Born Cwmgors, 14 February 1906; died Cwmgors, 5 October 1975
Career: Cwmgors School; Amman United; Swansea

Forward in 4 matches, against: South Africa, 1931; England, 1932; Scotland, 1932; Ireland, 1932 : Scored 1t - 3 points

At school and in his early years at senior level, Sgili Davies, who was a colliery official, had played at scrum-half and centre. He scored the Welsh try against the victorious Springboks, at St Helen's, in December 1931. His son Billy played at forward for Cwmgors and Swansea.

DAVIES, William Gareth
Born Carmarthen, 29 September 1955
Career: Gwendraeth Grammar School; University of Wales Institute of Science and Technology; Oxford University; Welsh Secondary Schools; Tumble; Llanelli; Cardiff; Barbarians; Carmarthenshire

Stand-off in 21 matches, against: Australia, 1978, 1978, 1981; New Zealand, 1978, 1980; Scotland, 1979, 1980,

1981, 1982, 1985; Ireland, 1979, 1982, 1985; France, 1979, 1980, 1982, 1985; England, 1979, 1980, 1981, 1982: Scored 1con 7dg 5pg - 38 points

British Isles 1980 tour South Africa: 1 cap

A former building society manager and assistant director of CBI Wales, Oxford Blue (1977) Gareth Davies was appointed Head of Sport for BBC Wales in May 1989. He is only the third BBC Wales Head of Sport, following Cliff Morgan and Onllwyn Brace, both former Welsh rugby internationals. He captained Cardiff in 1979-80. He played in only four matches for the 1980 British Isles tour of South Africa, but scored 37 points. He also played cricket for the Glamorgan 2nd XI. His autobiography, *Standing Off*, was published in 1986.

DAVIES, William Thomas Harcourt
Born Penclawdd, 23 August 1916
Career: Gowerton Grammar School; Penclawdd; Swansea; Headingley; London Welsh

Centre/stand-off in 6 matches, against: Ireland, 1936, 1937, 1939; England, 1937, 1939; Scotland, 1939: Scored 1t 1dg - 7 points

In 1939, schoolmaster Willie Davies scored the last drop-goal, valued at four points, for Wales in their final match. He joined Bradford Northern RLFC in August 1939 and represented both Wales (9 caps) and Great Britain at rugby league. The winner of the 1947 Lance Todd trophy, Davies is a cousin to Haydn Tanner [*qv*].

DAVIS, Clive Enoch
Born Tredegar, 17 September 1949
Career: Blackwood Secondary Modern School; Welsh Boys Clubs; Newbridge; Barbarians; Monmouthshire; Wales B

No 8/lock in 3 matches, against: Australia, 1978; England, 1981; Scotland, 1981: Scored 1t - 4 points

Brewery engineer Clive Davis took part in two Welsh tours: the first to Australia - where he won his first cap in the second meeting of the two countries at Sydney, and the second to North America in 1980. He scored Wales' only try in their win over England at Cardiff during the Welsh Centenary season. He captained Newbridge in the 1975-76 and 1978-80 seasons. In May 1991, he was appointed head coach at Ebbw Vale.

DAVIS, William Edward Norman
Born Birmingham, 7 September 1913
Career: Cardiff High School; King Edward's School, Camp Hill, Birmingham; Cardiff High School Old Boys; Penarth; Cardiff; Barbarians; North Midlands

Forward in 3 matches, against: England, 1939; Scotland, 1939; Ireland, 1939

'Wendy' Davis, who had a tannery, played in three Service and two Red Cross internationals. He made a total of 119 appearances for Cardiff between 1934 and 1940. Serving in the Royal Artillery during the Second World War, he played for the British Army against France in Paris in 1940. During the 1950s he was a rugby summariser on the Welsh Home Service. He retired to Cirencester where he spends a great deal of his time playing golf.

DAWES, Sydney John OBE
Born Chapel of Ease, Monmouthshire, 29 June 1940
Career: Lewis School, Pengam; University College, Aberystwyth; Loughborough College; Welsh Universities; Universities Athletic Union; Newbridge; London Welsh; Barbarians; Leicestershire; Surrey; Middlesex

Centre in 22 matches, against: Ireland, 1964, 1965, 1968, 1970, 1971; France, 1964, 1965, 1968, 1970, 1971; South Africa, 1964, 1970; England, 1965, 1969, 1970, 1971; Scotland, 1965, 1970, 1971; Australia, 1966, 1969; New Zealand, 1969: Scored 4t - 12 points

British Isles 1971 tour (captain) Australia, New Zealand: 4 caps

The captain of Wales on six occasions and the Barbarians in their memorable victory against the All Blacks at Cardiff in January 1973, John Dawes is a renowned name in British rugby both on and off the pitch. He captained the successful 1971 British Isles team that toured the Antipodes, leading the team in seventeen of the matches. He also captained London Welsh from 1965-71, the Wales tour to Argentina in 1968 and was the assistant to the Welsh team manager on the 1975 tour of the Far East and the 1978 tour of Australia, and coach to the 1977 British Isles team that toured New Zealand. After his international playing career ended, he was appointed coach to the national team and, in February 1980, Coaching Organiser for the WRU, a post which he held until October 1990. Formerly a schoolmaster; John Dawes is now involved in business. His son, Michael, has played for London Welsh.

DAY, Henry Thomas
Born Newport, September 1863; died Newport, 12 July 1911
Career: Cardiff; Newport

Forward in 5 matches, against: Ireland, 1892, 1894; England, 1893; Scotland, 1893, 1894

Carpenter Harry Day was an uncle of H T Phillips [*qv*]. He died from heart trouble after a long illness, leaving six children.

DAY, Hubert Charles
Born Griffithstown, 8 May 1908; died Salford, 27 June 1977
Career: Blaenavon; Pontypool; Newport

Forward in 5 matches, against: Scotland, 1930, 1931; Ireland, 1930; France, 1930; England, 1931

Hubert Day was a carpenter and licensee. In August 1931 he joined Salford RLFC where he played in 130 consecutive games. He gained three Wales RL caps.

DAY, Thomas Brynmor
Born Glanamman, c1907; died Swansea, 18 September 1980
Career: Coedffranc School, Skewen; Welsh Schools; Gorseinon; Swansea

Forward in 13 matches, against: England, 1931, 1932, 1935; Scotland, 1931, 1932, 1934, 1935; France, 1931; Ireland, 1931, 1932, 1934, 1935 ; South Africa, 1931

An oil refinery worker, Tom Day, who captained Swansea in 1933-34, was the son-in-law of W J Trew [qv].

DEACON, Thomas
Born 1868, registered in Swansea; died Morriston, 21 July 1921
Career: Morriston; Swansea

Forward in 4 matches, against: England, 1891, 1892; Scotland, 1892; Ireland, 1892

A carpenter by trade, Tom Deacon was employed as a building inspector by Swansea Corporation and was the secretary of the United Baptists National Benefit Society. He died as a result of injuries received in a car accident.

DELAHAY, William James
Born Bridgend, 2 September 1900; died Bridgend, 12 September 1978
Career: Penybont School; Bridgend; Cardiff; Torquay Athletic; Devon

Scrum-half/stand-off/centre in 18 matches, against: England, 1922, 1923, 1925, 1926; Scotland, 1922, 1923, 1925, 1926, 1927; Ireland, 1922, 1923, 1925, 1926; France, 1922, 1923, 1925, 1926; New Zealand, 1924: Scored 2t - 6 points

Bobby Delahay made a total of 148 appearances for Cardiff including the match against the 1924 All Blacks when, although Cardiff were beaten, he had an outstanding game and scored his team's try. He captained the club in 1926-27. At the age of 37 he was still playing rugby in Devon and captained Torquay Athletic from 1929-37. He was employed in the building trade.

DELANEY, Laurance
Born Llanelli, 8 May 1956
Career: Stebonheath Secondary Modern School; Welsh Youth; New Dock Stars; Llanelli; Wales B

Prop in 4 matches, against: Ireland, 1989; France, 1989; England, 1989, 1990

Laurance Delaney is employed as a welder. On 26 January 1991, he made his 450th appearance for Llanelli.

DEVEREUX, Donald Brian
Born 18 October 1932, registered in Neath
Career: Glynneath School; St Luke's College, Exeter; Welsh Schools; Welsh Youth; Glynneath; Neath; London Welsh

Prop in 3 matches, against: Australia, 1958; England, 1958; Scotland, 1958

Schoolmaster Don Devereux joined Huddersfield RLFC in February 1958 and later moved to Leeds RLFC. On returning to Wales, he coached the Welsh Secondary Schools team until 1973 when the WRU decided to sever the link because of his previous connection with the professional game.

DEVEREUX, John Anthony
Born Pontycymmer, 30 March 1966
Career: Ynysawdre Comprehensive School; South Glamorgan Institute; Blaengarw; Bridgend; Glamorgan Under 19

Centre in 21 matches, against: England, 1986, 1987, [1987 World Cup]; Scotland, 1986, 1987, 1989; Ireland, 1986, 1987, [1987 World Cup], 1989; France, 1986, 1987; Fiji, 1986; Tonga, 1986; Western Samoa, 1986; Canada, [1987 World Cup]; New Zealand, [1987 World Cup], 1988 (2); Australia, [1987 World Cup]; Romania, 1988: Scored 5t - 20 points

British Isles 1989 tour Australia

In 1986, John Devereux played at Cardiff for the British Isles against the Rest of the World XV. He scored two tries in five appearances during the 1989 British Isles tour of Australia. Like so many other rugby union players, Devereux was tempted north and joined Widnes RLFC in August 1989. He had played soccer for the Boys Clubs of Wales. He is now involved in business.

DIPLOCK, Richard S
Born 7 May 1965, registered in Bedwellty

Career: Glanafan Comprehensive School; Neath Tertiary College; Welsh Youth; Aberavon; Bridgend; Drummoyne (Australia)

Wing in 1 match, against: Romania, 1988

Richard Diplock is employed as a carpenter at Port Talbot Steelworks.

DOBSON, George Alexander
Born Pontypridd, 1873; died Cardiff, 8 June 1917
Career: Cardiff; Llwynypia

Forward in 1 match, against: Scotland, 1900

The brother of Tom Dobson [qv], he was employed as a coal trimmer and, after suffering long periods of ill health, died young.

DOBSON, Tom
Born Keiss, Caithness, 1871; died Cardiff, 4 July 1937
Career: Cardiff; Llwynypia

Forward in 4 matches, against: Ireland, 1898; England, 1898, 1899; Scotland, 1899: Scored 1t - 3 points

A coal trimmer at Cardiff Docks, Tom Dobson, one of the best scrummagers of his time, scored a try on his debut, against Ireland, at Limerick in March 1898. He was vice captain of Cardiff in 1898-99 and a brother to George Dobson [qv]. A great dog lover, he was especially fond of wire-haired terriers.

DONOVAN, Alun John
Born Abercrave, 5 October 1955
Career: Maesydderwen Comprehensive School; St Paul's College, Cheltenham; Swansea; Cardiff; Cheltenham; Breconshire; Wales B

Full back/centre in 5 matches, against: Australia, 1978, 1981; Ireland, 1981(r); England, 1982; Scotland, 1982

Schoolmaster Alun Donovan toured with Wales to Australia in 1978, winning his first cap, at full back, in the second encounter with Australia. In this match, the full back, J P R Williams [qv], appeared on the flank.

DONOVAN, Richard Evan
Born Llanharan, 20 January 1963
Career: Pencoed Comprehensive School; Welsh Schools Under 19; Welsh Youth; Llanharan; Swansea; South Wales Police; Welsh Police; British Police; Glamorgan; Wales B

Wing in 1 match, against: France, 1983(r)

Police officer Richard Donovan's only cap was as a replacement for Mark Wyatt against France, at Parc des Princes.

DOUGLAS, Mark Henry James
Born Aberystwyth, 10 December 1960
Career: Lampeter Comprehensive School; Welsh Secondary Schools; Lampeter; Carmarthen Athletic; Llanelli; London Welsh; Neath; Barbarians; Carmarthenshire

Scrum-half in 3 matches, against: Scotland, 1984; Ireland, 1984; France, 1984

Douglas was employed in an abattoir and now works as a butcher.

DOUGLAS, William
Born Barry, 2 July 1863; died Barry, 24 September 1943
Career: Cardiff

Back in 4 matches, against: England, 1886, 1887; Scotland, 1886, 1887

Employed as a traffic manager for David Davies & Sons, Ferndale Collieries Ltd, Cardiff, Billy Douglas gave distinguished service to sport both on and off the playing field. He was the captain of Cardiff in 1886-87, the chairman of Barry Football Club in 1891, president of Barry RFC from 1909-12, president of Barry Town RFC from 1912-14 and president of Barry Parade RFC from 1919-22. A referee of some repute, he officiated at four international matches: Ireland v England in 1891, England v Ireland in 1894, Scotland v England in 1896, England v Scotland in 1903. At the beginning of January 1902, Billy Douglas, a member of the Welsh Rugby Committee, walked out of the room where the Welsh team was being selected for the game against England on 11 January, in protest against John 'Strand' Jones being selected in preference to Bert Winfield. Douglas was also a representative on the International Board in 1914. He was a pioneer of water polo in Wales. His son, Bert, was secretary of Bryncethin RFC in the 1920s.

DOWELL, William Henry
Born Pontypool, 21 May 1885; died Newport, 9 November 1949
Career: Pontnewydd; Newport; Pontypool; Monmouthshire

Forward in 7 matches, against: England, 1907, 1908; Scotland, 1907, 1908; Ireland, 1907, 1908; France 1908

Firstly a collier and then a licensee, William Dowell played for Newport against South Africa in 1906. He joined Warrington RLFC in September 1908 and gained one Wales RL cap. His son, Dr Noel Dowell, after gaining a

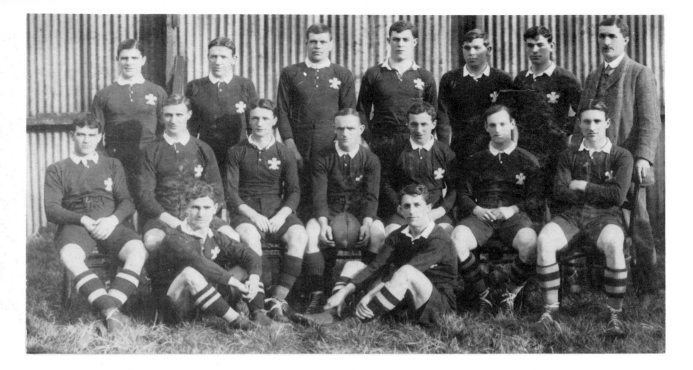

21. 1912 v Ireland
Back row: T Williams, W J Jenkins, L C Trump, G Stephens, J A Merry, H Hiams.
Middle row: F J Hawkins, H Uzzell, W Davies, J Bancroft (C), T H Vile, R C S Plummer, F Birt.
Front row: B R Lewis, W J Martin.
[*IRFU - Ulster Branch*]

22. 1914 v England
Top row: H Lewis, W H Evans, J Bancroft, W P Geen, G L Hirst.
Middle row: E Morgan, R Lloyd, J A Davies (C), J M C Lewis, T Williams (official).
Bottom row: H Uzzell, T J Lloyd, P L Jones, D Watts, J Jones.
[*Auty Collection*]
NB This was the original selected side before W J Watts replaced W P Geen.

23. 1919 v New Zealand Army
Back row: W G H Morris, J J Whitfield, A Rees, D G Francis, J Jones, E T Parker, W T Havard, unknown official.
Middle row: B M G Thomas, T J Nicholas, E B Rees, G Stephens (C), J Shea, E F Davies.
Front row: W J Martin, I J Fowler.
[*Wayne Thomas*]

48

secondary schools cap, played in the Welsh trials in the 1934-35 season.

DYKE, John Charles Meredith
Born 20 June 1884, registered in Narberth; died Westbourne, Bournemouth, 9 July 1960
Career: Christ College, Brecon; Penarth; London Welsh; Coventry; Barbarians; Glamorgan

Full back in 1 match, against: South Africa, 1906

Anglo-Welsh 1908 tour Australia, New Zealand

John Dyke, a solicitor, scored 9 points in eight appearances for the 1908 Anglo-Welsh tourists in New Zealand. He captained Penarth from 1905-07. He played for Glamorgan against New Zealand in December 1905. He was a brother of Louis Dyke [qv]. A third brother, G F E Dyke, won three Welsh hockey caps in 1907.

DYKE, Louis Meredith
Born Cardiff, 1888; died Llandough, 12 July 1961
Career: Christ College, Brecon; Penarth; Cardiff; London Welsh; Barbarians

Centre in 4 matches, against: Ireland, 1910, 1911; Scotland, 1911; France, 1911: Score 1t 2con - 7 points

Between 1908 and 1912, shipping clerk Louis Dyke made 107 appearances for Cardiff, scoring thirty-three tries and captaining the team in 1911-12. He was the brother of J C M Dyke [qv].

EDMUNDS, David Alan
Born Neath, 8 October 1961
Career: Neath Grammar School; Glamorgan Schools; Welsh Youth; Neath Athletic; Aberavon; Neath; Wales B

Wing in 2 matches, against: Ireland, 1990(r); Barbarians, 1990

Alan Edmunds is employed in the building trade. During the 1989-90 season he scored forty-five tries for Neath.

EDWARDS, Arthur Bernard
Born Bynea, 7 October 1927; died 19 September 1984
Career: Ebbw Vale Grammar School; University College Aberystwyth; London University; The Army; London Welsh; Llanelli; Ebbw Vale; Swansea; Headingley; Middlesex

Full back in 2 matches, against: England, 1955; Scotland, 1955: Scored 1pg -3 points

After a career in the Army, retiring as a Colonel in the Royal Army Education Corps, Arthur Edwards became the head of South London College of Further Education. In October 1951, he played for South Eastern Counties against South Africa and for the Combined Services team against the same opposition on Boxing Day, 1951 and kicked a penalty goal for Newport against the tourists in January 1952. He captained London Welsh in 1957-58.

EDWARDS, Benjamin Oswald
Born 29 May 1923, registered in Chepstow; died Cheltenham, 2 September 1978
Career: Newport; Ebbw Vale

Lock in 1 match, against: Ireland, 1951: Scored 1pg - 3 points

Ben Edwards, who made 115 appearances, scoring 383 points, for Newport, was employed as a foreman in a factory. He played for Abertillery and Ebbw Vale against New Zealand in December 1953. A bulky second row forward who kicked goals, Ben was probably the slowest player ever to represent Wales. His penalty goal against Ireland undoubtedly saved Wales that day. He served as the chairman of Cheltenham RFC.

EDWARDS, David
Born Glynneath, 21 March 1896; died Glynneath, 24 August 1960
Career: Glynneath; Neath; Rhigos

Forward in 1 match, against: England, 1921

Dai Edwards spent a short period as a labourer before becoming a collier and served in the Welsh Guards during the First World War. He captained Glynneath RFC from 1919 to 1921. Joining Rochdale Hornets RLFC in August 1921, he made his debut against Swinton on 27 August. He won two caps for Wales at RL. He returned to Wales in the late 1920s and coached Rhigos until stopped by the WRU for being an ex-professional player. He was however, permitted to play for Rhigos during the Second World War.

EDWARDS, Gareth Owen MBE
Born Gwaun-cae-Gurwen, 12 July 1947
Career: Pontardawe Technical School; Millfield School; Cardiff College of Education; Welsh Secondary Schools; Cardiff; Barbarians

Scrum-half in 53 matches, against: France, 1967, 1968, 1969, 1970, 1971, 1972, 1973, 1974, 1975, 1976, 1977, 1978; England, 1967, 1968, 1969, 1970, 1971, 1972, 1973, 1974 ,1975, 1976, 1977, 1978; New Zealand, 1967, 1969(2), 1972; Scotland, 1968, 1969, 1970, 1971, 1972, 1973, 1974, 1975, 1976, 1977, 1978; Ireland, 1968, 1969, 1970, 1972, 1973, 1974, 1975, 1976, 1977, 1978;

Australia, 1969, 1973, 1975; South Africa, 1970: Scored 20t 2con 3dg - 85 points

British Isles 1968 tour South Africa: 2 caps; 1971 Australia, New Zealand: 4 caps; 1974 South Africa: 4 caps

In the 1963-64 season Gareth Edwards appeared at full back for Glamorgan Secondary Schools against Munster and played in the centre for the Welsh Secondary Schools against their French counterparts in April 1966. He also had a final trial for the Welsh Youth soccer team. The Welsh Games Committee selected him the "most promising athlete of 1964" and he won the All England Schools 200 yards hurdles title. Currently employed in industrial management, he was appointed the chairman of the leisure company Hamdden, a subsidiary of Welsh Water, in May 1991 and is also a director of the Mercedes dealership Euro Commercials. He shares with Gerald Davies the Welsh try scoring record of twenty tries. He captained Wales on thirteen occasions (including the hundredth international match to be played at Cardiff Arms Park, on 19 January 1974), and made the following appearances for the British Isles: eight in South Africa in 1968; fifteen in New Zealand in 1971; fifteen in South Africa in 1974. He is a passionate angler, representing Wales in the sport, and in 1990 set a British angling record when he landed a 45lbs - 6ozs pike at Llandegfedd Reservoir in Gwent. His memoirs, *Gareth*, were published in 1978 and he is also the author of *Rugby Skills* (with Ian Robertson), published in 1979, *Forward Skills* (with Ian Robertson), published in 1980, *Golden Years of Welsh Rugby*, published in 1982, and *Gareth Edwards on Fishing* (with Tony Dawson), published in 1984. In 1975, he was awarded the MBE for his services to rugby.

EIDMAN, Ian Harold
Born Cardiff, 31 October 1956
Career: Stanwell School; Penarth Grammar School; University of Wales Institute of Science and Technology; Cardiff Schools; Glamorgan Schools; Welsh Secondary Schools; Cardiff Athletic; Dinas Powys, Universities Athletic Union, Cardiff, Wales B

Prop in 13 matches, against: Scotland, 1983, 1985, 1986; Romania, 1983; Ireland, 1984, 1985, 1986; France, 1984, 1986; England, 1984, 1986; Australia, 1986; Fiji, 1985

Ian Eidman, a sales representative, played for Cardiff against New Zealand in October 1980.

ELLIOT, John JP
Born 1872; died Cardiff, 30 March 1938
Career: Llandaff; Cardiff

Centre/scrum-half in 3 matches, against: Ireland, 1894, 1898; England, 1898

A director of Mountstuart Dry Docks and a property owner, Jack Elliot was a member of the all-Cardiff Welsh three quarter line against Ireland in 1894. He captained Cardiff in 1896-97. After retiring from playing, he refereed a number of first class matches and was a keen golfer, serving as captain of the Royal Porthcawl Golf Club in 1935. His daughter Betty married Welsh international William Roberts [*qv*].

ELSEY, William John
Born c1871; died Cardiff, 13 June 1936
Career: Cardiff; Surrey

Forward in 1 match, against: England, 1895 Scored 1t - 3 points

Despite scoring a try in his international debut, he was not selected to play again for Wales.

EMYR, Arthur
See JONES, A E

ESCOTT, Ralph Bond
Born Essington, Staffordshire, 11 January 1869; died Johannesburg, South Africa, 10 November 1907
Career: King Henry VII School, Coventry; Cambridge University; Blackheath; Cardiff; Penarth; Barbarians; Somerset

Half-back in 3 matches, against: Scotland, 1891; Ireland, 1894, 1895

Ralph Escott, the third son of the Rev William Sweet-Escott, JP (the family had assumed the additional surname Escott in 1810), after a career as an architect became an official in a gold mine. He played in the first ever Barbarians match, at West Hartlepool, on 27 December 1890 and captained Cardiff in 1895-96. He also played cricket for Glamorgan as did two of his brothers, Henry and William. He was related to Frank Hancock [*qv*], and his mother was a daughter of Lord Dynevor.

EVANS, Arthur
Born Abersychan, c1901; died Abersychan, 7 January 1952
Career: Abersychan Rovers; Pontypool

Forward in 3 matches, against: England, 1924; Ireland, 1924; France, 1924

Arthur 'Candy' Evans was a collier, publican and professional gambler. In 1924 he won the amateur heavyweight boxing championship of Wales, winning two bouts in the same evening after playing against Ireland in the afternoon! After turning professional, he was beaten inside two rounds by the famous Jack Doyle at the Crystal Palace in 1933. Weighing 16 stone and 6ft 1ins in height in his prime, he was nearly 20 stone at the time of his death. After signing for Halifax RLFC, he made his debut for the club against Bradford Northern in November 1924. He tragically took his own life in 1952 as a result of accumulating large gambling debts.

EVANS, Brinley
Born Felinfoel, 21 July 1906; died Felinfoel, 6 October 1978
Career: Welsh Schools; Llanelli

Forward in 6 matches, against: England, 1933, 1936, 1937; Scotland, 1933, 1936; Ireland, 1936

After working in the mines Bryn Evans became a steelworker. He was also a prominent darts player.

EVANS, Brinley Samuel MC
Born Felinfoel, 21 January 1894; died Llanelli, 28 June 1964
Career: Llanelli County School; London University; Llanelli; London Welsh

Wing/centre in 5 matches, against: England, 1920, 1922; Scotland, 1922; Ireland, 1922; France, 1922

Brinley Evans was the headmaster of Stradey Secondary Modern School. He received a battlefield commission from the ranks during the First World War and was decorated with the Military Cross for gallantry.

EVANS, Colin
Born Blaenavon, 20 November 1936
Career: Park Street Secondary Modern School, Blaenavon; Blaenavon; Tredegar; Newport; Pontypool

Scrum-half in 1 match, against: England, 1960

Colin Evans was employed as a fitter. On 6 February 1960, he made his rugby league debut for Leeds against Doncaster.

EVANS, Daniel Brinley
Born Penclawdd, 16 January 1902; died Penclawdd, 27 April 1970
Career: Edinburgh University; Penclawdd; Swansea

Scrum-half in 1 match, against: Scotland, 1933

Bryn Evans, formerly a collier, was a schoolmaster at Barry, and later, Penclawdd. He captained Swansea in 1932-33 and was the chairman of Penclawdd RFC.

EVANS, David
Born Maenclochog, 1872; died Maenclochog, 1 February 1912
Career: Clydach Vale; Penygraig; Barry; Penarth; Cardiff; Glamorgan Police

Forward in 4 matches, against: Scotland, 1896; Ireland, 1896; England, 1897, 1898

David Evans served as a police officer in the Glamorgan Constabulary after spending some time in the mines. He was the first policeman from the Glamorgan force to be capped by Wales. He succumbed to tuberculosis at the age of thirty-nine.

EVANS, David Benjamin
Born Llandybie, 3 September 1899; died Port Talbot, 23 June 1977
Career: Amman United; Llanelli; Swansea

Full back in 1 match, against: England, 1926

For many years 'D B' was a colliery fireman but later became an area manager for an insurance company.

EVANS, David Dan
Born Barry, 7 April 1909
Career: Barry Grange School; University College Cardiff; Old Caldeians; New Brighton; Birkenhead Park; Bath; Cheshire; Gloucestershire

Scrum-half in 1 match, against: England, 1934

David Evans was the captain of Bath in 1942-43. At one time a French master at Calday Grange Grammar School, he became the third, and last, headmaster of Oldfield Boys School, Bath. Evans also played cricket for Cheshire.

EVANS, Sir David William
Born Dowlais, 4 November 1866; died Cardiff 17 March 1926
Career: Llandovery College; Oxford University; Cardiff; London Welsh; Barbarians

Forward in 5 matches, against: Scotland, 1889; Ireland, 1889, 1890; England, 1890, 1891

Oxford Blue (1887 and 1888) David Evans, who captained Cardiff in 1891-92, was admitted as a solicitor in August 1893. His Barbarians cap is in the Twickenham rugby museum. He was chairman of the Musical Committee of the Cardiff Musical Festivals of 1902, 1904 and 1907 and was knighted in 1925.

EVANS, David Wyn
Born Wootton Bassett, 1 November 1965

Career: Aberdare Comprehensive School; University College, Swansea; Oxford University; Welsh Schools; Aberaman; Welsh Students; Welsh Universities; Cardiff

Centre/stand-off in 8 matches, against: France, 1989, 1990; England, 1989, 1990; New Zealand, 1989; Scotland, 1990; Ireland, 1990; Barbarians, 1990 Scored 2dg - 6 points

Graduating in management science from UC Swansea, David Evans pursued a post-graduate course in Social Studies at Oxford (where he won his Blue in 1988). In the summer of 1989, he toured Fiji and Australasia with the Oxbridge RFC. He was Cardiff's top scorer, with 102 points, in the 1990-91 Heineken League. He received his first cap one hundred years to the month after his namesake, David William Evans [qv], also an Oxford Blue and Cardiff player, received his. Previously employed as a financial representative, he is now a development officer with the Sports Council for Wales.

EVANS, Denis Pritchard
Born Scunthorpe, 19 March 1936
Career: Tredegar Grammar School; University College Aberystwyth; Oxford University; Welsh Secondary Schools; Ebbw Vale; Llanelli

Wing in 1 match, against: South Africa, 1960

After graduating from Aberystwyth University, Denis Evans went to Oxford where he gained a Blue in 1959. He was a training officer for the South Wales Electricity Board before becoming a management consultant. In 1965, he was elected chairman of Ebbw Vale. He coached the Japan XV against England during the 1972-3 season and was a member of the organising committee for the Hong Kong Sevens from its inception in 1976. He was also a founder of the Hong Kong Rugby Union and was the chairman from 1978 to 1980. In November 1989 he was appointed secretary of the Welsh Rugby Union.

EVANS, Emrys
Born Gwaun-cae-Gurwen, 24 April 1911; died Bristol, 23 June 1983
Career: Cwmgors; Amman United; The Army; Llanelli

Forward in 3 matches, against: England, 1937; Scotland, 1939; Ireland, 1939

Employed in the haulage industry, Emrys Evans played in two service internationals. In September 1939, he scored two tries in his debut for Salford RLFC against Rochdale Hornets. After the war, he rejoined the club before moving on to Wigan RLFC, and gained one cap for the Wales RL team.

EVANS, Frank
Born Dafen, 3 April 1897; died Llanelli, 30 November

1972
Career: Llanelli

Wing in 1 match, against: Scotland, 1921

Frankie 'Dafen' Evans was employed as a labourer before working for the Royal Naval Stores Depot in Llangennech. He signed for Swinton RLFC in August 1921, won seven RL caps for Wales and toured Australia with the Great Britain RL team in 1924. He also coached the Acton and Willesden RLFC.

EVANS, Gareth Lloyd
Born Newport, 2 November 1952
Career: Newport High School; Cross Keys; Newport; Barbarians

Wing in 3 matches, against: France, 1977(r), 1978; Australia, 1978(r)

British Isles 1977 tour New Zealand: 3 caps

Gareth Evans captained Newport in 1979-80 and coached the club until April 1991. He made seventeen appearances, and scored six tries, for the 1977 British Isles tourists in New Zealand. During the Welsh tour of Australia in 1978, he fractured his cheek bone. He was a financial representative in 1979.

EVANS, George Rosser
Born Dowlais, 1868
Career: Llandovery College; Cardiff

Half-back in 1 match, against: Scotland, 1889

Rosser Evans played in the Llandovery College-Christ College, Brecon match in 1885 and for the victorious Cardiff side against the New Zealand Natives in 1888.

EVANS, Gwyn
Born Maesteg, 6 September 1957
Career: Maesteg Comprehensive School; University College, Swansea; Universities Athletics Union; British Universities; Welsh Secondary Schools; Maesteg; Barbarians; Wales B

Full back/centre in 10 matches, against: Scotland, 1981(r), 1982; Ireland, 1981, 1982; France, 1981, 1982, 1983; Australia, 1981; England, 1982; Romania, 1983: Scored 4con 22pg - 74 points

British Isles 1983 tour New Zealand: 2 caps

Gwyn Evans scored eleven penalty goals in four matches for Wales in 1982 and appeared in twelve matches for the 1983 British Isles team in New Zealand. He plays cricket

24. 1923 v Ireland
Back row: T L Richards, W J Radford, S Morris, D D Pascoe, J H Davies, H S Davies.
Middle row: S G Thomas, J Powell, J Rees, A E Jenkins, R Harding, T Collins, A Baker.
Front row: D E John, W J Delahay. [*Hubert Price*]
NB As a consequence of the Irish 'Troubles', several players originally selected for this match, declined to travel.
Each member of the team was subsequently insured for £1,000 and six players - Richards, Radford, J H Davies,
H S Davies, Powell and Collins - made their only appearance for Wales in this match.

25. 1923 v Scotland
Back row: T Parker, S Morris, T Roberts, Ll Jenkins, A Baker, G Thomas, D B Jones (touch judge).
Middle row: R Harding, A Jenkins, T Johnson, C Lewis (C), R A Cornish, D G Davies, G M Michael.
Front row: B O Male, W J Delahay. [*G H Cornish*]

at club level and is employed as a sports centre manager.

EVANS, Gwynfor
Born Treherbert, 17 August 1918
Career: Clydach Boys School; Pontardawe Technical
College; Vardre United; Clydach; Swansea; Cardiff; Glam-
organ Police; Welsh Police; British Police; Barbarians

Flanker in 12 matches, against: England, 1947, 1948, 1949;
Scotland, 1947, 1948, 1949; France, 1947, 1948; Ireland,
1947, 1948, 1949; Australia, 1947 Scored 1t - 3 points

A police officer in the Cardiff City Force, Gwyn Evans
served in Italy and the Middle East during the Second
World War. He was chairman of the South Wales Police
RFC, 1971-9.

EVANS, Haydn Islwyn
Born Llanelli, 25 December 1898; died Llanelli, 13 May
1974
Career: Swansea; Llanelli; New Dock Stars

Centre in 4 matches, against: England, 1922; Scotland,
1922; Ireland, 1922; France, 1922: Scored 3t 1dg - 13
points

Islwyn Evans was an electrician at the Trostre Works

EVANS, Ieuan Cennydd
Born Capel Dewi, 21 March 1964
Career: Queen Elizabeth Grammar School, Carmarthen;
Salford University; Welsh Students; Llanelli; Barbarians;
Wales B

Wing in 22 matches, against: France, 1987, 1988, 1989,
1991; England, 1987, [1987 World Cup], 1988, 1989,
1991; Scotland, 1987, 1988, 1991; Ireland, 1987, [1987
World Cup], 1988, 1989, 1991; Canada, [1987 World Cup];
New Zealand, [1987 World Cup], 1988, 1988; Australia,
[1987 World Cup]: Scored 7t - 28 points

British Isles 1989 tour Australia: 3 caps

Ieuan Evans heads the Swansea operation of a leasing
company. In April 1985 he scored six tries for Wales B
against Spain and scored two tries in eight appearances for
the British Isles in Australia in 1989. His sister is a Welsh
international hurdler.

EVANS, Iorwerth
Born Trelewis, 1908; died Bedford, 18 September 1985
Career: Lewis School Pengam; Caerleon College; Bedford
Athletic; Bedford; London Welsh
Forward in 2 matches, against: Scotland, 1934; Ireland,
1934

Iorwerth Evans was a schoolmaster and swimming
instructor in Bedford. He was a member of the Champion
School relay team of Wales in 1924 and when capped was
the holder of the Caerleon College 440 yards record.

EVANS, John
Born Ammanford, 23 February 1871; died 19 July 1924,
registered in Prescot
Career: Ammanford; Llanelli; Llwynypia

Forward in 3 matches, against: Scotland, 1896; Ireland,
1896; England, 1897

After working as a collier Jack Evans became a tram track
layer. He signed for Swinton RLFC in October 1897. Both
his sons, Jack and Bryn, played rugby league in the 1920s
and 1930s.

EVANS, John Davies
Born Mountain Ash, 30 June 1926; died Velindre, 25
March 1989
Career: Pengeulan School, Mountain Ash; Mountain Ash;
Cardiff; Barbarians

Prop in 2 matches against: Ireland, 1958; France, 1958

After being a National Coal Board official and sales
manager, John Evans had his own grocery business. He
made 338 appearances for Cardiff between 1951 and 1961.

EVANS, John Elwyn
Born Brynamman, 1897; died Denbigh, 15 July 1941
Career: Brynamman; Amman United; Swansea; Llanelli

Centre in 1 match, against: Scotland, 1924

After retiring as a collier Jack Elwyn Evans became the
steward of Manselton Social Club. He signed for
Broughton Rangers RLFC and made his debut for them
against Widnes on 30 January 1926.

EVANS, John Hart
Born 9 April 1881, registered in Lampeter; died
Griffithstown, 9 August 1959
Career: Pontypool Thursdays; Pontypool; Monmouthshire

Centre in 3 matches, against: England, 1907; Scotland,
1907; Ireland, 1907

Jack Evans was employed in the mining industry. He
captained the Panteg Cricket Club for six years and played
cricket for Monmouthshire.

EVANS, John Raymond
Born Newport, 12 September 1911; killed in action North
Africa, 8 March 1943

Career: Newport High School; Welsh Secondary Schools; Newport; London Welsh; Barbarians

Forward in 1 match, against: England, 1934

A businessman on the Gold Coast before the war, John Evans, one of thirteen new caps, was appointed team captain in his only appearance for Wales. A natural second row forward, he was chosen as hooker in his only game for Wales. Evans captained Newport from 1935-37 which included the 1935 match against the the All Blacks. He was killed in action whilst serving as a Lieutenant in the 3rd Bn The Parachute Regiment during the Second World War.

EVANS, John William
Born Blaina, 26 May 1875; died Blaina, 5 July 1947
Career: Blaina

Forward in 1 match, against: England, 1904

Jack Evans, who spent his life working in collieries, turned down several offers to 'go North'. He was the first player to be capped directly from Blaina RFC and, in his later years, was a committee member at the club. He died just 100 yards from where he was born and international father and son Jack and Billy Gore were among the bearers at his funeral. His brother Alf captained Blaina in 1898-99 and 1908-09 and his son Bill played for the club and for Newport RFC.

EVANS, Owen James
Born Cardiff, 1867; died Griffithstown, 14 October 1942
Career: Cardiff Rangers; Cardiff

Half-back in 4 matches, against: England, 1887; Scotland, 1887, 1888; Ireland, 1888

Jem Evans, a marine engineer, was a referee in the Cardiff Division. His brother J D Evans, also played for Cardiff and was connected with Glamorgab CCC.

EVANS, Peter Denzil
Born Llanelli, 20 June 1928; died New Zealand, c1984
Career: St Michael's School, Bryn; Llanelli

Flanker in 2 matches, against: England, 1951; France, 1951

Peter Evans, who emigrated to New Zealand, ran his own business. He captained Llanelli from 1953-55. His brother Hagen played rugby league for Bradford Northern and Wales.

EVANS, Robert Thomas
Born Rhymney, 16 February 1921
Career: Rhymney School; Rhymney; Abergavenny; New-port; British Police; Monmouthshire

Flanker in 10 matches, against: France, 1947, 1950, 1951; Ireland, 1947, 1950, 1951; England, 1950, 1951; Scotland, 1950, 1951 Scored 1t - 3 points

British Isles 1950 tour New Zealand: 4 caps, Australia: 2 caps

Bob Evans was a police officer, retiring as a chief super-intendent in August 1976. He appeared in five Victory internationals, and played in twelve matches for the British Isles in New Zealand and five in Australia. He captained Newport RFC in 1951-52.

EVANS, Ronald BEM
Born Bridgend, 6 November 1941
Career: Tondu; Bridgend Sports; Neath; Bridgend; Cow-bridge; Glamorgan Police; Welsh Police; British Police; Glamorgan

Centre in 3 matches, against: Scotland, 1963; Ireland, 1963; France, 1963

Ron Evans is a police officer. On 15 February 1968, he scored 30 points for Bridgend against Penarth. He played stand-off for Neath.

EVANS, Stuart
Born Neath, 14 June 1963
Career: Dumbarton House School, Swansea; Welsh Youth; British Steel Corporation; Resolven; Swansea; Western Suburbs (Australia); Neath; Barbarians; Wales B

Prop in 9 matches, against: France, 1985, 1987; England, 1985, 1987; Fiji, 1986; Tonga, 1986, [1987 World Cup]; Western Samoa, 1986; Ireland, [1987 World Cup]

Stuart Evans was employed by the British Steel Corporation. In September 1987, he signed for St Helens RLFC.

EVANS, Thomas David
Born Neyland, 8 May 1902; died Carmarthen, 6 August 1969
Career: Neyland; Llanelli; Swansea; Plymouth Albion; Pembrokeshire; Breconshire; Devon

Centre in 1 match, against: Ireland, 1924

Tommy 'Pete' Evans was employed in Pembroke Dockyard, Devonport Dockyard, Neyland Gas Works and the Royal Naval Armaments Depot, Milford Haven. During the First World War he served as an apprentice shipwright. He played for Swansea against the 1924 All Blacks.

EVANS, Thomas Geoffrey
Born 1 May 1942
Career: Pembrey Comprehensive School; Llandovery College; University College of North Wales, Bangor; Universities Athletics Union; British Universities; Bangor; Llanelli; Bridgend; Neath; London Welsh; Barbarians; North Wales; Surrey

Lock in 7 matches, against: South Africa, 1970; Scotland, 1970, 1972; England, 1970, 1972; Ireland, 1970; France, 1972

British Isles 1971 tour(r) Australia, New Zealand

College lecturer Geoff Evans captained London Welsh in 1974-75 and coached them from 1978-82. He was one of seven London Welsh players to tour Australasia with the 1971 British Isles party, making six appearances in New Zealand.

EVANS, Thomas Henry
Born Ammanford, 31 December 1882; died Llanelli, 19 March 1955
Career: Ammanford County School; Ammanford; Llanelli

Forward in 18 matches, against: Ireland, 1906, 1907, 1908, 1909, 1910, 1911; England, 1907, 1909, 1910, 1911; Scotland, 1907, 1909, 1910, 1911; Australia, 1908; France, 1909, 1910, 1911   Scored 1t - 3 points

Police officer Tom Evans captained Ammanford RFC from 1902 to 1903 and Llanelli RFC from 1909 to 1911.

EVANS, Thomas Wynne
Born Llandybie, 13 August 1926; died Carmarthen, 8 May 1987
Career: Llandybie; Llanelli

Scrum-half in 1 match, against: Australia, 1958

Wynne Evans became a licensee after working as a collier. He captained Llanelli during the 1956-57 season.

EVANS, Trefor Pryce
Born Chorley, Lancashire, 26 November 1947
Career: Ammanford Grammar School; Welsh Youth; Amman United; Swansea; Barbarians; Wales B

Flanker in 10 matches, against: France, 1975, 1976; England, 1975, 1976; Scotland, 1975, 1976; Ireland, 1975, 1976, 1977; Australia, 1975: Scored 2 t - 8 points

British Isles 1977 tour New Zealand: 1 cap

Trefor Evans, who captained Swansea in 1976-77, is an estate agent in the city. He appeared in thirteen matches for the 1977 British Isles team in New Zealand.

EVANS, Vivian
Born Skewen, 14 July 1919
Career: Neath; Barbarians

Full back in 3 matches, against: Ireland, 1954; France, 1954; Scotland, 1954: Scored 2con 7pg - 25 points

After working in a steelworks, Viv Evans became the superintendent of a home for senior citizens. In November 1951, he played for Neath and Aberavon against South Africa and was aged 34 years and 183 days when he won his first cap. He captained Neath in 1947-48. He served in the Royal Navy as a seaman gunner during the Second World War and became a prisoner of war.

EVANS, Wilfred John
Born Griffithstown, 12 May 1914
Career: Pontnewydd; Abergavenny; Pontypool; Panteg

Prop in 1 match, against: Scotland, 1947

Wilf Evans is a retired chief inspector of police. He played in five Victory and two Red Cross internationals and captained Pontypool in 1945-46. In December 1947, he played for Pontypool, Blaenavon and Talywain against Australia.

EVANS, William Frederick
Born Rhymney, 24 April 1857; died c1935
Career: Christ College Brecon; Sherborne School; Oxford University; Rhymney; Newport; Gloucester; Cardiff; Gloucestershire

Back/half-back in 2 matches, against: Ireland, 1882; Scotland, 1883: Scored 1t

Bill Evans taught in Gloucestershire before moving to Australia where he was the headmaster of Fremantle Grammar School from 1887-90 and Adelaide Grammar School from 1890-91. He continued with his teaching career after returning to this country but, in his latter years, became something of a tramp, living rough in the hills near his home town. He played cricket for Dorset. His father, William Evans, was a clerk in holy orders.

EVANS, William George
Born 23 March 1886
Career: Blaina; Brynmawr; Aberavon

Forward in 1 match, against: Ireland, 1911

Collier William Evans, who gained his only cap when Rees Thomas [qv] pulled out of the Wales team following a bereavement, had been a reserve all season. He is the only player to have been capped directly from Brynmawr. He signed for Leeds RLFC, making his debut against

Warrington on 7 October 1911, and gained two RL caps for Wales.

EVANS, William Henry
Born Tonypandy, 9 February 1892; died Bryncethin, c1979
Career: Llwynypia; Penygraig

Centre in 4 matches, against: England, 1914; Scotland, 1914; France, 1914; Ireland, 1914: Scored 1t - 3 points

Collier William Evans served in the Welch Regiment during the Second World War.

EVANS, William Roderick
Born 19 December 1934
Career: Cowbridge Grammar School; Cambridge University; Welsh Secondary Schools; Porthcawl; Cardiff; Bridgend; London Welsh; Barbarians

Lock in 13 matches, against: Australia, 1958; England, 1958, 1961, 1962; Scotland, 1958, 1961, 1962; France, 1958, 1961; South Africa, 1960

British Isles 1959 tour Australia: 1 cap, New Zealand: 3 caps

After reading law at university, Cambridge Blue (1955) Roddy Evans qualified as a solicitor. He made fourteen appearances, one at No 8, for the 1959 British Isles tourists in New Zealand. He was the captain of Bridgend in 1961-62.

EVERSON, William Aaron
Born Rudry, March 1905; died Newport, 26 March 1966
Career: Caerphilly Grammar School; Newport

Full back in 1 match, against: Scotland, 1926: Scored 1con - 2 points

Between 1925-37 Bill Everson made 314 appearances, and scored 856 points, for Newport - a record which remained unbroken until 1962 - captained the club in 1930-31 and 1933-34 and played for the club against New South Wales in September 1927. He served on the committee at Newport RFC and was instrumental in founding the Snelling Sevens in 1954. After retiring from the police force, Everson had a tobacconist business.

FAULKNER, Anthony George
Born Newport, 27 February 1941
Career: St Mary's School, Newport; Newport Saracens; Cross Keys; Pontypool; Barbarians; Monmouthshire; Wales B

Prop in 19 matches, against: France, 1975, 1976, 1978, 1979; England, 1975, 1976, 1978; Scotland, 1975, 1976, 1978, 1979; Ireland, 1975, 1976, 1978, 1979; Australia, 1975, 1978, 1978; New Zealand, 1978: Scored 1t - 4 points

British Isles 1977 tour(r) New Zealand

Tony Faulkner was called out as a replacement for the British Isles during the 1977 tour of New Zealand playing in two matches. At the time of his final appearance in a Welsh jersey, against France in February 1979, he was ten days short of his thirty-eighth birthday. He coached Newport RFC from 1982-6. He has a black belt in judo. After working in the steel industry Faulkner is now a brewery representative.

FAULL, John
Born Morriston, 30 June 1933
Career: Bromsgrove School; Swansea; Barbarians

No 8/lock in 12 matches, against: Ireland, 1957, 1958, 1959; France, 1957, 1958, 1960; Australia, 1958; England, 1958, 1959, 1960; Scotland, 1958, 1959: Scored 1t - 3 points

British Isles 1959 tour Australia: 1 cap, New Zealand: 3 caps

John Faull is a company director. On 12 December 1953, playing at centre, he kicked two penalty goals for Swansea in their 6-6 draw with New Zealand. On the British Isles tour of Australasia he made nineteen appearances, three in Australia and sixteen in New Zealand. He captained Swansea in 1962-63. His father, Wilfred, refereed two international matches in 1936 and was president of the Welsh Rugby Union in 1962-63.

FAUVEL, Timothy John
Born Bridgend, 9 June 1960
Career: Cynffig Comprehensive School, Kenfig Hill; Cornelly Youth; Welsh Youth; Welsh Boys Clubs; Kenfig Hill; Aberavon; Woolongong (Australia); Pyle.

No 8 in 1 match, against: New Zealand, 1988(r)

Tim Fauvel is employed as a welder. He represented the Welsh Amateur Boxing Association Under 16 team, and appeared for the Welsh Basketball Under 16, 17 and 18 teams.

FEAR, Albert George
Born Abertillery, 25 August 1907
Career: Abertillery; Newport

Forward in 4 matches, against: Scotland, 1934, 1935; Ireland, 1934, 1935: Scored 1t - 3 points

Albert Fear was a collier before taking up employment in

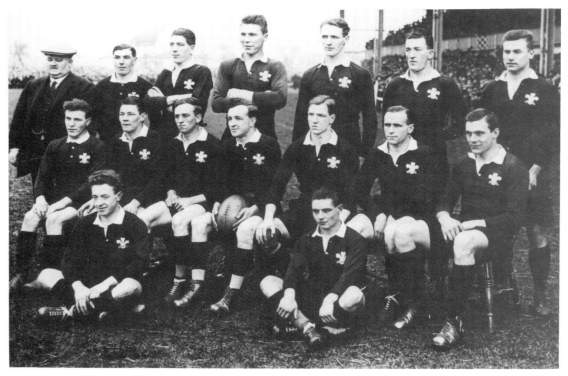

26. 1924 v England
Back row: J Darbyshire (touch judge), D H Davies, J I T Morris, A Evans, W I Jones, W J Ould, B M G Thomas.
Middle row: I Thomas, C H Pugh, T A W Johnson, J Rees (C), T Jones, R A Cornish, S Morris.
Front row: A D Owen, E Watkins.
[*Gareth Williams*]

27. 1925 v Ireland
Back row: Unknown official, B R Turnbull, R C Herrera, S D Lawrence, D N R Jones, D S Parker, unknown official.
Middle row: G E Beynon, E Finch, B Phillips, W I Jones (C), D H Davies, J Brown, S Hinam, R Harding.
Front row: D A John, W J Delahay.
[*Mrs B R Turnbull*]

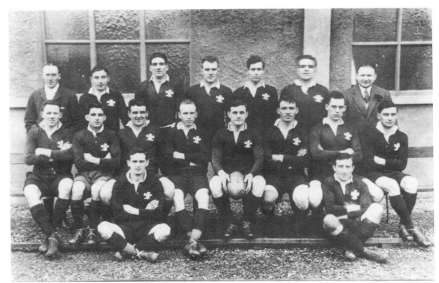

28. 1926 v Ireland
Back row: J N Jones (touch judge), S D Lawrence, D L Jones, J H John, E Watkins, D M Jenkins, S Hinam, R C Herrera.
Middle row: T E Rees, R A Cornish, C F Rowlands, R Harding (C), W J Delahay, T Hopkins.
Front row: W C Powell, W H Lewis.
[*Edward H Rees*]

the building industry. Converted from centre, he stood at 5ft 7 ins and weighed 11st. He played for Abertillery and Cross Keys against South Africa in 1931. His bother Jim had a Welsh trial as a wing forward.

FENDER, Norman Henry
Born Cardiff, 2 September 1910; died York, 24 October 1983
Career: Ninian Park School, Cardiff; Welsh Schools; Cardiff

Forward in 6 matches, against: Ireland, 1930, 1931; France, 1930, 1931; England, 1931; Scotland, 1931: Scored 1t - 3 points

Before becoming a licensee in York (after signing for York RLFC in August 1931), Norman Fender had worked as a labourer. He also played for the Wales and England RL teams and toured Australia with the 1932 Great Britain RL team.

FENWICK, Steven Paul
Born Nantgarw, 23 July 1951
Career: Caerphilly Grammar Technical School; Borough Road College; Taff's Well; Beddau; Mid Districts; Bridgend; Barbarians; Wales B

Centre in 30 matches, against: France, 1975, 1976, 1977, 1978, 1979, 1980; England, 1975, 1976, 1977, 1978, 1979, 1980, 1981; Scotland, 1975, 1976, 1977, 1978, 1979, 1980, 1981; Australia, 1975, 1978, 1978; Ireland, 1976, 1977, 1978, 1979, 1980; New Zealand, 1978, 1980: Scored 4t 11con 3dg 35pg - 152 points

British Isles 1977 tour New Zealand: 4 caps

Steve Fenwick, Wales' third highest points scorer, was a schoolmaster before going into business. He made twelve appearances for the British Isles tourists in 1977 and fifty one appearances for Beddau between 1971-73. He signed for Cardiff City RLFC in August 1981, and scored four goals on his debut against Salford. He made two appearances for the Wales RL team.

FINCH, Ernest JP
Born Pembroke Dock, 16 July 1899; died Haverfordwest, 1 October 1983
Career: Pembroke Dock County School; Monmouth Training College, Caerleon; Pembroke Dock Harlequins; Caerleon; Llanelli; Western Counties

Wing in 7 matches, against: France, 1924, 1925, 1926; New Zealand, 1924; Ireland, 1925, 1928; New South Wales 1927: Scored 4t - 12 points

Schoolmaster Ernie Finch served with the 5th (Royal Irish)

Lancers, during the First World War. He scored a try for Llanelli against New Zealand in 1924.

FINLAYSON, Alexander Alfred James
Born Cardiff, 18 March 1948
Career: St Illtyd's College, Cardiff; Old Illtydians; Cardiff; South Wales Police; Welsh Police; British Police; Barbarians; Wales B

Centre in 3 matches, against: Ireland, 1974; France, 1974; England, 1974

Alex Finlayson is a police inspector stationed in Cardiff City. He was a reserve for the British Isles team which toured South Africa in 1974 and vice-captain of Cardiff in 1980-81.

FITZGERALD, David
Born Cardiff, 1872; died Cardiff, 30 November 1951
Career: Grangetown; Cardiff Harlequins; Cardiff

Centre in 2 matches, against: Scotland, 1894; Ireland, 1894: Scored 1t 1dg - 7 points

Dai Fitzgerald was an agent for a coal company before working as a storeman. He joined the Leigh club in 1895, shortly before the schism, which led to the founding of the Northern Union (later the Rugby League). In February 1896, he joined Batley and remained with them until about 1903. In the years 1897, 1898 and 1901 he won three Challenge Cup winners medals. There was a halt in his career in 1898 when he had to appear before a Rugby League tribunal, and after being examined with regard to the nature of his employment he was refused permission to play against Huddersfield the following day. At a subsequent meeting when the whole matter was inquired into, the committee found both player and club guilty. They decided that Dai had not followed his employment as a coal agent in a bonafide manner and had committed a breach of the professional law. He was suspended until 1 May 1900, and the Batley club was fined £60. The money was recovered via a public subscription. He eventually returned to Cardiff to run a marine store business.

FORD, Frederick John Vivian
Born Redcar, 13 October 1917
Career: Imperial Service College; Royal Military Academy, Woolwich; Welch Regiment; The Army; Newport; Harlequins; Surrey

Wing in 1 match, against: England, 1939

John Ford served as an officer in the Welch Regiment and was taken prisoner of war on Crete in 1941. After retirement, he became a school administrator in the Imperial Service College. Despite his father being Irish, he qualified to play for Wales through his Welsh mother.

FORD, Ian Reginald
Born Cardiff, 6 June 1929
Career: Bassaleg County School; Nottingham University; Newport; Barbarians

Lock in 2 matches, against: England, 1959; Scotland, 1959

Qualified as a plant scientist, Ian Ford was a market gardener at St Mellons for many years. From 1967-71 he was the advisory officer to the Department of Horticulture in the Bay of Plenty, New Zealand. He once held the Newport appearances record with 482 games.

FORD, Stephen Paul
Born Cardiff, 15 August 1965
Career: Rumney High School; Rumney; Cardiff; Wales B

Wing in 7 matches, against: Ireland, 1990, 1991; Namibia, 1990, 1990; Barbarians, 1990; England, 1991; Scotland, 1991: Scored 2t - 8 points

After playing in two trial matches for Leeds RLFC in 1985, Steve Ford was suspended until April 1988. He is employed as a carpet-fitter. His brother Phil has played rugby league for the Great Britain side.

FORWARD, Allen
Born Cwmavon, Monmouthshire, 4 June 1921
Career: Varteg School; Abersychan Grammar Technical School; Pontypool; Monmouth Police; Welsh Police; British Police; Barbarians

Flanker in 6 matches, against: Scotland, 1951, 1952; South Africa, 1951; England, 1952; Ireland, 1952; France, 1952

Allen Forward is a retired police sergeant. In October 1951 he played for a Pontypool and Newbridge XV against South Africa. He captained Pontypool in 1953-54 and a combined Pontypool and Cross Keys XV against New Zealand in January 1954.

FOWLER, Isaac John
Born Pantyffynnon, 27 August 1894; died Batley, 17 June 1981
Career: Tycroes; Ammanford; Llanelli

Scrum-half in 1 match, against: New Zealand Army, 1919
Ike Fowler received his somewhat belated cap from the Welsh Rugby Union in 1975 - fifty six years after the game for which it was awarded. In August 1919, he made his debut for Batley RLFC against York. He also appeared for the Wales RL team in 1926. Fowler was employed in the mining industry before becoming a foreman in a textile factory in Batley.

FRANCIS, David Gwynn
Born Gorseinon, 2 February 1896; died Reading, 7 May 1987
Career: Gowerton Grammar School; University College Cardiff; Oxford University; Gorseinon; Loughor; Llanelli; London Welsh; Leicester; London Counties; Surrey

Forward in 2 matches, against: New Zealand Army, 1919; Scotland 1924

Oxford Blue (1919) Gwyn Francis was a schoolmaster. He captained London Welsh in 1924-25 and, after his playing career had ended, he became a referee and the president of Berkshire Rugby Union. He served as a staff sergeant in the Royal Welch Fusiliers during the First World War.

FRANCIS, Peter William
Born Cowbridge, 9 July 1957
Career: Cowbridge Grammar School; Barry Comprehensive School; Usk Agricultural College; Bridgend Sports Club; Maesteg; Llanelli; Kidwelly; Wales B

Prop in 1 match, against: Scotland, 1987

In January 1982, Peter Francis played for West Wales against Australia and, in October 1986, captained Wales B against France B at Pontypridd. He played 339 games for Maesteg, captaining the team from 1984-87. He is a farmer in Kidwelly.

GABE, Rees Thomas
(See Gape, R T)

GALE, Norman Reginald
Born Gorseinon, 24 July 1939
Career: Gowerton Grammar School; Gorseinon; Llanelli; Swansea

Hooker in 25 matches, against: Ireland, 1960, 1963, 1964, 1965, 1966; England, 1963, 1964, 1965, 1966, 1967, 1968; Scotland, 1963, 1964, 1965, 1966, 1967; New Zealand, 1963, 1967, 1969(r), 1969; France, 1964, 1965, 1966; South Africa, 1964: Australia, 1968: Scored 1t 1pg - 6 points

Formerly employed as a fitter, Norman Gale now has a public house in Llanelli. In November 1960, he played for Swansea against South Africa. He captained Llanelli in 1964-65 and 1967-68 and coached them in 1973-74.

GALLACHER, Ian Stuart
Born Llanelli, 22 May 1946

Career: Llanelli Grammar School; Welsh Youth; Felinfoel; Llanelli; Barbarians; Wales B

Lock in 1 match, against: France, 1970

Stuart Gallacher was employed as a sales representative before becoming a police officer. He captained Llanelli in 1968-70 and toured South Africa with the Barbarians in May 1969. After making his debut for Bradford Northern RLFC on 22 August 1970 and also winning four caps for the Wales RL team, Gallacher found employment in a carpet factory and now runs his own carpet business in Llanelli. In his spare time he coaches Llangennech RFC.

GAPE, Rees Thomas
(known as Gabe)
Born Llangennech, 22 June 1880; died Cardiff, 15 September 1967
Career: Llanelli Intermediate School; Borough Road College; Llangennech; Llanelli; London Welsh; Cardiff; Glamorgan; Middlesex

Wing/centre in 24 matches, against: Ireland, 1901, 1902, 1903, 1904, 1905, 1906, 1907, 1908; England, 1902, 1903, 1904, 1905, 1906, 1907, 1908; Scotland, 1902, 1903, 1904, 1905, 1907, 1908; New Zealand, 1905; South Africa, 1906; France, 1908: Scored 11t - 33 points

British Isles 1904 tour Australia: 3 caps, New Zealand: 1 cap

Rusty Gabe was a schoolmaster. He appeared four times against the 1906 Springboks, for Glamorgan, Wales, Llanelli and Cardiff. He scored a try for the 1904 British Isles touring team in the final match against Australia in Sydney, and played in all five matches in New Zealand. He captained Cardiff in 1907-08. He played in friendly cricket matches for Glamorgan and only ill health prevented him from winning fame on the cycle track. He was also a good billiards player and played water polo for Borough Road College.

GARRETT, Richard Marks
Born 1865, registered in Cardiff; died Penarth, 17 February 1908
Career: Penarth

Back in 8 matches, against: New Zealand Natives, 1888; Scotland, 1889, 1890, 1891; England, 1890, 1892; Ireland, 1890, 1891

Dickie Garrett was presented with a cup in 1890 following Penarth's third consecutive success in the Cardiff and District Championship. He worked as a tipper for the Taff Vale Railway Company at Penarth docks and was killed, working at Number 20 tip, when a truck ran over him. His son Tommy, who was also a Penarth player, won a Welsh schoolboys cap in 1910.

GEEN, William Purdon
Born Newport, 14 March 1891; killed in action Hooge, 31 July 1915
Career: Haileybury School; Oxford University; Newport; Blackheath; Barbarians; Monmouthshire

Wing/centre in 3 matches, against: South Africa, 1912; England, 1913; Ireland, 1913

Triple Blue winner (1910-12) Billy Geen had the misfortune to lose the ball as he crossed the Cambridge line on each appearance. In 1910 he played for England against the North. He played cricket for the Authentics and Monmouthshire. During the First World War he was commissioned into the King's Royal Rifle Corps and was killed in action. He was the nephew of Frank Purdon (*qv*).

GEORGE, Ernest Edward
Born Llantwit Major, 1871; died Cardiff, 28 November 1952
Career: Cardiff; Pontypridd; London Welsh; Plymouth Albion

Forward in 3 matches, against: Scotland, 1895; Ireland, 1895; England, 1896

After working as a mason Ernie George kept a hotel.

GEORGE, Glenn Maxwell
Born Newport, 30 September 1964
Career: Llyswerry High School; Newport Schools; Welsh Schools; Welsh Youth; Newport; Wales B

Flanker in 2 matches, against: England, 1991; Scotland, 1991

Glenn George, who is employed as a postal supervisor, captained Newport in 1990-91.

GETHING, Glyn Ivor
Born Neath, 16 June 1892; died Neath, 20 March 1977
Career: Skewen; Neath

Full back in 1 match, against: France, 1913

Glyn Gething was a bank official.

GIBBS, Ian Scott
Born Bridgend, 23 January 1971
Career: Ysgol Gyfun Llanharry; Pontypridd Schoolboys; Pencoed; Welsh Youth; Neath; Wales B

Centre in 4 matches, against: England, 1991; Scotland, 1991; Ireland, 1991; France, 1991

Scott Gibbs, who is a glazier, has been voted Welsh Brewers 'Player of the Year' for 1991, his first season in senior rugby and the youngest player ever to win the title. His father was an international gymnast.

GIBBS, Reginald Arthur
Born Cardiff, 1882; died Cardiff, 28 November 1938
Career: Queen's College, Taunton; Cardiff; Penarth; Barbarians; Glamorgan

Extra-back/stand-off/wing in 16 matches, against: Scotland, 1906, 1907, 1908, 1910, 1911; Ireland, 1906, 1908, 1910, 1911; England, 1907, 1908, 1910, 1911; France, 1908, 1910, 1911: Scored 17t 1con - 53 points

Anglo-Welsh 1908 tour Australia, New Zealand: 2 caps

Shipowner Reggie Gibbs appeared for Glamorgan against New Zealand in 1905 and scored a try for Cardiff against South Africa in 1907. He scored six tries in four matches in the 1908 season, which included four tries against France in their first ever match against Wales. He captained Penarth in 1903-04 and Cardiff in 1910-11 and Wales against Ireland in 1910. In January 1911 he scored 30 points for Cardiff against Moseley. He was the top scorer, with 28 points in ten appearances for the Anglo-Welsh team in New Zealand in 1908. He played cricket for Glamorgan and was a first class billiards player. His daughter, Shelagh, played golf for Glamorgan and Wales.

GILES, Raymond
Born Kenfig Hill, 15 January 1961
Career: Cynffig Hill Comprehensive School; Cornelly Youth; Kenfig Hill; Welsh Youth; Aberavon; Cardiff; Wales B

Scrum-half in 3 matches, against: Romania, 1983; Fiji, 1985(r); Canada, [1987 World Cup]

Ray Giles captained the Welsh Youth party to South Africa in 1980, the Wales B against Australia in October 1981 and on tour to Italy in 1986, and Aberavon from 1985-87. He was a member of the Welsh World Cup party in 1987. Appointed coach to Aberavon for 1991-92, he has been employed as a driver on an opencast mining site and is currently an area sales executive for Cae Garw Farm Sales, Pyle.

GIRLING, Barry Edward
Born 1857, registered in Bristol; died Algeria, 28 October 1905
Career: Cardiff

Forward in 1 match, against: England, 1881

Girling captained Cardiff RFC in 1881-2 after being vice-captain in 1879-80.

GOLDSWORTHY, Samuel James
Born Swansea, 1855; died Swansea, 28 September 1889
Career: Swansea; Newport

Forward in 3 matches, against: Ireland, 1884; England, 1885; Scotland, 1886

Employed as a ship's chandler, Samuel Goldsworthy was a prominent member of the Swansea Working Men's Club and a rugby referee at junior level. He was the first Welsh 'cap' to die.

GORE, John Henry
Born Blaina, 16 June 1899; died Bedwellty, 18 March 1971
Career: Blaina

Forward in 4 matches, against: Ireland, 1924; France, 1924; New Zealand, 1924; England, 1925

Licensee Jack Gore made his debut for Salford RLFC against St Helens on 31 January 1925, two weeks after making his final appearance for Wales at Twickenham. A number of sources claim that he had, in fact, played rugby league for St Helens some eighteen months before signing for Salford. He won three caps with the Wales RL team and also played for the English RL side. He was the father of Billy Gore [qv] and is a Gwent County Councillor.

GORE, William
Born Blaina, 19 November 1919
Career: Newbridge

Hooker in 3 matches, against: Scotland, 1947; France, 1947; Ireland, 1947

Before becoming a licensee Billy Gore worked as a foundryman. He was the first ever cap from the Newbridge club. In September 1947 he signed for Warrington RLFC. He is the son of Jack Gore [qv], and is a Gwent County Councillor.

GOULD, George Herbert
Born Newport, 1870; died Germiston, South Africa, 19 December 1913
Career: Newport, Wanderers (Johannesburg); Pirates (King William's Town, South Africa)

Centre in 3 matches, against: Ireland, 1892, 1893; Scotland, 1893: Scored 2t - 4points

29. 1927 v England
Back row: E G Nicholls (touch judge), T W Lewis, H T Phillips, J H John, W G Thomas, D L Jones, R C Herrera, R L Scott (SRU referee).
Middle row: G E Andrews, W H Lewis, B O Male, B R Turnbull (C), R Harding, S D lawrence, W C Powell.
Front row: W A Williams, J Roberts.
[*Mrs B R Turnbull*]

30. 1929 v Scotland
Back row: D Hellewell (referee), H J Jones, R J Barrell, A S Broughton, T Arthur, H Peacock, C C Pritchard, J Roberts, E Thomas (touch judge).
Middle row: F A Bowdler, J C Morley, T I Jones, W G Morgan (C), J A Bassett, W C Powell.
Front row: F L Williams, H M Bowcott.
[*Harold Jones*]

Bert Gould's work as a civil engineer took him to Barbados and South Africa where he died of pneumonia having played an important part in the development of rugby in that country. He was the brother of Arthur and Robert Gould [qv].

GOULD, Joseph Arthur
(known as GOULD A J)
Born Newport, 10 October 1864; died Newport, 2 January 1919
Career: Newport; London Welsh; Richmond; Southampton Trojans; Middlesex; Hampshire

Full back/centre in 27 matches, against: England, 1885, 1886, 1887, 1890, 1892, 1893, 1894, 1895, 1896, 1897; Scotland, 1885, 1886, 1887, 1888, 1890, 1892, 1893, 1894, 1895, 1896; Ireland, 1887, 1889, 1890, 1892, 1893, 1895, 1896: Scored 4t 1con 2dg

Arthur Gould, the first 'superstar' of Welsh rugby was a public works contractor before becoming a brewery representative. Together with five of his brothers he began his career with Newport, captaining them from 1893-95. He captained Wales in eighteen of his twenty-seven international matches. Acclaimed as a great athlete, he was a sprinter and hurdler of note, winning the Midland Counties AAA 100 yards and 120 yards hurdles in 1893. He was also proficient at billiards, hockey, golf and cards and was regularly in demand as a singer of comic songs. He is reputed to have won more than £1,000 in prize money for athletics and, though naturally left-footed, he could punt and drop kick a ball with both feet. In 1896, a newspaper opened a public subscription in his honour for services rendered to the nation and even the Welsh Rugby Union made a contribution. As a result of this, the International Board had to intervene after the WRU was accused of professionalism by the scandalised English Union, supported by the Scottish and Irish Unions who withdrew their teams to play against Wales in 1897. At a banquet held at the Royal Albert Hall Newport, on Easter Monday 1897, Gould was presented with the title deeds to a house in Clytha Park, Newport, to mark his retirement. He took up refereeing, and played cricket for Monmouthshire. The newspaper coverage of his death was probably the greatest ever given to a Welshman until the death of David Lloyd George, nearly thirty years later. He was a brother to Bert and Robert Gould [qv].

GOULD, Robert
Born Newport, 1863; died Nice, France, 29 December 1931
Career: Newport; London Welsh; Richmond

Forward in 11 matches, against: Ireland, 1882, 1884; England, 1882, 1884, 1885, 1886, 1887; Scotland, 1883, 1884, 1885, 1887

After working as a civil engineer, Bob Gould became a brewery representative. He captained Newport in 1886-87, Wales once in 1887 and was a member of the International Board in 1892. He was described by T B Jones as immensely strong and hard as nails, "...as good a forward as his brother was a back". He was a brother to Arthur and Bert Gould [qv]. Another brother, Wyatt, captained Newport in 1905-06 and ran for Great Britain in the 400 metres in the 1908 Olympics. A further brother, Gus, was a Welsh reserve.

GRAHAM, Thomas Cooper
Born c1866; died Cardiff, 1 December 1945
Career: Blaina; Newport; Barbarians

Forward in 12 matches, against: Ireland, 1890, 1891, 1893; Scotland, 1891, 1892, 1893, 1894, 1895; England, 1892, 1893, 1894, 1895: Scored 1t - 3 points

One of the first organisers and theorists of combined forward play, Thomas Graham was a minister of religion. He captained Blaina in 1887-88 and Newport from 1889-93, including their invincible season, 1891-92. He also played cricket for the Water Rats.

GRAVELL, Raymond William Robert
Born Kidwelly, 12 September 1951
Career: Burry Port Secondary Modern School; Queen Elizabeth Grammar School, Carmarthen; Welsh Youth; Llanelli; Barbarians; Wales B

Centre in 23 matches, against: France, 1975, 1976, 1978, 1981, 1982; England, 1975, 1976, 1978, 1982; Scotland, 1975, 1976, 1978, 1979, 1982; Ireland, 1975, 1976, 1978, 1979, 1981; Australia, 1975, 1978, 1978; New Zealand, 1978: Scored 1t - 4 points

British Isles 1980 tour South Africa: 4 caps(1r)

Ray Gravell, who had previously worked for an electricity board and had a spell as a sales representative, is now a radio and television broadcaster working for the BBC. He played in eleven matches on the 1980 British Isles tour of South Africa, and captained Llanelli in 1980-82. His autobiography, *Grav*, was published in 1986.

GRAY, Anthony John
Born Stoke on Trent, 14 June 1942
Career: Friars School, Bangor; Cardiff College of Education; London Welsh; Newbridge; Maesteg; Bridgend; London Counties; Eastern Counties

Flanker in 2 matches, against: England, 1968; Scotland, 1968

After leaving college, Tony Gray was employed as a

teacher and is now the Director of Physical Recreation at the University College of North Wales, Bangor. A wing forward who was faster than most wings, he made 250 appearances for London Welsh RFC and was their captain (1971-72) and then their coach. He was a member of the winning North Wales team against Monmouthshire in the final of the Welsh Counties Cup in 1967 and appeared for London Counties against South Africa in 1969. He became the district representative for North Wales on the Welsh Rugby Union, and served as Wales' coach from 1985 to 1988. In July 1990, he became part of a three man selection panel to choose the Welsh team.

GREENSLADE, Desmond
Born Cwmcarn, 11 January 1933
Career: Cwmcarn; Abercarn; Newbridge Youth; Newport; Barbarians

Prop in 1 match, against: Scotland, 1962

Des Greenslade is a collier. He made 286 appearances for Newport from 1955-63.

GREVILLE, Handel Glanffrwd
Born Drefach, 13 September 1921
Career: Gwendraeth Grammar School; Cefneithin; Carmarthen Athletic; Tumble; Llanelli Wanderers; Llanelli; Swansea; Pontyberem; Llandybie

Scrum-half in 1 match, against: Australia, 1947

Handel Greville was employed by the county council. He captained Llanelli in 1948-49 and has served as the club fixture secretary and chairman. In 1951, he played for Swansea against South Africa.

GRIFFIN, John
Born Southampton, 2 August 1859; died Southampton, 13 July 1895
Career: Epsom College; Edinburgh University

Forward in 1 match, against: Scotland, 1883

A Doctor of Medicine, John Griffin became, in June 1890, the visiting medical officer to the Provincial Hospital in Port Elizabeth, South Africa. Over a year later, on 30 July 1891, he refereed the first ever international match in the country, between South Africa and the British Isles. He later became vice-president of the Eastern Province Rugby Union. For over 100 years he was one of the 'unknowns' of Welsh rugby, appearing in the records as 'A Griffin'. His only cap came when he was drafted in as a late substitute, and the height of his previous rugby career had been as captain of Edinburgh University Third XV. To date, John Griffin appears to have had no Welsh connection whatsoever.

GRIFFITHS, Clive Ronald
Born Loughor, 2 April 1954
Career: Gowerton Grammar School; Cardiff College of Education; Welsh Secondary Schools, British Colleges; Penclawdd; Llanelli; Barbarians; Wales B

Full back in 1 match, against: England, 1979(r)

Clive Griffiths is a schoolmaster. Shortly after taking the field as a replacement for J P R Williams in the 1979 match with England, he made a scintillating run which ended in a try for Elgan Rees. In August 1979 he signed for St Helens RLFC. He has also represented Wales on two occasions at rugby league. At present he coaches Warrington RLFC.

GRIFFITHS, Daniel
Born Cwmduad, 20 June 1857; died Llanelli, 29 October 1936
Career: Llanelli

Forward in 2 matches, against: New Zealand Natives, 1888; Ireland, 1889

Dan Griffiths worked in the tinplate and iron works before becoming a coal trimmer at Llanelli docks. His wife, Catherine Jenkins, was a relative of Albert Jenkins [qv]. In June 1987, his great-great grandson, David Tucker, played as a replacement at scrum-half for Canada against Wales in the World Cup.

GRIFFITHS, Gareth Meredith
Born Penygraig, 27 November 1931
Career: Porth County School; Loughborough College; Welsh Secondary Schools; Dinas Powys; Cardiff; London Welsh; Barbarians; Devon

Wing/centre in 12 matches, against: England, 1953, 1957; Scotland, 1953, 1954, 1957; Ireland, 1953, 1954, 1955; France, 1953, 1954, 1955; New Zealand, 1953: Scored 5t - 15 points

British Isles 1955 tour(r) South Africa: 3 caps

A former schoolmaster, Gareth Griffiths is now employed in public relations. Called out to South Africa as a replacement, he appeared in eleven games for the 1955 British Isles, playing at centre, wing and full back. On 24 February 1954, he scored a try for the Barbarians against New Zealand. He has also represented Wales as a sprinter.

GRIFFITHS, Griffith
Born Llanelli, 15 September 1864; died Llanelli, 22 July 1938
Career: Llanelli

Half-back in 1 match, against: Ireland, 1889

Gitto Griffiths was employed in the South Wales Mills.

GRIFFITHS, Jonathan Lynn
Born Carmarthen, 23 August 1964
Career: Sandown School; Sandown-Shanklin; Welsh Youth; Carmarthen Quins; Llanelli; Barbarians; Wales B

Scrum-half in 2 matches, against: New Zealand, 1988; Scotland, 1989

Fireman, Jonathan Griffiths has played cricket for Wales Youth and Wales in the Minor Counties Championship. After signing for St Helens, he scored two tries on his debut against Sheffield Eagles on 3 September 1989. He appeared in the 1991 Silk Cut Challenge Cup final with St Helens.

GRIFFITHS, Michael
Born Tonypandy, 18 March 1962
Career: Blaenclydach Comprehensive School; Ystrad Rhondda; Bridgend; Cardiff; Barbarians; Wales B

Prop in 14 matches, against: Western Samoa, 1988; Romania, 1988; Scotland, 1989; Ireland, 1989, 1991; France, 1989, 1990, 1991; England, 1989, 1990; New Zealand, 1989; Namibia, 1990, 1990; Barbarians, 1990

British Isles 1989 tour Australia

Mike Griffiths made six appearances for the British Isles in Australia in 1989.

GRIFFITHS, Vincent Morgan
Born Pontypridd, 29 May 1901; died Newport, 7 January 1967
Career: West Monmouth School; Bristol University; Pontypool; Newport

Stand-off in 3 matches, against: Scotland, 1924; Ireland, 1924; France, 1924: Scored 1t 1dg - 7points;

British Isles 1924 tour South Africa: 2 caps

Schoolmaster Vince Griffiths played in thirteen matches during the 1924 British Isles tour of South Africa. Six of these appearances, including the two international matches, were in the centre position. In September 1927, he played for Newport against New South Wales. He captained Newport in 1928-29 and served on the Welsh selection committee after the Second World War.

GRONOW, Benjamin
Born Bridgend, 10 March 1887; died Huddersfield, 24 November 1967
Career: Bridgend; Glamorgan

Forward in 4 matches, against: France, 1910; England, 1910; Scotland, 1910; Ireland, 1910: Scored 1t - 3 points

Before working as a road haulier, Ben Gronow had been a stonemason. He captained Bridgend in 1908-09 and kicked off for Wales in the very first international match to be played at Twickenham in 1910. On 3 September 1910, he made his rugby league debut for Huddersfield against Ebbw Vale and gained a great reputation as a kicker. He remained at the club, scoring 1,701 points, before transferring to Batley in September 1928 and later to Featherstone Rovers. During the First World War he served in the Army Service Corps and played rugby union for various service teams. He spent some time as trainer to the Grenfell Club in Australia in 1926, having visited the country in 1920 and 1924 with the Great Britain tourists. He won eight Wales RL caps. Three of his brothers played for Bridgend and his sons for Huddersfield RLFC. He served in the Army Service Corps during the First World War.

GWILLIAM, John Albert
Born Pontypridd, 28 February 1923
Career: Monmouth School; Cambridge University; Newport; London Welsh; Wasps; Gloucester; Edinburgh Wanderers; Llanelli; Barbarians

Lock/No 8 in 23 matches, against: Australia, 1947; Ireland, 1948, 1949, 1950, 1951, 1952, 1953; England, 1949, 1950, 1951, 1952, 1953, 1954; Scotland, 1949, 1950, 1951, 1952; France, 1949, 1950, 1952, 1953; South Africa, 1951; New Zealand, 1953

John Gwilliam won a Welsh schoolboys cap during the Second World War and two Cambridge Blues (1947 and 1948). Under his captaincy Wales won the Triple Crown and Grand Slam in 1950 and 1952; in all he led Wales on thirteen occasions. He taught at Glenalmond and was later headmaster of Birkenhead School.

GWYN, David
(also known as GWYNN)
Born Swansea, 1862; died Swansea, 8 March 1910
Career: Swansea; Oldham; Exeter; Lancashire

Back in 6 matches, against: England, 1882, 1890, 1891; Scotland, 1887, 1891; Ireland, 1890

Dai, who was the brother of W H Gwynn [qv], played with Billy McCutcheon [qv] for Oldham. Until his death he was associated with Swansea Cricket Club for many years, particularly as club umpire.

GWYNN, William Henry
Born Swansea, 1856; died Bridgend, 1 April 1897
Career: Battersea College; Swansea

Half-back in 5 matches, against: England, 1884, 1885; Scotland, 1884, 1885; Ireland, 1884

Schoolmaster Gwynn captained Swansea in 1884-86, was the secretary of the WRU from 1892-96 and a representative on the International Board from 1892-95. He was one of the first and most able advocates of the passing game where the movement of the ball changed from one direction to the other across the field of play. During his playing career, he was renowned for passing the ball directly from the base of the scrum, between his legs, out to the backs. On 13 May 1893 he refereed the first ever soccer match between Swansea Town and Cardiff City on the Vetch Field. He played cricket for Swansea and Glamorgan and was a vice-president of the former. He also played soccer for Battersea College. The brother of David Gwyn [qv], he died as a result of a stroke which he suffered in 1895.

HADLEY, Adrian Michael
Born Cardiff, 1 March 1963
Career: Lady Mary High School, Cardiff; Cardiff Schools; South Glamorgan Schools; Welsh Youth; Cardiff; Barbarians; Wales B

Wing in 27 matches, against: Romania, 1983; Scotland, 1984, 1986, 1987(r), 1988; Ireland, 1984, 1986, 1987, [1987 World Cup], 1988; France, 1984, 1985, 1986, 1988; England, 1984, 1985, 1986, [1987 World Cup], 1988; Fiji, 1985, 1986; Tonga, 1986, [1987 World Cup]; Canada, [1987 World Cup]; New Zealand, [1987 World Cup]; Australia, [1987 World Cup]; United States, 1987: Scored 9t - 36 points

Adrian Hadley is a civil servant. After signing for Salford RLFC in March 1988, he had to wait until September of that year before he made his first-class debut for the club against Warrington.

HALL, Ian
Born Gilfach Goch, 4 November 1946
Career: Pontypridd; Aberavon; South Wales Police, Barbarians

Centre/wing in 8 matches, against: New Zealand, 1967; South Africa, 1970; Scotland, 1970, 1971, 1974; England, 1970; Ireland, 1974; France, 1974

Police officer Ian Hall captained Aberavon in 1971-72.

HALL, Michael Robert
Born Bridgend, 13 October 1965
Career: Brynteg Comprehensive School; University College, Cardiff; Cambridge University; Welsh Students; British Universities; Bridgend; Cardiff; Barbarians; Wales Under 21; Wales B

Wing/centre in 12 matches, against: New Zealand, 1988(r), 1988, 1989; Western Samoa, 1988; Romania, 1988; Scotland, 1989, 1990; Ireland, 1989; France, 1989, 1990; England, 1989, 1990: Scored 2t - 8 points

British Isles 1989 tour Australia: 1 cap

After graduating from Cardiff, Mike Hall pursued a two year post-graduate course in Land Economy at Cambridge where he gained two Blues (1987 and 1988) and is now employed as a surveyor. He scored three tries in six appearances for the British Isles in Australia.

HALL, Wayne Hopkin
Born Pencoed, 29 January 1958
Career: Pencoed Comprehensive School; Welsh Schools; Welsh Youth; Pencoed; Llanelli; Cardiff; Maesteg; Bridgend; Glamorgan; Wales B

Hooker in 1 match, against: Western Samoa, 1988

Wayne Hall is a wood machinist. He won his only cap two months short of his thirty-first birthday.

HANCOCK, Francis Escott
Born Wiveliscombe, 7 December 1859; died Wiveliscombe, 29 October 1943
Career: Wiveliscombe; Cardiff; Somerset

Back in 4 matches, against: Ireland, 1884; England, 1885; Scotland, 1885, 1886

Frank Hancock was a director in the Cardiff brewery owned by his father, William Hancock, a brewer and private bank owner from Wiveliscombe, who had purchased the Bute Dock Brewery in Cardiff. William later acquired the Anchor Brewery in Newport in 1884 which led to the foundation of William Hancock and Co Ltd. Early in 1884, Frank appeared for Cardiff against Cheltenham College scoring two tries and, in the next game, against Gloucester, the Cardiff selectors were reluctant to omit Frank from the team following this fine performance. A problem arose however because at that time the established format of a side was a full back, three three-quarters, two half-backs and nine forwards. So, in order to accommodate Frank in the backs, he was selected in addition to the three regulars, to the exclusion of the ninth forward. Thus was born the four three-quarters system as we know it today. He captained Cardiff in 1885-86 and, as a tennis player, won the Glamorgan singles title twice. His brother, Philip Froude Hancock, played for England and the British Isles from 1886 to 1890 and another brother Ernest, played for Cardiff.

HANNAN, James
Born Newport, 1864; died Newport, 22 June 1905

67

31. 1929 v England
Back row: R W Harland (IRFU referee), W G Thomas, C C Pritchard, H J Jones, T Arthur, R Jones, F A Bowdler, A W Jones (touch judge).
Middle row: J C Morley, E G Davies, J A Bassett, I E Jones (C), J Roberts, W G Morgan, D R Jenkins.
Front row: W Roberts, W C Powell.
[*Auty Collection*]

32. 1930 v Ireland
Back row: D Hellewell (referee), H C Day, A Skym, A W Lemon, D J Thomas, T Arthur, H Peacock, J S Jones (touch judge).
Middle row: W C Powell, J C Morley, W G Morgan, J Bassett (C), T E Jones-Davies, E H Jones, E M Jenkins.
Front row: N H Fender, F L Williams.
[*J B G Thomas*]

33. 1931 v France
Back row: Unknown official, D R James, A Skym, J Lang, E M Jenkins, T Arthur, A W Lemon, N H Fender, R W Harland (IRFU referee).
Middle row: R W Boon, C Davey, J C Morley, J A Bassett (C), F L Williams, T B Day.
Front row: A R Ralph, W C Powell.
[*Stephen Williams*]

68

Career: Newport; London Welsh; Newport Engineers

Forward in 19 matches, against: New Zealand Natives, 1888; Scotland, 1889, 1890, 1892, 1893, 1894, 1895; Ireland, 1889, 1890, 1892, 1893, 1894, 1895; England, 1890, 1891, 1892, 1893, 1894, 1895: Scored 2t - 6 points

A boilermaker by trade, Jim Hannan was a fine athletic forward, as was his brother Mat who also played for Newport. He died only six hours after his mother.

HARDING, Arthur Flowers

Born Market Rasen, 8 August 1878; died Martinborough, New Zealand, 15 May 1947
Career: Christ College Brecon; Llwynypia; London Welsh; Cardiff; Wanganui (New Zealand); Barbarians; Middlesex

Forward in 20 matches, against: England, 1902, 1903, 1904, 1905, 1906, 1908; Scotland, 1902, 1903, 1904, 1905, 1906, 1908; Ireland, 1902, 1903, 1904, 1905, 1906, 1907; New Zealand, 1905; South Africa, 1906: Scored 1t - 3 points

British Isles 1904 tour Australia: 3 caps, New Zealand: 1 cap; Anglo-Welsh 1908 tour (captain) Australia, New Zealand: 3 caps

Before emigrating to New Zealand in 1910, where he became a farm manager, 'Boxer' Harding had been an articled clerk. He captained London Welsh from 1903-07, played for Middlesex against the 1905 All Blacks and in 1906 he represented the same county against the Springboks. He played in all five matches in New Zealand during the 1904 British Isles tour, while four years later in New Zealand he appeared in eleven matches for the visiting Anglo-Welsh tourists. He served with the Imperial Yeomanry in South Africa in 1900. His Wales, 1908 tour and club caps are in the New Zealand Rugby museum at Palmerston North.

HARDING, Charles Theodore

Born Chorlton, Lancashire, 1860; died Newport, 13 July 1919
Career: Monmouth School; Newport

Forward in 3 matches, against: New Zealand Natives, 1888; Scotland, 1889; Ireland, 1889

Charles Harding worked in the docks and was a brother to George Harding [qv]. He captained Newport from 1887-89 and also led the Newport hockey team in its first season in 1895-96. He died on a train travelling from Cardiff to Newport.

HARDING, George Frederick JP

Born Chorlton, Lancashire, 1858; died Llantarnam, 8 July

1927
Career: Monmouth School; Newport

Forward/back/half-back in 4 matches, against: England, 1881, 1882; Ireland, 1882; Scotland, 1883

Company chairman of Lloyds and Yorath (brewers), George Harding was, with his brother Theo [qv], a founder member of Newport RFC. He also played cricket for Monmouthshire and South Wales at Lords and the Oval and was regarded as a good oarsman and miler.

HARDING, Rowe DL

Born Birchgrove, Swansea, 10 September 1901; died Gower, 10 February 1991
Career: Gowerton County School; Cambridge University; Gowerton; Loughor; Swansea; London Welsh; Llanelli; Barbarians

Wing in 17 matches, against: England, 1923, 1926, 1927, 1928; Scotland, 1923, 1927; France, 1923, 1924, 1925, 1926, 1927; Ireland, 1923, 1924, 1925, 1926, 1927; New Zealand, 1924: Scored 5t - 15 points

British Isles 1924 tour South Africa: 3 caps

Rowe Harding arrived at Cambridge University in 1924 having already appeared seven times in the Welsh jersey and fourteen times for the British Isles in South Africa. He won four Blues (1924-27) and was only on the losing side in the 1924 match. Representing Swansea Cricket and Football Clubs he won the Welsh AAA 100 yards in 1922 and 1926 and the 220 yards event in 1923. He captained Swansea in 1928-29 and published his lively survey of Welsh rugby in the twenties, *Rugby Reminiscences and Opinions,* in 1929. During the Second World War he served in the Home Guard. In 1945 he became a County Court judge, and in 1953 a Circuit Court judge. After the war Harding stood for Parliament in the National Liberal and Conservative interest, contesting Swansea East in the 1945 general election, and Gower in 1950 and 1951. He served as vice-president of the WRU from 1953-56 and sat on numerous committees, councils of institutions and charities in Wales. As president of the Royal Institution of South Wales in 1960 he helped in the revival of Swansea's Victorian Museum and was chairman of Swansea Porcelain from 1976. He was chairman and president of Glamorgan Cricket Club. In 1970 he was appointed a Deputy Lieutenant for Glamorgan. His father, Albert, a colliery manager, established Glais RFC in 1896.

HARRIS, Charles Albert

Born Maindy, Cardiff, 4 February 1902; died Aberavon, 1 October 1963
Career: Eastern School, Port Talbot; Seaside Albion; Neath; Aberavon; Maesteg; Briton Ferry; Cheltenham

Scrum-half in 1 match, against: New South Wales, 1927

Tal Harris, a former docker, had his own business. In 1931 he appeared for the Aberavon/ Neath XV against South Africa. Playing for Aberavon against Penarth, in January 1932, the game was held up for a while because Tal's alsatian dog had broken free from his leash and had joined his master on the field of play. Eventually Tal collared him and had him locked up in the dressing room.

HARRIS, Daniel John Edward
Born Penygraig, 27 May 1937
Career: Ferndale Grammar School; St Luke's College, Exeter; Pontypridd; Bridgend; London Welsh; Cardiff; Devon; Glamorgan

Lock in 8 matches, against: Ireland, 1959, 1960; France, 1959, 1960; Scotland, 1960, 1961; South Africa, 1960; England, 1961

After moving to Leigh RLFC, former schoolmaster Danny Harris left the profession to work in the hotel business. He made his debut for the club on 19 August 1961 against Swinton. At present he lives in Spain.

HATHWAY, George Frederick
Born 23 January 1897, registered in Newport; died Newport, 30 January 1971
Career: Cross Keys; Newport; London Welsh; Olympique (Paris)

Forward in 2 matches, against: Ireland, 1924; France, 1924

George Hathway won both his caps from the Newport club after trials from Cross Keys. On 2 October 1924, in front of a crowd of 27,948, he played for Newport against New Zealand. He captained Cross Keys in 1926-28. His brother Reg played for Newport against New South Wales in September in 1927, scoring the club's only try.

HAVARD, William Thomas MC, DD
Born Neuadd, Breconshire, 23 October 1889; died Gwbert-on-Sea, 17 August 1956
Career: Brecon Secondary School; University College Aberystwyth; Oxford University; St Michael's Theological College, Llandaff; Llanelli; London Welsh

Forward in 1 match, against: New Zealand Army, 1919

Bill Havard was the Bishop of St Asaph from 1934-50, and of St David's from 1950-56. Before winning his Blue in 1919, he had played rugby and soccer for Aberystwyth University and Town. He also played soccer for Swansea Town, and in September 1912, two days prior to the club's first Southern League match, when the reserve team was playing at Merthyr, Havard scored Swansea's first goal in competitive football. During the First World War Havard was commissioned as an army chaplain.

HAWKINS, Frank James MC
Born Wiveliscombe, Somerset, 1885   died: Treforest, 3 September 1960
Career: Glamorgan Police; Pontypridd; Somerset

Forward in 2 matches, against: Ireland, 1912; France, 1912

A police officer (No. 430) in the Glamorgan Constabulary, Frank Hawkins played for Somerset against South Africa in October 1906. He left the police and became a licensee in Pontypridd and Porth before the First World War. In 1911 he was the Pontypridd RFC treasurer. During the First World War he was wounded whilst serving as a 2nd Lieutenant in the 20th Bn, the Welch Regiment and ended the war with the rank of captain.

HAYWARD, David John
Born Crumlin, 1 March 1934
Career: Crumlin High Level School; Newbridge Grammar School; Loughborough College; Welsh Secondary Schools; Crumlin; Newbridge; Cardiff; Irish Wolfhounds; Leicestershire

Flanker in 6 matches, against: England, 1963; New Zealand, 1963; Scotland, 1964; Ireland, 1964; France, 1964; South Africa, 1964: Scored 1t - 3 points

After spending some time in the teaching profession David Hayward moved into interior design having also been employed as the manager of a drinks company. He captained Cardiff from 1962-64, coached the East Wales XV for their encounter with the All Blacks of 1967 and was chairman of Cardiff RFC in 1985-86. His contributions to rugby match programmes are regarded as masterpieces of humorous writing.

HAYWARD, Donald James
Born Pontypool, 30 June 1925
Career: Newbridge

Lock/prop in 15 matches, against: England, 1949, 1950, 1951, 1952; France, 1949, 1950, 1951, 1952; Scotland, 1950, 1951, 1952; Ireland, 1950, 1951, 1952; South Africa, 1951

British Isles 1950 tour New Zealand: 3 caps, Australia

Railway-fireman Don Hayward was recognised as a hard working forward, being one of the best of many good forwards in Wales at the time. During the 1950 British Isles tour of Australasia he made sixteen appearances for the visitors in New Zealand, and two in Australia. In October 1951, he played for the Pontypool and Newbridge

XV against South Africa and captained Newbridge in 1951-52. After leaving Wales to play rugby league he made his debut for Wigan RLFC against Leigh on 13 November 1954 and eventually emigrated to New Zealand where he continued to play rugby league.

HAYWARD, George
Born c1887; died Swansea, 14 February 1948
Career: Swansea

Forward in 5 matches, against: Scotland, 1908; France, 1908; Ireland, 1908; Australia, 1908; England, 1909

Four years after his final game for Wales, George Hayward, who was a butcher, joined Wigan RLFC, making his debut against Runcorn two days after Christmas day, 1913.

HELLINGS, Dick
Born Tiverton, 1 December 1873; died Pontyclun, 9 February 1938
Career: Llwynypia; Cardiff; Exeter; Devon

Forward in 9 matches, against: England, 1897, 1898, 1900, 1901; Ireland, 1898, 1899, 1900; Scotland, 1899, 1901: Scored 1t - 3 points

Coal cutter Dick Hellings scored a try whilst playing with a broken arm against England at Gloucester in January 1900.

HERRERA, Ronald Cecil
Born Wattsville, nr Newport, 16 January 1905; died Newport, 16 March 1973
Career: Wattsville School; Wattsville; Cross Keys; Newport

Forward in 8 matches, against: Scotland, 1925, 1926; France, 1925, 1926; Ireland, 1925, 1926; England, 1926, 1927: Scored 2t - 6 points

A former motor mechanic Ron Herrera became a police officer in the Newport Borough Force. Although losing to Scotland on their first visit to Murrayfield, on 6 February 1926, Wales scored a try through Herrera. He appeared for Newport against New South Wales in September 1927. He received a Royal Humane Society Award for saving a woman from drowning in the River Usk. His grandfather Patrico, a Spanish seaman, was shipwrecked off the coast of Cuba and, working his way back to Spain, was again shipwrecked, off Port Talbot, finally ending up in Wattsville. Ron's nephew John played in the second row for Newport and appeared in Welsh trials.

HIAMS, Harry
Born c1886; died Swansea, 10 April 1954

Career: Swansea; London Welsh; Llanelli; Aberafon

Forward in 2 matches, against: Ireland, 1912; France, 1912

Harry Hiams worked for ICI at Landore. He scored a long range drop goal while playing for Llanelli against South Africa in 1912. During the First World War he served in the Royal Field Artillery.

HICKMAN, Arthur
Born Skewen, 6 August 1910
Career: Neath County School; Welsh Secondary Schools; Neath

Wing in 2 matches, against: England, 1930; Scotland, 1933

Arthur Hickman was a transport manager for a building company. He won both his caps on home ground, Wales losing both games by 3 points to 11 points. He captained Neath in 1933-34 and, shortly after his 24th birthday, made his debut for Swinton RLFC against Halifax.

HIDDLESTONE, David Daniel
Born Hendy, 14 June 1890; died Hendy, 16 November 1973
Career: Llanelli; Neath; Hendy

Forward in 5 matches, against: England, 1922; Scotland, 1922; Ireland, 1922; France, 1922; New Zealand, 1924: Scored 1t - 3 points

Employed in the tinplate industry, Dai Hiddlestone won his first of four caps in an unbeaten Welsh XV. He was joint captain of Llanelli in 1918-19, captain the following season and captain of Neath in 1924-25. He won his final cap in November 1924 against a rampaging New Zealand team, who went on to complete an unbeaten tour. Over forty years later Dai's grandson, Terry Price [qv], made eight appearances for Wales.

HILL, Algernon Frank
Born Cardiff, 13 January 1866; died Cardiff, 20 April 1927
Career: Clifton College; Cardiff

Forward in 15 matches, against: Scotland, 1885, 1886, 1888, 1889, 1890, 1893, 1894; England, 1886, 1893, 1894; Ireland, 1888, 1890, 1893, 1894; New Zealand Natives, 1888

Frank Hill, a solicitor with an office in High Street, Cardiff was, according to the parish records for Llandaff, baptised as Alperus Frank Hill, in February 1866. He captained Wales against the New Zealand Natives, Cardiff in 1888-89 and 1894-95 and served on the committee of Cardiff RFC.

HINAM, Sydney
Born 29 August 1898, registered in Pontypool; died Cardiff, 16 August 1982
Career: Cardiff, British Police

Forward in 5 matches, against: Ireland, 1925, 1926; England, 1926; Scotland, 1926; France, 1926

Hinam, who served in the Royal Artillery during the First World War, obtained an early discharge by claiming to be a collier. He worked on the railways before becoming a police officer. On 11 September 1926 he made his first appearance for Rochdale Hornets RLFC against Castleford. After retiring from rugby league, he went to sea for a period before re-joining the police service where he was employed in airfield security.

HINTON, John Thomas
Born Bombay, India, 1860; died Cardiff, 4 February 1931
Career: Cardiff

Forward in 1 match, against: Ireland, 1884

John Hinton was employed as an agent for the Royal Liver Assurance Company and was chairman of the Roath Conservative Club.

HIRST, George Littlewood
Born Dowlais, 5 May 1890; died 30 July 1967, registered in Pontypool
Career: Emanuel School, Wandsworth; Pontypool; Newport; Barbarians

Wing in 6 matches, against: Scotland, 1912, 1913, 1914; England, 1914; France, 1914; Ireland, 1914: Scored 3t 2dg - 17 points

While a pupil at Emanuel School, George Hirst climbed the school tower and spire at night, with a cricket stump in his hand, and turned the weathervane in a different direction, collecting a twopenny bet for his daring. A trained engineer, he was employed by the Blaenavon Company but, after his marriage, became a partner in the business owned by his in-laws. He played in only one losing Welsh side, against England on 17 January 1914. He scored 75 tries for Newport in 121 games. His rugby career ended in 1919 when he broke his leg in a charity game at Bargoed. Both he and Jack Wetter [qv], who played together for Wales in three games in 1914, were buried on the same day in 1967. His son Geoff, a prop, captained Pontypool in 1948-49 and later played for Newport.

HODDER, Wilfred
Born Abersychan, 6 May 1896; died Lancaster, 12 November 1957

Career: Pontypool; Talywain

Forward in 3 matches, against: England, 1921; Scotland, 1921; France, 1921: Scored 1t - 3 points

After playing out his days in rugby league for Wigan, a club he had joined in August 1921, Wilf Hodder became a director of the club. Prior to moving north he had worked in the mines and during the First World War had served with the Royal Field Artillery. His brother Lester was in the Pontypool team that beat the Maoris on 1 January 1927 and New South Wales on 8 December 1927.

HODGES, Joseph Jehoida
Born Risca, 15 July 1876; died Ebbw Vale, 13 September 1930
Career: Pontymister; Newport; London Welsh

Forward in 23 matches, against: England, 1899, 1900, 1901, 1902, 1903, 1904, 1905, 1906; Scotland, 1899, 1900, 1901, 1902, 1903, 1904, 1905, 1906; Ireland, 1899, 1900, 1902, 1903, 1905, 1906; New Zealand, 1905: Scored 6t - 18 points

On 10 January 1903, Tom Pearson, the captain, and left wing of the Welsh side, and the scorer of the first Welsh try, was badly injured in a tackle. As a result of this, Jehoida Hodges was moved from the pack onto the wing. Obviously a fine finisher, he managed to cross the English line on no fewer than three occasions. He captained Newport in 1904-05 and appeared for them against South Africa in 1906. After working as a collier, he became a licensee and was later an agent for an insurance company. His funeral procession was enormous and the service was conducted by A A Mathews [qv] and attended by many former internationals. Coincidentally, the remains of fellow international Stan Winmill [qv] were laid to rest alongside his grave in Danygraig cemetery.

HODGSON, Grahame Thornton Ridgeway
Born Ogmore Vale, 1 December 1936
Career: Ogmore Vale Grammar School; St Luke's College, Exeter; Ogmore Youth; Bridgend; Exeter Saracens; Exeter; Torquay; Teignmouth; Aberavon; Llanelli; Neath; Barbarians; Glamorgan; Devon

Full back in 15 matches, against: Ireland, 1962, 1963, 1964, 1966, 1967; England, 1963, 1964; Scotland, 1963, 1964, 1966; France, 1963, 1964, 1966; New Zealand, 1963; South Africa, 1964: Scored 4pg - 12 points
Grahame Hodgson is a schoolmaster. In a four match tour of South Africa by Wales in May 1964 Hodgson played in all matches. He captained Neath in 1964-65 and played for Neath and Aberavon against South Africa in 1961 and New Zealand in 1963.

34. 1933 v England
Back row; B Evans, V G J Jenkins, W Wooller, I Isaacs, T Arthur, DJ Thomas, unknown official.
Middle row: A H Jones, R B Jones, R W Boon, W T Thomas, C Davey, E L Jones, A Skym.
Front row: H M Bowcott, M J L Turnbull.
[*Auty Collection*]

35. 1933 v Scotland
Back row: J S Jones (touch judge), E L Jones, W Wooller, I Isaacs, A Skym, T Arthur, R B Jones, J G Bott (RFU referee).
Middle row: G Bayllss, A H Jones, C Davey, W T Thomas (C), A Hickman, DJ Thomas, B Evans.
Front row: D B Evans, R R Morris.
[*Edgar Jones*]

36. 1935 v Ireland
Back row: D J Thomas, W Wooller, A M Rees, J Lang, T G Williams, T J Rees.
Middle row: C D Murphy, T B Day, C Davey (C), W C Jones, W C Powell, A Bassett, A G Fear.
Front row: T O James, G R R Jones.
[*Adam Machell*]

HOLLINGDALE, Bertie George

Born Swansea, 1889; died Waunarlwydd, 11 February 1961
Career: Waunarlwydd; Swansea

Forward in 2 matches, against: South Africa, 1912; England, 1913

Bert Hollingdale was one of a large family of boys, including Tom [qv], each of whom was a rugby player of above average ability.

HOLLINGDALE, Thomas Henry

Born Waunarlwydd, 12 November 1900; died Hounslow, 14 April 1978
Career: Waunarlwydd School; Gowerton County School; Waunarlwydd; Gowerton; Briton Ferry; Ammanford; Neath; Neath Borough Police; Glamorgan

Forward in 6 matches, against: New South Wales, 1927; England, 1928, 1930; Scotland, 1928; Ireland, 1928; France, 1928

Tom Hollingdale, who played for Neath and Aberavon against New South Wales in September 1927, was a police officer who joined the force on the spin of a coin - heads for the church, tails for the police. At the age of seventeenn he had passed his entrance examination to theological college, but sacrificed it for the police. After ten years on the Neath Borough force he resigned to take up theological studies at King's College, London. After ordination he became a curate in Forest Hill, London. Later, he became a vicar at St Peter's Church, Colchester and, during the years he was there, he became the second president of Colchester RFC.

HOLMES, Terence David

Born Cardiff, 10 March 1957
Career: Bishop Hannan School; Welsh Secondary Schools; Cardiff Youth; Welsh Youth; Cardiff; Barbarians

Scrum-half in 25 matches, against: Australia, 1978, 1981; New Zealand, 1978, 1980; Scotland, 1979, 1980, 1983, 1985; Ireland, 1979, 1980, 1982, 1983, 1985; France, 1979, 1980, 1982, 1983, 1985; England, 1979, 1980, 1982, 1983, 1984, 1985; Fiji, 1985: Scored 9t - 36 points

British Isles 1980 tour South Africa; 1983 New Zealand: 1 cap

In one hundred and ninety five appearances for Cardiff, which ended in November 1985, Holmes scored 123 tries and captained the team in 1984-85. On 3 December 1985, he signed for Bradford Northern RLFC and five days later made his first appearance for the club against Swinton. A mere thirteen minutes into the game his shoulder was dislocated. A further dislocation in a match five weeks

later, coupled to old injuries received on both British Isles tours, hampered his career and he retired from the game in October 1987. The followers of the northern game were never allowed to witness the full repertoire of one of the most talented rugby players of recent times. Like Gareth Davies, his half-back partner in the Welsh team, injuries restricted him to four appearances for the British Isles in South Africa. Again, three years later, in 1983, he played in only four matches for the British Isles XV on tour in New Zealand. A horrific injury in the seventh match, the first international against the All Blacks, in Christchurch, put an end to his tour. His autobiography, *My Life in Rugby*, was published in March 1988. Terry Holmes is now in business in Cardiff.

HOPKIN, William H

Born Newport, 1 July 1914
Career: Newport; Gloucester

Wing in 1 match, against: Scotland, 1937

Before making his debut for Swinton RLFC in November 1938, Bill Hopkin had worked for an omnibus company and was later employed in the British Railways buffet in Newport.

HOPKINS, Kevin

Born Cwmllynfell, 29 September 1961
Career: Maesydderwen Comprehensive School; South Glamorgan Institute; Welsh Secondary Schools; Ystradgynlais; Neath; Cardiff; Swansea; Barbarians; Wales B

Centre in 7 matches, against: England, 1985, 1987; France, 1987; Scotland, 1987; Tonga, [1987 World Cup]; Canada, [1987(r) World Cup]; United States, 1987

The great nephew of Thomas Hopkins [qv], Kevin Hopkins, a strong running centre and former schoolmaster, now works for Chartered Trust. He is the captain of Swansea for the 1991-92 season. His brother Cellan plays for Ystradgynlais.

HOPKINS, Philip

Born Pontardawe, 31 January 1880; died Swansea, 26 September 1966
Career: Collegiate School Tanyrallt, Alltwen; University College of North Wales, Bangor; Pontardawe; Swansea

Wing in 4 matches, against: Australia, 1908; England, 1909, 1910; Ireland, 1909: Score 3t - 9 points

An athlete of great ability, Phil Hopkins scored a try in each of his first three matches. Employed as a foreman, he played soccer, hockey, tennis and cricket, as well as rugby, to a high standard. He rowed for his college at Henley and had a handicap of four at Pontardawe Golf

Club. He was a reserve for the Wales hockey XI and the amateur soccer XI.

HOPKINS, Raymond
Born Maesteg, 8 July 1946
Career: Welsh Youth; Maesteg; Llanelli; Barbarians; Wales B

Scrum half in 1 match, against: England, 1970(r): Scored 1t - 3 points

British Isles 1971 tour Australia, New Zealand: 1 cap(r)

Ray 'Chico' Hopkins had toured Australasia and Fiji with the Welsh team in the summer of 1969 as cover for Gareth Edwards, but it was not until the following season that he replaced the injured Edwards at Twickenham to gain his only Welsh cap and become the first replacement to score a try for Wales. On 26 June 1971, he again replaced Gareth Edwards in the first British Isles-All Blacks encounter. Chico made one appearance in Australia and ten in New Zealand. He made his debut for Swinton RLFC against Huyton, on 3 December 1972. He was employed as a fitter before becoming a company representative.

HOPKINS, Thomas
Born 20 January 1903, registered in Pontardawe; died Ystradgynlais, 26 January 1980
Career: Cwmgiedd School; Penrhos School; Cwmgiedd; Ystradgynlais; Swansea

Forward in 4 matches, against: England, 1926; Scotland, 1926; Ireland, 1926; France, 1926: Scored 1t - 3 points

A colliery fireman, Tom Hopkins was one of the founders of Brecon County Rugby Union. He appeared for Swansea against the Maoris in 1926 and New South Wales in 1927. From 1946-70 he was the secretary of Ystradgynlais RFC. Tom Hopkins was the great uncle of Kevin Hopkins [qv].

HOPKINS, William John
Born c1898
Career: Aberavon

Stand-off in 2 matches, against: England, 1925; Scotland, 1925: Scored 1t - 3 points

Willie Hopkins was a docker, and later, a mechanic on the railways. He captained Aberavon in 1925-26.

HOWELL, William Henry
Born Swansea, December 1863
Career: Llandovery College; Swansea

Forward in 2 matches, against: Scotland, 1888; Ireland, 1888

HOWELLS, Brynmor
Born Hendy, 9 February 1911; died Llangyfelach, 6 June 1983
Career: Gorseinon; Hendy; Llanelli

Full back in 1 match, against: England, 1934

A steelworker, Bryn Howells played his first game for Broughton Rangers RLFC in January 1935. He then became a licensee, and in the summer months played cricket for Gorseinon and later Lancashire League club Enfield.

HOWELLS, William Geoffrey
Born Loughor, 29 October 1929
Career: Loughor; Swansea; Llanelli

Wing in 4 matches, against: England, 1957; Scotland, 1957; Ireland, 1957; France, 1957: Scored 1t - 3 points

Geoff Howells was employed in the tinplate and steelworks industry and later became a lorry driver. He was a committee member at Loughor RFC.

HUGHES, Dennis
Born Argoed, 3 July 1941
Career: Pengam Grammar School; University College Aberystwyth; Welsh Secondary Schools; Newbridge; Barbarians; Monmouthshire

Flanker in 6 matches, against: New Zealand, 1967, 1969; South Africa, 1970; Scotland, 1970; England, 1970; Ireland, 1970

Dennis Hughes, a bank clerk and then a business executive, made two tours with the Welsh team, the first to Argentina in 1968 and the second to Australasia and Fiji in 1969. He made 745 appearances for Newbridge, captained them from 1966-72 and appeared for Abertillery and Newbridge against Fiji in September 1964. He played first class rugby until he was forty and, in the mid 1960s, formed the best club back row in Britain with his brother Arthur and Ken Braddock [qv]. He was a member of the WRU rugby planning committee.

HUGHES, Gomer
Born Neath, 13 May 1910; died Salford, 14 November 1974
Career: Neath; Penarth

Forward in 3 matches, against: England, 1934; Scotland, 1934; Ireland, 1934

Employed as a builder's labourer, Gomer Hughes signed for Swinton RLFC and made his debut for them against Halifax on 25 August 1934.

HUGHES, Hugh
Born details unknown
Career: Cardiff

Full back in 2 matches, against: Scotland, 1887, 1889

'Sawdust' Hughes won both his caps in games played at Raeburn Place, Edinburgh. The match in February 1887 had been postponed from January because of frost, and the 1889 match, also in February, had to be restricted to two half-hours because of falling snow.

HUGHES, Keith
Born Glanamman, 15 December 1949
Career: Llanelli Grammar School; Cambridge University; Westminster Hospital; Welsh Secondary Schools; New Dock Stars; Llanelli; London Welsh; London Counties; Barbarians; Surrey

Wing/centre in 3 matches, against: Ireland, 1970; Australia, 1973; Scotland, 1974

Keith Hughes is a doctor in Ystradgynlais. He won two Blues in 1968-69 and was then capped from New Dock Stars. His father-in-law D L James was the president of the Welsh Rugby Union in 1978-79.

HULLIN, William G
Born Loughor, 2 January 1942
Career: Dynevor Grammar School; Welsh Secondary Schools; Mumbles; Aberavon; Cardiff; London Welsh; Barbarians; Surrey

Scrum half in 1 match, against: Scotland, 1967

Billy Hullin is the senior manager of Lloyds Bank, Newport. In 1969, he toured South Africa with a Barbarians party. On 10 May 1975 he captained the Welsh Presidents in the Ulster Invitation Centenary Sevens at Ravenhill, Belfast.

HURRELL, Richard John
Born Cwmcarn, 17 August 1933
Career: Welsh Youth; Cross Keys; Newport; Tredegar

Centre in 1 match, against: France, 1959
Jack Hurrell was an electrician. He captained Cross Keys from 1954-57 and played for Pontypool and Cross Keys against New Zealand in January 1954.

HUTCHINSON, Frederick Osborne
Born Maesteg, 1867; died Briton Ferry, May 1941
Career: Maesteg; Bridgend; Neath

Forward in 3 matches, against: Ireland, 1894, 1896;

Scotland, 1896

Fred Hutchinson was a stonemason like his father. He played cricket for Briton Ferry and the steelworks.

HUXTABLE, Richard
Born Swansea, 13 October 1890; died Swansea, 29 August 1970
Career: Glais; Swansea

Forward in 2 matches, against: France, 1920; Ireland, 1920

Dick Huxtable was employed as a tinplater and later, a collier. He captained Swansea in 1921-22.

HUZZEY, Henry Vivian Pugh
Born Varteg Hill, Monmouthshire, 24 July 1876; died Cardiff, 16 August 1929
Career: Canton; Cardiff; Glamorgan

Wing in 5 matches, against: Ireland, 1898, 1899; England, 1898, 1899; Scotland, 1899: Scored 4t 1dg - 16 points

Licensee Viv Huzzey was an accomplished athlete, scoring two tries for Oldham RLFC in his debut match against St Helens on 13 October 1900. He also played baseball for Wales.

HYBART, Albert John JP
Born Cardiff, 1865; died Cardiff, 28 January 1945
Career: Cardiff

Forward in 1 match, against: England, 1887

Hybart, a justice of the peace, was in the timber importing trade. He won his only cap in a drawn match, neither side scoring, played on the cricket pitch at Stradey Park, Llanelli. The severe weather necessitated the move from the rugby field which was unplayable.

INGLEDEW, Hugh Murray
Born Cardiff, 26 October 1865; died Cardiff, 1 February 1937
Career: St Edward's School, Oxford; Oxford University; Cardiff; Barbarians

Half-back in 3 matches, against: Ireland, 1890; England, 1891; Scotland, 1891

Hugh Ingledew, Knight of Grace, Order of St John of Jerusalem, was a solicitor, specialising in railway law. He was one of the original members of the Barbarian RFC, and was treasurer of Glamorgan cricket club from 1904-12. He also played cricket for the county, scoring 114 runs in seven innings. In the 1920s he played a leading role in the acquisition of the Arms Park from the Bute Estate. His son Kenneth was a well-known administrator in the hockey world.

ISAACS, Iorwerth
Born Cilfynydd, 4 October 1910; died Wrexham, 25 April 1966
Career: Pontypridd County School; Welsh Secondary Schools; Cilfynydd; Cardiff; Glamorgan Police; Pontypridd; Penarth

Forward in 2 matches, against: England, 1933; Scotland, 1933

After leaving the police force to sign for Leeds RLFC in August 1933, Iorrie Isaacs entered the teaching profession. From 1947 to 1966 he was Headmaster at Quinta School, Weston Rhyn, Oswestry.

JACKSON, Thomas Henry
Born Swansea, March 1870; died Llanelli, winter 1952
Career: Danygraig; Swansea

Forward in 1 match, against: England, 1895

Tom Jackson is believed to have been the first British international to score a try in France when he played for Swansea against Stade Français in 1899. He was employed as a dock labourer before becoming a licensee.

JAMES, Carwyn Rees
Born Cefneithin, 2 November 1929; died Amsterdam, 10 January 1983
Career: Gwendraeth Grammar School; University College Aberystwyth; Welsh Secondary Schools; Cefneithin; Llanelli; London Welsh; Devonport Services; Royal Navy; Barbarians

Stand-off/centre in 2 matches, against: Australia, 1958; France, 1958

Carwyn James taught at Llandovery College and Trinity College, Carmarthen. At the time of his death he contributed the rugby column for *The Guardian* which often contained brief comments of acute observation. A great nationalist, and a lover of Welsh literature, he stood as the Plaid Cymru candidate for the Llanelli seat in the 1970 General Election, polling 16.8% of the votes. During national service he learnt Russian. Possibly, his greatest achievements on the sporting front was preparing, in his capacity as coach, the British Isles XV of 1971 and the Llanelli team of October 1972, for their respective defeats of the All Blacks. He was the author of *The World of Rugby*, a history of rugby, written with John Reason, published in 1979, and *Focus on Rugby: an International*

Coaching Book, published in 1983, which accompanied a television series.

JAMES, David
Born Swansea, c1866; died Bonymaen, Swansea, 2 January 1929
Career: St Thomas Harlequins; Swansea; Broughton Rangers

Half-back in 4 matches, against: Ireland, 1891, 1892; Scotland, 1892; England, 1899

Like his brother Evan [*qv*], David James was a half-back. They were both employed in a copper works before moving on to a fuel works. They were not available to play for their country for a number of years as the Rugby Football Union had declared them to be professionals but, after their reinstatement they played in one further match, against England, at St Helen's, where they orchestrated the play to such an extent that England were overwhelmed by 26 points to 3 points. Six weeks after that Welsh win, David joined Broughton Rangers RLFC in February 1899. He was reported to have asked for the latest Test score a few minutes before he died. A younger brother Claude played inside right for the Swansea East XI, a forerunner of Swansea Town, and in the 1904 season, when the side played and won over twenty games, he scored thirty two goals. Another brother Sammy died of consumption in 1909.

JAMES, David Maldwyn
Born Cilfynydd, 28 June 1913
Career: Pontypridd Grammar School; Cilfynydd; Pontypridd; Cardiff; Mountain Ash

Hooker in 5 matches, against: Australia, 1947; England, 1948; Scotland, 1948; France, 1948; Ireland, 1948

Mal James worked for the National Coal Board. In 1937 he appeared in a final Welsh trial, ten years before winning his first cap at the age of 34 years and 5 months, which makes him Wales' third oldest first cap. He played in four Victory internationals after the Second World War, when ties were awarded in place of caps. From 1952-54 he was president of Tylorstown RFC. A useful tennis player, he appeared for Abercynon in the first division of the South Wales League.

JAMES, David Rees
Born Treorchy, 7 October 1906; died Rhondda, 1981
Career: Treorchy

Forward in 2 matches, against: France, 1931; Ireland, 1931

A colliery fireman, David James, who captained Treorchy in 1930-31, joined Leeds RLFC in September 1931.

37. 1935 v New Zealand
Back row: C H Gadney (referee), T J Rees, T G Williams, J Lang, A M Rees, E V Watkins, D J Tarr, M Moses (WRU touch judge).
Middle row: V G J Jenkins, H Payne, I G Prosser, C Davey (C), J I Rees, W Wooller, G R R Jones.
Front row: W C Jones, H Tanner.
[*Mrs Cliff Jones*]

38. 1938 v Ireland
Back row: R A Cornish (touch judge), C Davey, W Travers, A R Taylor, M E Morgan, W E Vickery, W Wooller, J C H Ireland (referee).
Middle row: F L Morgan, J I Rees, E V Watkins, W C Jones (C), H T Rees, A McCarley, W H Clement.
Front row: H Tanner, W S G Legge.
[*Mrs Cliff Jones*]

39. 1939 v Ireland
Back row: E R Price, E Evans, V J Law, M J Davies, L Manfield, L Davies, E Long, H Packer (touch judge).
Middle row: C H Davies, W Travers, W Wooller (C), S A Williams, W E N Davis, C M Matthews.
Front row: W T H Davies, H Tanner.
[*V J Law*]

78

JAMES, Evan
Born c1869; died Bonymaen, 18 August 1901
Career: St Thomas Harlequins; Swansea; Broughton Rangers

Half-back in 5 matches, against: Scotland, 1890, 1892; Ireland, 1891, 1892; England, 1899

Evan James was the brother of David [qv] and they appeared in four matches together. In his final match for Wales, against England, at St Helen's on 7 January 1899, he managed to outwit the opposition, despite being handicapped by a dislocated shoulder.

JAMES, John B
Born Blaengarw, 4 September 1938
Career: Blaengarw Youth; Pontycymmer; Bridgend; Glamorgan

Prop in 1 match, against: England, 1968

'Boyo' James, a blacksmith's striker, played for Bridgend from 1958-59 until 1970-71, making 426 appearances and captaining the club in 1968-69. He coached Nant-y-moel, Blaengarw and Bridgend and played for East Wales against the All Blacks in December 1967.

JAMES, Thomas Owen
Born Aberavon, 6 October 1904; died Port Talbot, 8 April 1984
Career: Aberavon

Full back in 2 matches, against: Ireland, 1935; Scotland, 1937: Scored 1pg - 3 points

A steelworker, Tommy was the brother of Will P James [qv]. He captained Aberavon in 1934-35, served on the club committee and was their baggage man for a number of years.

JAMES, William John
Born Port Talbot, 18 July 1956
Career: Dyffryn Comprehensive School; Welsh Secondary Schools; Welsh Youth; Taibach; Aberavon; Swansea; Barbarians; Wales B

Hooker in 21 matches, against: England, 1983, 1985, 1986, 1987; Scotland, 1983, 1984, 1985, 1986, 1987; Ireland, 1983, 1985, 1986, 1987; France, 1983, 1985, 1986; Romania, 1983; Fiji, 1985, 1986; Tonga, 1986; Western Samoa, 1986: Scored 1t - 4 points

Billy James, who is an architectural assistant, captained Wales in his final game, against Ireland in 1987. He represented the Combined Welsh Clubs against Japan in 1976. In 1980, he toured North America with Wales B,

and played for Wales B against France B at Pontypool in 1982. He captained Aberavon in 1979-81, 1984-85 and 1987-89.

JAMES, William P
Born c1902
Career: Aberavon

Wing in 2 matches, against: England, 1925; Scotland, 1925

A dock worker, Will James went north to join the paid ranks at Leeds RLFC in October 1925. He was the brother of Tommy O James [qv].

JARMAN, Henry
Born Talywain, 1883; died Talywain, 13 December 1928
Career: Pontypool; Talywain; Newport

Forward in 4 matches, against: England, 1910, 1911; Scotland, 1910; Ireland, 1910

British Isles 1910 tour South Africa: 3 caps

Collier Harry Jarman was described in the South African press as being one of the finest forwards in the 1910 British Isles team to tour that country. He died of pneumonia relatively young, in the same Talywain house in which he had been born.

JARRETT, Keith Stanley
Born Newport, 18 May 1948
Career: Monmouth School; Abertillery; Newport; London Welsh

Full back/centre in 10 matches, against: England, 1967, 1968, 1969; Scotland, 1968, 1969; Ireland, 1969; France, 1969; New Zealand, 1969, 1969; Australia, 1969 Scored 2t 17con 11pg - 73 points

British Isles 1968 tour South Africa

In his first appearance in the Welsh jersey, Keith Jarrett scored 19 points and the game, against England, was dubbed 'Jarrett's Match'. What promised to be a brilliant career in the game was cut short by a serious illness. In the summer of 1969 he toured Australasia and Fiji with the Welsh team. Seven matches were played and Jarrett played in every game, bar the opening one against Taranaki, scoring 52 points. In 1968 he played in five games for the British Isles in South Africa. An outstanding athlete, he played cricket for Glamorgan in 1967, as did his father before him. On 3 October 1969 he scored a try and kicked three goals in his first appearance for Barrow RLFC against Wigan and played twice for the Wales RL team. In May 1991, he relinquished his job as a marketing director of High Tower Development (a London bricklaying sub-contracting company) and is seeking a public house/restaurant business.

JEFFERY, James John
Born Oakdale, 26 February 1945
Career: Pontllanfraith Grammar School; Cardiff College of Education; Welsh Secondary Schools; Rhymney; Blackwood; Newport; Ebbw Vale; Barbarians; Monmouthshire

No 8 in 1 match, against: New Zealand, 1967

A schoolmaster, John Jeffery toured Argentina with a Wales XV in 1968 and South Africa with the Barbarians in May 1969. He scored twenty tries for Newport during the 1969-70 season and captained the club from 1970-72. Unfortunately, he is perhaps best remembered for dropping the ball on his goal line in his only appearance for Wales.

JENKIN, Albert Mortimer
Born Ibsley, Hampshire, 14 September 1872; died Bromley, 3 July 1961
Career: Northleach Grammar School; Llandovery College; Cambridge University; Swansea; Glamorgan

Forward in 2 matches, against: Ireland, 1895; England, 1896

Albert Jenkin qualified as a mining engineer and became the head surveyor for the Cymmer collieries. He captained Swansea in 1895-96. In 1902 he was ordained and two years later he went as a missionary to Nyasaland (now Malawi). During the First World War he served as an army chaplain in East Africa and, on returning to civilian life, he became Head of the Pretoria Native Mission. He later became Archdeacon of Pretoria.

JENKINS, Albert Edward
Born Llanelli, 11 March 1895; died Llanelli, 7 October 1953
Career: Seaside Stars; Llanelli

Centre in 14 matches, against: England, 1920, 1923; Scotland, 1920, 1921, 1923, 1928; France, 1920, 1921, 1922, 1923; Ireland, 1920, 1923, 1928; New Zealand, 1924: Scored 4t 7con 3dg 3pg - 47 points

Albert Jenkins, a docker, served with the 38th Infantry Division in France during the First World War. A skilful footballer who delighted the crowds, he suffered at the hands of the selectors who, for some unknown reason, chose him for only fourteen games in nine years. He captained Llanelli from 1921-22 and from 1923-25, and Wales against Ireland in 1923.

JENKINS, David Morgan
Born Pyle, 1901; died 22 April 1968

Career: Bryndu School, Kenfig Hill; Kenfig Hill; Treorchy; Glamorgan Police

Forward in 4 matches, against: England, 1926; Scotland, 1926; Ireland, 1926; France, 1926

David Jenkins, who had had trials for Swansea Town AFC in his youth, left the Glamorgan Constabulary in order to join the Hunslet RL club in August 1926. In 1931 he joined the Leeds RLFC and in 1934 Dewsbury RLFC. He won two caps for the Wales RL side. After his move north he became a licensee.

JENKINS, David Rees
Born Resolven, 12 April 1904; died Whitley Bay, 13 August 1951
Career: Resolven; Neath; Swansea

Forward in 2 matches, against: New South Wales, 1927; England, 1929

David Jenkins was a collier and later, a licensee. He played for Swansea against the Maoris in 1926 and New South Wales the following year. On 2 February 1929, he made his first appearance for Leeds RLFC.

JENKINS, Edward McDonald
Born Tonyrefail, 28 July 1904; died Porthcawl, 8 November 1990
Career: Cefn Cribbwr School; Cefn Juniors; Cefn Cribbwr; Bryncethin; Kenfig Hill; Cardiff; Bridgend; Aberavon; Glamorgan Police; British Police; Glamorgan

Forward in 21 matches, against: Scotland, 1927, 1928, 1930, 1931, 1932; France, 1927, 1928, 1929, 1930, 1931; Ireland, 1927, 1928, 1930, 1931, 1932; New South Wales, 1927; England, 1928, 1930, 1931, 1932; South Africa, 1932

Ned Jenkins, a police officer, was a tough, barrel-chested forward. He appeared for Neath and Aberavon against New South Wales in 1927. In a Welsh trial match in 1928 he was sent off, and received a two-month suspension for striking an opponent. In the 1930 match against France in Paris, Ned was 'sent off' a number of times but, pretending not to hear Ned carried on with taming the French forwards in a particularly rough clash. Mr Hellewell, the referee, blew up play ten minutes before the end, and went up to Ned saying, "don't go off without me". He captained Aberavon in 1929-30 and 1932-34. He was also a first class water polo player and swimmer, a natural boxer, and a shot and discus champion, winning the Glamorgan Police championship in 1947. After retiring from the police force he was a security officer with the Steel Company of Wales in Port Talbot.

JENKINS, Ernie
Born details unknown
Career: Pontnewydd; Newport

Forward in 2 matches, against: Scotland, 1910; Ireland, 1910

A dock worker, Ernie Jenkins played for Newport against New Zealand in 1905, South Africa in 1906 and Australia in 1908, all games which Newport narrowly lost. He made his debut for Rochdale Hornets RLFC on 17 September 1910.

JENKINS, John Charles
Born Newbridge, 19 April 1880; died Hounslow, winter 1971
Career: Long Ashton School, Bristol; Royal Military College, Sandhurst; Mountain Ash; London Welsh; New-port; Newbridge; Rosslyn Park; Barbarians; Middlesex; Monmouthshire

Forward in 1 match, against: South Africa, 1906

Jack Jenkins was commissioned into the South Wales Borderers at the age of eighteen. In 1903, he resigned from the Army, took an accountancy course and three years later joined the newly formed Territorial Army (Monmouthshire Regiment). He was promoted to Major in 1911 and, with the rank of Lieutenant Colonel, commanded the 2nd Bn Monmouthshire Regiment in France in 1915. In 1905 he played for Middlesex against New Zealand and, the following year, appeared for both Middlesex and Monmouthshire (captain) against South Africa. While with Newport he dropped four goals in one season, playing at forward or, occasionally, at centre. He made 200 appearances for London Welsh, captaining them in 1910-11. When winning his one cap for Wales he was handicapped with a septic hand. A great friend of Boxer Harding [*qv*], he was asked to join the Anglo-Welsh tour to Australia in 1908 but personal commitments did not allow him to go. While serving on the Middlesex Committee, he was involved in the negotiations for the purchase of the Twickenham ground. In 1926, aged 46, he played his fifty-third and final game for Middlesex, while his son, C R Jenkins, a medical student, played in his first game for the county. His son played for Bart's, Northampton, North of Ireland Football Club (captain 1933-34), Middlesex and for Ulster against the 1931 Springboks. Jack Jenkins married Helena, the sister of Leigh Richmond Roose, the Welsh soccer international. He contributed a chapter, 'Wales Past and Present' to *Rugby Football Up To Date*, written by E H D Sewell and published in 1921.

JENKINS, John Llewelyn
Born Maesteg, 12 March 1903
Career: Senghenydd; Pontypool; Cardiff; Aberavon

Forward in 2 matches, against: Scotland, 1923; France, 1923

John Jenkins was a collier before joining the Glamorgan Constabulary in June 1921. On 18 September 1925 he was ordered to resign for fighting with another police officer in a public place.

JENKINS, Leighton Hugh MBE
Born New Tredegar, 1 July 1931
Career: Monmouth Training College; Newport; Royal Air Force; Combined Services; Bath; London Welsh; Leicester

No 8/lock in 5 matches, against: Ireland, 1954, 1956; England, 1956; Scotland, 1956; France, 1956.

Leighton Jenkins was a squadron leader in the Royal Air Force which he joined after a period as a schoolmaster, having previously done his national service. He captained Newport in 1957-58 and was for a number of years the fixtures secretary of the Royal Air Force RU of which he was captain from 1962-64.

JENKINS, Neil Roger
Born Church Village, 8 July 1971
Career: Beddau Comprehensive School; Llantwit Fardre Youth; Welsh Youth; Pontypridd; Wales Under 21; Wales B

Stand-off in 4 matches, against: England, 1991; Scotland, 1991; Ireland, 1991; France, 1991: Scored 1t 1dg 1pg - 10 points

Neil Jenkins works in the family scrap metal business. He was Pontypridd's top scorer, with 127 points, in the 1990-91 Heineken League.

JENKINS, Thomas John Price
Born 1 February 1864, registered in Carmarthen; died London, 6 August 1922
Career: Queen Elizabeth Grammar School, Carmarthen; Llandovery College; Cambridge University; St Bartholomew's Hospital; United Hospitals; London Welsh; Blackheath; Middlesex

Back in 2 matches, against, Scotland, 1888; Ireland, 1888: Scored 1t

After qualifying as a Doctor of Medicine, T P Jenkins spent some years in Pembrokeshire and Radnorshire, before returning to London. As well as administering to the sick, he found time to take up acting. Appearing in *Follies of the Day* at the New Theatre, Swansea, the *Cambria Daily Leader* of 1 July 1890 wrote: "it is the football player who will most interest Welshmen ... Mr Jenkins has not been an actor long, yet his impersonation of Guy Livingston was fairly good". During the First World War he was a Medical Officer in the London Welsh Battalion. He was later the Medical Officer for the Port of Grimsby. In a number of written sources he is referred to as: Pryce-Jenkins, T J; Price-Jenkins, T J, and even Jenkins, Thomas Jehu Pryce. He was a founder of London Welsh RFC and captained the club in 1887-88.

JENKINS, Vivian Gordon James
Born Port Talbot, 2 November 1911
Career: Llandovery College; Oxford University; Cowbridge; Bridgend; London Welsh; Wasps; Barbarians; London Counties; Kent

Full back in 14 matches, against: England, 1933, 1935, 1936, 1937, 1938, 1939; Ireland, 19333, 1934, 1936; Scotland, 1934, 1935, 1936, 1938; New Zealand, 1935: Scored 1t 10con 1dg 3pg - 36 points

British Isles 1938 tour South Africa: 1 cap

Viv Jenkins won three Blues, playing in the centre (1930-32) and a cricket Blue (1933). He also played cricket for Glamorgan from 1931-37, scoring 1,072 runs in sixty-nine innings. He was vice-captain of the 1938 British Isles team in South Africa and scored 50 points (the second highest points scorer) in eleven games. In scoring the try against Ireland in March 1934, he became the first Welshman to score an international try from full back. He captained London Welsh in 1936-37. Jenkins was a schoolmaster and then a journalist and, until quite recently, he was the rugby correspondent of the *Sunday Times*, and editor of *Rothmans Rugby Yearbook*.

JENKINS, William Joseph
Born Cardiff, 1885; died Cardiff, 23 December 1956
Career: Cardiff; Barbarians

Forward in 4 matches, against: Ireland, 1912, 1913; France, 1912; Scotland, 1913

Billy Jenkins, who was employed in the building trade, captained Cardiff in 1913-14. His brother Eddie was a Welsh soccer international who won his only cap from Lovells Athletic as a right-half against England in 1925.

JOHN, Barry
Born Cefneithin, 6 January 1945
Career: Gwendraeth Grammar School; Trinity College Carmarthen; Cefneithin; Pontyberem; Llanelli; Cardiff; Barbarians

Stand-off in 25 matches, against: Australia, 1966, 1969; Scotland, 1967, 1968, 1969, 1970, 1971, 1972; New Zealand, 1967, 1968, 1968; England, 1968, 1969, 1970, 1971, 1972; Ireland, 1968, 1969, 1970, 1971; France, 1968, 1969, 1971, 1972; South Africa, 1970: Scored 5t

6con 8dg 13pg - 90 points

British Isles 1968 tour South Africa; 1971 Australia, New Zealand: 4 caps

'B J' or the 'King' as he became known after the historic 1971 British Isles tour of New Zealand, was one of the greatest Welsh players of the modern era. Possessing marvellous balance to his running he mesmerised opponents and thrilled spectators. Playing for the British Isles against South Africa in the opening international of the 1968 tour he dislocated his shoulder after fifteen minutes and took no further part in the tour. In the summer of 1969, he toured Australasia and Fiji with Wales. On the 1971 British Isles tour he amassed 188 points in seventeen appearances (this total included 30 points scored in the four international matches). Barry John is now a journalist and is the author of *The Barry John Story* and *O Gwmpas y Byd Gyda Barry John*, both published in 1974. He is the brother-in-law of Derek Quinnell [*qv*].

JOHN, David Arthur
Born Llanelli, 1900; died Chelsea, London, 16 August 1929
Career: Loughor; Gowerton; Llanelli; Bedford

Scrum-half in 4 matches, against: Ireland, 1925, 1928; England, 1928; Scotland, 1928

Arthur John was a steelworker.

JOHN, David Evan
Born Loughor, 1 March 1902; died Loughor, 20 November 1973
Career: Llanelli; Loughor

Stand-off in 5 matches, against: France, 1923; Ireland, 1923, 1928; England, 1928; Scotland, 1928: Scored 3t - 9 points

Dai John, like D A John, his namesake and half-back partner in the three 1928 matches, was a steelworker. He scored a try in each of these games and captained Llanelli in 1928-29. After retiring from the game he continued to serve Llanelli as a committee member.

JOHN, Ernest Raymond
Born Neath, 3 December 1925; died Neath, 30 September 1981
Career: Neath Grammar School; Crynant; Neath; Barbarians; Glamorgan

Lock/flanker in 19 matches, against: England, 1950, 1951, 1952, 1953, 1954; Scotland, 1950, 1951, 1952, 1953; Ireland, 1950, 1951, 1952, 1953; France, 1950, 1951, 1952, 1953; South Africa, 1951; New Zealand, 1953: Scored 1t - 3 points

**40. 1946 Victory International
v France**
Standing: Unknown, A S Bean (RFU
referee), unknown, W B Cleaver, W E
Williams, R T Evans, J Matthews, G W
PArsons, H Tanner, H C Jones, B L
Williams, W J Evans, L Williams, D J
Davies (obscured), L Manfield, J M
Bale, R A Cornish (WRU touch judge), I
Jones (WRU).
Kneeling: D G Davies, W G Jones.
[*Tony Lewis*]

*NB. Although the official records show
that Clifton Davies appeared as prop
forward , the position was actually taken
by his cousin, W G Jones who duly
travelled to Paris using Cliff Davies'
passport. This went undetected by the
French authorities..*

41. 1947 v Australia
Back row: A S Bean (RFU referee), J A
Gwilliam, L Manfield, E Davies, G
Evans, O Williams, C Davies.
Middle row: D M James, L Williams, B
L Williams, W E Tamplin (C), J Mattews,
K J Jones, W B Cleaver.
Front row: H Greville, G Davies.
[*Wayne Thoams*]

42. 1948 v Scotland
Back row: T N Pearce (RFU referee),
L Manfield, S Williams, W E Tamplin,
M James, O Williams, L Anthony, G
Evans, I Jones (WRU touch judge).
Middle row: W B Cleaver, K J Jones,
J Matthews, H Tanner (C), B L
Williams, R F Trott.
Front row: C Davies, G Davies.
[*Western Mail*]

British Isles 1950 tour New Zealand: 4 caps, Australia: 2 caps

Quantity surveyor Roy John, having played with distinction in all four matches which led to the Triple Crown and Grand Slam for Wales in his first international season, was selected to tour Australasia with the British Isles. He played in twenty one of the tour matches, seventeen in New Zealand and four in Australia, scoring a try in the second international against Australia. In November 1951, he played for Neath and Aberavon against South Africa and in January 1954 played for the same combination against New Zealand. He captained Neath in 1950-51.

JOHN, Glyndwr
Born Neath, 22 February 1932; died Bridgend, 7 June 1983
Career: Garw Secondary School; St Luke's College, Exeter; Welsh Secondary Schools; Tondu; Cross Keys; London Welsh; Royal Air Force; Cardiff; Devon

Centre/stand-off in 2 matches, against: England, 1954; France, 1954

Glyn John played soccer for Welsh Youth and joined the Leigh RLFC when he was a schoolboy. The Welsh Rugby Union granted him reinstatement after he had repaid the signing fee to Leigh. He taught at Sedbury Park School, Chepstow and Monmouth School.

JOHN, John Howell
Born Swansea, 31 August 1898; died 1977
Career: Loughor; Gendros; Ravenhill; Swansea; Glamorgan Police

Forward in 8 matches, against: England, 1926, 1927; Scotland, 1926, 1927; Ireland, 1926, 1927; France, 1926, 1927

Howell John was a collier before joining the Glamorgan Police. He captained Swansea in 1924-25, including the game against New Zealand in 1924, and played for the club against the Maoris in 1926 and New South Wales in 1927.

JOHNSON, Tom Albert W
Born 1893, registered in Cardiff; died Cardiff, 6 May 1948
Career: South Church Street Docks School, Cardiff; Welsh Secondary Schools; Penarth; Cardiff; Newport

Wing/full back in 12 matches, against: England, 1921, 1923, 1924, 1925; France, 1921, 1923, 1924; Ireland, 1921; Scotland, 1923, 1924, 1925; New Zealand, 1924: Scored 1t 1pg - 6 points

'Codger' Johnson, a ship's chandler, made one hundred and eighty seven appearances for Cardiff RFC between 1920 and 1927, captaining the club in 1924-25. He played in the Centenary match at Rugby School in 1923.

JOHNSON, William Dillwyn
Born Pontarddulais, 5 December 1923
Career: Gowerton Grammar School; Swansea; Pontarddulais; Swansea Police; Welsh Police; British Police; Barbarians

Flanker in 1 match, against: England, 1953

Dill Johnson had the distinction of scoring a try for Swansea against three touring sides: the 1945 New Zealand Kiwis, the 1948 Australians (an interception try, running 100 yards to the try-line) and the 1951 South Africans. In 1951 he scored a try from the kick off for the British Police against Devon which the referee timed at eight seconds. He captained Swansea in 1953-54. Formerly a police officer in the Swansea Borough Police, Johnson became, after retirement, a security consultant. He is the treasurer of the Swansea Old Players Association.

JONES, Anthony Windham
Born Llanelli, 1879; died Merthyr Vale, 23 October 1959
Career: Mountain Ash; Newport; Cardiff

Half-back in 1 match, against: Ireland, 1905: Scored 1t - 3 points

Windham Jones worked for a colliery manager in the Powell Dyffryn Colliery but later became an estate agent. He won his only cap after Billy Trew withdrew from the Welsh side. He served as a Welsh Rugby Union selector and was a representative for the Mid District and often acted as a touch judge for Wales.

JONES, Arthur Emyr
(Known as EMYR, Arthur)
Born Bangor, 27 July 1962
Career: Ysgol David Hughes, Menai Bridge; University College of Wales, Aberystwyth; Welsh Students; Welsh Universities; Menai Bridge; Swansea; Llanelli; Barbarians; Wales B

Wing in 9 matches, against: England, 1989, 1990; New Zealand, 1989; France, 1990, 1991; Scotland, 1990; Ireland, 1990; Namibia, 1990, 1990: Scored 3t - 12 points

Arthur Emyr read law at university and is now a broadcaster with BBC Wales. He has represented Wales in athletics and came third in the 100 metres in the 1988 Welsh Games.

JONES, Arthur Hugh
Born Bridgend, 2 October 1908; died Porthcawl, 26 June 1964

Career: Llandovery College; Welsh Secondary Schools; Bridgend; Cardiff; London Welsh; Eastern Counties

Wing in 2 matches, against: England, 1933; Scotland, 1933

Arthur Jones' first international appearance was in the side which defeated England for the first time at Twickenham. He was captain of London Welsh in 1931-32 and Cardiff during the 1937-8 season when they enjoyed their best season for 27 years. He had previously played hockey for Welsh public schools and was a fine golfer. He was the father-in-law of Howard Nicholls [qv].

JONES, Benjamin Lewis
Born Gorseinon, 11 April 1931
Gowerton Grammar School; Welsh Secondary Schools; Gorseinon; Neath; Devonport Services; Royal Navy; Llanelli

Full back/centre/wing in 10 matches, against: England, 1950, 1951, 1952; Scotland, 1950, 1951; Ireland, 1950, 1952; France, 1950, 1952; South Africa, 1951: Scored 9con 6pg - 36 points

British Isles 1950 tour(r) New Zealand: 1 cap, Australia: 2 caps

Schoolmaster Lewis Jones was a legend as both an amateur and professional rugby player. Shortly after his nineteenth birthday he joined the 1950 British Isles side at Gisborne for their thirteenth match as a replacement for the injured Irish full back Norton. He played in seven games in New Zealand, and scored 63 points, making him the second highest points scorer. On the Australian leg of the tour he was the leading scorer with 29 points in four games. In 1951, during his period of National Service he helped the Navy to their first Services championship since 1939. He played cricket for Cornwall and after signing for Leeds RLFC, scored seven goals in his first match, against Keighley, on 8 November 1952. He also played for the Wales RL side and made fifteen appearances for the Great Britain RL team. His book, *King of Rugger*, was published in 1958. His brother Allan captained Llanelli in 1952-53.

JONES, Brian James
Born Cwmcarn, 10 May 1935
Career: Cwmcarn School; Pontywaun Grammar School; St Luke's College, Exeter; Cwmcarn United; Cross Keys; Newport; Tredegar; Devonport Services; Combined Services; Royal Navy; Barbarians; Devon

Centre in 2 matches, against: Ireland, 1960; France, 1960

Whilst playing for Newport, Brian Jones had the distinction of appearing for a winning club side against the 'Big Two' touring sides from the Antipodes: Australia in 1957 and New Zealand in 1963; he also played for the

winning Barbarians side against the 1961 South Africans. Employed as a marketing director for a building company, Jones captained Newport from 1959-61 and coached the club in 1967-69 and Oxford University in 1968-69. He has served as secretary, and chairman of Newport and was chairman of Newport Athletic Club until October 1990.

JONES, Charles William
Born 18 June 1893; died Birkenhead, 19 January 1960
Career: Bridgend; Newport; The Army; Harlequins; Leicester; Birkenhead Park

Forward in 3 matches, against: England, 1920; Scotland, 1920; France, 1920

Charles Jones, who was in the army, served as a company sergeant-major in the Welch Regiment during the First World War. After the war he became the first non-officer to play in the Army side and played for the Mother Country in the rugby competition instituted by the Sports Control Board for the Services and the Dominions. He played for the Welch Regiment in five Army Cup finals, four times on the winning side. After leaving the army he became a physical training instructor at Birkenhead School.

JONES, Daniel
Born Taibach, 31 May 1875; died Taibach, 1 January 1959
Career: Taibach; Aberavon

Half-back in 1 match, against: England, 1897: Scored 1t - 3 points

Dan Jones, the first cap from the Aberavon club, worked as a millman at a tinplate works. He captained Aberavon in 1898-99. In 1954, he officiated at the opening of the Humphrey Leyshon and W R Thomas Commemorative Gates at the Talbot Ground, Aberavon.

JONES, Daniel
Born Neath Abbey, 2 March 1907; died November 1988
Career: Neath

Wing in 1 match, against: New South Wales, 1927

Dan Jones, a blacksmith, became a railwayman in later life. During the 1928-29 season, he scored fifty-nine tries for Neath.

JONES, David
Born c1881; died Aberdare, 21 January 1933
Career: Treherbert; Aberaman; Aberdare; Glamorgan Police; Glamorgan

Forward in 13 matches, against: England, 1902, 1903,

1905, 1906; Scotland, 1902, 1903, 1905, 1906; Ireland, 1902, 1903, 1905; New Zealand, 1905; South Africa, 1906

In October 1906 Dai 'Tarw' scored a try for Glamorgan against the touring Springboks. In October 1907, he joined the Merthyr Tydfil RL club. He was a collier before joining the Glamorgan Police who stationed him at Aberdare. After resigning from the police force he returned to Treherbert where he played for the local side. He went back to Aberdare to become licensee of the Eagle Hotel then returned once more to Treherbert to manage the Castle Hotel. He served with the Welsh Guards during the First World War and was seriously wounded during the Battle of the Somme. The effects of this injury caused him great suffering in later life.

JONES, David Charles Jenkin
Born Morriston, 30 April 1916
Career: Parc Llewellyn; Morriston; Swansea

Prop in 7 matches, against: England, 1947, 1949; France, 1947, 1949; Ireland, 1947, 1949; Scotland, 1949

Dai Jones was employed as a maintenance fitter by the Ford Motor Company in Swansea.

JONES, David Kenneth
Born Cross Hands, 7 August 1941
Career: Gwendraeth Grammar School; University College Cardiff; Oxford University; Welsh Secondary Schools; Penygroes; Llanelli; Cardiff; London Welsh; Barbarians

Centre/wing in 14 matches, against: England, 1962, 1963, 1964, 1966; Scotland, 1962, 1964, 1966; France, 1962, 1963, 1966; Ireland, 1962, 1966; New Zealand, 1963; South Africa, 1964: Scored 2t - 6 points

British Isles 1962 tour South Africa: 3 caps; 1966 tour Australia: 2 caps, New Zealand: 1 cap

After leaving Oxford, with a Blue won in 1963, Ken Jones taught at Bishop Hannon School but is now an industrialist. Touring South Africa with the 1962 British Isles team he played in twelve games, and scored a try in the first international; on the 1966 British Isles tour he made five appearances in Australia, scoring two tries in the second international and played in eleven games in New Zealand. He made two further tours of South Africa, with Wales in 1964, and Cardiff in 1967.

JONES, David L
Born c1901
Career: Newport

Forward in 5 matches, against: England, 1926, 1927; Scotland, 1926; Ireland, 1926; France, 1926

Dai Jones was a steelworker and later a labourer. Less than a month after winning his final cap against England, he made his debut, on 12 February 1927, for Wigan RLFC.

JONES, David Nathan Rocyn
Born Abertillery, 17 July 1902; died Ribchester, Lancashire, 26 January 1984.
Career: The Leys School; Cambridge University; St Mary's Hospital; Old Leysians; Newport; London Welsh; Middlesex

Full back in 1 match, against Ireland, 1925

Nathan Rocyn Jones, a Cambridge Blue (1923) was honorary medical officer to the WRU and served as president in 1964-65. He retired to Preston, Lancashire. His father, Sir David Rocyn Jones, was president of the WRU from 1947-53.

JONES, David Phillips
Born Pontypool, 10 December 1881; died Llantarnam, 9 January 1936
Career: Usk Grammar School; Pontypool; London Welsh; Barbarians; Monmouthshire

Wing in 1 match, against: Ireland, 1907: Scored 1t - 3 points

'Ponty' Jones, a mining surveyor, was a brother to Jack [qv] and 'Tuan' Jones [qv] and the first of the three to play for Wales. He captained Pontypool from 1904-07 and also played soccer for London Welsh and had a Welsh Amateur Soccer trial.

JONES, Edgar Lewis
Born Sketty, 4 May 1910; died West Cross, Swansea, 11 February 1986
Career: Gowerton; Llanelli; Barbarians

Forward in 5 matches, against: France, 1930; England, 1933, 1935; Scotland, 1933; Ireland, 1933

Edgar Jones worked as a collier, a steelworker, and later, a dock worker. He made his first appearance for Leeds RLFC in October 1935. He served in the Welch Regiment in the Second World War. He was also an accomplished cricketer, having played for Gowerton and had been involved in the Yorkshire League. His grandson played rugby for Clifton College.

JONES, Elfed Lewis MBE
Born Llanelli, 29 April 1912; died Llanelli, 5 October 1989
Career: Llanelli County School; Llanelli Harlequins; Llanelli

Wing in 1 match, against: Scotland, 1939

British Isles 1938 tour South Africa: 2 caps

Elfed Jones, who captained Llanelli in 1936-37, scored the first try for the 1938 British Isles tourists in the third and final international against the Springboks. He was the leading try scorer, with ten tries in eleven games - he scored three tries against SW Districts, and three tries against Rhodesia. After serving as a squadron leader in the Royal Air Force in the Second World War (receiving the Belgian Military Cross) he appeared in two Victory internationals. He worked as a magistrate's clerk, and became the chairman, and then the president of Llanelli.

JONES, Elwyn Howel
Born Glynneath, 8 September 1907; died Porthcawl, 4 May 1983
Career: Neath Grammar School; Neath Schoolboys; Welsh Secondary Schools; Swansea; Neath; Aberavon; Glamorgan

Wing in 2 matches, against: Ireland, 1930; France, 1930: Scored 1t - 3 points

Howie Jones was a bank official. He was the son of Howell Jones [*qv*].

JONES, Gary
Born Porth, 17 July 1960
Career: Porth Comprehensive School; Ystrad Rhondda; Pontypridd; Llanelli; Barbarians; Wales B

Flanker in 5 matches, against: New Zealand, 1988, 1989; France, 1989, 1990; England, 1989

Gary Jones, a fitter, toured Italy with Wales B in May 1986. A replacement for the Wales team in New Zealand in the summer of 1988, he won his cap in the second international against the host country.

JONES, Geoffrey Rippon Rees
Born Ipswich, 8 July 1914
Career: Ipswich School; Oxford University; London Welsh; Eastern Counties

Wing in 5 matches, against: England, 1934, 1936; Scotland, 1934; Ireland, 1935; New Zealand, 1935: Scored 2t - 6 points

Geoffrey Jones was the headmaster of Bembridge School before being appointed the principal of King William's College, Isle of Man. A triple Oxford Blue (1933-35) he also played cricket for the Cryptics and the Gentlemen of Suffolk. During the Second World War he served as a brigade major in the 4th Commando Brigade, receiving a

mention in despatches.

JONES, Glyn Graham
Born Morriston, 24 November 1906; died Morriston, 23 October 1987
Career: Llandovery College; Morriston; Cardiff; Cross Keys

Centre in 2 matches, against: Scotland, 1930; Ireland, 1931: Scored 1t 1dg - 7 points

'Chick' Jones, a clerk, captained Cardiff in 1933-34.

JONES, Graham
Born Garndiffaith, 24 November 1933
Career: Abersychan Grammar School; Abersychan Technical College; Garndiffaith; Pontypool; Ebbw Vale; Monmouthshire

Flanker in 3 matches, against: Scotland, 1963; Ireland, 1963; France, 1963: Scored 1t - 3 points

Graham Jones is a supervisor in a garage. He scored Wales' only try against Ireland in 1963.

JONES, Harold James
Born 22 December 1907; died 16 October 1955, registered in Staincliffe
Career: Maesteg; Neath; Cardiff; Glamorgan Police; Glamorgan

Forward in 2 matches, against: England, 1929; Scotland, 1929

Harold Jones was a collier. In December 1926 he joined the Glamorgan Constabulary where his career was somewhat short-lived and he resigned in May 1928. After joining Wigan RLFC at the beginning of the 1930s, he became a licensee. He also played three times for the Wales RL team. During the Second World War he was a flight sergeant and physical training instructor in the Royal Air Force. He was living in the Goat's Head Hotel in Steeton, Keighley at the time of his death.

JONES, Harry
Born Porthcawl, c1878
Career: Porth Scarlets; Penygraig; Glamorgan

Forward in 2 matches, against: Scotland, 1902; Ireland, 1902

Harry Jones had a reputation as a fine boxer.

JONES, Howell
Born Pontneddfechan, 5 April 1882; died Neath, 1

43. 1949 v England
Back row: N H Lambert (IRFU referee), W R Cale, E Coleman, J A Gwilliam, A Meredith, D J Hayward, C Evans, J W Faull (touch judge).
Middle row: D Jones, W H Travers, J Matthews, H Tanner (C), B L Williams, R F Trott, L Williams.
Front row: K J Jones, G Davies.
[*J B G Thomas*]

44. 1950 v Scotland
Back row: W R Willis, J D Robins, D Hayward, E R John, R T Evans, M C Thomas, M J Dowling (IRFU referee).
Middle row: W R Cale, D M Davies, C Davies, J A Gwilliam (C), J Matthews, K J Jones, W B Cleaver.
Front row: W C Major, B L Jones.
[*Western Mail*]

45. 1951 v South Africa
Back row: N H Lambert (IRFU referee), L Blyth, A Forward, E R John, J R G Stephens, D J Hayward, D M Davies, I Jones (WRU touch judge).
Middle row: M C Thomas, K J Jones, J A Gwilliam (C), B L Williams, B L Jones.
Front row: W O Williams, W R Willis, C I Morgan, G Williams.
[*Western Mail*]

December 1908
Career: Neath Intermediate School; Glynneath; Neath Excelsiors; Neath; Glamorgan

Forward in 1 match, against: Ireland, 1904

The father of Howie Jones [qv], Howell was a surveyor for Neath Rural District Council. He captained Neath RFC from 1903-05. His brothers Bill and Ivor also played for Neath, the former captaining the club from 1910-13 and serving on the committee at Glynneath RFC.

JONES, Ian Conin
Born Vryburg, South Africa, 2 March 1940
Career: Malmesbury School, Stellenbosch; South African College School; Stellenbosch University; Oxford University; London Welsh; Middlesex; Surrey

Lock in 1 match, against: Ireland, 1968

Employed as a merchant banker in Johannesburg, Ian Jones was a Rhodes Scholar at Oxford, where he won three rugby Blues (1962-64) and a boxing Blue.

JONES, Ivor Egwad CBE
Born Loughor, 10 December 1901; died Swansea, 16 November 1982
Career: Gowerton; Loughor; Swansea; Llanelli; Birmingham; London Welsh; North Midlands

Forward in 16 matches, against: England, 1924, 1928, 1929, 1930; Scotland, 1924, 1927, 1928, 1929, 1930; France, 1927, 1928, 1929; Ireland, 1927, 1928, 1929; New South Wales, 1927: Scored 1t 5con - 13 points

British Isles 1930 tour New Zealand: 4 caps, Australia: 1 cap

Furnaceman Ivor Jones' name is revered in New Zealand, a country he visited with the 1930 British Isles team. Showing a depth of versatility and great speed for a forward, he scored 28 points made up of three tries, six conversions, one drop goal and one penalty goal, in fourteen appearances. His all-round play had come to the attention of the selectors for the British Isles team to South Africa in 1924. Unfortunately he was unable to accept the invitation to tour. He captained Llanelli in 1926-28, 1930-32 and 1933-36. From 1962-65 he was a representative on the International Board and was the president of the Welsh Rugby Union in 1968-69.

JONES, James
Born c1893
Career: Cymmer; Aberavon

Forward in 6 matches, against: New Zealand Army, 1919;

England, 1920; Scotland, 1920, 1921; France, 1921; Ireland, 1921

Jim Jones, a licensee, captained Aberavon from 1921-23.

JONES, James Phillips MC
Born Pontypool, 23 November 1883; died South Yarra, Melbourne, Australia, 4 December 1964
Career: Christ College Brecon; Guy's Hospital; London Welsh; Blackheath; London; Barbarians

Centre in 1 match, against: Scotland, 1913: Scored 1t - 3 points

Anglo-Welsh 1908 tour Australia, New Zealand: 2 caps

'Tuan' Jones was a Doctor of Medicine and brother of D P ('Ponty') and J P ('Jack') [qv]. In October 1906 he played for Kent against South Africa. He made eleven appearances for the 1908 Anglo-Welsh tourists in New Zealand. He was also a useful cricketer. During the First World War he served in the Royal Army Medical Corps and was decorated for gallantry.

JONES, John
Born details unknown
Career: Aberavon; Devonport Albion; Glamorgan; Devon

Scrum-half in 1 match, against: England, 1901

'Bala Jones', was a general dealer. In 1897, when he moved to Devonport, he was declared a professional by the WRU but was later reinstated as an amateur.

JONES, John
Born Caio, Carmarthenshire, 2 December 1877; died Pencarreg, 3 April 1958
Career: St David's College School, Lampeter; St David's College, Lampeter; Oxford University; St Michael's College, Aberdare; Aberdare; Llanelli; Liverpool; London Welsh
Full back in 5 matches, against: England, 1902, 1903; Scotland, 1902, 1903; Ireland, 1902: Scored 4con 1pg - 11 points

'Strand' Jones was ordained a deacon in 1903 and a priest in 1904. From 1903-09 he was a curate in Mold and Corwen. In 1909, he was appointed as a chaplain (Ecclesiastical Establishment) in Karachi and he remained in India, ending up in Dalhousie, until 1929. Returning to this country he was the rector of Great Hanwood, Shropshire from 1929-34 during which time he was also chaplain of H M Prison, Shrewsbury. After retiring from the Church, he returned to Carmarthenshire to farm. He served as chairman of Lampeter RFC in 1947-8. He played Minor Counties Cricket for Carmarthenshire.

JONES, John

Born 25 January 1890
Career: Blackwood Crusaders; Tredegar; Abertillery; Pontypool; Brynmawr

Forward in 4 matches, against: England, 1914; Scotland, 1914; France, 1914; Ireland, 1914: Scored 1t - 3 points

Jack 'Bedwellty' Jones, a collier, was a member of the 'Terrible Eight', the scourge of the Scottish, French, and Irish packs in the 1914 season. The matches against Scotland and Ireland were, according to contemporary newspaper accounts, very abrasive contests. A little over two weeks after playing, and scoring a try, in his final game for Wales, against Ireland, 'Bedwellty' Jones signed for Oldham RLFC. Four days later, on 4 April 1914, he scored three tries on his debut against St Helens.

JONES, John Arthur

Born Risca, 1857; died Llandaff, 20 January 1919
Career: Monmouth School; Cardiff

Forward in 1 match, against: Scotland, 1883

Arthur Jones was firstly an admiralty agent and then a colliery director. A pioneer of rugby in Cardiff, he had played in the first ever game for Glamorgan FC against Cowbridge Grammar School in November 1874. He was also a keen tennis player. He was a governor of the University of South Wales and Monmouthshire and served as High Sheriff of Glamorgan.

JONES, John Phillips

Born Pontypool, 2 March 1886; died Llantarnam, 19 March 1951
Career: West Monmouth School; Christ College Brecon; Pontypool; London Welsh; Newport; Barbarians; Monmouthshire

Centre/wing in 14 matches, against: Australia, 1908; England, 1909, 1910, 1912, 1921; Scotland, 1909; France, 1909, 1910, 1912, 1913, 1920; Ireland, 1909, 1913, 1920: Scored 6t - 18 points

Anglo-Welsh 1908 tour Australia, New Zealand: 3 caps; British Isles tour 1910 South Africa: 3 caps

'Jack' Jones, the youngest of the Jones trio, D P 'Ponty' and J P 'Tuan' [qv], appeared for Monmouthshire against South Africa in 1906 and won three caps in New Zealand in the summer of 1908, representing the Anglo-Welsh in all three internationals against the All Blacks. In the second match with New Zealand, he scored the only try for the tourists. He appeared in a total of thirteen tour games. His brother 'Tuan' accompanied him on this tour. He won his first Welsh cap in December 1908 and he played his final game for Wales in the 1921 match against

England. In 1909-10, he scored four tries in three successive games: France (2t), Ireland (1t), France (1t). During the 1910 British Isles tour of South Africa, he appeared in twenty games, captaining the side in the first international. He captained Pontypool in 1907-08 and 1911-13. During the 1921-22 season he dislocated his collar bone three times. 'Jack' Jones was a colliery agent in partnership with his brother David.

JONES, Joseph

Born Pontardawe, 15 March 1899; died 27 January 1960, registered in Liverpool
Career: Swansea

Centre in 1 match, against: France, 1924

Licensee Joe Jones scored a try in his debut for Leeds RLFC against Huddersfield on 30 August 1924. He won one cap with the Wales RL team.

JONES, Kenneth Jeffrey OBE

Born Blaenavon, 30 December 1921
Career: West Monmouth Grammar School; St Paul's College, Cheltenham; Loughborough College; Talywain; Blaenavon; Pontypool; Newport; Barbarians

Wing in 44 matches, against: England, 1947, 1948, 1949, 1950, 1951, 1952, 1953, 1954, 1955, 1956; Scotland, 1947, 1948, 1949, 1950, 1951, 1952, 1953, 1954, 1955, 1956, 1957; France, 1947, 1948, 1949, 1950, 1951, 1952, 1953, 1954, 1955, 1956; Ireland, 1947, 1948, 1949, 1950, 1951, 1952, 1953, 1954, 1955, 1956; Australia, 1947; South Africa, 1951; New Zealand, 1953: Scored 17t - 51 points

British Isles 1950 tour New Zealand: 3 caps, Australia

Ken Jones played soccer before he appeared for a Blaenavon Sunday Schools XV at the age of nine. In 1940 he played for the Welsh Secondary Schools against the Anglo-Welsh Public Schools. During the Second World War, he served in India as a sergeant in the Royal Air Force. In 1950, he toured Australasia with the British Isles, scoring sixteen tries in sixteen games in New Zealand, and one appearance in Australia. The total of tries scored included a try in the first and final internationals against the All Blacks. He captained Newport in 1950-51 and 1953-54. A keen athlete, he was a member of the Newport Athletic Club and between 1946 and 1949 and between 1951 and 1953 he won both the Welsh AAA 100 and 220 yards. He also won the Welsh AAA long jump in 1949. Appearing in the 1948 Olympic Games, he won a silver medal in the 4 x 100 metres relay and, in the same year, won the Southern Counties 100 yards. Further honours came in 1954 when he captained the British team in the European Games and represented Wales in the 100 and 220 yards in the Empire Games, in Vancouver. In the 1958 Empire Games, held at Cardiff Arms Park, he was the manager of the Welsh team, and carried the baton into the stadium. Ken Jones, who was a teacher at Newport High School, resigned to run a tyre business in Newport. He has been the rugby corresppondent for the *Sunday Express* for a number of years.

JONES, Kenyon William James MBE (Military)
Born Llanishen, Monmouthshire, 5 September 1911
Career: Monmouth School; Oxford University; Monmouth; London Welsh; Headingley; Berlin; Yorkshire; Germany

Forward in 1 match, against: England, 1934

Twice an Oxford Blue (1931-2), Ken Jones was capped from London Welsh and was also selected to represent Wales as a high jumper but was unable to compete. His grandfather, James Jones, ran for Wales. A lieutenant colonel in the Welch Regiment in the Second World War, he served in Military Intelligence in Egypt and was awarded the American Bronze Star for his work in General Eisenhower's headquarters. He played his last game of rugby after the war when he appeared for an international XV in Cardiff. A management trainee in his post-graduate years, he became managing director at Unilever and later chairman and managing director of Ronson Products.

JONES, Kingsley Daniel
Born Pontypridd, 5 August 1935
Career: Llandovery College; Cardiff; Barbarians

Prop in 10 matches, against: South Africa, 1960; England, 1961, 1962, 1963; Scotland, 1961, 1963; Ireland, 1961, 1963; France, 1962; New Zealand, 1963

British Isles 1962 tour South Africa: 4 caps

Kingsley Jones, a nephew of W Cliff Jones [*qv*], is in the fruit retail business. He played in fourteen games for the 1962 British Isles XV in South Africa.

JONES, Mark Alun
Born Tredegar, 22 June 1965
Career: Tredegar Comprehensive School; Gwent Schools; Welsh Youth; Tredegar Ironsides; Tredegar; Neath; Wales B

No 8 in 14 matches, against: Scotland, 1987, 1989, 1990; New Zealand, 1988(r), 1989; Ireland, 1989, 1990; France, 1989, 1990; England, 1989, 1990; Namibia, 1990, 1990; Barbarians, 1990: Scored 2t - 8 points

Mark Jones was employed as a fitter, then became a groundsman at the Gnoll, Neath RFC's ground, before signing professional forms for Hull on 11 October 1990. He was a member of the Wales B side that toured Italy in May 1986, and Canada in the summer of 1989.

JONES, Marsden Douglas CBE
Born Swansea, 1893; died London, 5 January 1955
Career: Bishop Gore School, Swansea; University College Swansea; Cardiff; Blackheath; London Welsh; Barbarians

Forward in 2 matches, against: England, 1921; New Zealand, 1924

British Isles 1924 tour South Africa: 2 caps

Although registered as Marsden Douglas, he later became known as Douglas Marsden Jones. After training as a civil engineer, he became a manager with the Ford Motor Company. In 1923-25 he captained London Welsh and made twelve appearances for the 1924 British Isles tourists in South Africa where he remained for a short time working as a journalist. During the First World War he served in the Gloucestershire Yeomanry and during the Second World War he worked for the Ministry of Supply.

JONES, Paul Esmond Russell
Born Newport, 27 December 1894; died Quetta, India, 17 May 1934
Career: Blundell's School; The Army; Newport; London Welsh; Rosslyn Park; Barbarians

Centre in 1 match, against: Scotland, 1921

Paul Jones, a captain in the Royal Artillery, was the son of T B Jones [*qv*]. He died shortly after an operation for peritonitis.

JONES, Percy Llewellyn
Born Pontypridd, 23 March 1887; died Deal, 31 March 1969
Career: Rhydyfelin; Treorchy; Caerphilly; Tredegar; Newport; Pontypool; London Welsh

Forward in 8 matches, against: South Africa, 1912; England, 1913, 1914; Scotland, 1913, 1914; France, 1913, 1914; Ireland, 1914

Percy Jones, a member of the 'Terrible Eight' was a surface foreman in a colliery before becoming a hotelier. During the Second World War he instigated a Percy Jones XV, which raised money for charity by playing against a number of local teams in Gwent.

JONES, Raymond Bark
Born Blundellsands, 29 August 1911
Career: Uppingham School; Cambridge University; Waterloo; Lancashire

Forward in 2 matches, against: England, 1933; Scotland, 1933

A Cambridge Blue in 1931, 1932 and 1933, Raymond Jones became a solicitor. During the Second World War he was a Lieutenant in the Royal Naval Volunteer Reserve.

JONES, Richard

Born Shanghai, China, 5 January 1906; died Folkestone, 18 January 1986
Career: Perse School; London Welsh; Middlesex

Forward in 1 match, against: England, 1929

Born to a Welsh father and Japanese mother, Dick Jones and his three brothers and two sisters were orphaned at an early age. A guardian organised their journey, by train across Russia and Europe, to Britain where they were educated. A banker and director of an engineering company, Dick Jones made 135 appearances from 1926-32, scoring ten tries, for London Welsh, and was the brother of Robert Jones [qv]. He was a tank driver during the Second World War. He and his wife Dorothy accompanied the Welsh tour to Japan in 1975 but could recognise nothing of where he had lived for a time as a boy.

JONES, Richard Hughes

Born 27 November 1879; died Swansea, 24 November, 1958
Career: Swansea Trinity; Swansea; Glamorgan

Half-back in 15 matches, against: Ireland, 1901, 1904, 1908, 1909; England, 1902, 1904, 1905, 1909, 1910; Scotland, 1904, 1909; France, 1908, 1909, 1910; Australia, 1908: Scored 3t - 9 points

From 1899 Dick Jones played stand-off for Swansea. He worked as a stone mason before becoming a licensee.

JONES, Robert

Born Pontypridd, 3 June 1877
Career: Llwynypia; Cardiff; Glamorgan Police

Forward in 1 match, against: Ireland, 1901

Bob Jones was a police officer in the Glamorgan Constabulary.

JONES, Robert

Born Shanghai, October 1900; died Chessington, Surrey, February 1970
Career: Bedford School; Newport; Richmond; London Welsh; Northampton; Barbarians; East Midlands

Stand-off in 3 matches, against: England, 1926; Scotland, 1926; France, 1926

Bobby Jones, who scored a try and a drop-goal in December 1924 for East Midlands against the All Blacks,

had once played in an England trial He appeared in 1931, with his brother Harry, for Northampton against his brothers, Dick [qv] and Jack, who were representing London Welsh. A civil engineer, he worked at Northampton Town Hall and was later a purchasing manager for a shoe manufacturer.

JONES, Robert Nicholas

Born Trebanos, 10 November 1965
Career: Cwmtawe Comprehensive School; Welsh Secondary Schools; Swansea; Barbarians, Wales B

Scrum-half in 34 matches, against: England, 1986, 1987, [1987 World Cup], 1988, 1989, 1990, 1991; Scotland, 1986, 1987, 1988, 1990, 1991; Ireland, 1986, 1987, [1987 World Cup], 1988, 1989, 1990; France, 1986, 1987, 1988, 1989, 1990; Fiji, 1986; Tonga, 1986, [1987 World Cup]; Western Samoa, 1986, 1988; New Zealand, [1987 World Cup], 1988, 1989; Australia, [1987 World Cup]; United States, 1987; Romania, 1988: Scored 1t - 4 points

British Isles 1989 tour Australia: 3 caps

Robert Jones, currently the third most capped Welsh scrum-half, has captained Wales on five occasions. In 1989 he played in seven games for the British Isles team in Australia and has also appeared for the British Isles against an Overseas XV in 1986 and for the Home Unions against France, in Paris, in 1989. He captained Swansea in 1989-90 and was the club's top scorer, with 104 points, in the 1990-91 Heineken League. When first capped he was employed in a solicitor's office and was later a property manager in the BJ group. He now works for Stirling Finance. Robert has also played cricket for Glamorgan Colts and at three different age levels for Wales. He is the son-in-law of Clive Rowlands [qv].

JONES, Ronald Elvet

Born Neath, 24 February 1943
Career: Neath Grammar School; St Luke's College, Exeter; Crynant; Swansea; Neath; Coventry; Newbold-on-Avon; Devon; Warwickshire

Flanker/No 8 in 5 matches, against: France, 1967, 1968; England, 1967; Scotland, 1968; Ireland, 1968

Ron Jones teaches at Bablake School, Coventry. He played for East Wales against New Zealand in 1967.

JONES, Stephen Thomas

Born Ynysybwl, 4 January 1959
Career: Mill Street Comprehensive School, Pontypridd; Welsh Youth; Pontypool; East Glamorgan; Barbarians; Wales B

Prop in 10 matches, against: Scotland, 1983, 1984, 1988;

46. 1952 v Ireland
Back row: P F Cooper (RFU referee), A Forward, R C C Thomas, W O G Williams, D J Hayward, D M Davies, A G Thomas, I Jones (WRU touch judge).
Middle row: G Williams, M C Thomas, J R Stephens, J A Gwilliam (C), E R John, K J Jones, B L Jones.
Front row: W A Williams, C I Morgan.
[*Auty Collection*]

47. 1953 v France
Back row: I Jones (WRU touch judge), J R Stephens, J A Gwilliam, E R John, S Judd, R C C Thomas, D M Davies, G M Griffiths, O B Glasgow (IRFU referee).
Front row: W O G Williams, J D Robins, A G Thomas, T J Davies, B Williams (C), T Lloyd, K J Jones, C I Morgan.
[*Presse Sport*]
NB   The team wore black arm bands on their jerseys as a mark of respect for the recently deceased Queen Mary.

48. 1954 v France
Back row: I Jones (WRU touch judge), R C C Thomas, L M Davies, R J Robins, R H Williams, G Rowlands, C C Meredith, A I Dickie (SRU referee).
Middle row: W O G Williams, S Judd, W R Willis (C), V Evans, K J Jones.
Front row: G John, B V Meredith, A G Thomas, G M Griffiths.
[*Western Mail*]

Ireland, 1983; France, 1983, 1988; Romania, 1983; England, 1988; New Zealand, 1988, 1988: Scored 1t - 4 points

British Isles 1983 tour New Zealand: 3 caps

'Staff' Jones is a blacksmith's striker, employed by the National Coal Board. He toured the United States and Canada in 1980 with Wales B, played for Wales B against Australia in October the following year and made thirteen appearances for the British Isles in New Zealand in 1983.

JONES, Thomas
Born Pontnewydd, 13 December 1895
Career: Upper Cwmbran; Blaenavon; Pontnewydd; Pill Harriers; Newport; Glamorgan Police

Forward in 6 matches, against: England, 1922, 1924; Scotland, 1922, 1924; Ireland, 1922; France, 1922 Scored 1t - 3 points

Tom 'Cooking' Jones was a police officer in the Glamorgan Constabulary. For a period he was under a cloud after being suspended by the WRU in August 1922 for his alleged connection with rugby league agents. On the removal of the suspension he quickly rehabilitated himself into favour.

JONES, Thomas Baker
Born Newport, 16 September 1862; died Swansea, 26 May 1959
Career: Monmouth School; Newport

Forward in 6 matches, against: Ireland, 1882; England, 1882, 1885; Scotland, 1883, 1884, 1885: Scored 1t

Solicitor Tom Jones scored Wales' first try, against Ireland in 1882. He was the secretary of the Newport Athletic Club and, after moving to Swansea, president of the Gower Society. His son P E R Jones played for Wales in 1921 [*qv*]. He remains Wales' longest lived cap.

JONES, Thomas Iorwerth
Born Loughor, 3 April 1903; died Penclawdd, 31 August 1983
Career: Llanelli; Loughor

Forward in 5 matches, against: New South Wales, 1927; England, 1928; Scotland, 1928; Ireland, 1928; France, 1928

Iorwerth Jones, who worked in Bynea Steelworks, played soccer at an amateur level for Swansea Town and captained Llanelli in 1929-30. Less than four years after winning his final cap, against France in 1928, he played his first game for Leeds RLFC on 13 February 1932. After finishing in the professional game he returned to the Llanelli area where he had a grocery business.

JONES, W
Born c1872
Career: Cardiff; Leicester

Centre in 2 matches, against: Ireland, 1898; England, 1898

'Pussy' Jones worked for J Gibson, Building Contractors.

JONES, Walter Idris CBE
Born Llanelli, 18 January 1900; died Llandaff, 5 July 1971
Career: Llanelli County School; University College Aberystwyth; Cambridge University; Llanelli; London Welsh; Barbarians

Forward in 4 matches, against: England, 1925; Scotland, 1925; France, 1925; Ireland, 1925: Scored 1t - 3 points

Idris Jones gained a 1st Class degree in Chemistry at Aberystwyth and a doctorate at Cambridge where he won three Blues between 1923 and 1925. His first job was with ICI in Billingham where he remained until 1933 when he moved to Ystrad Mynach where he was the Director of Research for Powell Duffryn. From 1946 until his retirement in 1963, he was Director General of Research for the National Coal Board. He served on several bodies, including the Central Advisory Council for Education, the Honourable Society of Cymmrodorion, was chairman of the Appointments Board of the University of Wales from 1957-68 and a vice-president of the University College of Wales from 1968. He was created a CBE in 1954 and the University of Wales conferred an Honorary DSc on him in 1957. An avid mountaineer, he was a brother to the former Lord Chancellor, Lord Elwyn Jones. In 1924, due to pressure of work, he had to decline an invitation to tour South Africa with the British Isles and captained Wales against Ireland in 1925.

JONES, William Clifford OBE
Born Porth, 12 March 1914; died Bonvilston, 27 November 1990
Career: Porth County School; Llandovery College; Cambridge University; Welsh Secondary Schools; Cardiff; Bridgend; Pontypool; Pontypridd; London Welsh; Barbarians

Stand-off in 13 matches, against: England, 1934, 1935, 1936, 1938; Scotland, 1934, 1935, 1936, 1938; Ireland, 1934, 1935, 1936, 1938; New Zealand, 1935: Scored 2t - 6 points

Cliff Jones qualified as a barrister after leaving Cambridge with three Blues, awarded in 1933-35. He is the author of the book *Rugby Football*, which was published in 1937.

A series of injuries brought his promising playing career to a premature end. He was a WRU Selector from 1956-78 and served as president during the centenary year of 1981. He was the uncle of Kingsley Jones [qv].

JONES, William Desmond
Born Tumble, 25 October 1925; died Pontarddulais, 15 August 1987
Career: Gwendraeth Grammar School; Tumble; Aberavon; Llanelli; Welsh Police; British Police

Lock in 1 match, against: England, 1948

Des Jones, who captained Llanelli in 1949-50, worked as a collier in Tumble before joining the Carmarthenshire Constabulary where he became a police sergeant.

JONES, William Herbert
Born Llanelli, 1 May 1906; died Pontyberem, 31 July 1982
Career: Pontyberem; Llanelli

Scrum-half in 2 matches, against: Scotland, 1934; Ireland, 1934

Bert Jones, who was a collier at the Glynhebog and Pentremawr collieries, Pontyberem, played in two winning Welsh sides. On the 10 September 1934, he made his first appearance for St Helens RLFC but his professional career was rather short and he returned to Wales after playing in only thirteen games.

JONES, William John
Born Cefneithin, 4 February 1894; died Llanarthney, 15 July 1978
Career: Queen Elizabeth Grammar School, Carmarthen; Trinity College Carmarthen; Carmarthen Harlequins; Hendy; Llanelli
Forward in 1 match, against: Ireland, 1924

William Jones, the headmaster of Cefneithin primary school, was the chairman of the Welsh Schools Rugby Union. He saw active service in France during the First World War.

JONES, William Keri
Born 13 January 1945, registered in Neath
Career: Ystalyfera Grammar School; Cardiff College of Education; Neath; Cardiff; Barbarians

Wing in 5 matches, against: New Zealand, 1967; England, 1968; Scotland, 1968; Ireland, 1968; France, 1968: Scored 2t - 6 points

British Isles 1968 tour South Africa

Schoolmaster Keri Jones gave the Welsh back division an added dimension - pace. In the summer of 1968 he toured South Africa with the British Lions, playing in six games. On 16 November 1968 he made his debut for Wigan RLFC, against Rochdale Hornets.

JONES, William Roy
Born Swansea, 22 February 1903
Career: Brynmill School, Swansea; Mumbles; Bernard United; Swansea

Centre in 2 matches, against: New South Wales, 1927; France, 1928

Roy Jones, who captained Swansea in 1929-30, had shown promise as a soccer player, and had played for Swansea Schoolboys and Arcadia before turning to rugby. He appeared for Swansea against the Maoris in October 1926 and against New South Wales in October 1927. He was employed as the South Wales manager of Shell Mex and British Petroleum and served as both the chairman and later the president of the Swansea club.

JONES-DAVIES, Thomas Ellis DL, JP
Born Nantgaredig, 4 March 1906; died Swansea, 25 August 1960
Career: Queen Elizabeth Grammar School, Carmarthen; St George's School, Harpenden; Cambridge University; King's College London; St George's Hospital; United Hospitals; Llanelli; London Welsh; Barbarians; Middlesex

Centre in 4 matches, against: England, 1930, 1931; Ireland, 1930; Scotland, 1931: Scored 2t - 6 points

British Isles 1930 tour New Zealand, Australia

Tommy Jones-Davies read agriculture at university and sat papers in the Natural Sciences in 1928. The tragic death of his only brother (who was hoping to pursue a career in medicine) from a malignant disease caused him to change to medical studies. A good, all round sportsman, he had played tennis and cricket for his college and later became a first class golf player, appearing in the semi-finals of the Welsh Amateur Golf championships. He retained his early interest in agriculture - his father, Henry Jones-Davies, was a distinguished agriculturalist - and took great pleasure in his herd of pedigree Friesian cows. He captained London Welsh in 1929-30, scored eight tries and one dropped goal, in eight appearances, for the 1930 British Isles tourists in New Zealand. He was employed as the Assistant Medical Officer for Surrey and the County Medical Officer for Radnorshire. During the Second World War he served as a Lieutenant Colonel in the Royal Army Medical Corps. In 1952 he was appointed as High Sheriff of Carmarthenshire and was created an Officer of the Order of St John in 1959. Following in the strong Liberal traditions of his mother's family - her brother, Thomas Ellis, had been Liberal Chief Whip in Gladstone's fourth Government - he was president of the local Liberal Association.

JORDAN, Henry Martyn
Born Clifton, 7 March 1865; died Newport, 14 July 1902
Career: Monmouth School; Finchley School; Guy's Hospital; Newport; London Welsh

Back in 3 matches, against: England, 1885; Scotland, 1885, 1889: Scored 2t

Martyn Jordan qualified in medicine at Guy's Hospital and worked for a period as the Registrar in the Chelsea Hospital for Women. In 1895-96 he taught at Nizam's Medical School, Hyderabad. At the time of his death he was surgeon to the Westminster General Dispensary. He was the first Welsh player to score two international tries, an honour which he achieved on his debut against England in 1885. He was one of the smallest men to play for Wales but made up for this by his exceptional pace. In 1888-89 he captained London Welsh and was also a good cricketer. His brother Charles, who also played for Newport, played for Ireland against Wales in 1884 when the visitors arrived two players short. Some sources have given this 'cap' to Martyn but contemporary material states that it was his brother, a forward, who played in the Irish pack.

JOSEPH, William
Born Morriston, 10 May 1877; died Swansea, summer 1959
Career: Morriston; Swansea; Glamorgan

Forward in 16 matches, against: England, 1902, 1903, 1904, 1905, 1906; Scotland, 1902, 1903, 1904, 1905, 1906; Ireland, 1902, 1903, 1905, 1906; New Zealand, 1905; South Africa, 1906
Will Joseph, a cousin of R M Owen [qv], was employed as a steelworker. He appeared for Glamorgan against New Zealand in December 1905 and South Africa in October 1906. He also played quoits for Wales in 1901-02.

JOWETT, William Frederick
Born Swansea, 1879; died Clydach, 5 October 1939
Career: Morriston; Swansea; Glamorgan

Wing in 1 match, against: England, 1903

British Isles 1904 tour Australia, New Zealand

Schoolmaster Fred Jowett appeared in one match in New Zealand during the 1904 British Isles tour. He scored a goal on his first appearance for Hull Kingston Rovers RLFC on 23 September 1905. During the First World War he served as a corporal in the Welsh Ammunition Column.

JUDD, Sidney
Born Cardiff, 14 August 1928; died Llanrumney, 24 February 1959
Career: Cardiff High School; Trinity College Carmarthen; Welsh Secondary Schools; Carmarthen Athletic; Cardiff; Barbarians

Flanker/No 8 in 10 matches, against: England, 1953, 1954, 1955; Scotland, 1953, 1954, 1955; Ireland, 1953; France, 1953, 1954; New Zealand, 1953: Scored 1t - 3 points

Sid Judd, a schoolmaster, played for Cardiff, the Barbarians and Wales against the 1953-54 All Blacks, scoring a try in the latter game. He captained Cardiff in 1954-55. He died of leukemia.

JUDSON, Thomas Haigh
Born Ashton-under-Lyne, 1857; died Southport, 4 September 1908
Career: Oxford University; London Welsh; Rosslyn Park

Forward in 2 matches, against: England, 1882; Scotland, 1883: Scored 1t

There is some confusion over Judson's early life and career and, although strong evidence suggests that he was mistakenly recorded as "J H Judson, educated at Llandovery College", the school registers have no record of him attending the school as a pupil. It is however a fact that he did teach at the school for a period before being appointed a master at Highgate School where he was employed from 1883-April 1892. In 1891 he was a vice-president of Rosslyn Park RFC and a number of schoolmasters from Highgate School, all proposed by Judson, played for the club. He was also the first treasurer of London Welsh RFC. Judson, who took a first in natural sciences at Oxford, was teaching in Ashton-under-Lyne at the time of his death.

KEDZLIE, Quinton Dick
Born Scotland, c1861; died Cardiff, 3 May 1920
Career: Cardiff

Forward in 2 matches, against: Scotland, 1888; Ireland, 1888

Dick Kedzlie, a blacksmith, moved from Glasgow to Cardiff at the age of eight. He played in 119 games for Cardiff and was later chairman of the South Wales Baseball Association.

KEEN, Leslie
Born Port Talbot, 13 November 1954
Career: Sandfields Comprehensive School; Cardiff College of Education; British Colleges; Aberavon; Penarth

Wing in 4 matches, against: France, 1980; England, 1980; Scotland, 1980; Ireland, 1980: Scored 1t - 4 points

Schoolmaster Les Keen scored two tries for West Wales against Romania in October 1979. He currently coaches Aberavon RFC with fellow international Max Wiltshire. He is the brother-in-law of Allan Martin [qv].

KNIGHT, Paul
Born Tonypandy, 30 April 1959
Career: Porth Grammar School; Treorchy; Aberavon; Pontypridd; Barbarians

Prop in 5 matches, against: Namibia, 1990, 1990; Barbarians, 1990(r); England, 1991; Scotland, 1991

Paul Knight was a member of the Wales Squad in 1981-82 and appeared in the West Wales side against Australia in January 1982. He is the current captain of Pontypridd and is employed as a production controller.

KNILL, Franklyn Michael David
Born Monkton, Pembrokeshire, 22 December 1941
Career: Pembroke Grammar School; Pembroke; Canton; Cardiff; Penarth; South Wales Police; Barbarians; Pembrokeshire; Wales B

Prop in 1 match, against: France, 1976(r)

Mike Knill is a sergeant in the South Wales Police, stationed in Cardiff. He won his cap at the age of 34 years-74 days, as a replacement for Graham Price. He toured Canada with the 1976 Barbarians. He captained Penarth from 1978-80.

LANE, Stuart Morris
Born Tredegar, 12 November 1952
Career: Tredegar Grammar School; Cardiff College of Education; Welsh Secondary Schools; Cardiff; Newport; Newbridge; Wales B

Flanker in 5 matches, against: Australia, 1978(r), 1978; Ireland, 1979(r), 1980; Scotland, 1980

British Isles 1980 tour South Africa

Schoolmaster Stuart Lane toured Canada and South Africa with Cardiff RFC. Returning to South Africa in 1980 with the British Isles, he played less than one minute of rugby in the first match of the tour against Eastern Province - whilst attempting to tackle an opponent, he twisted his knee ligaments so badly that he had to return home for surgery. His elder brother Roger was also a prominent back row forward for Cardiff.

LANG, James
Born Garnant, 1 October 1909
Career: Hendy; Gorseinon; Llanelli; Swansea

Forward in 12 matches, against: France, 1931; Ireland, 1931, 1934, 1935, 1936; Scotland, 1934, 1935, 1936; England, 1935, 1936, 1937; New Zealand, 1935: Scored 1t - 3 points

Steelworker Jim Lang is best remembered for his domination of the lineout in the game against the 1935 All Blacks, which ensured victory for the Welsh team.

LAW, Vivian John
Born Cardiff, 11 June 1910; died Newport, 22 April 1989
Career: Newport High School; Newport High School Old Boys; Newport; The Army

Forward in 1 match, against: Ireland, 1939

Viv Law, a company representative, appeared in an Irish trial in 1934 and captained Newport from 1937-39. During the Second World War he served in the Monmouthshire Regiment and in the Royal Artillery. He played in four Service internationals and was chairman of Newport RFC in 1951-52.

LAWRENCE, Stephen David
Born Treorchy, 5 August 1899; died Merthyr, 13 February 1978
Career: Pontycymmer; Bridgend; Glamorgan Police

Forward in 6 matches, against: Scotland, 1925, 1926; Ireland, 1925, 1926; France, 1926; England, 1927

A one time collier, Steve Lawrence joined the Glamorgan Constabulary in January 1924 and retired in 1950 with the rank of sergeant. He captained Bridgend in 1926-27. During the Second World War he served as a sergeant pilot in the Royal Air Force.

LEGGE, Walter Sydney George
Born Risca, 11 November 1911; died 1984, registered in Newport
Career: Pontymister School; Risca; Cross Keys; Newport; Weston-super-Mare

Full back in 2 matches, against: Ireland, 1937, 1938: Scored 1con 1pg - 5 points

Walter Legge was employed as a steelworker. He captained Risca in 1946-47, following in the footsteps of his brother Ken who had captained the club in 1937-38. His son Gary played for Cross Keys and gained a Welsh Youth cap in 1951 and 1952.

49. 1956 v France
Back row: P F Cooper (RFU referee), R Richards, T R Prosser, G K Whitson, R J Robins, J R Stephens, L H Jenkins, I Jones (WRU touch judge).
Middle row: C D Williams, K J Jones, C I Morgan (C), B V Meredith, M C Thomas.
Front row: G D Owen, D O Brace, H P Morgan, G Rowlands.
[*Western Mail*]

50. 1958 v Australia
Back row: A I Dickie (SRU referee), T R Prosser, R H Davies, J Faull, R H Williams, W R Evans, D B Devereux, D O H Davies (WRU touch judge).
Middle row: T J Davies, B V Meredith, R C C Thomas (C), R H Williams, G Wells.
Front row: J E Collins, W R Evans, C R James, C A H Davies.
[*Western Mail*]

51. 1959 v France
Back row: N M Parkes (referee), T R Prosser, B V Meredith, R H Williams, D J E Harris, M J Price, M C Thomas, R C C Thomas (C), G D Davidge, D R Main, T J Davies.
Front row: J E Collins, W R Watkins, R J Hurrell, D I E Bebb, H J Morgan.
[*Presse Sport*]

LELEU, John
Born Bristol, 13 March 1935
Career: Bristol Grammar School; Bishop Gore School, Swansea; Mumbles; Swansea; Llanelli; London Welsh; The Army; Barbarians; Middlesex

Flanker in 4 matches, against: England, 1959; Scotland, 1959; France, 1960; South Africa, 1960

John Leleu, who captained London Welsh in 1958-59 and Swansea in 1960-61, works as a sales representative. His son Guy has played for London Welsh and Rosslyn Park.

LEMON, Arthur Whitelock
Born Tonna, 15 April 1905; died Neath, 28 May 1982
Career: Tonna; Briton Ferry; Neath; Glamorgan

Forward in 13 matches, against: Ireland, 1929, 1930, 1931, 1932, 1933; Scotland, 1930, 1931, 1932; France, 1930, 1931; England, 1931, 1932; South Africa, 1931

Arthur Lemon played for the combined Neath and Aberavon side against New South Wales in 1927 and against the 1931 Springboks. He worked as a tinplater before joining St Helens RLFC, making his debut for the club on 4 September 1933. He was employed as a drayman and carpenter at Greenalls Brewery until he returned to Neath where he was employed as a steelworker.

LEWIS, Arthur John Llewelyn
Born Crumlin, 26 September 1941
Career: Abertillery Technical College; Cross Keys Technical College; Hafodyrynys; Crumlin; Cross Keys; Ebbw Vale; Barbarians; Monmouthshire; Wales B

Centre in 11 matches, against: France, 1970, 1971, 1972, 1973; England, 1971, 1972, 1973; Ireland, 1971, 1973; Scotland, 1972, 1973: Scored 1t - 4 points

British Isles 1971 tour Australia, New Zealand

Electrician Arthur Lewis played in one game in Australia and nine in New Zealand with the 1971 British Isles team. He was chosen to captain Wales against New Zealand in December 1972 but had to withdraw through injury. In 1973 he was a member of the Welsh team which toured Canada.

LEWIS, Brinley Richard
Born Pontardawe, 4 January 1891; killed in action Ypres, 2 April 1917
Career: Swansea Grammar School; Cambridge University; Welsh Schools; Pontardawe; London Welsh; Barbarians

Wing in 2 matches, against: Ireland, 1912, 1913 Scored 2t - 6 points

Brinley Lewis, who won his first Blue in 1909 at the age of 18 and gained a further two Blues in 1910-11 and in 1915 played for a Wales XV against the Barbarians. He served as a Major in the Royal Field Artillery, 122 Brigade during the First World War. He was a cousin of Gwilym Michael [qv].

LEWIS, Charles Prytherch
Born Llangadog, 20 August 1853; died Llandovery, 28 May 1923
Career: Llandovery College; Cathedral School, Gloucester; Oxford University; London Welsh; Rosslyn Park; Llandeilo; Llandovery

Full back in 5 matches, against: Ireland, 1882; England, 1882, 1884; Scotland, 1883, 1884: Scored 4con

C P Lewis, probably the earliest born Welsh cap, won two Blues in 1876, the first in athletics (hammer) and the second in cricket. He also played cricket for the MCC and the South Wales Cricket Club, scoring a total of 1,609 runs for the latter, and for Carmarthenshire in the Minor Counties championship, topping the batting averages in 1909 at the age of 56. In 1881, he was elected a vice-president of the Welsh Rugby Union and in 1885 refereed the Wales v England game at Swansea. Returning as a master to his old school, Llandovery College, Lewis often assisted the rugby XV. He was Mayor of Llandovery in 1894-95 and 1904-05.

LEWIS, David Henry
Born Radyr, 4 December 1866; died Buffalo, New York State, USA, 8 September 1943
Career: Cardiff

Forward in 2 matches, against: England, 1886; Scotland, 1886

Dai Lewis began his working life as a junior clerk in the claims department of the GWR, Bute Docks, Cardiff. A fine athlete, he represented Cardiff Harriers in the hurdles. After "shuffling off to Buffalo" in the United States, he became secretary and later managing director of the Buffalo Automobile Club and president of the New York State Automobile Association. He was the author of *America Bids Me Welcome*, an autobiography, published in the USA. His father, Jacob Lewis, was a horse breeder; one of his horses, George Frederick, won the 1874 Derby. Dai's cousin, Sir Lewis Lougher, was the MP for Cardiff East and Crdiff Central from 1922-29.

LEWIS, Edward John
Born Llandovery, 5 December 1859; died London, 8 June 1925
Career: Llandovery College; Cambridge University; St Bartholomew's Hospital

Half-back in 1 match, against: England, 1881

E J Lewis, who played in the first Welsh XV of 1881, was the Honorary Consulting Physician to the Kilburn Dispensary and to the Clergy Orphan School.

LEWIS, Emyr Wyn
Born Carmarthen, 29 August 1968
Career: Ysgol Gyfun Bro Myrddin, Carmarthen; Carmarthen Athletic; Llanelli; British Police; Wales Under 21; Wales B

Flanker in 2 matches, against: Ireland, 1991; France, 1991

Emyr Lewis is a police officer in the Dyfed Powys Force, stationed in Aberaeron.

LEWIS, Geoffrey Windsor
Born Cambridge, 7 April 1936
Career: Maesteg Grammar Technical School; The Leys School; Cambridge University; English Public Schools; Richmond; Territorial Army; Barbarians; Eastern Counties; Oxfordshire

Centre in 2 matches, against: England, 1960; Scotland, 1960

A chartered surveyor, Geoffrey Lewis won three Cambridge Blues in 1956-58. He is the honorary secretary to the Barbarian RFC and was assistant manager of the Barbarians in South Africa in 1969 and Canada in 1976. He is the son of Windsor Hopkin Lewis [qv].

LEWIS, Howell
Born 24 May 1888; died Guildford, 29 May 1971
Career: Ystalyfera Grammar School; Cwmtwrch; Ystalyfera; Cwmllynfell; Swansea

Wing in 4 matches, against: Scotland, 1913, France, 1913, Ireland, 1913; England, 1914

Howell Lewis was the director of Brynhenllys Colliery. During the First World War he served as a captain in the Royal Welch Fusiliers. In April 1916 he captained West Wales against the Anzacs and also captained Swansea in the 1919-20 season.

LEWIS, John Goulston
Born Llanelli, 25 December 1859; died Llanelli, 9 May 1935
Career: Llanelli

Half-back in 1 match, against: Ireland, 1887

Johnny Lewis, who worked as a tinplater, also played

cricket for Llanelli and was the first player to score a century at Stradey. He captained Llanelli in 1887-88 and served as treasurer to the club. He played his only game for Wales at Birkenhead and so was the only Welshman in 100 years to gain a cap on a neutral ground.

LEWIS, John Morris Clement
Born 22 June 1890, registered in Bridgend; died Porthcawl, 25 October 1944
Career: Bridgend County School; Cambridge University; Porthcawl; Bridgend; Cardiff; London Welsh; Handsworth; Barbarians

Stand-off in 11 matches, against: England, 1912, 1914, 1923; Scotland, 1913, 1914, 1923; France, 1913, 1914; Ireland, 1913, 1914, 1921: Scored 3t 3con 1dg - 19 points

Clem Lewis won two Cambridge Blues, either side of the war, in 1913 and 1919. He served as a lieutenant in the Welch Regiment during the First World War. In 1919 he appeared for the Mother Country XV and captained Cardiff in 1920-21 and Wales twice in 1923. After working as a salesman for a colliery, he became a schoolmaster in Pyle.

LEWIS, John Rhodri
Born Maesteg, 25 February 1959
Career: Maesteg Comprehensive School; South Glamorgan Institute; Maesteg; Cardiff; Lydney; Wales B

Flanker in 7 matches, against: England, 1981, 1982; Scotland, 1981, 1982; Ireland, 1981; France, 1981, 1982: Scored 1t - 4 points

Rhodri Lewis toured the United States and Canada with the 1980 Wales B team.

LEWIS, Mark
Born March 1889, registered in Pontypridd; died Pontypridd, August 1968
Career: Treorchy; Llwynypia

Wing in 1 match, against: France, 1913

Mark Lewis won his only cap when Billy Geen [qv] dropped out of the Welsh side through injury. He spent all his working life at Scotch Colliery, Llwynypia and retired as head lampsman. In retirement, he studied maths and economics. In August 1968, he was found collapsed in Ynysangharad Park, Pontypridd and died shortly afterwards.

LEWIS, Phillip Ivor
Born Swansea, 6 January 1961
Career: Queen Elizabeth Grammar School, Carmarthen; Crewe and Alsager College; Welsh Schools; English

Colleges; British Colleges; Llanelli; Llandybie; Barbarians; Carmarthenshire; Wales B

Wing in 8 matches, against: Australia, 1984; Scotland, 1985, 1986; Ireland, 1985, 1986; France, 1985; England, 1985, 1986: Scored 2t - 8 points

Phil Lewis is a police officer.

LEWIS, Robert Allan
Born Pontypool, 7 October 1942
Career: Welsh Youth; Blaenavon; Abertillery; Monmouthshire

Scrum-half in 6 matches, against: England, 1966; Scotland, 1966; Ireland, 1966, 1967; France, 1966; Australia, 1966

British Isles 1966 tour Australia, New Zealand: 3 caps

Allan Lewis played in seventeen games for the British Isles in 1966, four in Australia and thirteen in New Zealand. He also toured South Africa in 1964 with the Welsh team, appearing in one game. He was one of the quickest passers in post-war Welsh rugby and played for a Welsh XV against Fiji in 1964 and it was thought that his performance would ensure that he would retain his place in the team in 1965 but he did not gain his first cap until 1966. Currently employed as a schools welfare officer, he previously worked as a carpenter. His brother Malcolm, a wing forward, has made over 500 appearances for Abertillery and still turns out occasionally in addition to serving as the club secretary.

LEWIS, Thomas William
Born Taff's Well, 7 June 1902
Career: Pentyrch; Taff's Well; Penylan; Cardiff; Glamorgan Police; British Police; Glamorgan

Forward in 3 matches, against: England, 1926, 1927; Scotland, 1927

Tom Lewis was a collier in Nantgarw Colliery before joining the Glamorgan Constabulary. When he won his first cap against England in 1926, he was one of six police officers in the team (five from Glamorgan and one from Newport). He played 260 games for Cardiff between 1924 and 1933, captaining them in 1932-33. After retiring from the Glamorgan Force in 1949 Lewis was employed by the Inland Revenue.

LEWIS, William
Born Morriston, 14 March 1899; died Swansea, 26 January 1927
Career: Ystalyfera Intermediate School; University College, Aberystwyth; Swansea; Llanelli

Forward in 1 match, against: France, 1925

Schoolmaster Will Lewis served in the Royal Naval Volunteer Reserve during the First World War.

LEWIS, Windsor Hopkin
Born Maesteg, 11 November 1906; died 30 November 1982, registered in Northampton
Career: Christ College Brecon; Cambridge University; Guy's Hospital; Welsh Secondary Schools; London Welsh; Maesteg; Barbarians

Stand-off in 6 matches, against: Ireland, 1926, 1927; England, 1927; France, 1927, 1928; New South Wales, 1927: Scored 1t 1dg - 7 points

Windsor Lewis played in the first Welsh Secondary Schools side in April 1924 and went on to win two Blues at Cambridge in 1926-27. He completed his medical training at Guy's Hospital, and later had a medical practice in Cambridge, where he was a consultant anaesthetist at Addenbrooke's Hospital. In the 1930s he coached the Cambridge University XV. He was a Major in the Royal Army Medical Corps during the Second World War. He was the father of G Windsor Lewis [qv].

LLEWELLYN, Gareth Owen
Born Cardiff, 27 February 1969
Career: Bryntirion Comprehensive School, Bridgend; Welsh Schools; Welsh Youth; Llanharan; Neath; Barbarians

Lock in 6 matches, against: New Zealand, 1989; England, 1990, 1991; Scotland, 1990, 1991; Ireland, 1990: Scored 1t - 4 points

After a fine display for Neath against the All Blacks in October 1989, Gareth Llewellyn won his first cap against the same opposition ten days later. In the opening match of the Five Nations Championship in 1991, against England, he partnered his brother Glyn [qv] in the second row. He is employed as a fitter and turner with British Steel.

LLEWELLYN, Glyn David
Born Bradford-on-Avon, 9 August 1965
Career: Bryntirion Comprehensive School; North East London Polytechnic; Bridgend Schools; Welsh Schools; Llanharan; London Welsh; Llanelli; Neath

Lock in 7 matches, against: Namibia, 1990, 1990; Barbarians, 1990; England, 1991; Scotland, 1991; Ireland, 1991; France, 1991

Glyn Llewellyn, an architect, toured Canada with the Welsh Schools side in 1983. He partnered his brother

Gareth [qv] in the Welsh team against England and Scotland in 1991, both playing at lock. He has also played basketball for the Welsh Schools team.

LLEWELLYN, Philip David
Born Swansea, 12 May 1947
Career: Penlan Comprehensive School; Welsh Youth; Morriston; Swansea; Barbarians

Prop in 5 matches, against: Ireland, 1973; France, 1973; Australia, 1973; Scotland, 1974; England, 1974

Phil Llewellyn, who is an electrician, toured Canada twice, firstly with Wales in 1973, and secondly with the Barbarians in 1976.

LLEWELLYN, Willie
Born Tonypandy, 1 January 1878; died Pontyclun, 22 March 1973
Career: Christ College, Brecon; Pharmaceutical College, Bloomsbury; Llwynypia; Ystrad; London Welsh; Cardiff; Newport; Penygraig; Glamorgan; Surrey

Wing in 20 matches, against: England, 1899, 1900, 1901, 1902, 1904, 1905; Scotland, 1899, 1900, 1901, 1902, 1904, 1905; Ireland, 1899, 1900, 1901, 1902, 1903, 1904, 1905; New Zealand, 1905: Scored 16t - 48 points

British Isles 1904 tour Australia: 3 caps, New Zealand: 1 cap

Willie Llewellyn was brought up playing a sort of rough and tumble rugby in the Rhondda. His obvious skills were honed at Christ College, Brecon. Shortly after his twenty-first birthday he was capped against England and celebrated the occasion by scoring four tries. In the 1902-04 seasons he scored six tries for Wales in four successive games. On tour in Australasia with the British Isles, he scored seven tries in Australia, (four of which were scored against Australia - two in the first encounter and one each in the following two internationals) but failed to score in his four appearances in New Zealand. He captained London Welsh from 1900-03. Willie Llewellyn, who was a nephew of Thomas Williams [qv], was a pharmacist. During the Tonypandy Riots of 1910, when over sixty properties were damaged, his chemist shop was left untouched. He was made the first life member of the Pontyclun Club and was the last survivor of the 1905 Welsh side which beat the All Blacks.

LLEWELYN, Donald Barry
Born Ashton, Lancashire, 6 January 1948
Career: Llanelli Grammar School; Loughborough College; Caerleon College; Hendy; Carmarthen Athletic; Newport; Llanelli; Newbridge; Barbarians; Pembrokeshire

Prop in 13 matches, against: South Africa, 1970; Scotland, 1970, 1971, 1972; England, 1970, 1971, 1972; Ireland, 1970, 1971; France, 1970, 1971, 1972; New Zealand, 1972: Scored 1t - 3 points

Barry Llewelyn toured Australasia and Fiji with Wales in 1969 and the Far East in 1975. He also played for a Wales XV against New Zealand in 1974 and captained Llanelli in 1971-72. He has a sports and leisure wear business.

LLOYD, David John
Born Pontycymmer, 29 March 1943
Career: Garw Grammar School; Cardiff Training College; Welsh Secondary Schools; Pontycymmer; Bridgend; Barbarians; Glamorgan

Prop in 24 matches, against: England, 1966, 1967, 1969, 1972, 1973; Scotland, 1966, 1967, 1968, 1969, 1972, 1973; Ireland, 1966, 1967, 1968, 1969; France, 1966, 1967, 1968, 1969, 1970, 1972; Australia, 1966, 1969; New Zealand, 1969

Schoolmaster John Lloyd toured Argentina in 1968, and Australasia and Fiji in 1969 with Wales. He captained Wales in three matches in 1972 and played 392 games for Bridgend, captaining them in 1966-68 and 1969-73, before being appointed the club coach. In 1980 he was assistant manager to the Welsh team which went to the United States and Canada. In December 1979, he was appointed coach to the Welsh team. His daughter, Alison, has represented Wales in basketball and netball.

LLOYD, David Percy Marmaduke
Born Ammanford, 5 January 1871; died Llanwrtyd Wells, 10 March 1959
Career: Carmarthen Grammar School; Pontardawe; Llanelli; Ammanford; Barbarians

Wing in 4 matches, against: Scotland, 1890; England, 1890, 1891; Ireland, 1891

In December 1888 Percy Lloyd, who was then a seventeen year old pupil at Carmarthen Grammar School, played for Llanelli against the New Zealand Natives in the thirty-second match of their tour. He captained the club from 1891-94. An athlete of note, he later became a hotelier in Llanwrtyd Wells.

LLOYD, Evan
Born Llanelli, 6 June 1871; died Llanelli, 28 February 1951
Career: Llanelli

Wing in 1 match, against: Scotland, 1895

52. 1960 v France
Back row: M R Jeffreys (WRU touch judge), T R Prosser, L J Cunningham, D J E Harris, J Faull, G D Davidge, B R Cresswell, N M Parkes (RFU referee).
Middle row: M J Price, D O Brace, B V Meredith (C), J Leleu, N H Morgan.
Front row: F G Coles, B J Jones, T B Richards, D I E Bebb.
[*Western Mail*]

53. 1961 v France
Back row: N M Parkes (RFU referee), T R Prosser, T J Davies, P E J Morgan, W R Evans, B Price, D Nash, H J Mainwaring, A E I Pask, unknown (WRU touch judge).
Front row: H M Roberts, W J Thomas, J E Collins, L H Williams, K H L Richards, D I E Bebb, H J Morgan.
[*Hubert Price*]

54. 1962 v Ireland
Back row: C E Harrison (WRU touch judge), D J Davies, W R Evans, K A Rowlands, A E I Pask, D J Warlow, J A S Taylor [SRU referee].
Middle row: L J Cunningham, K D Jones, A O'Connor, B V Meredith (C), C Ashton, H J Morgan, D B Davies, G T R Hodgson.
Front row: D I E Bebb, D R R Morgan.
[*Lafayette Photography*]
NB this match was postponed from the previous season due to a smallpox epidemic in the Rhondda.

Evan Lloyd, a tinplater at the Old Castle works in Llanelli, was also a noted sprinter. He captained Llanelli in 1897-98.

LLOYD, George Llewellyn
Born Newport, 1877; died Newport, 1 August 1957
Career: The Leys School; Newport; Kent

Half-back in 12 matches, against: Ireland, 1896, 1899, 1902, 1903; Scotland, 1899, 1900, 1901, 1902, 1903; England, 1900, 1901, 1903: Scored 3t - 9 points

Llewellyn Lloyd was a solicitor in Newport. He captained Newport RFC from 1899-1903, Wales once in 1893 and played cricket for Monmouthshire, as well as captaining Newport Cricket Club in 1899-1901.

LLOYD, Robert
Born 1888, registered in Crickhowell; died Halifax, 18 January 1930
Career: Pontypool

Scrum-half in 7 matches, against: Scotland, 1913, 1914; France, 1913, 1914; Ireland, 1913, 1914; England, 1914

It is reputed that Bobby Lloyd, who captained Pontypool in 1913-14, chose to join Halifax RLFC, after turning down offers from other rugby league clubs, as his former half-back colleague at Pontypool, Stuart Prosser, was playing for the club. He scored a try in his debut match against Keighley on 26 September 1914. He won one cap for the Wales RL side and toured Australia in 1920 with the Great Britain RL team. Initially Lloyd was employed as a collier but later became a licensee.

LLOYD, Thomas John
Born 1882; died Neath, 27 April 1938
Career: Glynneath School; Glynneath; Neath

Forward in 7 matches, against: France, 1909, 1913, 1914; Ireland, 1913, 1914; England, 1914; Scotland, 1914

'T C' Lloyd was a member of the 'Terrible Eight'. After working as a collier, he became a bookmaker. He captained Glynneath in 1903-04 and Neath in 1913-14.

LLOYD, Trevor
Born Taibach, 5 September 1924
Career: Eastern School, Taibach; Steel Company of Wales; Cwmavon; Aberavon; Maesteg; Bristol; Glamorgan

Scrum-half in 2 matches, against: Ireland, 1953; France, 1953

British Isles 1955 tour South Africa

Trevor Lloyd worked as a blast furnaceman and served in the Royal Navy during the Second World War. In celebration of the 75th anniversary of the Welsh Rugby Union in 1955, Wales, captained by Trevor Lloyd, played a British Isles XV. In the same year he toured South Africa with the British Isles, appearing in five games. He captained Maesteg in 1948-51, 1953-54, 1955-56 and coached them from 1956 until 1959.

LOCKWOOD, Thomas William
Born Cheshire, 1863
Career: Newport; London Welsh; Richmond; Middlesex Wanderers; Birkenhead Park; Middlesex; Cheshire

Forward in 3 matches, against: England, 1887; Scotland, 1887; Ireland, 1887

Lockwood, who captained Birkenhead Park in 1891-92, originally hailed from Cheshire. His father, an architect, designed Newport Town Hall.

LONG, Edgar Cecil
Born Gower, 1907; died Swansea, 31 January 1958
Career: Mumbles; Swansea

Forward in 7 matches, against: England, 1936, 1937; Scotland, 1936, 1937, 1939; Ireland, 1936, 1939

Edgar Long captained the Swansea team to a great victory over the 1935-36 All Blacks, having played for the club against the Maoris in 1926, New South Wales in 1927 and South Africa in 1931. He was employed at the Elba Works, Mumbles.

LYNE, Horace Sampson MBE
Born Newport, 31 December 1860; died Newport, 1 May 1949
Career: Plymouth School; Royal Naval College, Portsmouth; Newport

Forward in 5 matches, against: Scotland, 1883, 1884; England, 1884, 1885; Ireland, 1884

Horace Lyne, a solicitor, captained Newport in 1883-84. He served as a representative on the International Board from 1887-1938, was president of the Welsh Rugby Union from 1906-47 and chairman of Newport Athletic Club from 1894-1949. He refereed the game between England and Ireland in 1885. Off the rugby field, he served as the Chief Fire Officer for Newport for 50 years and was granted the Freedom of the Borough on 6 April 1934.

MADDOCK, Hopkin Thomas MC
Born Pontycymmer, 1881; died Cardiff, 15 December 1921
Career: Christ College, Brecon; Pontycymmer; London

Welsh; Middlesex; Glamorgan

Wing in 6 matches, against: England, 1906, 1907; Scotland, 1906, 1907; Ireland, 1906; France, 1910: Scored 6t - 18 points

Hop Maddock was employed by the London County Council. He played for Glamorgan against South Africa in 1906 and captained London Welsh in 1909-10 and 1911-12. He died from the effects of wounds sustained during the First World War during which he had served in the Royal Fusiliers (Public Schools Battalion) and in the Machine Gun Corps.

MADDOCKS, Keith
Born Resolven, 16 June 1927
Career: Cowbridge Grammar School; St Luke's College, Exeter; Resolven; Neath; Plymouth Albion; Devon

Wing in 1 match, against: England, 1957

Schoolmaster Keith Maddocks played for Neath and Aberavon against New Zealand in January 1954 and captained Neath in 1957-58. He was the Welsh AAA Junior 100 yards champion in 1944.

MAIN, Derrick Roy
Born Abbassia, Egypt, 29 November 1931
Career: King Henry VIII Grammar School, Abergavenny; St Luke's College, Exeter; Abergavenny Harlequins; Abergavenny; London Welsh; Royal Navy; Barbarians; Devon

Prop in 4 matches, against: England, 1959; Scotland, 1959; Ireland, 1959; France, 1959
Derrick Main was the master in charge of sport at Bancroft's School and later taught at The College, Bishop's Stortford. After a leg injury he took early retirement and now runs a woodworking factory, repairing kitchen and household fittings. His brother Gordon was a back row forward with Ebbw Vale for many seasons.

MAINWARING, Gwilym Thomas
Born Port Talbot, 24 January 1941
Career: Eastern School, Taibach; Taibach; Aberavon; Bridgend; Barbarians

Lock in 6 matches, against: Scotland, 1967; Ireland, 1967; France, 1967; England, 1967, 1968; New Zealand, 1967

Billy Mainwaring, a steelworker, toured Argentina with Wales in 1968. He captained Aberavon from 1969-71 and is a committee member at the club.

MAINWARING, Haydn James
Born Swansea, 10 June 1933

Career: Bishop Gore School; Welsh Secondary Schools; Swansea; Harlequins; London Welsh; Royal Navy; Combined Services; Barbarians; Hampshire

Centre in 1 match, against: France, 1961

Banker Haydn Mainwaring played at full back for the Barbarians against South Africa, in February 1961, and brought off two try-saving tackles. The first, against Avril Malan, the captain, hit the Springbok with such force that Malan was unable to make an appearance at the match dinner. The second tackle was on Michel Antelme, the winger. His cap later in the season was seen as a reward for these efforts.

MAJOR, Windsor Cynwyd
Born Llangynwyd, 15 June 1929
Career: Cwmfelin School; Maesteg Comprehensive School; Bridgend Technical College; Maesteg Celtic; Maesteg; London Welsh; Bridgend; Neath; Aberavon; The Army; Combined Services; Glamorgan; Eastern Counties

Wing in 2 matches, against: France, 1949; Scotland, 1950

Windsor Major was a carpenter before taking up farming. He captained Maesteg in 1957-58 and was the club president from 1979 until 1986.

MALE, Benjamin Oswald
Born 31 December 1893, registered in Newport; died Risca, 23 February 1975
Career: Cross Keys; Pontypool; Cardiff

Full back in 11 matches, against: France, 1921, 1927, 1928; Scotland, 1923, 1924, 1927, 1928; Ireland, 1924, 1927, 1928; England, 1927: Scored 6con 1pg - 15 points

In March 1924, Ossie Male was ignominiously dismissed from the Welsh party at Paddington Station, en route to Paris for the game against France. Representatives of the Welsh Rugby Union had convened a meeting on the train, and decided on this punishment after Male was found guilty of contravening a bye-law - he had played for Cardiff - which forbade players from playing in a game within one week of appearing in an international. In his appearance for Cardiff against New South Wales in December 1927, he kicked two penalty goals. He captained Wales on three occasions, in 1927 and 1928 and Cardiff in 1928-29. He also played soccer for Abertillery. A teacher, Male became the headmaster of Wattsville Secondary Modern School.

MANFIELD, Leslie DFC
Born Mountain Ash, 10 November 1915
Career: Mountain Ash County Intermediate School; University College Cardiff; Carnegie Physical Training

College, Leeds; Welsh Secondary Schools; Universities Athletics Union; Mountain Ash; Cardiff; Penarth; London Welsh; Otley; Neath; Bridgend; Royal Air Force; Combined Services; Barbarians; Yorkshire

No 8 in 7 matches, against: Scotland, 1939, 1948; Ireland, 1939, 1948; Australia, 1947; England, 1948; France, 1948

Teacher Les Manfield won the 1937 Welsh University Colleges light heavyweight boxing championship. In 1938 he was selected to play in an England trial but chose instead to play in a Wales trial. During the Second World War he was a squadron leader in the Royal Air Force and was decorated with the Distinguished Flying Cross. He appeared in two Red Cross internationals in 1939-40, two Service internationals in 1942, and eight Victory internationals in 1945-46.

MANN, B B
Born details unknown
Career: Cardiff

Forward in 1 match, against: England, 1881

B B Mann was a member of the first Welsh XV that played against England in 1881, the season in which he was vice captain of Cardiff. He did not play rugby for the Cardiff club after the end of the 1880-81 season and remains the number one mystery man of Welsh rugby, the only player in the first national side to remain unidentified.

MANTLE, John
Born Cardiff, 13 March 1942
Career: Bedwellty Comprehensive School; Loughborough College; Welsh Secondary Schools; British Universities; Bargoed; Newport; Leicestershire

Flanker/No 8 in 2 matches, against: England, 1964; South Africa, 1964

John Mantle played soccer for the Welsh Boys Clubs, and won the Welsh under-19 triple jump. He toured South Africa in 1964 with Wales, and played in all four games. On 23 January 1965, he made his debut for St Helens RLFC and went on to win sixteen caps for the Wales RL team, also playing in thirteen games for the Great Britain XIII. He was a member of the St Helens team in three winning RL Cup finals.

MARGRAVE, Frederick Lofthouse
Born Llanelli, 25 December 1858; died Llanelli, 1 January 1946
Career: Llandovery College; Llanelli

Forward in 2 matches, against: England, 1884; Scotland, 1884

Margrave was secretary of Llanelli RFC in 1876. He captained the club in 1877-78 and from 1880-81 to 1884-85. He was the proprietor of a wine business.

MARTIN, Allan Jeffrey
Born Port Talbot, 11 December 1948
Career: Sandfields Comprehensive School; Cardiff College of Education; Welsh Secondary Schools; Aberavon; Llanelli; Penarth; Barbarians; Wales B

Lock in 34 matches, against: Australia, 1973, 1975, 1978, 1978; Scotland, 1974, 1975, 1976, 1977, 1978, 1979, 1980; Ireland, 1974, 1975, 1976, 1977, 1978, 1979, 1980, 1981; France, 1975, 1976, 1977, 1978, 1979, 1980, 1981; England, 1975, 1976, 1977, 1978, 1979, 1980; New Zealand, 1978, 1980: Scored 1t 3con 5pg - 25 points

British Isles tour 1977 New Zealand: 1 cap; 1980 South Africa

Allan Martin, a qualified school teacher, shares with Robert Norster the honour of being Wales' most capped lock. A company representative, he made three tours with Wales: to Canada in 1973; the Far East in 1975, and Australia in 1978. He played in thirteen games for the British Isles in New Zealand in 1977 and, in South Africa three years later, he made eight appearances for the British visitors. In May 1979 he toured South Africa with Surrey. He captained Aberavon in 1981-82. He is the brother-in-law of Les Keen [qv]. His son Steven, has played for the Welsh Schools XV.

MARTIN, Walter John DCM
Born Woodford, Essex 14 May 1883; died Newport, 30 April 1933
Career: Evesham School; Newport High School; University College Cardiff; Newport; Monmouthshire

Stand-off in 3 matches, against: Ireland, 1912; France, 1912; New Zealand Army, 1919

Walter Martin, who won an exhibition to the University College, Cardiff, served as a company sergeant major in the South Wales Borderers during the First World War and was decorated for gallantry. He captained Newport in 1912-13, scoring a try for the club in the 9-3 win against South Africa in October 1912 (he had also played in the same fixture in October 1906), played cricket for Newport and was proficient in the long jump. When he played against New Zealand Army in 1919, aged 36, he became one of the oldest backs to represent Wales. He worked for a firm of acccountants before becoming a railways official in the Newport Docks. Tragically, Walter Martin took his own life in 1933.

MASON, Jonathan Edward
Born Aberdare, 13 June 1965

Career: Cynon Valley Schools; Mountain Ash; Pontypridd

Wing in 1 match, against: New Zealand, 1988(r)

Full back Jonathan Mason, a furniture design technician, won his cap as a replacement for Mike Hall.

MATHEWS, Alfred Augustus
Born Rhymney, 7 February 1864; died Malpas, Newport, 12 August 1946
Career: Llandovery College; St David's College, Lampeter; Swansea

Half-back in 1 match, against: Scotland, 1886

A A Mathews, who played for Swansea against the New Zealand Natives in 1888, was a clergyman. After ordination he was curate, and then vicar of Holy Trinity, Swansea, from 1887-97. He became vicar of Blaenavon in 1897 and remained in Monmouthshire until his death in 1946. His daughter Barbara, became Baroness Brooke of Ystradfellte after marrying Henry Brooke, Home Secretary in the Macmillan government. His grandson, Peter Brooke MP, is currently Secretary of State for Northern Ireland. Mathews was also well-known as a referee and regularly officiated at the funerals of former international rugby players.

MATHIAS, Roy
Born Llanelli, 2 September 1949
Career: Stebonheath School; Welsh Secondary Schools; Welsh Youth; Felinfoel; Llanelli; Barbarians
Wing in 1 match, against: France, 1970

Roy Mathias, an electrician, had converted to the wing position from that of flanker. He joined St Helens RLFC, making his debut on 22 August 1972, made one appearance for the Great Britain RL side and won twenty caps for the Wales RL team.

MATTHEWS, Christopher Mansel
Born Bridgend, 1911; died Cardiff, 5 December 1965
Career: Porthcawl; Maesteg; Bridgend; Cardiff

Wing in 1 match, against: Ireland, 1939

Chris Matthews, a commission agent, captained Bridgend in 1936-37 as did his father Thomas. Jenkin Matthews, an uncle, played in a Welsh trial. Chris won the Welsh Powderhall sprint in 1932.

MATTHEWS, Jack OBE
Born Bridgend, 21 June 1920
Career: Bridgend County School; University College Cardiff; Welsh Secondary Schools; Cardiff; Bridgend; The

Army; Combined Services; Barbarians; Hampshire

Centre/wing in 17 matches, against: England, 1947, 1948, 1949, 1950, 1951; Australia, 1947; Scotland, 1948, 1949, 1950, 1951; France, 1948, 1949, 1950, 1951; Ireland, 1949, 1950, 1951: Scored 4t - 12 points

British Isles 1950 tour New Zealand: 4 caps, Australia: 2 caps

Jack Matthews practices medicine in Cardiff. He won the Welsh AAA Junior 220 yards title in 1937 and served in the Royal Army Medical Corps during the Second World War. He had played in five Victory internationals before winning his first cap and captained Cardiff in 1945-47 and 1951-2. On 27 September 1947, he played for Cardiff against Australia and four days later appeared for the Combined Services against the same tourists. In Australasia with the 1950 British Isles team, he made fifteen appearances in New Zealand and five in Australia. He was the Medical Officer to the 1980 British Isles team in South Africa and, for many years, for the Welsh section of the British Boxing Association. He was awarded the OBE in the Queen's Birthday Honours List in 1981.

MAY, Phillip Stephen
Born 1 July 1956, registered in Carmarthen,
Career: Llanelli Grammar School; University College Swansea; University College, Aberystwyth; Welsh Universities; British Universities; New Dock Stars; Llanelli; Barbarians; Welsh B

Lock in 6 matches, against: England, 1988; Scotland, 1988; Ireland, 1988; France; New Zealand, 1988, 1988

Phil May made his debut for Llanelli in October 1974 and went on to captain the club in 1982-83 and 1986-87. During the latter season he played his 400th game for the club, and he made his 450th appearance in the match with London Welsh, on Boxing Day, 1988. He has now played in 519 games and been a member of three Schweppes Cup winning sides. Formerly a brewery executive, he is now the Commercial and General Manager to Llanelli RFC

MAYNARD, Edwin Thomas
(Known as THOMAS, Edwin)
Born Upper Cwmbran 21 March 1878; died Cwmbran, 20 November 1961
Career: Upper Cwmbran Juniors; Pontnewydd; Newport

Forward in 6 matches, against: Scotland, 1904, 1909; Ireland, 1904, 1909; France, 1909, 1910

'Beddoe' Thomas played in 320 games for Newport from 1899 to 1912. He is believed to be the first Welshman to score a try at Twickenham, while playing for Newport against the Harlequins. He was in the Newport team

55. 1963 v Ireland
Back row: A C Luff (RFU referee), N R Gale, D Williams, B Thomas, K A Rowlands, W J B Morris, K D Jones, H C Young (WRU touch judge).
Middle row: D R R Morgan, H J Morgan, D C T Rowlands (C), A E I Pask, H M Roberts.
Front row: G Jones, D Watkins, R Evans, G T R Hodgson.
[*Hubert Price*]

56. 1965 v France
Back row: R W Gilliland (referee), N R Gale, A E I Pask, J Uzzell, S J Dawes, T G Price, K A Rowlands, D Williams, R G Waldron, B Price, H J Morgan, R Lewis (WRU touch judge).
Front row: S J Watkins, G J Prothero, D Watkins, D C T Rowlands (C), D I E Bebb.
[*Presse Sports*]

57. 1966 v Scotland
Back row: M H Titcomb (RFU referee), N R Gale, S J Watkins, B Thomas, B Price, D Williams, G J Prothero, I Davies (WRU touch judge).
Middle row: D J Lloyd, D Watkins, A E I Pask (C), H J Morgan, G T R Hodgson.
Front row: D K Jones, R A Lewis, L Davies, K Bradshaw.
[*Western Mail*]

against New Zealand in 1905, South Africa in 1906 and Australia in 1908. Before becoming the licensee of the Bridgend Inn, Pontnewydd (which was used by Pontnewydd RFC as their club headquarters and changing rooms) he was employed as a labourer. 'Beddoe' Thomas was made a life member of Pontnewydd RFC in 1949.

McCALL, Barney Ernest Wilford MC
Born Clifton, 13 May 1913; died Cardiff, 31 March 1991
Career: Weymouth School; Royal Military College, Sandhurst; The Army; London Welsh; Newport

Wing in 3 matches, against: England, 1936; Scotland, 1936; Ireland, 1936

Barney McCall was an officer in the Army. His selection for Wales caused a fuss in the press as he had no Welsh blood. He played cricket for the Army, Combined Services and Dorset. Resigning from the Army in 1937, he became the games master at King's School, Canterbury but was recalled to the colours on the outbreak of the Second World War. Following his retirement in 1958, he became the Cadet Force Executive Officer in Glamorgan. He was mistakenly declared as having died in 1982 by Robert Brooke, who edits the obituaries for *Wisden's Cricketing Almanac*.

McCARLEY, Allen
Born Port Talbot, 5 December 1914; died Port Talbot, 25 July 1963
Career: Central School, Port Talbot; Taibach; Neath; Aberavon
Forward in 3 matches, against: England, 1938; Scotland, 1938; Ireland, 1938: Scored 3t - 9 points

Allen McCarley was employed as a fitter/turner in the Port Talbot steelworks. He was elected captain of Neath for the 1939-40 season but, due to the war, did not actually take up the captaincy. He was assistant coach to Aberavon in 1951-52.

McCUTCHEON, William Morgan
Born Swansea, 1870; died Oldham, 3 July 1949
Career: Swansea; Oldham; Lancashire

Wing in 7 matches, against: Scotland, 1891, 1892, 1893; England, 1892, 1893, 1894; Ireland, 1893: Scored 1t - 2 points

Billy McCutcheon, who was employed as a clerk, started playing at full back for Swansea. On moving to Oldham in December 1888, where he played for nine seasons and was captain, he played in the centre and on the wing. He and Dai Gwyn remodelled the kind of game played at Oldham in the 1890s. After his playing days were over he took up refereeing in Lancashire and was the president of Oldham RLFC from 1924-26.

MEREDITH, Alun
Born Ystrad, 1919
Career: Pentre County School; Bristol University; Welsh Secondary Schools; Bristol; Rosslyn Park; London Welsh; Waterloo; Cardiff; Devonport Services; Royal Navy; Gloucestershire; Devon; Yorkshire

Lock in 3 matches, against: England, 1949; Scotland, 1949; Ireland, 1949: Scored 1t - 3 points

Alun Meredith, who won the Welsh Schools high jump championship in 1936, was a director of sport in the Royal Navy. He captained Bristol in 1945-46 and appeared for Gloucestershire and Somerset against Australia on 20 September 1947.

MEREDITH, Brinley Victor
Born Cwmbran, 21 November 1930
Career: West Monmouth Grammar School; St Luke's College, Exeter; Welsh Secondary Schools; London Welsh; Newport; Devonport Services; Royal Navy; Barbarians; Devon; Hertfordshire

Hooker in 34 matches, against: Ireland, 1954, 1955, 1956, 1957, 1958, 1959, 1961, 1962; France, 1954, 1955, 1956, 1957, 1959, 1960, 1962; Scotland, 1954, 1955, 1956, 1957, 1958, 1959, 1960, 1961, 1962; England, 1955, 1956, 1957, 1958, 1959, 1960, 1961, 1962; Australia, 1958; South Africa, 1960: Scored 3t - 9 points

British Isles 1955 tour South Africa: 4 caps; 1959 Australia, New Zealand; 1962 South Africa: 4 caps

Bryn Meredith is Wales' most capped hooker. He appeared for the South Western Counties against New Zealand in December 1953. In two British Isles tours to South Africa he played in twenty-eight games, fourteen on each tour. On the first tour he scored a try in the second international match. On the tour of Australasia in 1959 he appeared in two games in Australia nine in New Zealand but had to stand down in favour of the tour captain, also a hooker (and considered by many to be an inferior player), in the major games. He captained Newport in 1958-59 and 1961-62. A former teacher, he left the profession to become a representative.

MEREDITH, Courtenay Charles
Born Pontypridd, 23 September 1926
Career: Neath Technical College; University College Cardiff; Crynant; Steel Company of Wales; Neath; Barbarians

Prop in 14 matches, against: Scotland, 1953, 1954, 1955, 1957; New Zealand, 1953; England, 1954, 1955, 1956,

1957; Ireland, 1954, 1955, 1956; France, 1954, 1955:
Scored 1t - 3 points

British Isles 1955 tour South Africa: 4 caps

Courtenay Meredith, a steelworks official at the Steel
Company of Wales, Margam, was joint captain of Crynant
in 1948-49. He played for a Neath and Aberavon XV
against New Zealand in January 1954 and in fourteen
games for the 1955 British Isles tourists in South Africa.
Hatained Neath in 1955-56.

MEREDITH, John
Born Swansea, 1863; died Swansea, 30 November 1920
Career: Swansea

Forward in 4 matches, against: Scotland, 1888, 1890;
Ireland, 1888; England, 1890

John Meredith was the secretary of the West Glamorgan
Friendly Society under the National Health Insurance. A
literary adjudicator in eisteddfodau, he also took a great
interest in horticulture.

MERRY, James Augustus
Born Newport, 1888; died Newport, 14 December 1943
Career: Pill Harriers

Forward in 2 matches, against: Ireland, 1912; France, 1912

Crane driver Gus Merry played thirty-five games for the
Hull RL club after making his debut on 5 September 1912
and also made one appearance for the Wales RL side. His
1919 application for reinstatement as an amateur was
refused following the war years when he played for Pill
Harriers during a period when the professional laws were
suspended.

MICHAEL, Gwilym Morgan
Born 1892, registered in Pontardawe; died Pontardawe, 24
May 1941
Career: Pontardawe; Swansea

Forward in 3 matches, against: England, 1923; Scotland,
1923; France, 1923: Scored 1t - 3 points

Gwilym Michael, who was the cousin of Brinley Lewis
[qv], was the manager of a tinplate company. He played
in the Centenary match at Rugby School in 1923. During
the First World War he served in Palestine and
Mesopotamia and, during the Second World War,
commanded a Home Guard signals detachment.

MICHAELSON, Roger Carl Brandon
Born Porthcawl, 31 March 1941

Career: Clifton College; Cambridge University; Welsh
Secondary Schools; Porthcawl; Aberavon; London Welsh;
Barbarians; Surrey

No 8 in 1 match, against: England, 1963

Roger Michaelson won three Blues in 1960-62 and in
November 1960 played for Cambridge University against
South Africa. He is the proprietor of a wholesale fruit
business.

MILLAR, William Henry
Born Derby, 1873
Career: Mountain Ash

Forward in 7 matches, against: Ireland, 1896, 1900, 1901;
England, 1900, 1901; Scotland, 1900, 1901

Fred Millar, played soccer for Derby Junction Juniors,
Mountain Ash - he was one of the founders of the club -
and Glamorgan. He captained Mountain Ash RFC in 1897-
98. An apprentice coach builder before he became a collier
in Nixon's Navigation Colliery, Mountain Ash, he joined
Hull RL club, making his debut on 7 September 1901.

MILLS, Frank Musgrave
Born Gloucester, 1871; died Porthcawl, 17 February 1925
Career: Swansea; Cardiff

Forward in 13 matches, against: England, 1892, 1893,
1894, 1895, 1896; Scotland, 1892, 1893, 1894, 1895;
Ireland, 1892, 1893, 1894, 1895
Frank Mills, a licensee, was the vice captain of Cardiff in
1895-96.

MOORE, William John
Born Garw Valley, 17 February 1910; died Oldham, 31
March 1976
Career: Bridgend; Glamorgan

Forward in 1 match, against: Ireland, 1933

Billy Moore, a quarryman, made his first appearance for
Rochdale Hornets RLFC on 20 January 1934. He was once
a sparring partner to the boxer Jack Doyle and fought Jack
Peterson at Weston-Super-Mare, a bout which ended in 'no
decision' - a result which is not recorded in Peterson's
official record. He served in the Royal Air Force during
the Second World War.

MORGAN, Charles Henry
Born Carmarthen, 22 December 1932
Career: Clifton College; Welsh Secondary Schools;
Carmarthen Athletic; Llanelli; Barbarians

Prop in 2 matches, against: Ireland, 1957; France, 1957

Henry Morgan played for a Welsh XV against a Rest of Britain XV in 1958, a match organised to celebrate the Cardiff Empire Games. He is employed in the textile business.

MORGAN, Clifford Isaac CVO, OBE
Born Trebanog, 7 April 1930
Career: Tonyrefail Grammar School; University College Cardiff; Welsh Secondary Schools; Cardiff; Bective Rangers; Barbarians

Stand-off in 29 matches, against: Ireland, 1951, 1952, 1953, 1954, 1955, 1956, 1957, 1958; France, 1951, 1953, 1955, 1956, 1957, 1958; South Africa, 1951; England, 1952, 1954, 1955, 1956, 1957, 1958; Scotland, 1952, 1953, 1954, 1955, 1956, 1957, 1958; New Zealand, 1953: Scored 3t - 9 points

British Isles 1955 tour South Africa: 4 caps

Cliff Morgan captained Wales on four occasions, and is the country's most capped stand-off. He made three appearances for the Barbarians against touring teams: South Africa in 1952, New Zealand in 1954 and Australia in 1958. In 1955, watched by a crowd of 90,000, he scored a try for the British Isles in their first international against South Africa and captained the tourists in the third international - one of fourteen games that he played in during the tour. He edited *Rugby: the Great Ones*, published in 1970. He received the OBE in 1977, the CVO in 1986, an Honorary MA from the University of Wales in 1988, an Honorary Doctorate from Keele University in 1989 and was made an Honorary Fellow of the Polytechnic of Wales in 1989. Having commenced his career with the South Wales Electricity Board, he joined the BBC in 1958 as the Sports Organiser for Wales. He became the editor of Sportsview and Grandstand, the producer of This Week, editor of Sport Radio, Head of Outside Broadcasts (Radio) and, from 1975 until his retirement in 1987, was the Head of Outside Broadcasts for BBC Television. Currently the presenter of the radio programme *Sport on 4* every Saturday and a freelance writer, he is the president of the London Glamorgan Society and the Welsh Sports Association for Mental Handicap and a vice president of the National Children's Home.

MORGAN, D
Born details unknown
Career: Swansea

Forward in 7 matches, against: Scotland, 1885, 1886, 1887; England, 1886, 1887; Ireland, 1887, 1889: Scored 1t

MORGAN, David
Born Llanelli, 14 July 1872; died Pemberton, 13 September 1933

Career: Seaside Stars; Llanelli

Half-back in 2 matches, against: Ireland, 1895; England, 1896

Dai Morgan was employed as a tinplater in Llanelli.

MORGAN, David Edgar
Born Llanelli, 17 May 1896; died Llanelli, 9 September 1983
Career: Park Street School; Welsh Schools; New Dock Stars; Llanelli

Forward in 4 matches, against: Ireland, 1920; England, 1921; Scotland, 1921; France, 1921

At the age of eleven years Edgar Morgan played for Welsh Schools against English Schools and also played soccer for Llanelli. He served in the Royal Engineers during the First World War. On 27 August 1921, he played his first game for Hull RLFC and went on to play five games for the Wales and two games for the Great Britain RL sides. On returning to live in South Wales he became a police officer.

MORGAN, David Robert Ruskin
Born Pontyberem, 29 August 1941
Career: Gwendraeth Grammar School; Cardiff College of Education; Pontyberem; Llanelli; Cardiff; Barbarians

Wing in 9 matches, against: England, 1962, 1963; Scotland, 1962, 1963; France, 1962, 1963; Ireland, 1962; New Zealand, 1963

Robert Morgan was a schoolmaster before becoming a supervisor for British Petroleum.

MORGAN, Edgar MC
Born Pontardawe, April 1882; died c1962
Career: Collegiate School, Tanyrallt; University College of North Wales, Bangor; Alltwen; Pontardawe; Swansea

Forward in 4 matches, against: England, 1914; Scotland, 1914; France, 1914; Ireland, 1914

Anglo-Welsh 1908 tour Australia, New Zealand: 2 caps.

Edgar Morgan, one of the famed 'Terrible Eight', made fourteen appearances, more than anyone else, on the New Zealand leg of the 1908 Anglo-Welsh tour of Australasia but had to wait a further six years before he played his first game for Wales. During the First World War he was commissioned as an infantry officer and later transferred to the Royal Engineers. One of his Anglo-Welsh jerseys is on display in the Abercrave RFC clubhouse. In his early days he was a deckhand on a barque and sailed around Cape Horn. In later life he was a mechanical engineer.

MORGAN, Edward

Born Aberdare, 22 May 1880; died North Walsham, 1 September 1949

Career: Christ College Brecon; Guy's Hospital; United Hospitals; London Welsh; Sketty; Newport; Surrey; Kent

Wing in 16 matches, against: England, 1902, 1904, 1905, 1906; Scotland, 1902, 1904, 1905, 1906; Ireland, 1902, 1903, 1904, 1905, 1906; New Zealand, 1905; South Africa, 1906; France, 1908: Scored 14t - 42 points

British Isles 1904 tour Australia: 3 caps, New Zealand: 1 cap

Teddy Morgan was a Doctor of Medicine and the brother of W LL Morgan [*qv*]. It was he who scored the only try of the 1905 Wales - All Blacks match. From 1903-05 he scored eight tries in five successive international games and captained Wales against France in 1908 in the first match between the two countries. While playing for London Welsh he sometimes played under the nom-de-plume of 'W E S Digby', or 'W E Smart'. On the British Isles tour of Australasia, Teddy Morgan took over the captaincy after Bedell-Sivright, the tour captain, was injured. Teddy Morgan had a medical practice in Sketty for a number of years. In October 1938 he lost the sight of his right eye in a shooting accident. He was the uncle of W Guy Morgan [*qv*]. His son Guy who, after a period as a journalist on the *Manchester Guardian,* became the *Daily Express* film critic (1933-40) and wrote a number of film scripts, including *Albert RN* which was adapted from his own play.

MORGAN, Frederick Luther

Born Pontyberem, 11 February 1915; died Llanelli, 29 December 1988

Career: Gwendraeth Grammar School; Pontyberem; Llanelli; Police Union

Forward in 4 matches, against: England, 1938, 1939; Scotland, 1938; Ireland, 1938

Fred Morgan was a police officer in the Carmarthenshire Constabulary. He captained Llanelli in 1939-40.

MORGAN, Gerwyn Rhys

Born Southerndown, 9 June 1954

Career: Caerleon Comprehensive School; Newport College of Education; Caerleon; Newport; Barbarians; Wales B

Prop in 1 match, against: Scotland, 1984

Rhys Morgan, a plumber, won his only cap as a late replacement. In his first season for Newport in 1973-74, straight from Youth rugby, he was the club's top scorer with 126 points. He went on to make over 500 appearances for the club, was captain in 1987-88 and

retired in 1990.

MORGAN, Harry Perrott

Born Goytre, Pontypool, 16 June 1930

Career: Wycliffe College; Cambridge University; Newport; Cardiff; Usk

Centre in 4 matches, against: England, 1956; Scotland, 1956; Ireland, 1956; France, 1956   Scored 1t - 3 points

Harry Morgan, who won two Blues in 1952-53, was employed as a company representative.

MORGAN, Haydn John

Born Oakdale, 30 July 1936

Career: Newbridge Grammar School; Oakdale; Abertillery; Irish Wolfhounds; The Army; Trinant; Barbarians

Flanker in 27 matches, against: England, 1958, 1960, 1961, 1962, 1965, 1966; Scotland, 1958, 1961, 1962, 1963, 1965, 1966; Ireland, 1958, 1959, 1961, 1962, 1963, 1965, 1966; France, 1958, 1959, 1961, 1962, 1963, 1965, 1966; Australia, 1966   Scored 3t - 9 points

British Isles 1959 tour Australia, New Zealand: 2 caps; 1962 South Africa: 2 caps

Haydn Morgan is in the car sales business and was employed for a number of years by a motor company in Johannesburg. He made thirty one appearances for the British Isles: two in Australia, sixteen in New Zealand, and thirteen in South Africa. He also visited South Africa with the 1958 Barbarians and the 1964 Welsh tourists. He captained Abertillery in 1959-60 and 1964-65. In November 1960, he played for Ebbw Vale and Abertillery against South Africa and in February 1961 scored a try for the Barbarians against the same opposition at Cardiff Arms Park.

MORGAN, John Lewis

Born Alejandra, Argentina, 23 October 1892; died Campo Largo, Chaco, Argentina, 7 July 1947

Career: Llandovery College; Carmarthen Grammar School; Oriental Stars; Llanelli

Forward in 2 matches, against: South Africa, 1912; England, 1913

During his schooldays at Carmarthen, Johnnie Morgan was a hooker and, in the summer months, an important member of the cricket XI. In the school sports in May 1909, he won the 'throwing the cricket ball' competition, with a throw of over eighty-one yards. He was employed as an engineer at the Thomas and Clement Foundry, Llanelli. In May 1913 he returned to live in Alejandra, Argentina where he took up farming before moving, in 1932, to

58. 1967 v Scotland
Back row: K D Kelleher (referee), J P O'Shea, J Taylor, G T Mainwaring, B Price, S J Watkins, D J Lloyd, A H D North (WRU touch judge).
Middle row: B I Rees, T G R Davies, W G Hullin, A E I Pask (C), T G Price, K J Braddock, W H Raybould.
Front row: D I E Bebb, B John.
[*E Yerbury & Co*[

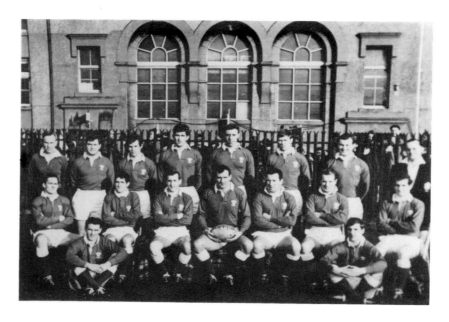

59. 1968 v Scotland
Back row: G D Francis (WRU touch judge), S J Watkins, R E Jones, W D Thomas, W D Morris, A J Gray, M L Wiltshire, G C Lamb (RFU referee).
Middle row: K S Jarrett, T G R Davies, G O Edwards (C), D J Lloyd, B John.
Front row: W K Jones, J P O'Shea, J Young, D Rees.
[*Western Mail*]

60. 1969 v Ireland
Back row: D C T Rowlands (coach), D A Bidder (WRU touch judge), S J Watkins, D Williams, B E Thomas, T M Davies, W D Morris, D J Lloyd, D C J McMahon (SRU referee).
Middle row: K S Jarrett, M C R Richards, B E V Price (C), G O Edwards, J Taylor.
Front row: J P R Williams, T G R Davies, B John, J Young.
[*Western Mail*]

Chaco in the north of Argentina, where he became a police officer.

MORGAN, Morgan Edward
Born 18 December 1913, registered in Pontardawe; died Abercrave, 16 April 1978
Career: Abercrave School; Swansea Borough Police; Swansea; Police Union; Barbarians

Forward in 4 matches, against: England, 1938, 1939; Scotland, 1938; Ireland, 1938

British Isles 1938 tour South Africa: 2 caps

Eddie Morgan served in the Swansea Borough Police Force from February 1937 until August 1967 when he took up an appointment as usher at Neath Magistrate's Court as well as farming in Abercrave. He played in fourteen games for the 1938 British Isles in South Africa and captained Swansea in 1939-40.

MORGAN, Norman Henry
Born 26 March 1935, registered in Pontypool
Career: Llanhilleth School; Llanhilleth; Newport; Barbarians

Full back in 3 games, against: Scotland, 1960; Ireland, 1960; France, 1960: Scored 4con 2pg - 14 points
Steelworker Norman Morgan, who was a left-footed kicker, holds the scoring record for Newport, with 951 points scored between 1955 and 1962.

MORGAN, Peter John
Born Broadhaven, 1 January 1959
Career: Sir Thomas Picton School; Welsh Youth; Haverfordwest; Llanelli; Sydney Welsh (Australia); Pembrokeshire; Wales B

Centre/stand-off/wing in 4 matches, against: Scotland, 1980(r); Ireland, 1980, 1981; New Zealand, 1980(r)

British Isles 1980 tour South Africa

Peter Morgan is a coal merchant. He was chosen as an utility back by the British Isles for their 1980 tour of South Africa, playing in seven games and was a member of the Llanelli side which won the 1979 Snelling Sevens. His brother Anthony also played for Llanelli.

MORGAN, Philip Edward John
Born Hereford, 21 December 1937
Career: Welsh Youth; Steel Company of Wales; Aberavon

Prop in 3 matches, against: England, 1961; Scotland, 1961; France, 1961

Phil Morgan, a steelworker, captained Aberavon in 1963-64 and is a committee member at the club.

MORGAN, Thomas
Born Llannon, 14 November 1866; died Bridgend, 22 March 1899
Career: Morfa Rangers; Llanelli

Back in 1 match, against: Ireland, 1889

Tom Morgan was employed in a colliery in Pentre.

MORGAN, William Guy
Born Garnant, 26 December 1907; died Carmarthen, 29 July 1973
Career: Christ College Brecon; Cambridge University; Guy's Hospital; Welsh Secondary Schools; Swansea; London Welsh; Barbarians

Centre in 8 matches, against: France, 1927, 1929, 1930; Ireland, 1927, 1929, 1930; Scotland, 1929: Scored 3t 1dg - 13 points

Guy Morgan, who was the nephew of E Morgan [qv] and W Ll Morgan [qv], won four Blues in 1926-29 and captained Wales on four occasions. He also made forty-five appearances for Glamorgan Cricket Club. In May 1941 he changed his name, by deed poll, to W Guy Stewart-Morgan. He was a schoolmaster at Radley for thirty-two years.

MORGAN, William Ivor
Born Haverfordwest, August 1884; died Blackpill, Mumbles, 10 December 1943
Career: Danygraig Board School; Danygraig; Swansea

Forward in 13 matches, against: Australia, 1908; England, 1909, 1910, 1911; Scotland, 1909, 1910, 1912; France, 1909, 1910, 1911; Ireland, 1909, 1910, 1911: Scored 6t - 18 points

Ivor Morgan was a coal trimmer.

MORGAN, William Llewellyn
Born Aberdare, 9 January 1884; died Sketty, 11 April 1960
Career: Christ College Brecon; Aberdare; Cardiff; London Welsh; Racing Club de Paris; Barbarians; Glamorgan; Kent

Scrum-half in 1 match, against: Scotland, 1910

Anglo-Welsh 1908 tour Australia, New Zealand: 2 caps

After some years in the Royal Navy, Morgan became the landlord of the Lamb & Flag in Aberaman and later, the steward of the Liberal club in Aberdare. He was the brother of E Morgan [qv], and the uncle of W Guy Morgan [qv]. He appeared in ten matches in New Zealand during the 1908 Anglo-Welsh tour of Australasia.

MORIARTY, Richard Daniel
Born Gorseinon, 1 May 1957
Career: Bishop Vaughan School, Morriston; Clase; Morriston; Swansea; Western Suburbs (Australia); Wales B

Lock/flanker/No 8 in 22 matches, against: Australia, 1981, [1987 World Cup]; Ireland, 1982, 1984, 1985, [1987 World Cup]; France, 1982, 1984, 1985; England, 1982, 1983, 1984, [1987 World Cup]; Scotland, 1982, 1984, 1985; Fiji, 1986; Tonga, 1986, [1987 World Cup]; Western Samoa, 1986; Canada, [1987(r) World Cup]; New Zealand, [1987 World Cup]: Scored 2t - 8 points

Dick Moriarty toured North America and Canada with Wales in 1980 having made an appearance as a replacement for the West Wales XV against the All Blacks in 1978. He has also played for a Wales XV against the Maoris in 1972 and a WRU President's XV in 1984. He captained Wales on seven occasions and Swansea from 1986-89. Employed as an electrician, he is the brother of W Paul Moriarty [qv].

MORIARTY, William Paul
Born Morriston, 16 July 1964
Career: Penlan Comprehensive School; Morriston; Swansea; Western Suburbs (Australia); Barbarians; Wales B

Flanker/No 8 in 21 matches, against: Ireland, 1986, 1987, [1987 World Cup], 1988; France, 1986, 1987, 1988; Fiji, 1986; Tonga, 1986, [1987 World Cup]; Western Samoa, 1986; England, 1987, [1987 World Cup], 1988; Scotland, 1987, 1988; Canada, [1987 World Cup]; New Zealand, [1987 World Cup], 1988; Australia [1987 World Cup]; United States, 1987: Scored 4t - 16 points

Paul Moriarty appeared for Wales in nine matches, all played overseas, with his brother, Dick Moriarty [qv]. He signed for Widnes RLFC, making his debut on 30 March 1989.

MORLEY, John Cuthbert
Born Newport, 28 July 1909; died Newport, 7 March 1972
Career: Newport Secondary School; Welsh Secondary Schools; Newport

Wing in 14 matches, against: England, 1929, 1930, 1931, 1932; Scotland, 1929, 1931, 1932; France, 1929, 1931; Ireland, 1929, 1930, 1931, 1932; South Africa, 1931: Scored 5t - 15 points

British Isles 1930 tour New Zealand: 3 caps, Australia

Dentist Jack Morley scored a try for the 1930 British Isles

in their first international against the All Blacks. In all, he appeared in thirteen games in New Zealand. He captained Newport in 1931-32 before joining Wigan RLFC, and played his first game for them on 7 September 1932. He also played for the Welsh, English, and Great Britain RL teams with great success.

MORRIS, Sir George Lockwood Bart
Born Swansea, 29 January 1859; died Henley, 23 November 1947
Career: Clifton College; Swansea

Forward in 5 matches, against: Ireland, 1882; England, 1882, 1884; Scotland, 1882, 1884

George Morris, who succeeded as eighth Baronet in 1947, on the death of a cousin, was the manager of an engineering works. He captained Swansea in the 1881-83 seasons.

MORRIS, Haydn Thomas
Born Mountain Ash, 14 July 1928
Career: Mountain Ash Grammar School; Bangor Normal College; Cardiff Training College; Mountain Ash; Beaumaris; Barry; Cardiff; Barbarians

Wing in 3 matches, against: France, 1951, 1955; Ireland, 1955: Scored 2t - 6 points

British Isles 1955 tour South Africa

Haydn Morris was a schoolmaster in Barry and Lancashire. Later he was appointed PE Adviser to the Norfolk Education Authority, and was Director of PE at the University of East Anglia. He scored nine tries in eight appearances for the British Isles in South Africa.

MORRIS, Joseph Ivor Thomas
Born Burry Port, 4 August 1901; died Paddington, 10 September 1964
Career: Bynea; Burry Port; Loughor; Ystalyfera; Swansea; Aberavon; Llanelli; Cheltenham; Glamorgan Police

Forward in 2 matches, against: England, 1924; Scotland, 1924

Glyn Morris worked as a steelworker before joining the Glamorgan Constabulary. After a disciplinary hearing in November 1928, he was ordered to resign from the force and later worked as an engineer in Cheltenham.

MORRIS, Martyn Stuart
Born Neath, 23 August 1962
Career: St Joseph's Comprehensive School, Port Talbot; Welsh Youth; South Wales Police; Neath; Barbarians;

Wales B

Flanker in 9 matches, against: Scotland, 1985; Ireland, 1985, 1990, 1991; France, 1985, 1991; Namibia, 1990, 1990; Barbarians, 1990

Martyn Morris is a police officer in the South Wales Constabulary.

MORRIS, Ronald Rhys
Born Carmarthen, 13 June 1913; died Westbury on Trym, February 1983
Career: Queen Elizabeth Grammar School; Welsh Secondary Schools; Swansea; Bristol; Saracens; London Welsh; Gloucestershire

Stand-off in 2 matches, against: Scotland, 1933, 1937

Ron Morris was a company representative before starting his own building business in Bristol. He served on the committee at Bristol RFC.

MORRIS, Stephen
Born autumn 1896, registered in Newport; died Newport, 29 May 1965
Career: Pill Harriers; Cross Keys

Forward in 19 matches, against: England, 1920, 1922, 1923, 1924, 1925; Scotland, 1920, 1922, 1923, 1924, 1925; France, 1920, 1922, 1923, 1924, 1925; Ireland, 1920, 1922, 1923; New Zealand, 1924

A former collier, Steve Morris became an education welfare officer with Monmouthshire County Council until retiring in June 1961. He captained Cross Keys in 1922-23 and was appointed chairman in 1947. He played in the William Webb Ellis Centenary match at Rugby School in 1923 and for Abertillery and Cross Keys against New South Wales in 1927 and South Africa in 1931. He was the number one choice as forward for Wales for several seasons and captained his country against Scotland in 1925. He was also a fine boxer. His ashes were scattered on Pandy Park.

MORRIS, William
Born Llanelli, 29 October 1869; died Gellideg, 4 November 1946
Career: Llanelli

Forward in 3 matches, against: Scotland, 1896; Ireland, 1896; England, 1897

Bill Morris, a plasterer, was the uncle of 'Gipsy' Daniel, the British light-heavyweight boxing champion.

MORRIS, William David
Born Rhigos, 11 November 1941
Career: Gladlys Secondary Modern School; Glynneath; Rhigos; Penarth; Neath; Ebbw Vale

No 8/flanker in 34 matches, against: France, 1967, 1968, 1969, 1970, 1971, 1972, 1974; England, 1967, 1968, 1969, 1970, 1971, 1972, 1973, 1974; Scotland, 1969, 1970, 1971, 1972, 1973, 1974; Ireland, 1968, 1969, 1970, 1971, 1973, 1974; New Zealand, 1969, 1969, 1972; Australia, 1969, 1973; South Africa, 1970: Scored 6t - 19 points

Although winning his first two caps as a No 8, Dai Morris is Wales' most capped flanker. Touring Argentina with Wales in 1968, he played in both unofficial internationals. On the seven match tour of Australasia and Fiji with Wales in 1969, he appeared in six matches, and scored a try against Australia. A welder, he still turns out for charity and 'Golden Oldies' games.

MORRIS, William George Henry
Born Abertillery, 1894; died Bournemouth, 14 July 1967
Career: Blaenau Gwent; Pill Harriers; Abertillery; London Welsh

Forward in 3 matches, against: New Zealand Army, 1919; France, 1920; Ireland, 1921

A former collier, Bill Morris became an education welfare officer. Described as 5ft 11ins, and 13st in 1919 and a speedy player, he captained Abertillery in 1919-20 and 1925-28. He also captained Abertillery and Cross Keys against New South Wales in 1927 and was also well known as a very fine billiards player and boxer.

MORRIS, William James Bunce
Born Borth, Cardiganshire, 21 May 1940
Career: Ardwyn Grammar School; Cardiff Training College; Aberystwyth; Pontypool

Wing in 2 matches, against: Scotland, 1963; Ireland, 1963

Bill Morris, a youth and community education advisor in Cardiff, is the cousin of John Morris, QC, the MP for Aberavon and former Secretary of State for Wales (1974-79).

MORRIS, William John
Born Melbourne, 16 June 1941
Career: Grove Park School, Wrexham; New Brighton; Wrexham; Newport; Barbarians

Lock in 2 matches, against: Scotland, 1965; France, 1966

Solicitor Bill Morris toured South Africa with the Barbarians in 1969 shortly before announcing his retirement from the game "because of pressure of work".

MOSELEY, Kevin
Born 2 July 1963, registered in East Glamorgan,
Career: Blackwood; Pontypool; Bay of Plenty (New
Zealand); Newport; Wales B

Lock in 5 matches, against: New Zealand, 1988; Romania,
1988; Scotland, 1989; Ireland, 1989; France, 1990

Printer Kevin Moseley, who captained Pontypool in 1989-
90, was sent off in the game against France in 1990.

MURPHY, Cornelius Denis
Born Aberfan, 3 September 1908; died Leeds, 13 July
1964
Career: Ynysddu; Cross Keys

Forward in 3 matches, against: England, 1935; Scotland,
1935; Ireland, 1935

Con Murphy worked as a collier before becoming a
licensee. He joined Acton & Willesden RLFC, making his
debut on 31 August 1935, transferred to Streatham &
Mitcham in 1936-37, before making his first appearance
for Leeds RLFC on New Year's Day 1937. He had a
successful career with the northern club until June 1947,
winning eleven Wales RL caps. He was a police reservist
during the Second World War. His son John played for
Headingley and Yorkshire as did his grandson Adam
Machell.

NASH, David
Born Markham, Monmouthshire, 15 July 1939
Career: Nantyglo Grammar School; Cardiff College of
Education; Welsh Secondary Schools; Cardiff Athletic;
Crumlin; Ebbw Vale; Barbarians; Monmouthshire

No 8/lock in 6 matches, against: South Africa, 1960;
England, 1961; Scotland, 1961; Ireland, 1961; France,
1961, 1962

British Isles 1962 tour South Africa

David Nash, who was the first forward of the Ebbw Vale
club to be capped, was appointed Wales' first national
coach in 1967. He made two appearances for the 1962
British Isles in South Africa. After a period as the head
of the PE department at Croesyceiliog Grammar School,
he was appointed the facilities manager at the National
Sports Centre Wales, Cardiff, in 1971 and is now the sports
director in Ebbw Vale.

NEWMAN, Charles Henry
Born Newport, 28 February 1857; died Lucerne, 28

September 1922
Career: Monmouth School; Cambridge University; Abergavenny; Newport; North Durham; County Durham

Back/half-back in 10 matches, against: England, 1881,
1882, 1884, 1885, 1886, 1887; Ireland, 1882; Scotland,
1883, 1884, 1885

Charlie Newman, who gained a Blue in 1882 and captained
Newport in 1882-83, was one of three clergymen in the
first Welsh XV. He was one of the founders of the Newport
RFC but gained most of his caps from the North Durham
club in Gateshead.

NICHOLAS, David Llewellyn
Born Llanelli, 3 March 1955
Career: Stradey Secondary Modern School; Welsh
Secondary Schools; Welsh Youth; Llanelli; Felinfoel;
Wales B

Wing in 4 matches, against: England, 1981; Scotland,
1981; Ireland, 1981; France, 1981

David Nicholas, who worked as an engineer for the British
Steel Corporation, coached Felinfoel RFC in 1985-86.

NICHOLAS, Trevor John
Born Sudbrook, 7 January 1894; died Minehead, 13 March
1979
Career: Cardiff; Ebbw Vale; Penarth

Wing in 1 match, against: New Zealand Army, 1919

A clerk in the National Coal Board, Nicholas served in the
38th Welsh Division during the First World War. His
Wales cap and jersey are in the Gilbert Museum, Rugby.

NICHOLL, Charles Bowen
Born Llanegwad, 19 June 1870; died 9 July 1939,
registered in Tiverton
Career: Llandovery College; Cambridge University; Black-
heath; London Welsh; Llanelli; Glasgow; Monkstown;
Barbarians

Forward in 15 matches, against: Ireland, 1891, 1892, 1893,
1895, 1896; England, 1892, 1893, 1894, 1895, 1896;
Scotland, 1892, 1893, 1894, 1895, 1896

'Boomer' Nicholl, a clergyman, won three Blues in 1890-
93, and two Athletics Blues (putting the shot) in 1892 and
1893. He played in the Barbarians team which lost a rugby
match against the Corinthians soccer team in April 1892.
He was the brother of DW Nicholl [qv].

NICHOLL, David Wilmot
Born Llanegwad, 14 June 1871; died Llanelli, 11 March

61. 1970 v Ireland
Back row: D C T Rowlands (coach), G C Lamb (RFU referee), D Williams, T G Evans, T M Davies, W D Thomas, D B Llewellyn, W D Morris, W Hitchings (WRU touch judge).
Middle row: S J Watkins, J P R Williams, B John, G O Edwards (C), J Young, S J Dawes, D Hughes.
Front row: K Hughes, W H Raybould. *[Lafayette Photography]*

62. 1972 v France
Back row: M H Titcomb (RFU referee), A Cuny (FRF touch judge), A J L Lewis, R T E Bergiers, J Young, T M Davies, D B Llewelyn, T G Evans, W D Thomas, W D Morris, R Lewis (WRU touch judge), D C T Rowlands (coach).
Front row: J P R Williams, T G R Davies, B John, D J Lloyd (C), J Taylor, G O Edwards, J C Bevan.

[Western Mail]

118

1918
Career: Llandovery College; Llanelli

Forward in 1 match, against: Ireland, 1894

David Nicholl was a bank cashier in Llanelli. He was the brother of C B Nicholl [qv] and a keen angler and golfer.

NICHOLLS, Erith Gwynne
Born Westbury on Severn, 15 July 1874; died Dinas Powys, 24 March 1939
Career: Newport; Cardiff Stars; Cardiff Harlequins; Cardiff; Barbarians; Gloucestershire

Centre in 24 matches, against: Scotland, 1896, 1899, 1900, 1901, 1902, 1906; Ireland, 1896, 1898, 1899, 1900, 1901, 1902, 1903, 1905, 1906; England, 1897, 1898, 1899, 1901, 1902, 1904, 1906; New Zealand, 1905; South Africa, 1906: Scored 3t 1dg - 13 points

British Isles 1899 tour Australia: 4 caps

Gwyn [sic] Nicholls, who captained Cardiff RFC in 1898-99, 1899-1900, 1900-01, 1903-04, had a laundry business with his brother in law Bert Winfield [qv]. He had the honour of being the first Welsh player to appear in an international for a British Isles side and was also the first person to score a try against Australia in that country's first international in 1899. He also scored a try in the second international and was the leading British try scorer, with twelve tries. He captained the Welsh side against the All Blacks in the famous 1905 match and, playing for Cardiff against the tourists on Boxing Day 1905, he scored a try. On 1 January 1907, he scored a brilliant try for the club in the 17-0 win against South Africa. Nicholls refereed the 1909 Calcutta match at Richmond, and served as a Welsh Rugby Union selector from 1925-31. On 18 August 1923, he dived, fully clothed, into the sea at Weston-Super-Mare and rescued two girls who were in difficulties. He was the vice-president of Dinas Powys RFC. He was the author of *The Modern Game of Rugby*, published in 1916. A brother to S H Nicholls [qv] he was also the father-in-law of Frank Williams [qv]. As a lasting tribute to Nicholls, the Gwyn Nicholls Memorial Gates were opened at Cardiff Arms Park on Boxing Day, 1949.

NICHOLLS, F E
Born details unknown
Career: Cardiff Harlequins

Centre in 1 match, against: Ireland, 1892

Nicholls' Wales cap and jersey are in the Bridgend RFC clubhouse.

NICHOLLS, Howard Charles Warrender
Born Maesteg, 2 June 1931
Career: Maesteg Grammar School; Hereford Cathedral School; Maesteg Celtic; Maesteg; Bridgend; Cardiff

Wing in 1 match, against: Ireland, 1958

Howard Nicholls, started his career with Lloyd's Bank and later entered the family business of wholesale butchers from which he retired in 1990. In 1969, following an x-ray on a knee that had been troubling him for many years, he discovered that the knee had been fractured and had knitted together without medical assistance, the injury having occured during the 1958 game against Ireland. At Hereford Cathedral School he played in the same XI as the future Test cricketing brothers, Peter and Dick Richardson. His son Richard played for Cross Keys in 1990-91. He is the son-in-law of A H Jones [qv].

NICHOLLS, Sydney Herbert
Born 1868, registered in Newent, Gloucestershire; died Cardiff, 24 November 1946
Career: Cardiff

Forward in 4 matches, against: New Zealand Natives, 1888; Scotland, 1889, 1891; Ireland, 1889

Syd Nicholls was a hotelier. In 1901 he was the secretary of the Hull RLFC. He also served as the chairman of the Welsh Football Association and of Cardiff City Football Club. Outside of sport, he was the chairman of the Grangetown Conservative Association. He was the older brother of E G Nicholls [qv]. His son Jack gained four consecutive soccer caps for Wales as an inside right in 1924-25 from Newport County and then Cardiff City, despite having only appeared a few times in football league games.

NORRIS, Charles Howard
Born Porth, 11 June 1934
Career: Porth Secondary School; St Luke's College, Exeter; Welsh Secondary Schools; Tylorstown; Cardiff; Barbarians

Prop in 2 matches, against: France, 1963, 1966

British Isles 1966 tour Australia, New Zealand: 3 caps

Howard Norris, a schoolmaster, made 413 appearances for Cardiff, captaining them from 1967-69, and played in all three rows of the pack. On tour in Australasia he made three appearances for the British Isles in Australia and thirteen in New Zealand.

NORSTER, Robert Leonard
Born Ebbw Vale, 23 June 1957
Career: Nantyglo Grammar School; Gwent College of

Higher Education; South Glamorgan Institute; University College Cardiff; Abertillery; Cardiff; Barbarians; Wales B

Lock in 34 matches, against: Scotland, 1982, 1983, 1984, 1985, 1987, 1988; England, 1983, 1984, 1985, 1987, [1987 World Cup], 1988, 1989; Ireland, 1983, 1984, 1985, 1987, [1987 World Cup], 1988; France, 1983, 1984, 1985, 1987, 1988, 1989; Australia, 1984; Fiji, 1985, 1986; Tonga, 1986; Western Samoa, 1986, 1988; Canada, [1987 World Cup]; United States, 1987; New Zealand, 1988: Scored 2t - 8 points

British Isles 1983 tour New Zealand: 2 caps; 1989 Australia: 1 cap

Bob Norster, who shares the record as the most capped Welsh lock with Allan Martin, made a great contribution to lineout play in the 1980s. He toured the United States and Canada with Wales in 1980 and played for Cardiff against New Zealand in October the same year. On the first British Isles tour in 1983, he played in six matches, and on the second tour made five appearances. He captained Cardiff from 1987 to 1989. He now works for Chartered Trust.

NORTON, William Barron

Born Carmarthen, 28 April 1862; died Niger, West Africa, 17 December 1898
Career: Queen Elizabeth Grammar School, Carmarthen; Carmarthen; Cardiff

Back in 6 matches, against: Ireland, 1882, 1884; England, 1882, 1884; Scotland, 1883, 1884: Scored 1t

A brewer by trade, Norton was employed, at the time of his death, by the Public Works Department, Old Calabar, Niger.

O'CONNOR, Anthony

Born 24 April 1934, registered in Neath,
Career: Duffryn Grammar School; Bristol University; Oxford University; Aberavon; Barbarians; Glamorgan

Scrum-half in 5 matches, against: South Africa, 1960; England, 1961; Scotland, 1961; France, 1962; Ireland, 1962

British Isles 1962 tour South Africa

After graduating, Oxford Blue (1958) Tony O'Connor joined ICI and later moved to the British Steel Corporation. He captained Aberavon in 1957-58 and in January 1961 played for Neath and Aberavon against South Africa. He played in nine matches for the British Isles in South Africa.

O'CONNOR, Rory

Born 14 September 1932, registered in Neath; died 7

March 1986, registered in Neath
Career: Welsh Youth; Bridgend; Aberavon

Flanker in 1 match, against: England, 1957

Steelworker Rory O'Connor, who played for Welsh Youth against France in 1951, was the first Welsh Youth player to win a senior cap. In January 1961, he played for Neath and Aberavon against South Africa and captained Aberavon in 1960-62. He was the club steward at Aberavon Green Stars RFC.

OLIVER, George

Born Pontypool, 3 April 1891; died Pontypool, 21 July 1977
Career: Talywain; Pontypool; Pill Harriers

Forward in 4 matches, against: England, 1920; Scotland, 1920; France, 1920; Ireland, 1920

During the space of a fortnight in August 1921, Pontypool RFC lost eight players to rugby league. One of these was George Oliver who had signed for Hull RLFC. He won four caps for the Wales RL team. Oliver, who worked as a collier and later a process worker with ICI, won the Northern Command heavyweight boxing title during the First World War and the Welsh amateur heavyweight boxing championship in 1920. His brother Elijah played in the Pontypool team that beat the Maoris in 1927.

O'NEIL, William

Born Cardiff, 5 June 1878; died Cardiff, 2 April 1955
Career: St Peter's R C School, Cardiff; St Peter's, Cardiff; Cardiff; Aberavon; Glamorgan

Forward in 11 matches, against: Scotland, 1904, 1905, 1908; Ireland, 1904, 1905, 1907, 1908; England, 1905, 1907, 1908; France, 1908

Billy O'Neil's family originally hailed from Cork. His parents and sister, who were emigrating to the United States, landed at Milford Haven in 1874 after the ship they were travelling in foundered in the Irish Sea. From there they made their way to Cardiff where William was born. Before playing his first game for Warrington RLFC on 17 October 1908, he had been a member of the Welsh side which won the Triple Crown in 1905 and the Grand Slam in 1908, the first country to do so. In fact he only played in one losing side, ironically, against Ireland in 1904. O'Neil was a crane driver in the Cardiff docks.

OSBORNE, William T

Born Mountain Ash, c1879
Career: Mountain Ash; Glamorgan Police

Forward in 6 matches, against: England, 1902, 1903; Scotland, 1902, 1903; Ireland, 1902, 1903: Scored 1t - 3 points

In 1902, the Scottish RU informed the WRU that they would refuse to play Wales if Will Osborne was selected claiming that he had signed professional forms. He made a full statement denying the allegation and the game went ahead with him in the Welsh side. He made his debut for Huddersfield RLFC on 5 September 1903 after moving from South Wales where he had worked as a collier and a police officer. He transferred to Hull RLFC in October 1906.

O'SHEA, John Patrick
Born Weston-Super-Mare, 2 June 1940
Career: Lewis School, Pengam; St Luke's College, Exeter; Welsh Secondary Schools; Penzance-Newlyn; Cardiff; Newbridge; Barbarians; Monmouthshire; Cornwall

Prop in 5 matches, agaainst: Scotland, 1967, 1968; Ireland, 1967, 1968; France, 1968

British Isles 1968 tour South Africa: 1 cap

'Tess' O'Shea made two tours of South Africa, the first in 1968, when he made eight appearances (and a sending off in the twelfth match, against Eastern Transvaal) and the second with the Barbarians in 1969. He captained Cardiff in 1969-70.

OULD, William John
Born Glyncorrwg, 6 May 1899; died Cardiff, 19 October 1960
Career: Treherbert; Resolven; Aberavon; Cardiff; Glamorgan Police; British Police

Forward in 2 matches, against: England, 1924; Scotland, 1924

W J Ould retired in 1952, after twenty nine years in the Glamorgan Constabulary. He appeared for Cardiff against New South Wales in December 1927 and played amateur soccer in the Welsh League and was the first captain of the British Police XV.

OWEN, Albert David
Born Gurnos Cross, 31 July 1898; died Cimla, 14 June 1964
Career: College School, Ystradgynlais; University College Cardiff; Ystalyfera; Swansea; Cinderford

Stand-off in 1 match, against: England, 1924

Schoolmaster and Civil Service International, Albert Owen served in the South Wales Borderers during the First World War. He was the brother-in-law of 'Gwenallt'- the writer Thomas Morris Jones.

OWEN, Garfield David
Born Llanharan, 20 March 1932
Career: Cowbridge Grammar School; Shoreditch College, Carnegie College; Llanharan; Newport; Cardiff Athletic; Wrexham; Maesteg; Barbarians

Full back in 6 matches, against: Ireland, 1955, 1956; France, 1955, 1956; England, 1956; Scotland, 1956: Scored 7con 4pg - 26 points

At the age of fifteen, Garfield Owen played rugby for the Welsh Army Cadets against the English Army Cadets. In 1953, he won the Welsh AAA Senior Javelin competition. On 1 November 1956, he scored two goals in his first game for Halifax RLFC. Initially a schoolmaster, he later became the director of a tool manufacturing company.

OWENS, Richard Morgan
Born Llandore, Swansea, 17 November 1876; died Swansea, 27 February 1932
Career: Hafod Rangers; Swansea

Scrum-half in 35 matches, against: Ireland, 1901, 1902, 1903, 1904, 1905, 1906, 1908, 1909, 1911; England, 1902, 1903, 1904, 1905, 1906, 1907, 1909, 1910, 1911, 1912; Scotland, 1902, 1903, 1904, 1905, 1906, 1907, 1909, 1911, 1912; New Zealand, 1905; South Africa, 1906; France, 1908, 1909, 1910, 1911; Australia, 1908: Scored 2t - 6 points

Although registered as Owens, he is always referred to as Owen. A cousin of William Joseph [qv], he was over thirty-five years old when he won his final cap against Scotland in 1912. He is described as "Diminutive Dicky" on an Ogden's cigarette card, in a 'Famous Footballers' series. The *Cambria Daily Leader* of 6 February 1906 disparagingly describes a lecture Dicky Owen had delivered on "how Wales beat New Zealand", stating that "...[his] attempt at oratory was, of course, amateurish...'. He captained Swansea in 1911-12 and was employed as a steelworker before becoming a licensee. Tragically, he took his own life in 1932.

PACKER, Harry
Born Chipping Norton, 3 September 1868; died Newport, 25 May 1946
Career: Devon County School; West Buckland School; Newport

Forward in 7 matches, against: England, 1891, 1896, 1897; Scotland, 1895, 1896; Ireland, 1895, 1896

Harry Packer, a wholesale grocer, served on the Welsh Rugby Union committee and was a selector. He served in the Sportsmen's Battalion during the First World War. He was the Manager of the 1924 British Isles tourists in South Africa and, even at the age of sixty-five in 1934, was a touch judge for the Wales - England game. Packer was the president of the South Wales and Monmouthshire AAA from 1919 to 1945. He was also the president of the Welsh Cross-Country Association for a number of years and the International president in 1921 and 1927.

PALMER, Frank Cyril MC
Born Swansea, 26 June 1896; died Swansea, 16 October 1925
Career: Swansea Grammar School; Taunton College; Swansea

Wing in 3 matches, against: England, 1922; Scotland, 1922; Ireland, 1922: Scored 1t - 3 points

Estate agent Frank Palmer, who captained Swansea in 1923-24, was decorated for gallantry while serving with the 15th Bn, the Welch Regiment, during the First World War.

PARFITT, Frederick Charles
Born Pontnewydd, 12 August 1869; died Newport, 20 March 1953
Career: Pontnewydd School; Pontnewydd; Maindee; Newport; Bath; Somerset

Half-back in 9 matches, against: England, 1893, 1894; Scotland, 1893, 1894, 1895, 1896; Ireland, 1893, 1894, 1896: Scored 1t - 3 points

Fred Parfitt, who worked as a builder, captained Newport at bowls and represented Wales at that sport from 1908-28 and was the president of the Welsh Bowling Association.

PARFITT, Stuart Ashley
Born Usk, 4 March 1966
Career: Bryntirion Comprehensive School, Bridgend; Welsh Schools; Bridgend; Swansea

Centre in 2 matches, against: Namibia, 1990(r); Barbarians, 1990

Stuart Parfitt, previously a financial consultant, is now a police officer.

PARKER, David Stewart
Born Llansamlet, 8 August 1904; died Swansea, 16 June 1965
Career: Llansamlet; Swansea

Forward in 10 matches, against: Ireland, 1924, 1925, 1929; France, 1924, 1925, 1929; New Zealand, 1924; England, 1925, 1930; Scotland, 1925: Scored 4con 1pg - 11pts

British Isles 1930 tour New Zealand: 4 caps, Australia: 1 cap

Dai Parker, who captained Swansea in 1927-28, including the game against New South Wales in October 1927, worked as a docker before becoming the licensee of the Cricketers Hotel, Swansea. On tour with the 1930 British Isles to Australasia, he played in fifteen games in New Zealand (scoring a penalty in the final international) and the one game in Australia, against the national XV. He was the brother of E T Parker [qv], and was for a number of years, a Labour member of Swansea Borough Council. His brother Alf played for Llanelli against South Africa in 1931.

PARKER, Edwin Thomas
Born Llansamlet, 29 March 1891; died Tredegar, 25 November 1967
Career: Llansamlet School; Swansea

Forward in 15 matches, against: New Zealand Army, 1919; England, 1920, 1921, 1922, 1923; Scotland, 1920, 1921, 1922, 1923; Ireland, 1920, 1921, 1922; France, 1921, 1922, 1923: Scored 2t - 6 points
Tom Parker, who captained Swansea in 1920-21 and Wales seven times, coached the St Samlet XV. An official in a tinplate factory, he moved to Tredegar in order to find work at the new steel works in Ebbw Vale where he was a pickler. He was the brother of Dai Parker [qv].

PARKER, William James
Born Swansea, winter 1873; died Penmaen, Gower, 10 November 1955
Career: Swansea

Forward in 2 matches, against: England, 1899; Scotland, 1899

Will Parker, who served on the Swansea RFC committee, worked in a fuel works. He captained Swansea in 1903-04 when the side only lost one match.

PARSONS, George
Born Newbridge, 21 April 1926
Career: Abertillery County School; Abertillery; Cardiff; Newport

Lock in 1 match, against: England, 1947

George Parsons, who had played in two Victory internationals, was chosen to play against England in 1947, but was denied the opportunity of adding to his one cap as, en route to France, it was rumoured that he had negotiated with rugby league officials. Despite his protestations he was asked to leave the Paris-bound train. In September 1947, he played for Abertillery and Cross Keys against Australia. He joined St Helens RLFC, making his debut

63. 1971 v Ireland
Back row: D B Llewelyn, T M Davies, M G Roberts, D Williams, W D Thomas, D C T Rowlands (coach).
Middle row: J P R Williams, J C Bevan, B John, S J Dawes (C), J Taylor, G O Edwards, T G R Davies.
Front row: J Young, A J L Lewis.
[*Crealey Studios*]

on 24 January 1948. He appeared in twelve games for the Wales RL team. Parsons worked in a glassworks, having previously served as both a police officer (ten months) and in the Royal Fusiliers.

PASCOE, Daniel
Born Llanharan, 7 July 1900; died Leeds, 19 May 1971
Career: Llanharan School; Llanharan; Bridgend; Neath

Forward in 2 matches, against: France, 1923; Ireland, 1923

Dan Pascoe captained Bridgend in 1923-24 and Neath in 1926-27. On 5 February 1927, nearly four years after winning his final cap, he scored four goals in his first game for Leeds RLFC. He worked as a collier before becoming a licensee.

PASK, Alun Edward Islwyn
Born Blackwood, 10 September 1937
Career: Pontllanffraith Grammar School; Loughborough College; Welsh Schools; University Athletics Union; Abertillery; Barbarians; Leicestershire; Monmouthshire
Flanker/No 8 in 26 matches, against: France, 1961, 1962, 1963, 1964, 1965, 1966; England, 1962, 1963, 1964, 1965, 1966; Scotland, 1962, 1963, 1964, 1965, 1966, 1967; Ireland, 1962, 1963, 1964, 1965, 1966, 1967; New Zealand, 1963; South Africa, 1964; Australia, 1966: Scored 2t - 6 points

British Isles 1962 tour South Africa: 3 caps; 1966 Australia: 2 caps, New Zealand: 4 caps

Alun Pask, who was originally a schoolmaster, is now employed in the production department of the BBC. In November 1960, he played for Ebbw Vale and Abertillery against South Africa and in September 1964 appeared for Abertillery and Newbridge against Fiji. He played seventeen games in South Africa (fourteen for the British Isles in 1962, and three for Wales two years later). On the 1966 British Isles tour of Australasia he appeared in six games in Australia, and sixteen in New Zealand. He also appeared in a Welsh XV against Fiji in 1964. Pask captained Wales in six games and Abertillery in 1962-63. His brother David was also a good back row forward who played for Glamorgan Wanderers.

PAYNE, Gareth Webb
Born 8 September 1935, registered in East Glamorgan
Career: Pontypridd Grammar School; Welsh Secondary Schools; Pontypridd; Newport; London Welsh; Stroud; The Army; Barbarians; Glamorgan; Gloucestershire; Hampshire

Lock in 3 matches, against: England, 1960; Scotland, 1960; Ireland, 1960

Gareth Payne trained as a civil engineer before joining the Royal Engineers. In 1960, he played for London Counties and Combined Services against South Africa and, in 1961, for South Eastern Counties against the same opposition.

PAYNE, Harry
Born Treboeth, 10 December 1907
Career: Swansea; Royal Navy

Forward in 1 match, against: New Zealand, 1935

Harry Payne, who served in the Royal Marines during the Second World War, played in two Service internationals and captained Swansea in 1937-38. His son, Jeffrey Payne, was appointed, in a "receivership capacity" to Swansea AFC in the 1980s. In March 1991 Harry played for twenty minutes in a Swansea 'past' XV in Bordeaux.

PEACOCK, Harry
Born Newport, 14 February 1909
Career: St Woolos School; Municipal Secondary School, Newport; Pontypool; Newport; Monmouthshire Police
Forward in 6 matches, against: Scotland, 1929, 1930; France, 1929, 1930; Ireland, 1929, 1930: Scored 2t - 6 points

Harry Peacock played for the Newport schoolboys at the age of ten, and the Newport 1st XV at the age of seventeen, appearing in 117 games for the club. He appeared for Newport against New South Wales in September 1927. From school he became an apprentice engineer before joining the Monmouthshire Constabulary in 1929. He was in the Army from 1943 to 1946 and, on demobilisation, held the rank of Major. He was then seconded to the Allied Military Government of Germany where he served for eleven years. Harry now lives on Jersey and leads an active life playing golf.

PEAKE, Edward
Born Tidenham, 29 March 1860; died Bluntisham, 3 January 1945
Career: Marlborough College; Oxford University; Chepstow; Newport

Back in 1 match, against: England, 1881

Edward Peake's family, which originally hailed from Denbighshire, was entitled to bear heraldic arms and the family motto was *Heb Dduw Heb Ddim* (Without God there is nothing). He played in Wales' first international and his cap from that game is in the Welsh Folk Museum at St Fagan's Castle. He won four Blues at Oxford - three in cricket from 1881-83 and an athletics Blue in the 120 yards hurdles in 1883. He captained Chepstow against Monmouth in January 1881, played cricket for Chepstow, Newport, Gloucestershire and Berkshire, and for the Free Foresters against a Cambridge XI when he was still able to score 75 runs at the age of seventy-five! In his 1st Class cricket career he was known as a right hand fast bowler and took 116 wickets for 2,551 runs - an average of 21.9 runs per wicket. Peake held a number of teaching posts before becoming the rector of Bluntisham cum Erith.

PEARCE, Peter Gareth
Born Laugharne, 11 November 1960
Career: Laugharne School; Ysgol St Clears; Welsh Secondary Schools; Welsh Youth; Laugharne; Carmarthen Athletic; Dinas Powys; Bridgend; Llanelli; Sydney Welsh (Australia); Barbarians; Wales B

Stand-off in 3 matches, against: Ireland, 1981, 1982(r); France, 1981: Scored 2dg - 6 points

In May 1980 Gary Pearce, who was nineteen years of age, travelled to North America with a Welsh party. In 1981-82 he was the leading scorer in Wales with 391 points and in 1985-86 scored 420 points for Llanelli. On 21 September 1986 he kicked three goals in his debut game for Hull RLFC. He is employed as a sales representative.

PEARSON, Thomas William CB, DSO, TD, DL
Born Bombay, 10 May 1872; died Newport, 12 September 1957
Career: Mill Hill School; Cardiff; Newport; Blackheath; Barbarians; Middlesex

Wing in 13 matches, against: England, 1891, 1892, 1895, 1897, 1898, 1903; Ireland, 1891, 1894, 1895, 1898; Scotland, 1892, 1894, 1895: Scored 4t - 12 points

Thomas Pearson scored forty tries for Cardiff during 1892-93, the season he captained the club. He was a fine athlete, representing Wales sixteen times at hockey between 1899 and 1910, captaining the side in six games, and scoring five goals in four consecutive games. He also captained the Welsh XV in the game against England in 1903. Not wishing to neglect his sporting skills in the summer months, he played lawn tennis and won the men's Welsh doubles title. He served as a Lieutenant Colonel in the Royal Field Artillery attached to the 4th Welsh Brigade, in the First World War. He was also the captain of Newport Golf Club.

PEGGE, Edward Vernon
Born Briton Ferry, 5 June 1864; died Neath, 21 March 1915
Career: King's College, London; Heidelberg University; London Welsh; Neath

Forward in 1 match, against: England, 1891

Edward Pegge, whose father kept the last private lunatic asylum in Wales, was a Doctor of Medicine and one of a number of WRU vice-presidents. In 1887, after failing to catch a train carrying his Neath colleagues to Devon for a rugby tour, he chartered a train and set off in pursuit. Pegge captained Neath from 1889-92 and was the brother-in-law of Field Marshal Sir George White VC, the defender of Ladysmith in the Boer War. He was a great hunting and fishing man and a point-to-point jockey.

PEREGO, Mark Angelo
Born Winchester, 8 February 1964
Career: Graig Comprehensive School; Welsh Schools; Welsh Youth; South Wales Police; Llanelli; Burry Port

Flanker in 1 match, against: Scotland, 1990

Formerly a police officer in the South Wales Constabulary, Mark Perego is currently a fireman. He was a member of the Dyfed Fire Brigade team which won the seven-a-side world championship at the World Police and Fire Games held in Vancouver in 1989.

PERKINS, Sydney John
Born Blaenavon, 27 February 1954
Career: Blaenavon Secondary School; Trinity College, Carmarthen; Blaenavon; Pontypol; Barbarians; Gwent; Wales B

Lock in 18 matches, against: Scotland, 1983, 1984, 1985, 1986; Ireland, 1983, 1984, 1985, 1986; France, 1983, 1984, 1985, 1986; Romania, 1984; England, 1984, 1985, 1986; Australia, 1984; Fiji, 1985

Carpenter John Perkins was a member of the Pontypool XV which won the Schweppes Cup in 1983. He is coach to the Pontypool club and has taken them to the final of the Schweppes Cup in 1991. This is quite an achievement for Perkins after he was left with a squad in disarrray following defections early in the season. In May 1983, he played for a Wales B side in Spain - which was in reality a team containing all Welsh players who had not been selected for the 1983 British Isles tour. He captained Pontypool from 1985-87.

PERRETT, Fred Leonard
Born Briton Ferry, 9 May 1891; died France, 1 December 1918
Career: Briton Ferry; Neath; Aberavon; Glamorgan

Forward in 5 matches, against: South Africa, 1912; England, 1913; Scotland, 1913; France, 1913; Ireland, 1913

Fred Perrett joined the Leeds RLFC, making his debut on 6 September 1913. Tragically, he died after the end of hostilities, of wounds sustained in the First World War while serving as a 2nd Lieutenant in the 17th Bn, Royal

Welch Fusiliers.

PERRINS, Victor Charles
Born Newport, 3 September 1944
Career: Stow Hill Selective Secondary Modern School, Newport; Newport Youth; Welsh Youth; Newport United; Newport

Hooker in 2 matches, against: South Africa, 1970; Scotland, 1970

Vic Perrins joined the Welsh party as a replacement for Jeff Young on the 1969 tour to Australasia and Fiji, playing in the final game of the tour against Fiji. Following a period as a bricklayer, he is now employed as an engineer. He is a keen coarse fisherman. Brother Brian, who was also a hooker and prop, played for Newport and gained Welsh Youth caps in 1961.

PERRY, William John
Born 22 September 1886; died Neath,16 February 1970
Career: Neath Borough Police; Neath; Glamorgan

Forward in 1 match, against: England, 1911

Bill Perry was a police officer in Neath. He captained Neath RFC in 1911-12.

PHILLIPS, Allan John
Born Kenfig Hill, 21 August 1954
Career: Kenfig Comprehensive School; Cornelly Youth; Welsh Youth; Kenfig Hill; Cardiff; Barbarians; Glamorgan; Wales B

Hooker in 15 matches, against: England, 1979, 1980, 1981, 1982; France, 1980, 1981, 1982; Scotland, 1980, 1981, 1982; Ireland, 1980, 1981, 1982; New Zealand, 1980; Australia, 1981

British Isles 1980 tour South Africa

Allan Phillips is the chief sales executive for BET Services, a construction company. In 481 appearances for Cardiff he scored 130 tries, was captain from 1985-87 and has coached the club since 1989-90. He toured South Africa with Surrey in May 1979 and with the 1980 British Isles team when he played in seven games.

PHILLIPS, Brinley
Born Merthyr, 11 October 1900; died Neath, 1980
Career: Aberavon; Taibach; Glamorgan Police

Forward in 5 matches, against: England, 1925, 1926; Scotland, 1925; France, 1925; Ireland, 1925

Phillips was a labourer before joining the Glamorgan Constabulary in June 1921. One week after resigning from the police force in January 1926, he made his debut for Huddersfield RLFC, scoring a try. He played one game for the Wales RL side.

PHILLIPS, David Horace
Born Swansea, 24 August 1928
Career: Dynevor Grammar School; Trinity College, Carmarthen; Vardre United; Swansea

Wing in 1 match, against: France, 1952

Horace Phillips is a schoolmaster.

PHILLIPS, Henry Percy OBE
Born Machen, 1869; died Newport, 26 February 1947
Career: Clytha School, Newport; Neuchatel, Switzerland; Newport

Half-back in 6 matches, against: England, 1892, 1893, 1894; Scotland, 1893, 1894; Ireland, 1893

Percy 'Sparrow' Phillips worked as a stonemasonbefore becoming a salesman for a firm of colliery proprietors and later a coal shipping agent. He was awarded the OBE for work as the honorary secretary of the Belgian Relief Commission at Newport during the First World War. He served as the Belgian vice-consul for many years.

PHILLIPS, Henry Thomas
Born Cross Keys, 22 June 1903; died Newport, 16 December 1978
Career: Cross Keys; Newport

Forward in 9 matches, against: England, 1927, 1928; Scotland, 1927, 1928; France, 1927, 1928; Ireland, 1927, 1928; New South Wales, 1927

Harry Phillips, who was the nephew of H T Day [qv], worked as a collier before becoming a police officer in the Newport Borough Force. He appeared for Newport against New South Wales in September 1927 and captained the club in 1929-30.

PHILLIPS, Kevin Huw
Born Hebron, Whitland, 15 June 1961
Career: Glandwr School; Preseli Comprehensive School; Cardigan; Neath

Hooker in 19 matches, against: France, 1987, 1990, 1991; Ireland, [1987 World Cup], 1990, 1991; Tonga, [1987 World Cup]; New Zealand, [1987 World Cup], 1988, 1989; United States, 1987; England, 1988, 1990, 1991; Scotland, 1990, 1991; Namibia, 1990, 1990; Barbarians, 1990

Kevin Phillips captained Wales on their tour to Namibia in 1990. Like his two props in the Neath front row, who are fellow internationals, he farms in Pembrokeshire. He led Neath to their first premiership title in the inaugural Heineken league in April 1991. He has been a member of the Welsh Tug-of-War team.

PHILLIPS, Louis Augustus
Born Newport, 24 February 1878; killed in action Cambrai, 14 March 1916
Career: Monmouth School; Newport

Half-back in 4 matches, against: England, 1900; Scotland, 1900, 1901; Ireland, 1900

Louis Phillips, an architect by profession, won the amateur golf championship of Wales in 1907 and 1912, and was runner-up in the Irish championship in 1913. In August of the same year he played for the Welsh golf team against the Irish team. Phillips joined the Public Schools Battalion of the Royal Fusiliers during the First World War and was a sergeant at the time of his death.

PHILLIPS, Rowland David
Born St David's, 28 July 1965
Career: St David's Comprehensive School; Welsh Schools; Neath

Flanker in 10 matches, against: United States, 1987; England, 1988; Scotland, 1988, 1989; Ireland, 1988, 1989; France, 1988; New Zealand, 1988, 1988; Western Samoa, 1988

Rowland Phillips was a police officer in the South Wales Police before leaving for Warrington RLFC in September 1990. He is the son-in-law of Brian Thomas [qv].

PHILLIPS, William David
Born Cardiff, 16 August 1855; died Cardiff, 15 October 1918
Career: Bridgend School; Cardiff

Forward in 5 matches, against: England, 1881, 1884; Ireland, 1882, 1884; Scotland, 1884

Phillips was elected to a Welsh Rugby Union vice-presidency and was a Welsh representative on the International Board from 1887-1907. He captained Cardiff in the 1879-81 and 1882-83 seasons and refereed the Ireland - Scotland game in 1889. After working as an official on the railways, he became an accountant and was a member of Cardiff Conservative Club.

PICKERING, David Francis
Born Briton Ferry, 16 December 1960

Career: Cwrt Sart Comprehensive School; Dwr-y-Felin School; Neath VI Form College; University of Wales Instititute of Science and Technology; Welsh Secondary Schools; Welsh Universities; Llanelli; Neath; Barbarians; Wales B

Flanker in 23 matches, against: England, 1983, 1984, 1985, 1986, 1986; Scotland, 1983, 1984, 1985, 1986, 1987; Ireland, 1983, 1984, 1985, 1986; France, 1983, 1984, 1985, 1986, 1987; Romania, 1983; Australia, 1984; Fiji, 1985, 1986: Scored 3t - 12 points

Dai Pickering captained Wales in eight matches, including the short tour to the South Pacific Islands in 1986. Following a serious head injury on this tour he handed over the captaincy to Dick Moriarty before leaving for home. He was appointed coach to Neath RFC for the season 1991-92 and now runs a sports outfitting business.

PLUMMER, Reginald Clifford Stanley
Born Newport, 29 December 1888; died Newport, 18 June 1953
Career: Long Ashton School, Bristol; Newport Athletic; Newport; London Welsh; Barbarians
Wing in 5 matches, against: Scotland, 1912; Ireland, 1912; France, 1912; South Africa, 1912; England, 1913: Scored 2t - 6 points

British Isles 1910 tour South Africa

Reggie Plummer played his first game for Newport in March 1906, appeared for the club against South Africa in October of the same year and captained the team in 1920-21. In 1910, he toured South Africa with the British Isles, scoring six tries in twelve appearances. He served as a corporal in the Royal Engineers in the First World War. He was a brother-in-law of T H Vile [qv].

POOK, Thomas Richard
Born Plymouth, 1869; died Newport, 21 February 1948
Career: Newport; Maindee

Forward in 1 match, against: Scotland, 1895

Tom Pook joined Holbeck RLFC, making his first appearance for them on 3 September 1898. After his rugby career was over he became attached to the Newport Cricket section. His son Reg became Mayor of Newport.

POWELL, Graham
Born Ebbw Vale, 17 November 1932
Career: Ebbw Vale Grammar School; Bristol University; English Universities; Ebbw Vale; Clevedon; Gloucestershire; Somerset

Centre in 2 matches, against: Ireland, 1957; France, 1957

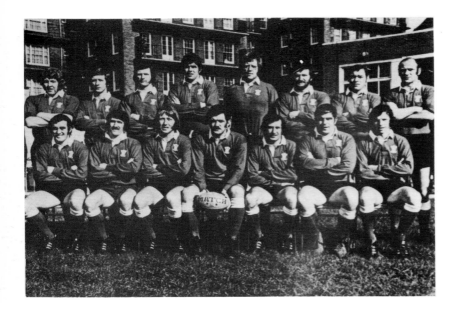

64. 1975 v Ireland

Back row: G Price, R T E Bergiers, T P Evans, A J Martin, G A Wheel, R W R Gravell, A J Faulkner, T J Cobner.

Front row: P Bennett, T G R Davies, J P R Williams, T M Davies (C), G O Edwards, R W Windsor, J J Williams.

[*Western Mail*]

65. 1976 v France

Back row: F M D Knill, S P Fenwick, G Price, T P Evans, A J Martin, A G Faulkner, T J Cobner, R W Windsor.

Front row: T G R Davies, J P R Williams, G O Edwards, T M Davies (C), P Bennett, J J Williams, R W B Gravell.

[*Western Mail*]

66. 1978 v Scotland

Back row: J D Bevan (replacement), D M D Rea (IRFU touch judge), M J Watkins, J R West (IRFU referee), G Price, J Squire, D L Quinnell, A J Martin, G A Wheel, A G Faulkner, T J Cobner, S J Richardson, A W Bevan (WRU touch judge), T P Evans (replacement).

Front row: G L Evans (replacement), R W R Gravell, T G R Davies, J P R Williams, P Bennett (C), G O Edwards, R W Windsor, J J Williams, S P Fenwick, D B Williams.

[*Auty Collection*]

128

Graham Powell was the first Ebbw Vale player to play for Wales. He appeared in a Welsh Schools soccer trial, in opposition to Phil Woosnam the future Welsh soccer international. He was Victor Ludorum in athletics at Bristol University. He captained Ebbw Vale in 1957-58, including an Abertillery and Ebbw Vale XV against Australia. He taught Physics in a secondary school for three years before going into industry, eventually retiring as a director of Total Oil. He was related to the brothers Jack and Wickham Powell [qv].

POWELL, John
Born details unknown
Career: Cardiff

Wing in 1 match, against: Ireland, 1923: Scored 1dg - 4 points

Jack Powell, like his brother W J Powell [qv], was a licensee. He was related to Graham Powell [qv].

POWELL, John A
Born Merthyr
Career: Cardiff; London Welsh; Glamorgan

Forward in 1 match, against: Ireland, 1906

Jack Powell, a Cardiff RFC committeeman, was a coal trimmer. He played for Glamorgan against New Zealand in December 1905 and for Cardiff against South Africa on 1 January 1907.

POWELL, Richard Whitcomb
Born 1864, registered in Abergavenny; died Llanwenarth Citra, 11 January 1944
Career: Abergavenny Grammar School; Abergavenny; Newport

Forward in 2 matches, against: Scotland, 1888; Ireland, 1888

Dick Powell, who was the steward at Abergavenny Asylum, was a fine cricketer and, with his brother C Powell, played for Abergavenny Cricket Club. He served on the Abergavenny RFC committee. His sister-in-law married Jack Jonathan who played hockey for Wales in 1903.

POWELL, Wickham James
Born Cardiff, 13 September 1892; died Cyncoed, 20 March 1961
Career: Cardiff

Wing in 4 matches, against: England, 1920; Scotland, 1920; France, 1920; Ireland, 1920: Scored 2t - 6 points

Wick Powell, Jack Powell's brother [qv], served with the 38th Division in France during the First World War. He captained Cardiff in 1919-20 before joining Rochdale Hornets RLFC where he played his first game on 4 September 1920. Returning to Cardiff in 1922, he became a licensee. He was related to Graham Powell [qv].

POWELL, William Charles
Born Aberbeeg, c1905; died South Africa, 1973
Career: Abertillery; London Welsh; Northampton; Wasps; The Army; Barbarians; Middlesex

Wing/scrum-half in 27 matches, against: Scotland, 1926, 1928, 1929, 1930, 1931, 1932, 1935; Ireland, 1926, 1927, 1928, 1929, 1930, 1931, 1932, 1933; France, 1926, 1927, 1928, 1929, 1930, 1931; England, 1927, 1929, 1931, 1932, 1935; South Africa, 1931: Scored 1t 2con 2dg 1gm - 18 points

'Wick' Powell toured Cornwall with Captain Crawshay's side in 1922. In 1926-27 he captained London Welsh and, in the 1931 match against England, became the last Welshman to score a goal from a mark. He had served in the Welsh Guards before qualifying as an architect in 1933. He emigrated to South Africa in 1946 where he had his own practise in Johannesburg.

PRICE, Brian
Born Bargoed, 30 October 1937
Career: Cardiff College of Education; St Luke's College, Exeter; Cross Keys; Newport; Vichy (France); Barbarians

Lock in 32 matches, against: Ireland, 1961, 1964, 1965, 1966, 1967, 1969; France, 1961, 1963, 1964, 1965, 1966, 1967, 1969; England, 1962, 1963, 1964, 1965, 1966, 1967; Scotland, 1962, 1963, 1964, 1965, 1966, 1967, 1969; New Zealand, 1963, 1969, 1969; South Africa, 1964; Australia, 1966, 1969

British Isles 1966 tour Australia: 2 caps, New Zealand: 2 caps

Brian Price, captained Newport in 1963-64 and 1968-69. Formerly a P E master at a Gwent School, he is now employed as a rugby analyst by BBC Radio Wales. He played in seventeen games for the British Isles in Australasia, five in Australia, and twelve in New Zealand. He has played on winning sides against the 'Big Three': for the Barbarians against South Africa in 1961, Newport against the All Blacks in 1963 (captain) and played against Australia twice in 1966. He is the cousin of John Uzzell [qv].

PRICE, Edwin Ronald
Born Trealaw, 16 September 1915
Career: Porth Secondary School; Merchant Venturers

Technical College, Bristol; Penygraig; Weston-super-Mare; Royal Air Force; Somerset

Forward in 2 matches, against: Scotland, 1939; Ireland, 1939

Ron Price played in four Service, and one Red Cross international games. During the Second World War he served in the Royal Air Force in South Africa where he played the best rugby of his career until a shoulder injury put an end to his days on the rugby field. Whilst there, he played alongside rugby league stalwarts like Gus Risman and Alan Edwards who were, in his opinion, magnificent players. He was employed as an electrician and unfortunately had a leg amputated in 1949.

PRICE, Graham
Born Moascar, Egypt, 24 November 1951
Career: West Monmouth Grammar School; Crewe and Alsager College; Nash College, Newport; University of Wales Institute of Science and Technology; Welsh Secondary Schools; Pontypool United; Pontypool; Barbarians; Monmouthshire; Wales B

Prop in 41 matches, against: France, 1975, 1976, 1977, 1978, 1979, 1980, 1981, 1982, 1983; England, 1975, 1976, 1977, 1978, 1979, 1980, 1981, 1982, 1983; Scotland, 1975, 1976, 1977, 1978, 1979, 1980, 1981, 1982; Ireland, 1975, 1976, 1977, 1978, 1979, 1980, 1981, 1982, 1983; Australia, 1975, 1978, 1978, 1981; New Zealand, 1978, 1980: Scored 2t - 8 points

British Isles 1977 tour New Zealand: 4 caps; 1980 South Africa: 4 caps; 1983 New Zealand: 4 caps

A member of the legendary Pontypool front row, Graham Price played in thirty-nine consecutive international games. On three British Isles tours he played in thirty-six games: fourteen in 1977, twelve in 1980, and ten in 1983. In October 1989, one month short of his thirty-eighth birthday, he played for Pontypool against the touring All Blacks. In 1970 he won the Welsh schools shot and discus titles. Graham Price worked as a laboratory technician for two years, but is now the deputy manager of the Cwmbran New Town Centre.

PRICE, Malcolm John
Born Pontypool, 8 December 1937
Career: Welsh Youth; Pontypool; Royal Air Force; Barbarians

Centre in 9 matches, against: England, 1959, 1960, 1962; Scotland, 1959, 1960; Ireland, 1959, 1960; France, 1959, 1960: Scored 2t - 6 points

British Isles 1959 tour Australia: 2 caps, New Zealand: 3 caps

Malcolm Price played in four games in Australia, and fourteen in New Zealand for the 1959 British Isles side. He scored four tries in two consecutive internationals, two tries in the second, and final, match with Australia, and two tries in the first game against New Zealand. He captained Pontypool from 1960-62 and, in November 1960, played for Pontypool and Cross Keys against South Africa. On 3 February 1962 he scored a try in his first appearance for Oldham RLFC and went on to play for the Great Britain team.

PRICE, Terence Graham
Born Hendy, 16 July 1945
Career: Llanelli Grammar School; Leicester University; Welsh Secondary Schools; New Dock Stars; Hendy; Llanelli; London Welsh; Leicestershire

Full back in 8 matches, against: England, 1965, 1966; Scotland, 1965, 1967; Ireland, 1965; France, 1965, 1967; Australia, 1966: Scored 9con 1dg 8pg - 45 points

British Isles 1966 tour(r) Australia, New Zealand

Terry Price never realised his full potential as a player of exceptional skills. A gregarious character, he seemed to possess an insouciant air on the playing field. Following a period in rugby league - he had joined the Bradford Northern club, kicking five goals in his debut match on 23 August 1967 - he flirted very briefly with American football before returning to Hendy, his home village, where he coaches the first XV. He played in three games for the British Isles in New Zealand after being called out as a replacement. He is the grandson of Dai Hiddlestone [qv].

PRIDAY, Alun James
Born Whitchurch, Cardiff, 23 January 1933
Career: Glanynant School; Whitchurch Boys School; Whitchurch Grammar School; Penarth; Aberavon; Royal Air Force; Cardiff; Rhiwbina; Barbarians; Glamorgan

Full back in 2 matches, against: Ireland, 1958, 1961

Company director Alun Priday was appointed the secretary of Cardiff RFC in 1972.

PRITCHARD, Cecil Clifford
Born Tranch, Pontypool, 1 May 1902; died Newport, 27 August 1966
Career: Blaenavon; Talywain; Cross Keys; Pontypool; Barnstaple; Monmouthshire

Hooker in 8 matches, against: England, 1928, 1928; Scotland, 1928, 1929; Ireland, 1928, 1929; France, 1928, 1929

Cecil Pritchard, a goal kicking hooker, played for Pontypool against the New South Wales visitors in 1927, his brother George 'Cogley', who played for Barnstaple, played for Devon and Cornwall against the tourists, and a third brother, Royce, appeared for Abertillery and Cross Keys against the same opposition. He captained Pontypool in 1928-29. Originally employed as a collier, he later became a council worker.

PRITCHARD, Charles Meyrick
Born Newport, 30 September 1882; died No 1 Casualty Clearing Station, France, 14 August 1916
Career: Newport Intermediate School; Long Ashton School, Bristol; Newport; Monmouthshire

Forward in 14 matches, against: Ireland, 1904, 1906, 1907; England, 1905, 1906, 1907, 1908, 1910; Scotland, 1905, 1906, 1907; New Zealand, 1905; South Africa, 1906; France, 1910: Scored 1t - 3points

Charlie Pritchard, who served as a captain in the South Wales Borderers, was killed during the Battle of the Somme in 1916. In civilian life he had been the proprietor of a shop. He captained Newport in 1906-09, having made his debut for the club against Swansea on 25 January 1902.

PRITCHARD, Clifford Charles
Born Pontypool, 1 October 1881; died Pontypool, 14 December 1954
Career: West Monmouth Grammar School; Newport; Pontypool; Race Wanderers

Centre/extra back in 5 matches, against: Scotland, 1904, 1906; Ireland, 1904; New Zealand, 1905; England, 1906: Scored 2t - 6 points

When Wales beat New Zealand in 1905, undertaker Cliff Pritchard was carried home shoulder high from the station through the streets of Pontypool. His son Harold obtained a double first at Jesus College, Oxford and was one of Britain's leading rocket scientists, working at Woomera, Australia. Another son, Fred, also had a brilliant career at Jesus College, Oxford.

PROSSER, David Rees
Born 13 October 1912, registered in Neath; died York, 6 May 1973
Career: Glynneath; Neath; Swansea; Glamorgan

Forward in 2 matches, against: Scotland, 1934; Ireland, 1934

Dai Prosser played for a combined Neath and Aberavon XV against South Africa in 1931. His brother, Glyn [qv], also played in the same two games for Wales. Prosser scored a try on his debut for York RLFC on 15 September 1934 and won eight caps for the Wales RL team. Following a move to the Leeds club he became their coach. He was employed as a blacksmith in a colliery and later kept a fish shop.

PROSSER, Frederick John
Born Newport, 15 December 1892; died Penarth 15 June 1947
Career: Cardiff; Glamorgan Police

Forward in 1 match, against: Ireland, 1921

Jack Prosser was a police officer.

PROSSER, Idris Glyn
Born Glynneath, 27 November 1907; died Glynneath, 13 November 1972
Career: Crown School, Glynneath; Glynneath; Neath

Forward in 4 matches, against: England, 1934; Scotland, 1934; Ireland, 1934; New Zealand, 1935

Glyn Prosser, Dai's brother [qv], was vice-captain of the combined Neath and Aberavon side against the 1935 All Blacks. He was a founder member of the Welsh Academicals and was the team's first captain. He was employed as a collier and was a Sunday School teacher. Glyn made his debut for Huddersfield RLFC on 4 January 1936.

PROSSER, Thomas Raymond
Born Pontypool, 2 March 1927
Career: George Street School, Pontypool; Pontypool United; Pontypool; Barbarians; Monmouthshire

Prop in 22 matches, against: Scotland, 1956, 1957, 1958, 1959, 1960; France, 1956, 1957, 1958, 1959, 1960, 1961; England, 1957, 1958, 1959, 1960; Ireland, 1957, 1958, 1959, 1960, 1961; Australia, 1958; South Africa, 1960: Scored 1t - 3 points

British Isles 1959 tour Australia, New Zealand: 1 cap.

Ray Prosser was 34 years and 23 days when he won his final cap against France, on 25 March 1961. He has always been a great advocate of forward play as demonstrated by the New Zealand teams down the years. He captained Pontypool in 1956-58 and made one appearance for the 1959 British Isles side in Australia, and eleven in New Zealand. He appeared for Pontypool and Cross Keys against New Zealand in January 1954. Prosser coached Pontypool RFC from 1970-86. He was employed as an excavator driver and is now a foreman in a steel recovery plant, the graphically named Slag Reduction Company, at the Panteg Works.

PROTHERO, Gareth John
Born Beddau, 7 December 1941

Career: Welsh Youth; Beddau; Cardiff; Bridgend

Flanker in 11 matches, against: Scotland, 1964, 1965, 1966; Ireland, 1964, 1965, 1966; France, 1964, 1965, 1966; England, 1965, 1966: Scored 1t - 3 ponts

British Isles 1966 tour Australia, New Zealand

Gary Prothero made one appearance during the Welsh four match tour of South Africa in May 1964. In 1966 he played in one match for the British Isles in Australia, and seven in New Zealand. A serious eye injury, sustained in a club match against Llanelli in October 1966, put an end to his playing days. He now works in a factory.

PUGH, Charles Henry
Born 7 March 1896, registered in Pontypridd; died Gowerton, 23 January 1951
Career: Port Talbot County School; Maesteg; Aberavon; Neath; Glamorgan Police; Glamorgan
Forward in 7 matches, against: England, 1924, 1925; Scotland, 1924, 1925; Ireland, 1924; France, 1924; New Zealand, 1924: Scored 1t - 3 points

Charlie Pugh was a police officer in the Glamorgan Constabulary.

PUGH, Jeremy David
Born Builth Wells, 4 March 1960
Career: Builth Wells High School; Swansea Youth; Builth Wells; Pontypridd; Neath; Breconshire; Wales B

Prop in 3 matches, against: United States, 1987; Scotland, 1988(r), 1990

Jeremy Pugh, who coaches the Builth Wells club, is an entrepreneur. During his free time he takes part in enduro racing - cross country motor-cycling.

PUGH, Phillip
Born Seven Sisters, 8 October 1959
Career: Llangatwg Comprehensive School; Cadoxton Comprehensive School, Neath; Seven Sisters Youth; Welsh Youth; Neath; Eastern Suburbs (Australia); Aberavon; Wales B

Flanker in 1 match, against: New Zealand, 1989

Phil Pugh, who is a colliery worker at Blaenant, toured with Wales to the South Pacific Islands in 1986.

PUGSLEY, Joseph
Born Swansea, 10 May 1885; died Cardiff, 13 June 1976
Career: St Saviour's; Grange Stars; Cardiff; London Welsh

Forward in 7 matches, against: England, 1910, 1911; Scotland, 1910, 1911; Ireland, 1910, 1911; France, 1911: Scored 2t - 6 points

Joe Pugsley worked as a docker, before becoming a boilermaker. He played for Cardiff against the Springboks on 1 January 1907. On 2 September 1911, he made his first appearance for Salford RLFC and went on to win one Wales RL cap.

PULLMAN, Joseph John
Born Cardiff, 19 June 1876; died Sully, July 1955
Career: Neath; Glamorgan Police

Forward in 1 match, against: France, 1910

Joe Pullman, who was 33 years - 6 months old when he was capped, joined the Glamorgan Constabulary in March 1908 where he became a sergeant. In 1914-15 he was the elected captain of Neath RFC.

PURDON, Frank T
Born County Westmeath, Ireland, c1857
Career: Machen; Newport; Swansea

Forward in 4 matches, against: England, 1881, 1882; Ireland, 1882; Scotland, 1883

Frank Purdon, a clerk, played six consecutive seasons for Newport as a half-back and as a forward although he played as a forward only for Wales. He lived very close to Rodney Parade and was a cricketer of some note, trialling for the South Wales Cricket Club, the forerunner of Glamorgan. He was the uncle of W P Geen [qv] and a relative of the two Purdons who were capped for Ireland.

QUINNELL, Derek Leslie
Born Llanelli, 22 May 1949
Career: Coleshill School; Welsh Youth; Llanelli; Barbarians; Wales B

No 8/flanker/lock in 23 matches, against: France, 1972(r), 1974, 1977, 1978, 1979; New Zealand, 1972, 1978, 1980; England, 1973, 1975(r), 1977, 1978, 1979; Scotland, 1973, 1974, 1977, 1978, 1979; Australia, 1973, 1978; Ireland, 1977(r), 1978, 1979: Scored 1t - 4 points

British Isles 1971 tour Australia, New Zealand: 1 cap; New Zealand 1977: 2 caps; South Africa 1980: 2 caps

Derek Quinnell played in four winning sides against the All Blacks - for the British Isles in 1971 and 1977, Llanelli in 1972, and the Barbarians in 1973. As well as a trip to the Far East in 1975 and Australia in 1978 with a Welsh team, he played for a Welsh XV against: Japan in 1973, Tonga in 1974, New Zealand in 1974, Argentina in 1976,

67. 1980 v New Zealand
Back row: M D M Rea (IRFU touch judge), D I H Burnett (IRFU touch judge), E T Butler (replacement), G Price, C Williams, G P Williams, A J Martin, J P R Williams, P Ringer, R Ackerman, I Stephens (replacement), J R West (IRFU referee).
Middle row: H E Rees, T D Holmes, W G Davies, D L Quinnell, S P Fenwick (C), J Squire, A J Phillips, D S Richards.
Front row: P G Pearce (replacement), S T Jones (replacement), G Williams (replacement), P J Morgan (replacement).
[*David Williams Photography*]

68. 1983 v England
Back row: J R West (IRFU referee), G Price, C Williams, D F Pickering, R D Moriarty, R L Norster, J Squire,
Middle row: T D Holmes, M Dacey, M A Wyatt, E T Butler (C), D S Richards, C W F Rees, M G Ring.
Front row: W J James, H E Rees.
[*Auty Collection*]

133

and Romania in 1979. He captained the Barbarians against New Zealand in December 1978 and Llanelli in 1979-80. His three overseas tours with the British Isles brought him thirty-two appearances for the visitors: nine in New Zealand in 1971, fourteen in New Zealand in 1977 and nine in South Africa in 1980. He is a national selector, and is the brother-in-law of Barry John [qv]. Formerly a sales representative, he is now a company director. His son Scott, who has played for Welsh Youth and Wales Under 19, was named the Outstanding Young Player of the Year in April 1991, at the Welsh Brewers Annual Rugby Dinner in Cardiff.

RADFORD, William John
Born Cardiff, 8 April 1888; died Newport, 2 January 1924
Career: Newport; Pill Harriers

Forward in 1 match, against: Ireland, 1923

Radford was a member of the unbeaten Newport XV in the 1922-23 season. A docker, he died in an accident in Newport docks less than a year after he had become Wales' oldest first cap, a record which he still holds.

RALPH, Albert Raymond
Born Abercarn, 21 January 1908; died Leamington Spa, 5 October 1989
Career: Pontywaun Grammar School; Caerleon Training College; Caerleon; Abercarn; Newport; London Welsh

Stand-off in 6 matches, against: France, 1931; Ireland, 1931, 1932; South Africa, 1931; England, 1932; Scotland, 1932: Scored 1t 1dg - 7 points

Dicky Ralph was a schoolmaster and later, until his retirement in 1968, the headmaster of Thorp Arch Grange School, Yorkshire. He captained Newport in 1932-33 before joining Leeds RLFC where he made his debut on 26 August 1933. In December of the same year he won his one Wales RL cap against Australia. He won a Challenge Cup Final medal with Leeds against Warrington in 1936. From August 1937 to February 1939 he appeared in forty-five games for Batley RLFC. He also played cricket for Monmouthshire. His son, Mike, an Oxford double Blue, competed in the triple jump at the 1964 Tokyo Olympics and was the AAA triple jump champion in 1966.

RAMSAY, Samuel
Born Scotland, 1873; died Rhiwbina, 14 January 1956
Career: Treorchy

Forward in 2 matches, against: England, 1896, 1904

Sam Ramsay, a colliery official, captained Treorchy during the 1896-97 season. After winning his first cap in 1896,

eight years elapsed before he won his second, against England in 1904. His brother-in-law Harry James was a half-back with Treorchy at the turn of the century.

RANDALL, Robert John
Born Neath, 1891; died Port Talbot, 7 July 1965
Career: Aberavon

Forward in 2 matches, against: Ireland, 1924; France, 1924

Bob Randall was the head annealer in the Borough Tinplate works and later worked in the Abbey Works, Port Talbot. He captained Aberavon in 1923-24.

RAPPS, John
Born Aberaman, July 1876; died Stretford, Manchester, 23 January 1950
Career: Penygraig

Forward in 1 match, against: England, 1897

Following his move to rugby league, the first Welsh international to do so after the schism, Jack Rapps became known as 'The Salford Lion'. He made his first appearance for Salford RLFC on 4 September 1897. He played for Lancashire RL, and appeared in the Cup Final in 1900, 1902, 1903, and 1906. Employed as a collier in South Wales, he became a licensee after his move to Salford. He also worked as a groundsman at the Ardwick Athletic ground, Manchester, until its closure in the 1920s.

RAYBOULD, William Henry
Born Cardiff, 6 March 1944
Career: Cathays High School, Cardiff; Cambridge University; Welsh Secondary Schools; Cathays High School Old Boys; London Welsh; Newport; Bridgend; Cardiff; Barbarians

Centre in 11 matches, against: Scotland, 1967; Ireland, 1967, 1968, 1970; France, 1967, 1968, 1970(r); England, 1967, 1970; New Zealand, 1967; South Africa, 1970: Scored 1dg - 3 points

British Isles 1968 tour South Africa

Billy Raybould gained a Blue in 1966. He played in seven games for the British Isles XV in South Africa. After teaching he became an inspector of schools and is now the director of the Welsh Language Education Development Committee. His father played soccer for Cardiff City and his brother Phil made twelve league appearances for Swansea Town and six for Newport County and was a Welsh schools and amateur international.

REES, Aaron
Born details unknown

Career: Kenfig Hill; Maesteg

Forward in 1 match, against: New Zealand Army, 1919

Collier Aaron Rees captained Maesteg from 1912-14 and 1919-20.

REES, Alan
Born Port Talbot, 17 February 1938
Career: Glanafan Grammar School; Welsh Secondary Schools; Aberavon; Maesteg; Llanelli

Stand-off in 3 matches, against: England, 1962; Scotland, 1962; France, 1962: Scored 1dg - 3 points.

Alan Rees captained Maesteg in 1961-62 before joining Leeds RLFC where he made his debut on 1 September 1962. An excellent cricketer, regarded as one of the finest cover fielders in UK cricket during the 1960s, he fitted in 216 appearances, scoring 7,681 runs, for Glamorgan CCC between 1955 and 1968. He is the cousin of Keith Barnes, who played rugby league for Australia and managed the Australian tour to Britain in 1990. He is the Sports Officer for Afan Borough Council.

REES, Arthur Morgan CBE, QPM, DL
Born Llangadog, 20 November 1912
Career: Llandovery College; Cambridge University; Welsh Secondary Schools; Royal Air Force; Metropolitan Police; London Welsh; Stoke; Wrexham; Barbarians; Sussex; Middlesex

Forward in 13 matches, against: England, 1934, 1935, 1936, 1937, 1938; Scotland, 1935, 1936, 1937, 1938; Ireland, 1935, 1936, 1937; New Zealand, 1935

Arthur Rees played for the Welsh Schools hockey XI, and won two rugby Blues in 1933 and 1934. When a schoolboy at Llandovery he was given the nickname 'Hairpin' for his thin, lithe build. During the Second World War he served as a pilot in the RAF, holding the rank of squadron leader (acting wing commander). Following service with the Metropolitan Police Force, he was appointed Chief Constable of Denbighshire in 1956 and, in 1964, Chief Constable of Stafford and Stoke-on-Trent where he remained until 1977. He has been a director of Stoke City AFC, a life member of the Midlands Sports Advisory Council and chairman of both the British and English Karate Boards. He was awarded the OBE in 1960, the CBE in 1963, the Queen's Police Medal in 1970, appointed a Deputy Lieutenant of Staffordshire in 1967 and has been made a Knight of St John. In May 1977 he was granted the Freedom of the City of London.

REES, Brian Idris
Born 28 August 1942, registered in Neath

Career: Neath Grammar School; University College, Aberystwyth; Cambridge University; Bryncoch; London Welsh

Hooker in 3 matches, against: Scotland, 1967; Ireland, 1967; France, 1967

Brian Rees is an orthopaedic consultant at the Welsh School of Medicine in Cardiff. He gained 4 Blues in 1963-66. In 1968 he toured Argentina with a Welsh XV.

REES, Clive Frederick William
Born Singapore, 6 October 1951
Career: Llanelli Grammar School; Loughborough College; Llanelli Wanderers; Llanelli; London Welsh; Reading; Barbarians; Berkshire; Wales B

Wing in 13 matches, against: Ireland, 1974, 1982, 1983; Australia, 1975, 1981; New Zealand, 1978; France, 1981, 1982, 1983; England, 1982, 1983; Scotland, 1982, 1983

British Isles 1974 tour South Africa

Clive 'Billy Whizz' Rees is the master in charge of rugby at the Haberdashers Aske's School, Elstree. Following his first cap, against Ireland, in 1974, he was selected for the British Isles tour of South Africa, (appearing in six matches) and toured the Far East with Wales in 1975. He also represented a Welsh XV against the Maoris in 1982 and travelled with a Wales B selection to Spain the following year and had the honour of captaining the London Welsh side during their centenary season in 1985-86. He was a fine 7-a-side player who, oddly, failed to touch down for Wales.

REES, Daniel
Born c1876
Career: Hafod Rovers; Swansea

Centre in 5 matches, against: England, 1900, 1903, 1905; Scotland, 1903, 1905

Dan Rees played his first game for Swansea against Devonport Albion on 23 October 1897. He later 'moved north' and made his debut for Hull Kingston Rovers RLFC on 21 October 1905.

REES, Douglas
Born Swansea, 15 January 1944
Career: Penclawdd; Swansea; Aberavon; Llanelli

Full back in 3 matches, against: Scotland, 1968; Ireland, 1968; France, 1968: Scored 3pg - 9 points.

Doug Rees is employed as a tinplate worker at British Steel.

REES, Evan B
Born Cwmavon
Career: Swansea

Centre in 1 match, against: New Zealand Army, 1919

Evan Rees joined Dewsbury RLFC, making his first appearance for the club on 13 December 1919. He was employed as a clerical assistant in a textile company.

REES, Harold Elgan
Born Clydach, 5 January 1954
Career: Clydach Secondary School; Cwmtawe Comprehensive School; Borough Road College, London; Welsh Secondary Schools; Vardre Youth; Neath; Middlesex; Wales B

Wing in 13 matches, against: Scotland, 1979, 1980, 1983; Ireland, 1979, 1980, 1983; France, 1979, 1980, 1983; England, 1979, 1980, 1983; New Zealand, 1980: Scored 6t - 24 points
British Isles 1977 tour New Zealand: 1 cap; 1980 tour(r) South Africa

Elgan Rees played three seasons for Wales, scoring two tries in each season. He made eighteen appearances for the British Isles: twelve in New Zealand, scoring eight tries, making him the fifth highest points scorer for the British team, and six games in South Africa. Rees captained Neath from 1982-83 to 1984-85, and was the chairman of Neath RFC until resigning the post in April 1991.

REES, Henry Tudor
Born Pontypridd, 9 May 1908; died Pentyrch 3 June 1978
Career: Nottage; Taff's Well; Aberdare; Porthcawl; Aberavon; Cardiff; Glamorgan Police; British Police; Glamorgan

Forward in 5 matches, against: Scotland, 1937, 1938; Ireland, 1937, 1938; England, 1938

Harry Rees, who joined the Glamorgan Constabulary in 1927, retired as a sergeant and was then employed as a police officer in a colliery.

REES, John Conway
Born Llandovery, 13 January 1870; died Westminster, 30 August 1932
Career: Llandovery College; Oxford University; Morriston; Blackheath; Richmond; Llanelli; Cardiff; London Welsh; Barbarians

Back in 3 matches, against: Scotland, 1892; England, 1893, 1894

Conway Rees gained three Blues in 1891-93 and is credited with introducing the four threequarter line to Oxford University. In 1891 he played cricket for the MCC against Glamorgan. He was the headmaster of a college in Aligarh in India from 1903-11 and later founded a school, Colvin Talugdar, in Lucknow, basing it on the English public school system, and was principal there for twenty-one years. He played cricket for Carmarthenshire in the Minor Counties Championship.

REES, John Idwal
Born Swansea, 25 July 1910
Career: Swansea High School; University College, Swansea; Cambridge University; Swansea; London Welsh; Edinburgh Wanderers; Barbarians

Centre/wing in 14 matches, against: England, 1934, 1936, 1937, 1938; Scotland, 1934, 1935, 1936, 1937, 1938; Ireland, 1934, 1936, 1937, 1938; New Zealand, 1935: Scored 1t - 3 points

Idwal Rees gained two Blues in 1931 and 1932. After graduating, he entered the teaching profession and was assistant master at Fettes College from 1933-38. From 1938 to 1971 he taught at Cowbridge Grammar School, where he became the headmaster. He was the co-author, with H F Macdonald, of the book *Rugger Practice and Tactics,* published in 1938.

REES, Joseph
Born 3 June 1893; died Swansea, 12 April 1950
Career: Amman United; Ammanford; Swansea

Full back in 12 matches, against: England, 1920, 1921, 1922, 1923, 1924; Scotland, 1920, 1921; France, 1920, 1923; Ireland, 1920, 1921, 1923: Scored 2con 1pg - 7 points

Joe Rees, a school attendance officer, was the brother of Billo Rees, the Wales and Great Britain rugby league international. He captained Swansea in 1922-23.

REES, Lewis Morgan
Born Treherbert, 17 January 1910; died Manchester, 21 December 1976
Career: Treorchy; Cardiff

Forward in 1 match, against: Ireland, 1933

Lewis Rees worked in a dyeing works before becoming a brewery drayman. On 25 August 1934 he made his debut for Oldham RLFC against Wigan.

REES, Peter
Born Penygroes, 8 February 1925
Career: Gwendraeth Grammar School; Llanelli; Tumble;

Penygroes

Wing in 2 matches, against: France, 1947; Ireland, 1947

Peter Rees, a power station manager, captained Tumble in 1952-53. He was the chairman of Llanelli from 1967-71, and became the president of the club in 1983.

REES, Peter Maxwell
Born 14 October 1937, registered in East Glamorgan
Career: Lewis School, Pengam; Sheffield University; Universities Athletic Union; Newbridge; Newport

Wing in 4 matches, against: England, 1961; Scotland, 1961; Ireland, 1961, 1964

Former civil engineer Peter Rees travelled to South Africa in May 1964 on a four match tour with Wales, but did not play in any of the games. He made 330 appearances for Newport between 1960-71 but only one appearance against a major touring team - South Africa in 1961. He is a development officer for Newport.

REES, Theophilus Aneurin
Born Llandovery, 1858; died Merthyr, 11 September 1932
Career: Llandovery College; Sherborne School; Oxford University

Forward in 1 match, against: England, 1881

Aneurin Rees, a solicitor, was the town clerk of Merthyr for thirty years. He served as a Welsh Rugby Union selector, played cricket for the MCC and the Gentlemen of South Wales and was a keen angler. He was instrumental in establishing the Tenby, Morlais Castle Club, near Dowlais, and the Cilsanws (Merthyr) Golf Clubs.

REES, Thomas Edgar
Born Pontyclun, 22 August 1904; died Oldham, 10 November 1968
Career: Pontyclun; London Welsh; The Army

Full back in 4 matches, against: Ireland, 1926; France, 1926; New South Wales, 1927; England, 1928

After a period as a collier, Tommy Rees served in the Welsh Guards. Later, he was employed by the gas board, and a sheet metal works. He joined Oldham RLFC, making his debut on 25 August 1928, and played for the English RL team against Australia in 1929. He also played baseball for Oldham Greyhounds and became a rugby league referee.

REES, Thomas James
Born Fleur de Lys, Monmouthshire, 8 May 1913; died

Fleur de Lys, 19 February 1990
Career: Fleur de Lys Council School; Bargoed; Cross Keys; Mountain Ash; Abertillery; Ebbw Vale; Newport; Pontypool

Forward in 8 matches, against: Scotland, 1935, 1936, 1937; Ireland, 1935, 1936; New Zealand, 1935; England, 1936, 1937

TJ Rees weighed 14st 12lbs when he won his first cap in 1935. Two years later he weighed 18st 10lbs when he won his final cap against Scotland. He had been a collier before joining the Monmouthshire Constabulary. He won the Monmouthshire Police heavyweight boxing championship and was a prominent member of their tug-of-war team. Selected for the British Isles tour to South Africa in 1938, he was unable to go for financial reasons.

REEVES, Frederick Charles
Born Cross Keys, 12 June 1892; died Pontywaun, 5 August 1976
Career: Cross Keys; Newbridge; Pill Harriers

Scrum-half in 3 matches, against: France, 1920; Ireland, 1920; England, 1921

Fred Reeves was a collier. He captained Cross Keys in 1924-25.

REYNOLDS, Alan David
Born Carmarthen, 24 January 1966
Career: Ysgol Gruffydd Jones, St Clears; Laugharne; Whitland Youth; Whitland; Swansea; Carmarthenshire Districts; Pembrokeshire

Flanker in 2 matches, against: Namibia, 1990, 1990(r)

Alan Reynolds was a plasterer before becoming a self-employed builder.

RICHARDS, David Stuart
Born Cwmgwrach, 23 May 1954
Career: Neath Grammar School; Cardiff College of Education; Welsh Secondary Schools; Cwmgwrach; Swansea; Barbarians; Wales B

Centre/wing in 17 matches, against: France, 1979, 1980, 1981, 1982; England, 1979, 1980, 1981, 1983; Scotland, 1980, 1981, 1983; Ireland, 1980, 1981, 1982, 1983; New Zealand, 1980; Romania, 1983(r): Scored 4t - 16 points

British Isles 1980 tour South Africa: 1 cap

David Richards, who is currently a national selector, was a sports teacher but now works for the BJ Group in Swansea. He toured Australia with Wales in 1984, and

69. 1985 v Ireland

Back row: J B Anderson (SRU reserve touch judge), J M Fleming (SRU touch judge), D J Bishop (replacement), P I Lewis, J Whitefoot, S J Perkins, R L Norster, R D Moriarty, M S Morris, I H Eidman, W G Davies, I Stephens (replacement), K V J Fitzgerald (ARU referee), J Bevan, unknown official.

Front row: B Bowen (replacement), H Davies, M H Titley, R Ackerman, M G Ring, T D Holmes (C), M A Wyatt, W J James, D F Pickering, G J Roberts (replacement), M Richards (replacement).

[*David Williams Photography*]

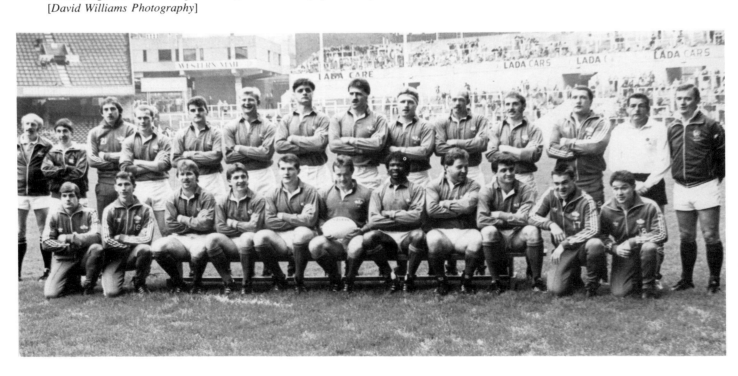

70. 1987 v United States of America

Back row: B Williams (WRU reserve touch judge), D W Matthews (touch judge), P T Davies (replacement), P H Thorburn, R D Phillips, W P Moriarty, S Russell, R L Norster, D Young, R G Collins, K H Phillips, M Pugh (replacement), C High (RFU referee), J A F Trigg (touch judge).

Front row: I J Watkins (replacement), P I Lewis (replacement), K Hopkins, R N Jones, A M Hadley, B Bowen (C), G M C Webbe, J D Pugh, M G Ring, A Clement (replacement), C Jonathan (replacement).

[*David Williams Photography*]

South Africa with the British Isles in 1980, where he played in seven games. He captained Swansea for the 1981-82 and the 1983-84 seasons.

RICHARDS, Ernest Gwyn
Born Bryncethin 22 December 1905; died Bridgend 17 December 1985
Career: Bryncethin; Bridgend; Cardiff; Torquay Athletic; Devon

Stand-off in 1 match, against: Scotland, 1927

Gwyn Richards was a collier. He played his first game for Huddersfield RLFC on 17 October 1931. He served in the Welch Regiment during the Second World War, and led the Regiment XV to victory in the Army Cup. He was the uncle of Ken Richards [*qv*].

RICHARDS, Evan Sloane
Born 1862, registered in Swansea; died Llandaff, 19 April 1931
Career: Swansea

Forward in 2 matches, against: England, 1885; Scotland, 1887

Evan Richards was a mining engineer. He captained Swansea in 1883-84 and 1886-88 and refereed both Cardiff and Newport against the New Zealand Natives in 1888. His father, E M Richards, was the Liberal Member of Parliament for Cardiganshire from 1868-74.

RICHARDS, Huw David
Born 9 October 1960, registered in Carmarthen
Career: Maesydderwen Comprehensive School; Neath; Brecon; Wales B

Lock in 4 matches, against: Tonga, 1986(r), [1987 World Cup]; England, [1987(r) World Cup]; New Zealand, [1987 World Cup]

Huw Richards formerly a storekeeper, is now a farmer. He was sent off in the game against New Zealand, in the World Cup in 1987.

RICHARDS, Idris
Born Pontypridd, c1898; died c1962
Career: Cardiff

Forward in 3 matches, against: England, 1925; Scotland, 1925; France, 1925

Idris Richards was an official with the Midland Bank. He captained Cardiff in 1923-24, and was chairman of Merthyr RFC during the 1930s.

RICHARDS, Kenneth Henry Llewellyn
Born 29 January 1934, registered in Bridgend; died Bridgend, 8 January 1972
Career: Bridgend Grammar School; Welsh Secondary Schools; Tondu; Bridgend; Cardiff; Royal Air Force; Maesteg; Glamorgan

Stand-off in 5 matches, against: South Africa, 1960; England, 1961; Scotland, 1961; Ireland, 1961; France, 1961: Scored 1t 2pg - 9 points

Schoolmaster Ken Richards, who was tragically killed in a car accident, was the nephew of E G Richards [*qv*]. On 19 August 1961 he scored a try and kicked two goals in his debut match for Salford RLFC.

RICHARDS, Maurice Charles Rees
Born Ystrad, 2 February 1945
Career: Tonypandy School; Cardiff

Wing in 9 matches, against: Ireland, 1968, 1969; France, 1968, 1969; Scotland, 1969; England, 1969; New Zealand 1969, 1969; Australia, 1969: Scored 7t - 21 points

British Isles 1968 tour South Africa: 3 caps

Maurice Richards scored four tries against England in the 1969 match. He toured South Africa with the British Isles in 1968 and played in eleven games. In the summer of 1969 he was a member of the Welsh team that toured Australasia and Fiji, playing in six of the seven games. He made his debut for Salford RLFC on 15 October 1969 and went on to gain three Wales RL and two Great Britain RL caps. In 1963, he won the junior grade Welsh long jump championship. Initially employed in the scientific section of a steel company, he is now a computer consultant.

RICHARDS, Rees
Born c.1888
Career: Cymmer; Aberavon

Forward in 3 matches, against: Scotland, 1913; France, 1913; Ireland, 1913

Collier Rees Richards captained Aberavon in 1910-11 and 1912-13. He made his first appearance in the Wigan RLFC colours on 6 September 1913. He also won one Wales RL cap.

RICHARDS, Rex Clive
Born Newport, 4 February 1934; died Miami, Florida, 6 March 1989
Career: Maindee Junior School; Stow Hill Secondary Modern School; Cross Keys; Monmouthshire

Prop in 1 match, against: France, 1956

Rex Richards worked as an aqua-diver in summer shows. He began playing rugby during his National Service in the South Wales Borderers, when he also had a successful career in athletics. Normally a second row forward in club rugby, Richards played his only international game out of position and played in seventy-nine games for Cross Keys. On moving to the United States he worked as a diver and a stuntman, and appeared in a number of films, including *The Wild Women of Wonga*, voted in a poll as one of the worst films ever made. In his final years he worked as a cruise director, arranging entertainment on ships sailing from Florida to the Bahamas.

RICHARDS, Thomas Bryan
Born Neath, 23 November 1932
Career: Neath Grammar School; Cambridge University; Neath; Swansea; London Welsh; Royal Air Force; Barbarians; Hampshire

Stand-off in 1 match, against: France, 1960

Bryan Richards, a schoolmaster at Rugby, gained his Blue in 1955. He captained Swansea in 1958-59 and London Welsh in 1963-64.

RICHARDS, Thomas Lewis
Born Maesteg, 13 October 1895; died Maesteg, 25 May 1975
Career: Maesteg; London Welsh

Forward in 1 match, against: Ireland, 1923

Tom Richards was a National Coal Board platelayer in a colliery. He captained Maesteg in 1923-24. During the Second World War he worked in an explosives factory at Waltham Abbey.

RICHARDS, William Clifford
Born Hafodyrynys, 28 March 1901; died Crumlin, 13 February 1964
Career: Crumlin; Pontypool

Wing in 5 matches, against: England, 1922; Scotland, 1922; Ireland, 1922, 1924; France, 1922: Scored 2t - 6 points

Cliff 'Ginger' Richards was employed as a steelworker before becoming a collier. He captained Pontypool in 1923-25 and scored a try for the club against the Maoris in a 6-5 win on 1 January 1927 and was the outstanding player in the Pontypool side that beat New South Wales in December of the same year. He was killed in an accident at the Navigation Colliery, Crumlin.

RICHARDSON, Stanley John
Born Blaencwm, 1 April 1947

Career: Treherbert Secondary Modern School; Tondu; Aberavon; Barbarians; Wales B

Prop in 2 matches, against: Australia, 1978(r); England, 1979

John Richardson won his first cap on the summer tour of Australia in 1978 when he came on as a replacement for Graham Price who had his jaw fractured by a punch. In May 1979, he toured South Africa with Surrey. He has coached the Wick club, near Bridgend, Bridgend RFC and is presently one of the coaches at Pyle RFC.

RICKARDS, Arnold Robert
Born 17 August 1901, registered in Thornbury, Gloucestershire; died Cardiff, 18 June 1966
Career: Cardiff; Glamorgan Police; Gloucestershire

Forward in 1 match, against: France, 1924: Scored 1t - 3 points

Arnold Rickards played in a winning Welsh XV at the Stade Colombes on the last Thursday of March 1924. He played for Gloucestershire against New Zealand on 25 September 1924. He was a police officer in the Glamorgan Constabulary.

RING, John
Born Port Talbot, 13 November 1900; died Wigan, 10 November 1984
Career: Aberavon Quins; Aberavon

Wing in 1 match, against: England, 1921: Scored 1t - 3 points

Johnny Ring scored seventy-six tries for Aberavon during the 1920-21 season. On 26 August 1922, he made his first appearance for Wigan RLFC. In 1932 he was playing for Rochdale Hornets. He won six Wales RL caps and also appeared for the England and Great Britain RL teams. A prolific rugby league try scorer, he topped the try scoring charts during four consecutive seasons, 1922-26 and broke the try scoring records of Aberavon, Wigan and Rochdale Hornets. He had worked as a shunter at the Port Talbot Steelworks and later became a groundsman, an employee of Leyland Motors and practiced as a professional masseur in Wigan.

RING, Mark Gerarde
Born Cardiff, 15 October 1962
Career: Lady Mary High School, Cardiff; Cardiff Youth; Welsh Youth; Cardiff; Pontypool; Barbarians; Wales B

Centre/full back in 28 matches, against: England, 1983, 1988, 1990, 1991; Australia, 1984, [1987 World Cup]; Scotland, 1985, 1988, 1990, 1991; Ireland, 1985, 1987,

[1987 World Cup], 1988, 1990, 1991; France, 1985, 1988, 1990, 1991; Tonga, [1987 World Cup]; United States, 1987; New Zealand, 1988, 1988, 1989; Namibia, 1990, 1990; Barbarians, 1990: Scored 1t 1con 2pg - 12 points

Mark Ring was a member of the Wales B team that went to Spain in 1983. A serious leg injury in 1985, and a subsequent operation, has restricted his international appearances. Blessed with great vision, often coupled with outrageous displays of individuality, he is guaranteed to entertain. He plays baseball for Grange Albion and Wales. He has been employed in the Civil Service and worked with disabled youngsters in Cardiff. He has set up his own business, Ringdale Industrial Roofing.

RINGER, Paul
Born Leeds, 28 January 1948
Career: Cardigan Grammar School; Madeley College; Polytechnic of Wales; Cardigan; Leicester; Ebbw Vale; Vichy (France); Llanelli; Wales B

Flanker in 8 matches, against: New Zealand, 1978, 1980; Scotland, 1979; Ireland, 1979; France, 1979, 1980; England, 1979, 1980: Scored 2t - 8 points

Paul Ringer played for a Welsh XV against Romania in 1979. He was sent off for an alleged late tackle in the 1980 England - Wales match. He made his debut for the Cardiff City RLFC on 30 August 1981 and won two Wales RL caps. He is employed in the property business. His brother Tim was on the coaching staff at the University College of Wales, Aberystwyth.

ROBERTS, Cyril Richard
Born Neath, 19 December 1930
Career: Bryncoch; Neath

Wing in 2 matches, against: Ireland, 1958; France, 1958: Scored 1t - 3 points

Cyril Roberts, whose father John gained a Welsh schoolboys cap in 1910, worked for the Metal Box Company.

ROBERTS, David Edward Arfon
Born Llanelli, 23 January 1909
Career: Llandovery College; Oxford University; Welsh Secondary Schools; London Welsh; Waterloo; Langholm; Llanelli

Scrum-half in 1 match, against: England, 1930

Roberts taught at Felsted School before being appointed a schools inspector. He served as a captain in the Royal Artillery during the Second World War.

ROBERTS, Edward John
Born Llanelli, c.1867; died Llanelli, 14 June 1940
Career: Morfa Rangers; Llanelli

Full back in 3 matches, against: Scotland, 1888; Ireland, 1888, 1889

Ned Roberts worked as a millman in a tinplate works. He helped coach Hendy RFC. Three of his sons played for Llanelli.

ROBERTS, Evan
Born Llanelli, 19 September 1861; died Llanelli, 16 October 1927
Career: Llanelli
Forward in 2 matches, against: England, 1886; Ireland, 1887

Evan Roberts was employed in a tinplate works. He was the Hon Treasurer to Llanelli RFC.

ROBERTS, Gareth John
Born Pontlliw, 15 January 1959
Career: Gowerton Comprehensive School; University of Wales Institute of Science and Technology; Welsh Secondary Schools; Universities Athletics Union; Pontarddulais; Swansea; Cardiff; Llanelli; Barbarians; Wales B

Flanker in 7 matches, against: France, 1985(r); England, 1985, [1987 World Cup]; Ireland, [1987 World Cup]; Tonga, [1987 World Cup]; Canada, [1987 World Cup]; Australia, [1987 World Cup]: Scored 2t - 8 points

Pharmacist Gareth Roberts appeared in twenty-one games for the Welsh Schools, at various age levels. He was a member of the Wales B team to Spain in 1983. A series of injuries deprived him of further international appearances.

ROBERTS, Hugh Meirion
Born Abergwyngregin, Caernarfonshire, 11 September 1934
Career: Cardiff High School; Cardiff High School Old Boys; Welsh Secondary Schools; Cardiff; London Welsh; Barbarians

Centre in 8 matches, against: South Africa, 1960; England, 1961; Scotland, 1961, 1962; Ireland, 1961, 1963; France, 1961, 1962

Meirion Roberts, a sales representative, captained Cardiff 1964-65.

ROBERTS, John
Born Toxteth, 4 April 1906; died Hawick, 31 October 1965

Career: Cardiff High School; Cambridge University; Welsh Secondary Schools; London Welsh; Cardiff; Barbarians

Centre/wing in 13 matches, against: England, 1927, 1928, 1929; Scotland, 1927, 1928, 1929; France, 1927, 1928, 1929; Ireland, 1927, 1928, 1929; New South Wales, 1927: Scored 5t - 15 points

John Roberts was ordained into the ministry of the Presbyterian Church. He gained two Blues in 1927-28. In the latter match his brother, William [qv], appeared on the Oxford side. In 1932, he travelled to Amoy in China to do missionary work and in 1937 he was appointed minister at Otterburn, Northumberland, transferring to Southdean, near Hawick, in 1951. He was a keen supporter of Jedforest RFC, giving his services on many occasions as a coach. A former moderator of the Hawick Presbytery, he was also the industrial chaplain to the knitwear firm of Lyle & Scott. A keen golfer, there were few courses in the south of Scotland he had not played on. He was also an enthusiastic huntsman and was often seen at the meets of the Jedburgh pack. During the Second World War he served as a lieutenant in the Home Guard in the Otterburn area as well as serving in the Royal Observer Corps.

ROBERTS, Michael Gordon
Born St Asaph, 20 February 1946
Career: Colwyn Bay County School; Ruthin School; Trinity College, Dublin; Oxford University; Colwyn Bay; Liverpool; Birkenhead Park; London Welsh; Barbarians; London Counties; Surrey; Wales B

Lock in 8 matches, against: England, 1971, 1979; Scotland, 1971, 1975; Ireland, 1971, 1973; France, 1971, 1973: Scored 1t - 4 points

British Isles 1971 tour Australia, New Zealand

Mike Roberts, the director of a sports travel company, gained a Blue in 1968. He appeared for the London Counties against Fiji in 1970 and played in eleven games for the 1971 British Isles team, one in Australia, and ten in New Zealand. He captained London Welsh in 1975-76 and in 1979 played in a North Wales XV against Romania.

ROBERTS, Thomas
Born Risca, 1897; died Feniton, Devon, 28 September 1972
Career: Danygraig School, Risca; Risca; Newport

Forward in 9 matches, against: Scotland, 1921, 1922, 1923; France, 1921, 1922; Ireland, 1921, 1922; England, 1922, 1923

Tom Roberts worked as a collier before joining the Newport Borough Police Force. He is the only player to be capped directly from the Risca club, which he captained

in 1921-22. He played in the William Webb Ellis Centenary match at Rugby in 1923. His brother Dai was said by some to have been an even better player. His wife, Irene (neé Morris) played hockey for Wales. His rugby collection was stolen after his death.

ROBERTS, William
Born Toxteth, 20 February 1909
Career: Cardiff High School; Oxford University; Royal University of Rome; Welsh Secondary Schools; Cardiff; London Welsh

Stand-off in 1 match, against: England, 1929

Bill Roberts read Classics and Law at Oxford where he gained four Blues between 1928-31, captaining the university XV in the 1931 game. He also served as the secretary of the Oxford University RUFC in 1931. In 1934 he married Betty, the daughter of John Elliot [qv]. He served as an acting captain in the Welsh Guards in the Second World War. Roberts was a free lance journalist and a breeder of prize Welsh sows. He was the brother of John Roberts [qv].

ROBINS, John Denning
Born Cardiff, 17 May 1926
Career: Birkenhead Park; Bradford; Coventry; Sale; London Welsh; Cardiff; Leicester; Royal Navy; Barbarians; Cheshire; Yorkshire

Prop in 11 matches, against: England, 1950, 1951, 1953; Scotland, 1950, 1951; Ireland, 1950, 1951, 1953; France, 1950, 1951, 1953

British Isles 1950 tour New Zealand: 3 caps, Australia: 2 caps

John Robins was a games master. He was the assistant manager and coach to the 1966 British Lions, and coached Loughborough College, Sheffield University, and Cardiff University rugby XVs. He played in two Services internationals for England against Wales and Scotland in 1945, and appeared in an England trial in 1948. He had the added ability of being a reliable place kicker and during the British Isles tour of Australasia in 1950, he scored nine conversions and six penalty goals in sixteen appearances.

ROBINS, Russell John
Born Pontypridd, 21 February 1932
Career: Pontypridd Grammar School; Welsh Secondary Schools; Pontypridd; The Army; Barbarians; Yorkshire

No 8/lock/flanker in 13 matches, against: Scotland, 1953, 1954, 1955, 1957; France, 1954, 1955, 1956, 1957; England, 1955, 1956, 1957; Ireland, 1955, 1957: Scored 1t - 3 points

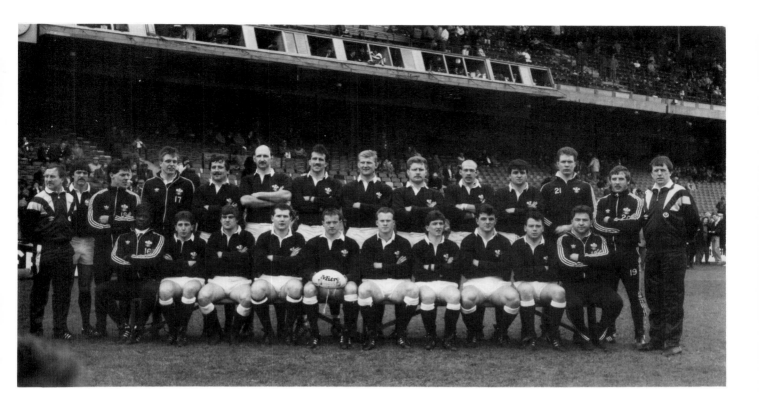

71. 1988 v Ireland
Back row: Unknown (SRU touch judge), R J Megson (SRU referee), J L Griffiths (replacement), M R Hall (replacement), D A Buchanan, P S May, R L Norster, W P Moriarty, D Young, R G Collins, R D Phillips, M A Jones (replacement), K H Phillips (replacement), unknown (SRU touch judge).
Front row: G M C Webbe (replacement), J Davies, I J Watkins, A M Hadley, B Bowen (C), P H Thorburn, R N Jones, M G Ring, I C Evans, J D Pugh (replacement).
[*Lafayette Photography*]

72. 1990 v Ireland
Back row: B R Williams, G O Llewelyn, M A Jones, A G Allen, M S Morris, A E Jones, R G Collins, H Williams-Jones.
Front row: S P Ford, D W Evans, R N Jones (C), M G Ring, P H Thorburn, K H Phillips, A G Bateman.
[*Lafayette Photography*]

British Isles 1955 tour South Africa: 4 caps

Russell Robins worked for the National Coal Board before becoming a lecturer in the Army. A backrow forward of great versatility and stamina, he appeared in seventeen games for the British Isles on the hard grounds of South Africa, playing in more games than anyone else. On 14 February 1959 he scored a try on his debut for Leeds RLFC.

ROBINSON, Ian Robert
Born Cardiff, 21 February 1944
Career: Rumney Junior School; Caer Castell High School; Cardiff; Barbarians; Wales B

Lock in 2 matches, against: France, 1974; England, 1974

Ian Robinson is the sales manager for an industrial clothing company in Cardiff.

RODERICK, William Buckley VD
Born Llanelli, 17 January 1862; died Llanelli, 1 February 1908
Career: Bath School; Sidney College, Llanelli; Llanelli

Forward in 1 match, against: Ireland, 1884

Buckley Roderick was admitted a solicitor in July 1885. He served as the Coroner for Kidwelly, the Registrar and High Bailiff of Llanelli County Court, and vice-consul for Spain. He was a Lieutenant Colonel in the 1st Volunteer Battalion, Welch Regiment and was awarded the Volunteer Decoration for his services; Past Master of the Prince of Wales Lodge of Freemasons; a member of the Council of the English Jersey Cattle Society - he bred Jersey cattle for eighteen years. In 1881, he received a gold medal for winning the five mile Amateur Cycling Championship of South Wales in Cardiff and represented Wales in that sport.

ROSSER, Melvin Aaron
Born Machen, 18 April 1901; died York, 8 September 1988
Career: Machen; Cardiff; Penarth; Glamorgan Police; Glamorgan

Centre/full back in 2 matches, against: Scotland, 1924; France, 1924

Mel Rosser was a police officer in the Glamorgan Constabulary. Following his move to Leeds RLFC he became a licensee. He made his debut for the club on 6 September 1924 and went on to gain two Wales RL caps and toured Australia in 1928 with the Great Britain RL team.

ROWLAND, Ernest Melville
Born 21 September 1864, registered in Neath

Career: Chardstock College; Llandovery College; St David's College, Lampeter; London Welsh

Forward in 1 match, against: England, 1885

Ernest Rowland, whilst a student reading for a career in the Church, was sent down for a term by the authorities of St David's College who deemed that he had abused certain privileges.

ROWLANDS, Charles Foster
Born 1899, registered in Merthyr; died Morriston, 10 November 1958
Career: Cowbridge Grammar School; Treforest School of Mines; Welsh Schools; Cymmer; Swansea; Aberavon

Wing in 1 match, against: Ireland, 1926

Charles Rowlands was employed as a surveyor with HM Office of Works.

ROWLANDS, Daniel Clive Thomas OBE
Born Upper Cwmtwrch, 14 May 1938
Career: Ystradgynlais Grammar School; Cardiff College of Education; Welsh Secondary Schools; Cwmllynfell Youth; Cwmtwrch; Abercrave; Pontypool; Llanelli; Swansea

Scrum-half in 14 matches, against: England, 1963, 1964, 1965; Scotland, 1963, 1964, 1965; Ireland, 1963, 1964, 1965; France, 1963, 1964, 1965; New Zealand, 1963; South Africa, 1964

Clive Rowlands, who was a schoolmaster, is the proprietor of a sports shop in Ystalafera and is also employed selling grandstands for the Gwent company Brohome. After captaining Wales in every game he played, he has been involved in the game as coach and selector. He captained Pontypool in 1962-63, Swansea in 1967-68 and was the National Coach to the Wales team from 1968-1974. He was the manager of the Welsh team to Australia in 1978, the British Isles to Australia in 1989 and will manage the Welsh team to Australia in the summer of 1991. He was also the manager of the British Isles team against the Rest of the World XV in 1986 and managed Wales in the 1987 World Cup. He was the president of the Welsh Rugby Union in 1989 and is currently the president of Welsh Districts and Brecon County. When awarded the OBE for services to rugby, he is reported to have exclaimed "Oh, bloody 'ell" The father-in-law of Robert Jones [qv], he edited (with David Farmer) Giants of Post-War Welsh Rugby, which was published in 1990.

ROWLANDS, Gwyn
Born Berkhamsted, 19 December 1928
Career: Berkhamsted School; London Hospital; London Welsh; Civil Service; Royal Air Force; Cardiff

Wing in 4 matches, against: New Zealand, 1953; England, 1954; France, 1954; 1956: Scored 1t 2con 2pg - 13 points

Gwyn Rowlands is a Doctor of Medicine in Berkhamsted and is the medical adviser to a London pharmaceutical company. He had two trials for England during the 1948-49 season and was the vice-captain of Cardiff in 1955-56. His daughter Jane has played lacrosse for Wales.

ROWLANDS, Keith Alun
Born Brithdir, 7 February 1936
Career: Cowbridge Grammar School; Aberdare Grammar School; London University; Welsh Secondary Schools; Aberaman; Llanelli; Cardiff; London Welsh; Barbarians

Lock in 5 matches, against: France, 1962, 1965; Ireland, 1962, 1963, 1965

British Isles 1962 tour South Africa: 3 caps

Keith Rowlands, after serving as a commercial representative for several years, was appointed the secretary of the International Board in 1988. He has been a Welsh selector and is the president of Aberaman and Rhiwbina RFCs. In 1962 he played in seventeen games for the British Isles team in South Africa, scoring a try in the final international. He captained Cardiff in 1965-67, including the game against Australia in November 1966.

ROWLES, George Albert
Born Pontypool, 1866; died Cadoxton, 12 September 1922
Career: Penarth

Half-back in 1 match, against: England, 1892

George Rowles, a boiler maker and carpenter, captained Penarth in 1885-86. Following the withdrawal of the James brothers from the game against England, the Welsh Committee met hurriedly and selected Percy Phillips of Newport and George Rowles to fill the gap.

RUSSELL, Stuart
Born Kenya, 29 May 1963
Career: Burford School; South Bank Polytechnic; London Welsh; Barbarians; Wales B

Lock in 1 match, against: United States, 1987

Stuart Russell played in an England Under 19 Group final trial. His brother Mark plays for Harlequins.

SAMUEL, David
Born Swansea, 1869; died Killay, 15 September 1943
Career: Morriston; Swansea

Forward in 2 matches, against: Ireland, 1891, 1893: Scored 1t - 1 point

David Samuel worked in a tinplate works at the Cwmbwrla works, subsequently at Cwmfelin and finally, until his retirement, as an assorter at the King's Dock in Swansea. In the 1891 international against Ireland, he appeared alongside his brother John [qv] scoring a try on his debut. Another brother, Jacob, also played for Swansea. David was a deacon at the Mount Calvary Baptist Chapel in Manselton and, in addition to his rugby prowess, played cricket for Swansea and was a keen quoits player.

SAMUEL, John
Born Swansea, 1868; died Manselton, 23 December 1947
Career: Swansea

Forward in 1 match, against: Ireland, 1891

John Samuel, the brother of David Samuel [qv], was a life deacon at the Manselton Congregational Church. He was a great pigeon fancier.

SAMUEL, Thomas Frederick
Born Llanelli, 8 January 1897; died c1941
Career: New Dock Stars; Llanelli; Mountain Ash

Full back in 3 matches, against: Scotland, 1922; Ireland, 1922; France, 1922: Scored 2con - 4 points

Fred Samuel was employed as a pipe fitter in a colliery. He signed professional forms for the Hull RLFC, and made his debut on 11 October 1922. In the following summer he played in the rugby league Cup Final against Leeds at Wakefield and later emigrated to Australia for a brief period. He was last seen in Coventry during the Blitz of 1941.

SCOURFIELD, Thomas Brinley
Born 1909, registered in Pontypridd; died Canada, February 1976
Career: London Welsh; Torquay Athletic; Devon

Full back in 1 match, against: France, 1930

Tommy Scourfield joined Huddersfield RLFC and made his first appearance against Bradford Northern on 26 November 1932. In 1933, he won a Cup Final winners medal against Warrington, played at Wembley, in front of a crowd of 41,874 - at the time a record attendance for this fixture. He won one Wales RL cap, in April 1935. He worked as a builder's labourer but, after his move North, became a groundsman.

SCRINE, Frederick George
Born Swansea, 25 March 1877; died Parkmill, Swansea, 8

June 1962
Career: Swansea; Coventry; Cumberland; Gloucestershire;

Forward in 3 matches, against: England, 1899; Scotland, 1899; Ireland, 1901

Fred Scrine scored the only try of the game for Swansea against the 1905 All Blacks. In 1907, he received a temporary suspension by the Welsh Rugby Union for using 'improper language to a referee'. Originally a plasterer, he later became a licensee.

SHANKLIN, James Llewellyn
Born East Williamston, Tenby, 11 December 1948
Greenhill Grammar School, Tenby; Welsh Secondary Schools; Tenby; London Welsh; London Counties; Middlesex

Wing/centre in 4 matches, against: France, 1970, 1973; New Zealand, 1972; Ireland, 1973: Scored 1t - 4 points

Jim Shanklin, who was employed by Guinness as a trainee brewer, now owns a sports goods business in Acton, London. He played for London Welsh from 1968-80, captaining the side in 1976-77.

SHAW, Glyndwr
Born Rhigos, 11 April 1951
Career: Cwmddulais Secondary School; Welsh Youth; Neath

Prop in 12 matches, against: New Zealand, 1972; England, 1973, 1974; Scotland, 1973, 1974; Ireland, 1973, 1974, 1977; France, 1973, 1974, 1977

National Coal Board employee Glyn Shaw captained Neath in 1977-78. On 13 November 1977, he made his debut for Widnes RLFC against New Hunslet. He made one appearance for the Great Britain team and seven for the Wales RL side.

SHAW, Terence Windsor
Born Ystrad Mynach, 9 August 1962
Career: Blackwood; Welsh Youth; Newbridge; Cardiff; South Canterbury (New Zealand); Barbarians; Wales B

Lock in 1 match, against: Romania, 1983

In October 1983, following a tour to Spain in the summer with Wales B, Terry Shaw played for a Wales XV against Japan.

SHEA, Jeremiah
Born Newport, August 1892; died Caerleon, 30 June 1947
Career: Pill Harriers; Newport

Centre in 4 matches, against: New Zealand Army, 1919; England, 1920, 1921; Scotland, 1920: Scored 1t 1con 2dg 2pg - 19 points

Playing in his second game, against England, in 1920, Jerry Shea scored a 'full-set' - a try, a conversion, two dropped goals, and a penalty goal. On Christmas Eve 1921, he scored a try in his debut game for Wigan RLFC where he remained for three seasons - two as captain - and went on to gain two caps for the Wales RL side. He never lived in the 'North' and always travelled to matches. He helped to form Pontypridd RLFC (only lasted for two years). Only 5ft 6ins tall and weighing under 10st 7lbs, he was a well known and very successful welter weight boxer, noted for his remarkable hitting powers. In February 1920, at Mountain Ash, he lost in a fight with Ted Kid Lewis, the former world welterweight champion, in a non-title bout. Among his successful fights were defeats of Frank Moody, Gypsy Daniels and Johnny Basham (over fifteen rounds at Stow Hill Pavilion, Newport, on 17 November 1924) Shea's last contest. He was also a professional runner, winning three open professional handicaps at 440 yards and several other competitions up to 1,000 yards. Also a noted swimmer, he gave up sport at the age of thirty-three.

SHELL, Robert Clive
Born Pyle, 9 September 1947
Career: Pyle; Aberavon; Barbarians

Scrum-half in 1 match, against: Australia, 1973(r)

Clive Shell won his only cap as an injury-time replacement for Gareth Edwards. In 1973, he also appeared for the Wales XV against Japan. A schoolmaster, he captained Aberavon from 1976-77 to 1978-79. He coaches Pyle RFC.

SIMPSON, Henry Joseph
Born Sedgefield, Durham, 1856; died Penarth 22 March 1911
Career: Cardiff

Forward in 3 matches, against: England, 1884; Scotland, 1884; Ireland, 1884

Joe Simpson, came to live in Cardiff in 1870 when his father was appointed Assistant Manager of the *Western Mail* where he was also employed, for a short time, as an apprentice before the family moved to England, returning to Wales a few years later. He was Wales' fourth captain (against Ireland in 1884), the first non-Oxbridge educated player to be so honoured. In this game Ireland arrived at Cardiff two players short and consequently had to borrow from the locality. They were given the services of C Jordan (the brother of H M Jordan [*qv*]), and Harry McDaniel, both from the Newport club. Simpson captained Cardiff from 1883-85 and is reputed to have worn spectacles whilst playing! He served as an auditor for the Welsh Rugby

Union and was employed in the offices of Tellefsen, Willis & Co, coal exporters of Cardiff and was subsequently appointed chartering clerk to Hacquoil Brothers, a firm in which he eventually became a partner. Simpson was declared a bankrupt in November 1905 and, according to the *Evening Express* of 15 January 1906,"on or about the 21st November 1905, with intent to defeat or delay his creditors, despatched from his dwelling-house, or otherwise absented himself". In a later newspaper report, in November 1906, it was revealed that Simpson had fled, for a brief time, to Saskatchewan and then Winnipeg in Canada. The press recorded that, after recovering from a serious illness, he returned to Britain, with the intention of associating "... himself with a business altogether apart from the coal trade; and his only solicitude is that he may be able ultimately to pay all his creditors in full - this is his great ambition". He started his own business, Simpson, Holdaway & Co with which he was involved until his death in 1911.

SKRIMSHIRE, Reginald Truscott
Born 30 January 1878, registered in Crickhowell; died Worthing, 20 September 1963
Career: Monmouth School; Newport; Blackheath; Villagers (South Africa); Western Province (South Africa); Barbarians; Kent

Centre in 3 matches, against: England, 1899; Scotland, 1899; Ireland, 1899

British Isles 1903 tour South Africa: 3 caps

Civil engineer Reg Skrimshire was the son of Charles Skrimshire who had a medical practice in Blaenavon. He was the only Welshman on the 1903 British Isles tour to South Africa and was the top points and try scorer with 59 points. As well as appearing in all twenty-two games he scored a try in the first international. It was often written that he was too fast for his wings, who consequently regarded him as a selfish player.

SKYM, Archibald
Born Drefach, 12 July 1906; died Cardiff, 15 June 1970
Career: Drefach; Tumble; Llanelli; Cardiff; Carmarthenshire Police; Glamorgan Police; British Police; Barbarians

Forward in 20 matches, against: England, 1928, 1930, 1931, 1932, 1933, 1935; Scotland, 1928, 1930, 1931, 1932, 1933; Ireland, 1928, 1930, 1931, 1932, 1933; France, 1928, 1930, 1931; South Africa, 1931: Scored 2t - 6 points

Archie Skym, a former collier, joined the Carmarthenshire Police in 1927 and, in 1929, transferred to the Glamorgan Constabulary. He captained Cardiff in 1934-35 and in January 1935, one week before the game against Scotland, a broken ankle put an end to his international career. He was the Glamorgan Police bowls singles champion in

1947, 1948 and 1950 and represented the county in the same sport.

SMITH, J Sidney
Born c1858
Career: Cardiff

Forward in 3 matches, against: England, 1884, 1885; Ireland, 1884

Smith, articled to a clerk in Cardiff, was secretary of Cardiff RFC in 1883-84.

SPARKS, Brian Anthonie
Born Llanharan, 23 June 1931
Career: Cowbridge Grammar School; St Luke's College, Exeter; Neath; Pontypool; Bridgend; Royal Air Force; Glamorgan Police; Barbarians; Glamorgan; Devon

Flanker in 7 matches, against: Ireland, 1954, 1956; England, 1955, 1956; France, 1955; Scotland, 1956, 1957

Brian Sparks, a police officer before becoming a schoolmaster, played for Neath and Aberavon against New Zealand in January 1954. He captained the winning St Luke's team in the final of the Middlesex Sevens in 1957. On 28 December 1957, he appeared in his first game for Halifax RLFC, celebrating the occasion with a try. He was founder-chairman of the Welsh Schools Basketball Association in 1963. In 1978 he was the Headmaster of Tynyrheol Primary School, Llangeinor.

SPILLER, William
Born St Fagans, 8 July 1886; died Cardiff, 9 June 1970
Cardiff: Lansdowne School, Cardiff; Barry; Cardiff

Centre in 10 matches, against: Scotland, 1910, 1911; Ireland, 1910, 1911; England, 1911, 1912, 1913; France, 1911, 1912; South Africa, 1912: Scored 4t 1dg - 16 points

Police officer Billy Spiller retired from the Glamorgan Police Force with the rank of inspector. He scored the only try of the match for Cardiff against South Africa in December 1912 and captained Cardiff in the same season. He has the distinction of being the first Glamorgan cricketer to score a century in the County Championship, a milestone which was achieved against Northamptonshire in June 1921. Spiller also played bowls for Glamorgan.

SQUIRE, Jeffrey
Born Pontywaun, Monmouthshire, 23 September 1951
Career: Newbridge Grammar School; St Luke's College, Exeter; Cross Keys; Newport; Pontypool; Barbarians; Monmouthshire; Devon; Wales B

73. 1990 v Namibia
The eight players that received their first cap during this tour were:
O L Williams, D A Williams, A D Reynolds, S A Parfitt, G D Llewellyn, P Knight, P Arnold, C J Bridges.
[*Western Mail*]

74. 1991 v Ireland
Back row: J M Fleming (SRU touch judge), A J Carter (replacement), B R Williams (replacement), M Griffiths, J D Davies, E W Lewis, G D Llewelyn, P Arnold, M S Morris, P T Davies, N R Jenkins, K Waters (replacement), D J Bishop (NZRFU referee), J B Anderson (SRU touch judge).
Front row: R N Jones (replacement), D W Evans (replacement), S P Ford, I S Gibbs, I C Evans, P H Thorburn (C), M G Ring, C J Bridges, K H Phillips, A Clement (replacement).
[*David Williams Photography*]

148

No 8/flanker in 29 matches, against: Ireland, 1977, 1978, 1979, 1980, 1981, 1982, 1983; France, 1977, 1978, 1979, 1980, 1981, 1982, 1983; England, 1978, 1979, 1980, 1981, 1982, 1983; Scotland, 1978, 1979, 1980, 1981, 1983; Australia, 1978, 1981; New Zealand, 1978, 1980: Scored 2t - 8 points

British Isles 1977 tour(r) New Zealand: 1 cap; 1980 South Africa: 4 caps; 1983 New Zealand: 1 cap

Following an early teaching career, and a period as manager of a building society, Jeff Squire is now a director of a sportswear company. He captained Pontypool from 1979-82. Both his tries for Wales were scored in a space of four games in the 1983 season, the first was against England, and the second, against Ireland, in his final game. He made three tours with the British Isles, and one with Wales, in Australia, in 1978. He played in twenty games in New Zealand, fourteen on the 1977 tour, and six on the 1983 trip; while in South Africa in 1980 he played in eleven games, and captained the tourists in one game, against the Junior Springboks. He also played for a Welsh XV against Argentina in 1976, Romania in 1979, and the Maoris in 1982. He has served as a Welsh selector and is a useful opening bowler for Cross Keys Cricket Club.

STADDAN, William James
Born Cardiff, 1861; died Dewsbury, 30 December 1906
Career: Cardiff; Dewsbury

Half-back in 8 matches, against: Ireland, 1884, 1887; England, 1886, 1890; Scotland, 1886, 1888, 1890; New Zealand Natives 1888: Scored 1t 1dg - 1 point

'Buller' Stadden - his name is usually written with this spelling - opened his international career in 1884 with a drop goal (the first scored by a Welshman) against Ireland, and closed it with a try at Dewsbury in 1890 enabling Wales to claim their first victory over England. Both the second and third drop goals kicked by Welshmen were also scored against Ireland, in 1887 and 1891. Stadden, who took his own life, was a butcher and later a grocer and licensee in Dewsbury.

STEPHENS, Glyn
Born Neath, 29 November 1891; died Neath, 22 April 1965
Career: Cadoxton Church School; Welsh Schools; Neath

Forward in 10 matches, against: England, 1912, 1913; Scotland, 1912, 1913; Ireland, 1912,1913; France, 1912, 1913; South Africa, 1912; New Zealand Army, 1919

Glyn Stephens was a mining engineer. In April 1919 he captained Wales against the New Zealand Army in the first post War international - over six years after he had won his previous cap, against Ireland in 1913. His son, J Rees Stephens [qv], captained Wales in 1954, 1955 and 1957. They are the first, and only, father and son to captain the Welsh team. Stephens was a representative on the International Board in 1954-55 and served as president of the Welsh Rugby Union in 1956-57. He was the chairman of Port Talbot County Magistrates Bench, a director of several companies and a member of the Governing Body of the Church in Wales. He was the brother-in-law of Eric Evans, secretary of the WRU from 1948-55.

STEPHENS, Ian
Born Tongwynlais, 22 May 1952
Career: Whitchurch Comprehensive School; Taff's Well; Bridgend; Barbarians; Wales B

Prop in 13 matches, against: England, 1981, 1982, 1984; Scotland, 1981, 1982; Ireland, 1981, 1982, 1984; France, 1981, 1982, 1984; Australia, 1981, 1984

British Isles 1980 tour(r) South Africa; 1983 New Zealand: 1 cap

In May 1980, 'Ikey' Stephens was in Canada on a five match tour of North America with Wales B, ostensibly a Welsh team containing a number of full internationals. Having played in one game in the United States, and one in Vancouver, he was requested to leave the tour party to join the British Isles side in South Africa to replace the injured English prop, Phil Blakeway. He was called on to play in five games. A back injury during the 1983 British Isles tour restricted his appearances to four in New Zealand. He captained Bridgend in 1985-86. Stephens, who is a cabinet maker, is a member of the Bridgend coaching team.

STEPHENS, John Griffith
Born Llanbadarn Fawr, 30 October 1893; died Barton-le-Willlows, Yorkshire, 14 May 1956
Career: Aberystwyth County School; St David's College School, Lampeter; St David's College, Lampeter; Llanelli; London Welsh; Royal Air Force

Forward in 4 matches, against: England, 1922; Scotland, 1922; Ireland, 1922; France, 1922

John Stephens, who served in the Royal Flying Corps in the First World War, was ordained into the Church as a deacon in 1919 and priest one year later. He was a curate in Llanelli from 1919-22, chaplain to the Royal Air Force from 1922-28, curate in New Brighton in 1928-29, vicar in Darlington from 1929-54, and was, on his death, vicar of Bossall with Buttercrambe, near York. In an interview with 'Argus' of the *Llanelli Star*, he claimed that he and not William Cummins, scored the try against France in 1922. He played several matches at full back for the Royal Air Force.

STEPHENS, John Rees
Born Neath, 16 April 1922
Career: Llandovery College; Welsh Schools; Neath; Barbarians

No 8/lock in 32 matches, against: England, 1947, 1952, 1953, 1954, 1955, 1957; Scotland, 1947, 1949, 1952, 1953, 1955, 1956, 1957; France, 1947, 1949, 1951, 1952, 1953, 1955, 1956, 1957; Ireland, 1947, 1948, 1949, 1952, 1953, 1954, 1955, 1956, 1957; South Africa, 1951; New Zealand, 1953: Scored 2t 1con - 8 points
British Isles 1950 tour New Zealand, Australia: 2 caps

Rees Stephens, who is the son of Glyn Stephens [qv], captained Wales in six games, five of which were wins, and appeared in four Victory internationals. He was the first Welshman to score a try for Wales in the first post-Second World War game, against England, in January 1947 and captained Neath and Aberavon against Australia in October of the same year. In 1950 he played in thirteen games for the British Isles, eight in New Zealand, and five in Australia. He played in the Barbarians matches against the South Africans in 1952 and against New Zealand in 1954. On 23 January 1954, he made his second appearance for Neath and Aberavon when the combined side played against New Zealand. He captained Neath from 1951-54. For a number of years he served as a selector for the Welsh Rugby Union. He was praised for his heroic efforts during the disastrous floods at Neath in July 1955, when he mustered a party of YMCA youth to open a mobile canteen at night time. Rees Stephens gave up farming to manage a café in Neath.

STOCK, Albert
Born Newport, 21 April 1897; died Newport, 4 May 1969
Career: Pill Harriers; Newport

Centre in 4 matches, against: France, 1924; New Zealand, 1924; England, 1926; Scotland, 1926

Stock started playing rugby in Egypt during the First World War. In September 1927, he appeared for Newport against New South Wales. A butcher by trade, he was chairman of the Newport and District Junior Rugby Union, and chairman of Newport Athletic Club Old Players Association.

STONE, Peter
Born Loughor, 20 June 1924; died Bideford, 10 July 1971
Career: Gowerton Grammar School; University College Aberystwyth; Loughor; Llanelli; Swansea

Flanker in 1 match, against: France, 1949

Peter Stone was capped while a student at Aberystwyth. He taught in Swansea before moving to Devon to teach at Bideford and Barnstaple. During the Second World War

he served in the Royal Navy. He captained Loughor in 1953-54.

SUMMERS, Richard Henry Bowlas
Born Haverfordwest, 30 July 1860; died Haverfordwest, 22 December 1941
Career: Cowbridge Grammar School; Cheltenham College; Haverfordwest

Back in 1 match, against: England, 1881
Richard Summers served in the Army. Shortly after winning his only cap in Wales' first international, he left for India where he remained for a number of years before returning to Wales. He recorded an interview of early rugby memories for the BBC.

SUTTON, Stephen
Born Abertillery, 17 February 1958
Career: Nantyglo Comprehensive School; Talywain; Pontypool; South Wales Police; Welsh Police; British Police; Monmouthshire; Barbarians; Wales B

Lock in 9 matches, against: France, 1982, 1987; England, 1982, 1987; Scotland, 1987; Ireland, 1987; Canada, [1987 World Cup]; New Zealand, [1987(r) World Cup]; Australia, [1987 World Cup]

Steve Sutton, who worked for a motor components company before becoming a police officer in the South Wales Police, did not take up playing rugby until he began working. In 1978, he played for Monmouthshire against New Zealand and in October and November 1981 for Wales B and Pontypool against Australia. He captained the South Wales Police in 1984-85, and now assists with coaching the side. He toured New Zealand with the British Police in 1988.

TAMPLIN, William Ewart
Born Risca, 10 May 1917; died Pontypool, 20 October 1989
Career: Abergavenny; Pontypool; Newport; Cardiff; Barbarians

Lock in 7 matches, against: Scotland, 1947, 1948; France, 1947, 1948; Ireland, 1947; Australia, 1947; England, 1948: Scored 3con 6pg - 24 points

Bill Tamplin captained Wales against Australia in December 1947. He scored 883 points for Cardiff and captained the club in 1950-51. He kicked two penalty goals for Cardiff against the Springboks in October 1951. A police officer, who later became a solicitor's clerk, he played in five Services internationals, and one Victory international. Tamplin was a cousin of Bleddyn Williams [qv].

TANNER, Haydn
Born Gowerton, 9 January 1917
Career: Gowerton Grammar School; University College Swansea; Welsh Secondary Schools; Swansea; Cardiff; London Welsh; Bristol; Penclawdd; Barbarians

Scrum-half in 25 matches, against: New Zealand, 1935; England, 1936, 1937, 1938, 1939, 1947, 1948, 1949; Scotland, 1936, 1937, 1938, 1939, 1947, 1948, 1949; Ireland, 1936, 1937, 1938, 1939, 1947, 1948, 1949; France, 1947, 1948, 1949

British Isles 1938 tour South Africa: 1 cap

Haydn Tanner's international career spanned fourteen seasons, beginning in December 1935, against New Zealand, a little over two weeks before his nineteenth birthday. Tanner tasted victory for a second time against the tourists, as he and his cousin, W T H Davies [qv], who partnered him at half back, had figured in Swansea's win by 11 points to 3 points in September 1935. He captained Wales on twelve occasions, and also captained the Barbarians against Australia in 1948, in the first ever meeting between the club and an overseas side. In 1938, Tanner toured South Africa with the British Isles, playing in ten games. During the Second World War he served in the Royal Corps of Signals and appeared in eight Service and four Victory internationals. He captained Cardiff from 1947-49. Having commenced his working life as a schoolmaster at Bristol Grammar School, Tanner worked as an industrial chemist and eventually became the purchasing director of Reed Paper and Board (UK). He retired in November 1980. He has also dabbled in journalism.

TARR, Donald James
Born Llandeilo Fawr, 11 March 1910; died Fareham, 4 June 1980
Career: Ammanford County School; Welsh Secondary Schools; Ammanford; Swansea; Cardiff; United Services Portsmouth; Royal Navy; Barbarians; Hampshire

Forward in 1 match, against: New Zealand, 1935

Don Tarr broke his neck in the game against the All Blacks in 1935, having played against them for Swansea three weeks previously. He had served in the Royal Navy before taking up a career as a teacher.

TAYLOR, Albert Russell
Born Risca, 2 December 1914; died Abergavenny, 9 October 1965
Career: Pontywaun Grammar School; Cross Keys; Welsh Police; Abergavenny; Barbarians; Monmouthshire

Forward in 3 matches, against: Ireland, 1937, 1938; England, 1939: Scored 1t - 3 points

British Isles 1938 tour South Africa: 2 caps

Russell Taylor was the top scorer, with a tally of 53 points in twelve games, for the 1938 British Isles team in South Africa, the only Cross Keys player to make a British Isles tour. Serving on the Abergavenny RFC committee, he was secretary in 1945, and vice-president a year later. He was a sergeant in the Monmouthshire Constabulary.

TAYLOR, Charles Gerald
Born Ruabon, 1863; killed in action Dogger Bank, 24 January 1915
Career: Royal Naval Engineering College, Portsmouth; Royal Naval College, Greenwich; Ruabon; Blackheath; London Welsh; United Services

Back in 9 matches, against: England, 1884, 1885, 1886, 1887; Scotland, 1884, 1885, 1886; Ireland, 1884, 1887

At the time of his death, on board *HMS Tiger* at the Battle of the Dogger Bank (during which action the German Battle Cruiser *SMS Blücher* was sunk), Taylor was Engineer-Captain of the 1st Battle Cruiser Squadron. An athlete of some note, he was the Welsh pole vault champion.

TAYLOR, John
Born Watford, 21 July 1945
Career: Watford Grammar School; Loughborough College; Old Fullerians; London Welsh; London Counties; Surrey

Flanker in 26 matches, against: Scotland, 1967, 1969, 1971, 1972, 1973; Ireland, 1967, 1968, 1969, 1971, 1973; France, 1967, 1968, 1969, 1970, 1971, 1972, 1973; England, 1967, 1969, 1971, 1972, 1973; New Zealand, 1967, 1969, 1972; Australia, 1969: Scored 4t 3con 2pg - 25 points

British Isles 1968 tour South Africa; 1971 Australia, New Zealand: 4 caps

John Taylor complemented Dai Morris and Mervyn Davies in the Welsh back row in eighteen matches. Though small in stature for a modern break away forward, he was a player of great talent and agile in mind. His speed around the field, in support and in defence, ensured a plentiful supply of good ball for his team mates. In 1968 he played in five games for the British Isles in South Africa, and in fifteen games in Australasia in 1971. He captained a Welsh XV against Japan in 1973, and captained London Welsh in 1972-74 and in 1977-78. He was a schoolmaster before becoming a sports journalist for the *Mail on Sunday* newspaper and a commentator for Harlech Television and Eurosport. He is the author of *Decade of the Dragon: a Celebration of Welsh Rugby 1969-79*, published in 1980. He has been appointed a member of the Independent Television team of commentators for the forthcoming 1991 World Cup.

THOMAS, Alan Robert Francis
Born Beckenham, Kent, 16 April 1940
Career: Alexander School, Beckenham; Pontlottyn School; Bargoed Technical School; Tredegar; Pontypool; Newport; Neath; Ebbw Vale; Cross Keys

Flanker in 2 matches, against: New Zealand, 1963; England, 1964

Alan Thomas, formerly employed as a mining engineer, now owns the BEWA Electronics factory. He made 212 appearances for Newport.

THOMAS, Alun Gruffydd
Born Cwmavon, 3 February 1926; died Swansea, 8 May 1991
Career: Port Talbot County School; University College Aberystwyth; Welsh Secondary Schools; Llanelli Wanderers; Llangennech; Swansea; Cardiff; Llanelli; Barbarians

Centre/wing/stand-off in 13 matches, against: England, 1952, 1954; Scotland, 1952, 1953, 1955; Ireland, 1952, 1953, 1954, 1955; France, 1952, 1953, 1954, 1955: Scored 1t 1dg - 6 points

British Isles 1955 tour South Africa

Alun Thomas had been employed as a sales manager and an oil company representative, and was latterly an appeals officer for the National Trust. During his time as a national selector, from 1963-68, he was the assistant manager to the Wales team on the 1964 tour to South Africa and in 1974, returned to the same country as the manager of the British Isles party. His first visit to South Africa in 1955 was as a player with the British Isles tourists when he appeared at full back on five occasions. He was the brother-in-law of Len Blythe and the uncle of Roger Blyth [qv].

THOMAS, Beriah Melbourne Gwynne
Born Nantymoel, 11 June 1896; died Pontypridd, 23 June 1966
Career: Bridgend County School; University College Cardiff; St Bartholomew's Hospital; London University; Ogmore Vale; Bridgend; London Welsh; Cardiff; Barbarians

Wing in 6 matches, against: New Zealand Army, 1919; Scotland, 1921; France, 1921, 1923; Ireland, 1921; England, 1924: Scored 2t - 6 points

Melbourne Thomas, who hailed from Nantymoel, was a Doctor of Medicine. During the First World War, he served as a surgeon sub-lieutenant in the Royal Navy.

THOMAS, Brian
Born 18 May 1940, registered in Neath

Career: Neath Grammar School; Cambridge University; Welsh Secondary Schools; Neath

Lock/prop in 21 matches, against: England, 1963, 1964, 1965, 1966, 1969; Scotland, 1963, 1964, 1966, 1969; Ireland, 1963, 1964, 1966, 1969; France, 1963, 1964, 1969; New Zealand, 1963, 1967, 1969, 1969; South Africa, 1964: Scored 1t - 3 points

Brian Thomas, who won three Blues in 1960-62, played for Cambridge University in November 1960 and Neath and Aberavon in January 1961 against South Africa. He went on two tours with Wales. In the first, in 1964 to South Africa, he played in all four games. During the second, the 1969 visit to Australasia and Fiji, his four appearances were all in New Zealand, where he played at lock in three games, and once as prop in the second international. He captained Neath from 1966-68. He was the team manager at Neath in the 1980s and in April 1991 returned to the club in the same role on a salary of £36,000. He is the father-in-law of Rowland Phillips [qv].

THOMAS, Charles James
Born Newport, 1864; died Usk, 8 March 1948
Career: Newport; Barbarians

Half-back/wing/centre in 9 matches, against: Ireland, 1888, 1889, 1890, 1891; New Zealand Natives, 1888; Scotland, 1889, 1890; England, 1890, 1891

Charlie 'Moose' Thomas was one of the people who introduced rugby to Resolven in the Neath Valley. He also played at forward for Newport. He worked as a boiler-maker until 1922 whereupon, despite being a teetotaller, he took over the New Court Hotel, and later the Greyhound public house in Usk. In 1938, he and O J Evans [qv] posed for a fiftieth anniversary photograph of their partnership, wearing Welsh jerseys and caps. He died on the sixtieth anniversary of his debut for Wales.

THOMAS, Cyril Rhys
Born Bridgend, 27 March 1902; died Newport, 5 December 1977
Career: Blaengarw; Kenfig Hill; Maesteg; Bridgend; Pontycymmer; Glamorgan Police; British Police; Glamorgan

Wing in 2 matches, against: England, 1925; Scotland, 1925: Scored 1t - 3 points

Cyril Thomas, the son of the editor of the *Glamorgan Gazette*, was a police officer in the Glamorgan Constabulary. During the 1924-25 season, when he captained the club, he scored fifty-eight tries for Bridgend. His son, Gwyn, played for Guy's Hospital, Bridgend, London Counties and Kent.

THOMAS, David John
Born Dunvant, 15 March 1879; died 19 October 1925, registered in Llanelli
Career: Pontarddulais; Gowerton; Dunvant; Swansea

Forward in 10 matches, against: England, 1904, 1910, 1911, 1912; Australia, 1908; Scotland, 1910, 1911; Ireland, 1910, 1911; France, 1911

David Thomas scored the try for Swansea which defeated South Africa 3-0 on Boxing Day 1912. Employed as a collier, he captained Swansea during the 1913-14 season.

THOMAS, David John
Born Swansea, 30 March 1909
Career: Swansea; Glamorgan Police

Forward in 11 matches, against: Scotland, 1930, 1932, 1933, 1935; Ireland, 1930, 1932, 1935; England, 1932, 1933, 1934, 1935

On retiring from the Glamorgan Constabulary, Dai Thomas became a security officer. He captained Swansea during the 1934-35 season.

THOMAS, David Leyshon
Born Neath, March 1909; died Neath, 28 May 1952
Career: Briton Ferry; Bridgend; Neath

Forward in 1 match, against: England, 1937

Thomas, who was employed at BP Llandarcy, was the brother of H W Thomas [qv].

THOMAS, David Lynn
Born Pontrhydyfen, 29 April 1941
Career: Dyffryn Grammar School; Port Talbot; Bridgend Technical College; Welsh Secondary Schools; Aberavon; Maesteg;

Centre in 1 match, against: Ireland, 1961

Dave Thomas, a civil engineer, played at scrum-half for Welsh Secondary Schools and represented Glamorgan at schoolboy level in the 200 yards hurdles. He played for Neath and Aberavon against South Africa in January 1961 and for a Welsh XV against Fiji in 1964.

THOMAS, Edward John
Born 14 October 1883; killed in action Mametz Wood, France, 7 July 1916
Career: Ferndale Board School; Ferndale; Penygraig; Mountain Ash; Bridgend; Glamorgan Police; Glamorgan

Forward in 4 matches, against: South Africa, 1906; France, 1908; Ireland, 1908; Scotland, 1909

Dick Thomas joined the Glamorgan Constabulary on 4 November 1904. In December 1905 he played for Glamorgan against New Zealand and in October and December of the following year he appeared for Glamorgan and Monmouthshire respectively, against South Africa. On 16 August 1913, he was promoted to acting sergeant. He won the Glamorgan Police heavyweight boxing championship and the Glamorgan and Monmouthshire Assault at Arms competition. Enlisting in the Welch Regiment in January 1915, he was promoted to the rank of Company Sergeant Major and was killed in action with the 16th Battalion in the first suicidal attack of the 38th (Welsh) Division against the prepared German positions at Mametz Wood during the Battle of the Somme.

THOMAS, Edwin
See MAYNARD, Edwin Thomas

THOMAS, George
Born 1857; died Newport, 14 June 1934
Career: Newport

Back in 3 matches, against: New Zealand Natives, 1888; Ireland, 1890; Scotland, 1891: Scored 1t

George Thomas, one of eight new caps, scored a try on his debut against the New Zealand Natives. He was a sprinter of note, competing on the professional circuit and, after retiring from the track, became a trainer in athletics. He was a regular attender at sporting funerals.

THOMAS, Harold
Born details unknown
Career: Swansea; Morriston; Llanelli

Full back in 1 match, against: France, 1912: Scored 1con - 2 points

Harold 'Drummer' Thomas served with the Welch Regiment. He joined Llanelli from the Morriston club for the 1909-10 season and later moved to Haverfordwest.

THOMAS, Harold Watkin
Born Neath, 19 February 1914; died 10 December 1989
Career: Neath Schoolboys; Briton Ferry; Neath; Cimla; Glamorgan

Forward in 6 matches, against: England, 1936, 1937; Scotland, 1936, 1937; Ireland, 1936, 1937

Metal worker Harold Thomas played for Neath and Aberavon against the All Blacks in 1935 and captained Neath in 1936-37. He made his debut for the Salford RFLC on 9 October 1937, played in two games for the Wales RL side and received a winners medal from Don Bradman after the 1938 rugby league Cup Final, when he played for

Salford against Barrow. During the Second World War he served as a regimental sergeant major in the maritime branch of the Royal Artillery and saw action in the Atlantic, Russian and Indian waters and the ship on which he was serving was sunk by a Japanese submarine. Before the end of the war he played in two Services internationals. Harold Thomas was the brother of D L Thomas [qv] and the son of Tom Thomas of Neath's 'Terrible Eight'.

THOMAS, Horace Wyndham
Born Cardiff, 28 July 1890; killed in action Guillemont, France, 3 September 1916
Career: Bridgend County School; Monmouth School; Cambridge University; Swansea; London Welsh; Barbarians

Stand-off in 2 matches, against: South Africa, 1912; England, 1913

Thomas, whose father was a clegyman in Bettws, Bridgend, was a choral scholar at Cambridge where he collected a Blue in 1912. Prior to the First World War, he spent some time in India where he was in business and from 1906-1909 had served as a private in the Calcutta Harbour Defence Force. He was killed in action at Guillemont, during the Battle of the Somme, whilst serving as a temporary 2nd Lieutenant in the 11th Bn, the Rifle Brigade.

THOMAS, Ivor
Born Pontyrhyl, Bridgend, 30 April 1900
Career: Pontycymmer; Bryncethin; Bridgend; Cardiff; Torquay Athletic; Devon

Forward in 1 match, against: England, 1924

Ivor Thomas originally a collier, later worked for a building company. Now aged 91, he is the oldest surviving Welsh cap and lives in Torquay.

THOMAS, James Denzil
Born Llandyfriog, 21 April 1929
Career: Llandeilo Grammar School; Ystalyfera Grammar School; Bangor Normal College; Cardiff College of Education; Cwmgors; Brynamman; Skewen; Neath; Llanelli; Bath; Tenby

Centre in 1 match, against: Ireland, 1954: Scored 1dg - 3 points

Schoolmaster Denzil Thomas taught in Bridgend and Greenhill Grammar School, Tenby.

THOMAS, Lewis Cobden
Born Merthyr Tydfil, 6 August 1865; died Neath, 14 April 1928

Career: Merthyr College; Wesleyan College, Taunton; Llandovery College; University College Aberystwyth; University College Cardiff; Neath; Cardiff

Forward in 2 matches, against: England, 1885; Scotland, 1885

L C Thomas, a solicitor, who founded a legal firm which still bears his name, was elected onto Neath Town Council in 1897 and became the Mayor of the town in November 1901. A powerful swimmer, he was presented with the Certificate of the Royal Humane Society for saving a man from drowning in the Blue Pool, Pontsarn, Merthyr. His Wales cap and jersey are in the Neath RFC clubhouse.

THOMAS, Malcolm Campbell
Born Machen, 25 April 1929
Career: Bassaleg Grammar School; Welsh Secondary Schools; Newport; Devonport Services; London Welsh; Barbarians; Cornwall

Centre/wing/stand-off in 27 matches, against: France, 1949, 1950, 1951, 1952, 1956, 1958, 1959; England, 1950, 1951, 1952, 1953, 1956, 1957, 1958; Scotland, 1950, 1951, 1952, 1956, 1957, 1958; Ireland, 1950, 1951, 1952, 1956, 1958, 1959; South Africa, 1951: Scored 4t 2con 2pg - 22 points

British Isles 1950 tour New Zealand: 2 caps, Australia: 1 cap; 1959 Australia, New Zealand: 1 cap

Malcolm Thomas, who was an instructor lieutenant in the Royal Navy at the time of his selection, was the youngest member of the British Isles touring party to Australasia in 1959 (Lewis Jones, who was younger than Thomas by nearly two years, did not join the touring side until the thirteenth match). His skills with the boot had not been tested by Wales as he was one of a number of kickers in the team. With 96 points in fifteen games - 69 points from kicks (73 points scored in twelve games in New Zealand, and 23 points in three games in Australia) - Thomas was the leading points scorer. Nine years later Malcolm Thomas returned to Australasia with the British Isles team. when he appeared in seventeen games, scoring 56 points in the fifteen games he played in New Zealand. Having been passed over by the selectors for the British Isles tour of South Africa in 1955, Thomas had some compensation by touring that country in 1958 with a Barbarians party. After leaving the Navy he entered the teaching profession and later became the managing director of a paper company. He is also a part-time rugby journalist.

THOMAS, Rees
Born Caldicot, 1882; died Pontypool, 15 June 1926
Career: Pontnewydd; Pontypool; Talywain

Forward in 8 matches, against: France, 1909, 1911; Ireland,

1909; Scotland, 1911, 1912; England, 1912, 1913; South Africa, 1912: Scored 1t - 3 points

Rees Thomas, formerly a collier, worked in the Panteg Steel Works. He captained Pontypool from 1908-11 and joined Warrington RLFC, making his debut against Wigan on 5 October 1912.

THOMAS, Richard Clement Charles
Born Cardiff, 28 January 1929
Career: Blundell's School; Welsh Secondary Schools; Cambridge University; Brynamman; Swansea; Harlequins; London Welsh; Barbarians

Flanker in 26 matches, against: France, 1949, 1952, 1953, 1954, 1958, 1959; Ireland, 1952, 1953, 1954, 1955, 1956, 1958, 1959; Scotland, 1953, 1954, 1955, 1956, 1958, 1959; New Zealand, 1953; England, 1954, 1956, 1957, 1958, 1959; Australia, 1958: Scored 1t - 3 points

British Isles 1955 tour South Africa: 2 caps

Clem Thomas is in the wholesale meat business, and is the rugby correspondent on *The Observer*, a regular contributor to *The Guardian* and a commentator on radio and television. A hard, banging (to borrow a phrase from his own vocabulary) back row forward, he gained a Blue in 1949 and captained Swansea in 1954-55. On tour with the British Isles in South Africa in 1955, he played in nine games. During his tenure as captain of Wales in nine games during the 1958-59 season, he led the national team to five victories and one draw. He also captained Harlequins, Barbarians and the British Isles. His son Mark, also a Cambridge Blue, played for University College, Aberystwyth, Swansea and London Welsh. In the 1974 General Election, standing as the Liberal candidate for the Gower constituency, he polled 19.4% of the votes. He also stood as the Liberal candidate for Wales Mid and West in the European Parliamentary Election in July 1979. Among his published works are: *Rugby Wales '87* (co-edited with Barry John) and *Welsh Rugby: The Crowning Years, 1968-80*, written with Geoffrey Nicholson and published in 1980.

THOMAS, Robert
Born 1871; died Brynhyfryd, Swansea, 7 March 1910
Career: Manselton Rangers; Mynyddbach; Morriston; Swansea

Forward in 4 matches, against: England, 1900, 1901; Scotland, 1900; Ireland, 1900

Robert Thomas, a steel tube millman at the Mannesmann Tube Works, Landore, was a member of the 1900 Triple Crown side. Tragically, an accident in August 1905 at his place of employment, when a pair of tongs went through the palm of his right hand severely injuring him, scarred

him mentally as well as physically.

THOMAS, Rowland Lewis
Born Henllan Amgoed, 11 July 1864; died Whitland, 21 January 1949
Career: Llandovery College; University College Hospital, London; London Welsh; Llanelli; Middlesex

Forward in 7 matches, against: Scotland, 1889, 1891; Ireland, 1889, 1890, 1891; England, 1891, 1892

Thomas was a Doctor of Medicine at St Clears for more than forty years. During the First World War he was the Medical Officer for the Welsh Horse. He was a founder member and first secretary of London Welsh RFC. In 1925, he was appointed the coroner for West Carmarthenshire, and served on the Carmarthenshire County Council. A Welsh Rugby Union referee he also served as president of Whitland RFC. Rowley Thomas, a descendant of the Methodist cleric, Daniel Rowlands of Llangeitho, was a well-known figure in local hunting circles. His hunting clothes and boots were placed alongside him in his coffin and the hunting horn was sounded at the end of the funeral service.

THOMAS, Samuel Gethin
Born Llwynhendy, 24 April 1897; died Westminster Hospital, 1 February 1939
Career: Bynea; Llanelli

Forward in 4 matches, against: England, 1923; Scotland, 1923; France, 1923; Ireland, 1923

Gethin Thomas, was a grocer and sub-postmaster in Llwynhendy. He served with the 4th Bn, Welch Regiment during the First World War. His brother Ewart played for Llanelli.

THOMAS, Stephen
Born Kidwelly, 22 August 1865; died Gowerton, 23 October 1937
Career: Llanelli; Gowerton

Forward in 3 matches, against: Scotland, 1890; England, 1890; Ireland, 1891

Stephen Thomas worked in the tinplate works in Gowerton. He was Gowerton RFC's first trainer.

THOMAS, Watkin Gwyn
Born Llanelli 16 January 1906; died Birmingham 10 August 1977
Career: Llanelli County School; University College Swansea; Welsh Secondary Schools; Llanelli; Swansea; Waterloo; London Welsh; Barbarians; Lancashire

Forward in 14 matches, against: England, 1927, 1929, 1931, 1932, 1933; Scotland, 1927, 1931, 1932, 1933; France, 1927; Ireland, 1927, 1932, 1933; South Africa, 1931: Scored 2t - 6 points

Watcyn Thomas - he spelled his name this way - was a schoolmaster at Cowley Grammar School, St Helens and the King Edward VI Grammar School, Aston, for 42 years. He captained Wales in their first victory at Twickenham in 1933 and in the two remaining games of that season. In the match at Twickenham, Watcyn Thomas, one of six Welsh speakers in the side, bellowed out his exhortations to the front row in Welsh. In his final match for Wales, against Ireland in March 1933, he played Bob Barrell and Archie Skym in their proper positions, which went against the wishes of 'the men in overcoats'. Shaken by this show of insolence, the selectors decided to dispense with his services. He was chairman of the English Schools RU selectors and coached the 19 age group. He played in twenty-five games for Lancashire and wrote his memoirs, *Rugby-Playing Man*, which was published in the year of his death.

THOMAS, William Delme BEM
Born Bancyfelin, 12 September 1942
Career: St Clears School; Welsh Youth; Carmarthen Athletic; Llanelli; Barbarians

Lock in 25 matches, against: Australia, 1966, 1969; Scotland, 1968, 1970, 1971, 1972, 1973; Ireland, 1968, 1970, 1971, 1973; France, 1968, 1970, 1971, 1972, 1973; England, 1969, 1970, 1971, 1972, 1973, 1974; New Zealand, 1969, 1972; South Africa, 1970

British Isles 1966 tour Australia, New Zealand: 2 caps; 1968 South Africa: 2(1r) caps; 1971 Australia, New Zealand: 3(1r) caps

Delme Thomas captained Llanelli in 1972-73 season which included the club's defeat of the All Blacks in October 1972 and was awarded the BEM as a result of this momentous victory. This followed the highly successful tour he undertook to the Antipodes with the British Isles party when he had played in fifteen games - one in Australia and fourteen in New Zealand. Five years earlier, he had appeared in seventeen games for the British Isles on his first visit to Australasia - three in Australia and fourteen in New Zealand. In South Africa with the British Isles in 1968, he played in twelve matches. Although a lock forward, he came on as a replacement prop in the third international against the Springboks and retained this position for the fourth and final international. He also played in three games for Wales in their visit to South Africa in 1969. He is employed as an electricity linesman.

THOMAS, William Henry
Born Fishguard, 22 March 1866; died Beccles, 11 October

1921
Career: Llandovery College; Cambridge University; Welsh Secondary Schools; Haverfordwest; London Welsh; Weston-super-Mare; Llanelli; Somerset

Forward in 11 matches, against: Scotland, 1885, 1886, 1887, 1888, 1891; England, 1886, 1887, 1890; Ireland, 1888, 1890, 1891

British Isles 1888 tour Australia, New Zealand

Schoolmaster W H Thomas gained two Cambridge Blues in 1886-87, as well as a cross country Blue in 1887. He was the first Welshman to tour Australia and New Zealand with a British team, playing in fifteen games on the New Zealand leg of the tour. Thomas captained Wales on two occasions and may well have been capped whilst still at Llandovery College.

THOMAS, William James
Born Bargoed, 1 September 1933
Career: Lewis School, Pengam; Welsh Schools; Welsh Youth; Bargoed; Newport United; Newport; Abertillery; Cardiff; Barbarians

Hooker in 2 matches, against: France, 1961, 1963

Engineer's toolmaker Billy Thomas is the son of Billy 'Deri' Thomas, the one time middleweight boxing champion of Wales, and the last Welshman to defeat Tommy Farr. His uncle Tom won the Welsh welterweight boxing title. He was a member of the coaching team at Bedwas RFC.

THOMAS, William Llewelyn
Born Brecknock, 6 May 1872; died Bootle, Cumberland, 19 January 1943
Career: Christ College Brecon; Oxford University; Newport; Barbarians

Wing in 3 matches, against: Scotland, 1894; England, 1895; Ireland, 1895

Thomas won two Blues in 1893-94. After leaving Oxford he returned to his old school in Brecon as an assistant master. Following his ordination into the Church in 1899 he became a curate in Rushall. In 1910, when he held a living in Llandrindod Wells, he was the captain of Llandrindod Wells Golf Club. From 1912 to 1924 he was vicar of Irton and was then vicar of Bootle in Cumberland until his death in 1943. He was the cousin of R T D Budworth, the English rugby international (1890-91) who had also attended Christ College, Brecon.

THOMAS, William Trevor
Born Merthyr, c1909

Career: Oakdale Elementary School; Oakdale; Blackwood; Abertillery

Forward in 1 match, against: England, 1930

'Ocker' Thomas, a collier, played for Abertillery and Cross Keys against South Africa in October 1931, kicking two enormous penalties - one from inside his own half - in a 9-10 loss. He signed professional forms for Oldham RLFC and made his debut for the club on 21 November 1931.

THOMPSON, Joseph Francis
Born Hambrook, near Bristol, 22 December 1902; died Leeds, 13 October 1983
Career: Abercarn; Cross Keys

Forward in 1 match, against: England, 1923

Joe Thompson did not receive the cap which he had won in 1923, until it was presented by the Welsh Rugby Union in 1975. He made his first appearance for Leeds against Huddersfield RLFC on 10 February 1923 and there followed a very distinguished career in the professional game. Over ten years later, in April 1933, he played his last game for Leeds, having amassed 1,883 points in 390 games. At the end of his first season with Leeds he won a Cup Winners medal against Hull in a resounding 28-3 victory and later captained the club to victory against Swinton in the Rugby League Cup Final of 1932. He played in twenty five RL internationals, eight for Wales, five for Other Nationalities, and twelve for Great Britain. Despite having participated in three tours "Down Under" with the British side, becoming the first forward to play in internationals on three successive visits, he played in only one game for Britain on home soil.

THORBURN, Paul Huw
Born Rheindalen, Germany, 24 November 1962
Career: Hereford Cathedral School; University College, Swansea; Welsh Universities; Universities Athletic Union; Ebbw Vale; Neath; Barbarians; Wales B

Full back/wing in 36 matches, against: France, 1985, 1986, 1987, 1988, 1989, 1990, 1991; England, 1985, 1986, [1987 World Cup], 1989, 1990, 1991; Fiji, 1985; Scotland, 1986, 1988, 1989, 1990, 1991; Ireland, 1986, [1987 World Cup], 1988, 1989, 1990, 1991; Tonga, [1987 World Cup]; Canada, [1987 World Cup]; New Zealand, [1987 World Cup], 1989; Australia, [1987 World Cup]; United States, 1987; Western Samoa, 1988; Romania, 1988(r); Namibia, 1990, 1990; Barbarians, 1990: Scored 2t 43con 69pg - 301 points

Paul Thorburn is Wales' highest international points scorer, and needs only another eight points to overhaul the British Isles record of 308 points held by Michael Kiernan of Ireland. In 1986, he scored a Welsh record of 52 points in the championship, including a penalty kick against Scot-

land which measured over 64 metres. He held the Five Nations record of sixteen penalty goals, scored in 1986, until Hodgkinson, the England full back, kicked eighteen in the 1991 championship. He was the replacement wing for Glen Webbe in the game against Romania in 1988. Thorburn has captained Wales in nine games, and led a Wales team to Canada in 1989. At club level, he holds the Neath record of 438 points in 1984-85 and was Neath's leading scorer, with 166 points, in the 1990-91 Heineken League. He made an unusual appearance at Wembley Stadium in August 1987 when, kitted out in gridiron kit, he was brought on to the field during part of the play by the Los Angeles Rams to kick off against the Denver Rams. In May 1991, he was appointed a regional sales executive by Welsh Development International, the sales arm of the Welsh Development Agency.

TITLEY, Mark Howard
Born Swansea, 3 May 1959
Career: Ysgol Gyfun Rhydfelen; North Surrey College of Technology; Mid Wales Schools; East Wales Schools; London Welsh; Bridgend; Swansea; Barbarians; Surrey; Wales B

Wing in 15 matches, against: Romania, 1983; Scotland, 1984, 1985; Ireland, 1984, 1985; France, 1984, 1986, 1990; England, 1984, 1990; Australia, 1984; Fiji, 1985, 1986; Tonga, 1986; Western Samoa, 1986: Scored 4t - 16 points

Mark Titley, who is employed in the estate business, played his early rugby in the outside-half position. Moving from London Welsh to Bridgend, he secured the 'Man of the Match' award in the 1982 Schweppes final, despite being on the losing side against Cardiff. In the season 1983-84, he scored forty-two tries, including seven hat tricks. He is also a fine cricketer and has played for the Bridgend XI for a number of years.

TOWERS, William Hunter
Born Hartlepool, 1861
Career: Swansea; Hartlepool Rovers; Durham County

Forward in 2 matches, against: Ireland, 1887; New Zealand Natives, 1888

Both of Towers' appearances for Wales were in winning sides. He captained Swansea in 1888-89, a season which included the match against New Zealand Natives on Christmas Eve. He also refereed the match between Llanelli and the New Zealand Natives during the same month.

TRAVERS, George
Born Newport 9 June 1877; died Newport, 26 December 1945

Career: Trinity Church School, Newport; Pill Harriers; Mountain Ash; Newport

Hooker in 25 matches, against: England, 1903, 1905, 1906, 1907, 1908, 1909; Scotland, 1903, 1905, 1906, 1907, 1908, 1909, 1911; Ireland, 1903, 1905, 1906, 1907, 1908, 1909, 1911; New Zealand, 1905; South Africa, 1906; France, 1908, 1911: Scored 1t - 3 points

'Twyber' Travers, a coal trimmer at the Alexandra Docks, Newport, played for Monmouthshire against South Africa in 1906, appeared in two Triple Crown sides (1905 and 1909), and one Grand Slam side (1908), captaining Wales against Scotland in 1908. Although Wales won the Grand Slam in 1909 and 1911, Travers appeared only in six of the eight matches played. His international playing record includes only four losses. He was the father of eight sons, including W Travers [qv], and the brother-in-law of L C Trump [qv].

TRAVERS, William
Born Newport, 2 December 1913
Career: Newport; Pill Harriers; Cardiff; Barbarians

Hooker in 12 matches, against: Scotland, 1937, 1938, 1939, 1949; Ireland, 1937, 1938, 1939, 1949; England, 1938, 1939, 1949; France, 1949

British Isles 1938 tour South Africa: 2 caps

'Bunner' Travers was 35 years and 3 months when he played in his final international match, against France in March 1949. Eleven years earlier he had undertaken a tour of South Africa with the British Isles during which he was only rested in three of the twenty-three games played by the tourists, a record which gave him the highest tally of appearances of the tour. He captained Newport in 1939-40. During the Second World War he served in the Monmouthshire Regiment, and played in four Service, two Red Cross, and one Victory international games. Like his father, George Travers [qv], he was employed as a coal trimmer but later became a licensee. Three of his brothers played for Newport.

TREHARNE, Edward
Born Merthyr, 1862; died Barry, 29 December 1904
Career: Cowbridge Grammar School; St Bartholomew's Hospital; Pontypridd; Cardiff

Forward in 2 matches, against: England, 1881, 1882

Treharne, a Doctor of Medicine, was the president of Cadoxton Junior Conservative Club, a member of the Barry Lodge of Freemasons and Barry District Council.

TREW, William James
Born Swansea, 1878; died Swansea, 20 August 1926

Career: Swansea

Wing/stand-off/centre in 29 matches, against: England, 1900, 1901, 1907, 1908, 1909, 1910, 1911; Scotland, 1900, 1901, 1903, 1905, 1906, 1907, 1908, 1909, 1910, 1911, 1912, 1913; Ireland, 1900, 1908, 1909, 1911; France, 1908, 1909, 1910, 1911, 1913: Scored 11t 1con 1dg - 39 points

Billy Trew captained Swansea from 1906-11 and in 1912-13, taking in the wins against Australia and South Africa on Boxing Day 1908 and 1912, as well as Wales in fourteen matches between 1907-1913. He was also a member of the Swansea side that played against the 1905 All Blacks and appeared for Glamorgan against South Africa in 1906. Between January 1908 and January 1910 he scored ten tries in ten games, figuring in two Triple Crown successes. Playing in only four defeats, he was a member of the Triple Crown sides of 1900, 1908, 1909, and 1911. As well as winning the Grand Slam in 1908, 1909, and 1911, Trew captained the 1909, and 1911 sides, but was not the captain in the game against France in 1911. A boilermaker and later a licensee, he was the father-in-law of T B Day [qv] and his son, W J Trew junior, captained Swansea and played for the club against the Maoris in October 1926. His brothers Harry and Bert also played for Swansea.

TROTT, Richard Frank
Born Cardiff, 14 March 1915; died 28 March 1987
Career: Cardiff; Penarth; Waterloo; Barbarians

Full back in 8 matches, against: England, 1948, 1949; Scotland, 1948, 1949; France, 1948, 1949; Ireland, 1948, 1949

Frank Trott captained Penarth in 1938-39. He played in two Services, and two Victory internationals. An administrator employed by the electricity board, he served as secretary to the Cardiff Athletic RFC.

TRUMAN, William Henry
Born Porth, 11 December 1909; died Tenby, 23 June 1984
Career: London Welsh; Llanelli

Forward in 2 matches, against: England, 1934, 1935

Harry Truman had his own building and contracting business in Tenby. He weighed 22 stone in later years. His son Mike played for Cardiff, Neath, Swansea and Llanelli.

TRUMP, Leonard Charles
Born Newport, 23 April 1887; died Newport, 9 June 1948
Career: Pill Harriers; Newport

Forward in 4 matches, against: England, 1912; Scotland,

1912; Ireland, 1912; France, 1912

Len Trump became a professional player and made his first appearance for Hull Kingston Rovers RLFC on 14 September 1912. His service in the Royal Artillery during the First World War broke his contract with Hull Kingston Rovers and he did not receive the full signing on fee. He worked for a potato merchant and was the brother-in-law of George Travers [*qv*] and the uncle of W Travers [*qv*].

TURNBULL, Bernard Ruel
Born Cardiff, 16 October 1904; died Lymington, Hampshire, 7 April 1984
Career: Downside School; Cambridge University; St Peter's, Cardiff; London Welsh; Cardiff; Barbarians

Centre in 6 matches, against: Ireland, 1925; England, 1927, 1928; Scotland, 1927, 1930; France, 1928: Scored 1t - 3 points

Bernard Turnbull scored a try against Ireland in his debut match in 1925. He gained two Cambridge Blues in 1924-25. He captained Cardiff in 1927-28, including the match against New South Wales in December 1927, and in 1930-31 and Wales in one match, against England in 1927. He was one of six brothers, including M J L Turnbull [*qv*], who played for the club and was a company director of Currans, Cardiff.

TURNBULL, Maurice Joseph Lawson
Born Cardiff, 16 March 1906; killed in action near Montchamp, Normandy, 5 August 1944
Career: Downside School; Cambridge University; St Peter's, Cardiff; London Welsh; Cardiff; Somerset

Scrum-half in 2 matches, against: England, 1933; Ireland, 1933

Maurice Turnbull gained three cricket Blues in 1926, 1928-29 before going on to play for Glamorgan from 1924-39 (scoring 14,431 runs) and England in nine Tests. He was the secretary of Glamorgan from 1933 until 1939 and a Test selector from 1938-39. An officer in the Regular Army, he won three caps in 1929 for the Welsh hockey XI - scoring a goal against Scotland in his first appearance. He also won the South Wales Squash Racquets championship, founded the Cardiff Squash Club and was a member of the Welsh Squash team. Turnbull served as a Major in the 1st Bn, The Welsh Guards during the Second World War and was killed by a sniper during the intense fighting for the French village of Montchamp in Normandy. He was the author, with Maurice Allom, of two books on cricket: *The Book of of the Two Maurices* (MCC tour to Australasia in 1929-30), published in 1930 and *The Two Maurices Again* (MCC tour to South Africa in 1930-31) published in 1931. He was the brother of B R Turnbull [*qv*].

TURNER, Paul
Born Newport, 13 February 1959
Career: Newbridge Comprehensive School; Newport; Newbridge; London Welsh; Barbarians; Wales B

Stand-off in 3 matches, against: Ireland, 1989(r); France, 1989; England, 1989

Paul Turner, a civil servant, is set to become the most prolific points scorer in the history of Welsh rugby. He is less than 200 points short of the 3,513 held by Peter Lewis the former Pontypool and Wales B full back. He was the leading scorer, with 127 points, for Newport in the 1990-91 Heineken League. Turner holds the Newbridge and Newport record of points scored in one season, scoring respectively 405 in the 1983-84 season and 368 in the 1986-87 season. He captained Newbridge in 1984-85 and 1989-90. He won his first cap against Ireland, as a replacement for Paul Thorburn, the captain and full back. He has been appointed the coach of the Newport backs.

UZZELL, Henry
Born Shirehampton, 6 January 1883; died Bassaleg, 20 December 1960
Career: Crindau School, Newport; Tredegar; Newport; London Welsh; Gloucestershire

Forward in 15 matches, against: England, 1912, 1914, 1920; Scotland, 1912, 1913, 1914, 1920; Ireland, 1912, 1913, 1914, 1920; France, 1912, 1913, 1914, 1920 Scored 2t - 6 points

One of eleven children, Harry Uzzell might have been lost to Welsh rugby as, when he was very young, his father took the family to Motherwell in Scotland but did not like it there and returned to live in Crindau, Newport. A member of the 'Terrible Eight', Uzzell played in Wales' final game prior to the outbreak of the First World War and in their first post-War championship game in January 1920 when he captained Wales against England and was the captain of the side in the three remaining games that year. He captained Newport in 1913-14 and made 229 appearances for the club. When playing for Gloucestershire he had been invited to trial for England but declined saying that he only knew Welsh players. In 1907, he won the Welsh AAA 880 yards and followed this up with the Welsh AAA 440 title in 1908. He was a fruiterer until 1940, when, due to a shortage of fruit, he became the licensee of the Tredegar Arms, Bassaleg. His brother Ben had played for Newport and Pontypool.

UZZELL, John
Born Deri, Bargoed, 28 March 1942
Career: Bargoed Grammar School; St Luke's College, Exeter; Welsh Secondary Schools; Cardiff; Newport; Cross Keys; Caldicot; Devon

Centre in 5 matches, against: New Zealand, 1963; England, 1965; Scotland, 1965; Ireland, 1965; France, 1965

Dick Uzzell's drop goal for Newport against New Zealand in October 1963, scored in the first twenty minutes, ensured a famous victory for the Gwent club and the only defeat suffered by the tourists in twenty-seven games. His cousin and fellow international, Brian Price [qv], captained the Newport team in this match. Currently a regional account manager for the Forward Trust Finance Company, he was formerly a representative for a tyre company and then for a brewery. He is a keen squash player.

VICKERY, Walter Elias
Born Port Talbot, 25 October 1909
Career: Central School, Port Talbot; Taibach; Cwmavon; Aberavon

Forward in 4 matches, against: England, 1938, 1939; Scotland, 1938; Ireland, 1938

Walter Vickery was a docker. He captained Aberavon in 1936-37 and 1945-46. His father, George Vickery, who had captained Aberavon in 1903-05, won one cap for the England XV in 1905.

VILE, Thomas Henry
Born Newport, 6 September 1882; died Newport, 30 November 1958
Career: Newport Intermediate School; Portishead College, Somerset; Pill Harriers; Newport; Blackheath; London Welsh; Barbarians; Monmouthshire

Scrum-half in 8 matches, against: England, 1908, 1913; Scotland, 1908, 1921; Ireland, 1910, 1912; France, 1912; South Africa, 1912

British Isles 1904 tour Australia: 2 caps, New Zealand: 1 cap

Tommy Vile's long international career covered the years from 1904-21. He won three caps for the British Isles in Australasia in 1904 and appeared in all five games in New Zealand - four years before making his debut for Wales, against England, in 1908. He was almost 38 years and 5 months when he gained his final cap in 1921, and captained Wales in his last four appearances. He played for Newport against the All Blacks in 1905 and the following year against the Springboks. He captained Newport from 1909-12, making 298 appearances for the club. Appointed a referee, from 1923-31 he officiated at twelve international games and all nine games of the British tour of Argentina in July 1927. In the years 1946-53 he was a representative on the International Board and the president of the WRU during 1955-56. He was a lieutenant in the Royal Field Artillery in the First World War and served as a major in the Intelligence Corps in the

Second World War. A manufacturer of soft drinks, Vile (who was the brother-in-law of R G S Plummer) was appointed president of the National Union of Mineral Water Manufacturers in 1934 and served as the High Sheriff of Monmouthshire. As well as writing regular articles for the *South Wales Argus*, he contributed a chapter 'The Man With the Whistle' to Teddy Wakelam's *The Game Goes On*, published in 1936.

VINCENT, Sir Hugh Corbet
Born Caernarfon, 27 April 1862; died Treborth, Bangor, 22 February 1931
Career: Worcester Cathedral School; Friar's School, Bangor; Sherborne School; Trinity College Dublin

Forward in 1 match, against: Ireland, 1882

One of eight children, Hugh Vincent was the son of a vicar who held the living of Caernarfon for many years. After graduating with an arts degree, Vincent entered the legal profession and served his articles in his home town where he opened his own practice in 1886 and later took charge of a branch of the firm in Bangor. He was appointed Clerk to the Bangor Bench of Magistrates, was Mayor of Bangor on three occasions and was a member of the Representative Body and of the Governing Body of the Church in Wales. A good all-round sportsman, he won his cap in 1882 because he happened to be in Dublin at the time of the international. A member of the Bangor Cricket Club and St Deiniol's Golf Club, he even appeared in a FA Cup tie for Caernarfon. In the General Election of 1910, he stood as the Conservative candidate for Caernarfon Boroughs, in opposition to David Lloyd George. He was knighted in 1924 in recognition of his public service.

WAKEFORD, John Donald Marshall
Born Cardiff, 29 September 1966
Career: Bishop of Llandaff High School; South Wales Police; Wales Under 21; Wales B

Lock in 2 matches, against: Western Samoa, 1988; Romania, 1988

John Wakeford is an officer in the South Wales Police.

WALDRON, Ronald Gwyn
Born Neath Abbey, 14 December 1933
Career: Neath Abbey School; Dwr-y-felin School; Neath YMCA; Neath; Royal Navy; Glamorgan

Prop in 4 matches, against: England, 1965; Scotland, 1965; Ireland, 1965; France, 1965

Ron Waldron captained Neath in 1959-60, played for Neath and Aberavon against South Africa in January 1961 and played in two matches for Wales in South Africa in

1964. He was appointed coach to the National XV in February 1990. At the time he was still the coach to the Neath club, and served on their committee. In November 1990, after also taking on the mantle of team manager of the National XV, he resigned from Neath in order to concentrate on the development of the Welsh Squad. Waldron was employed as a steelworker and now works as a storeman. He was coach to Resolven RFC in 1976-78. His son Tim played for Welsh Schools and London Welsh.

WALLER, Phillip Dudley
Born Bath, 28 January 1889; killed in action Arras, France, 14 December 1917
Career: Carmarthen Intermediate School; Newport; Wanderers (Johannesburg); Monmouthshire; Somerset

Forward in 6 matches, against: Australia, 1908; England, 1909; Scotland, 1909; France, 1909, 1910; Ireland, 1909

British Isles 1910 tour South Africa: 3 caps

Phil Waller, an engineer, never appeared in a losing Welsh XV and was a member of the Triple Crown and Grand Slam XV in 1909. He played in twenty-three games for the British Isles in their twenty-four match tour of South Africa in 1910. He remained in that country at the end of the tour serving as a 2nd Lieutenant in the South African Heavy Artillery in the First World War and was killed in action at Arras on the Western Front.

WALTERS, Nathaniel
Born Llanelli, 23 May 1875; died Llanelli, 22 February 1956
Career: Llanelli

Forward in 1 match, against: England, 1902

Llanelli licensee 'Danny' Walters won his only cap in Wales' first victory against England at Blackheath. He captained Llanelli in 1901-02, 1902-03, and 1906-07.

WANBON, Robert
Born Port Talbot, 16 November 1943
Career: St Josephs School, Port Talbot; Aberavon Boys Club; Aberavon Green Stars; Aberavon

No 8 in 1 match, against: England, 1968: Scored 1t - 3 points

Bobby Wanbon joined St Helens RLFC and made his debut on 17 February 1968 and later played for Warrington. He won eight caps for the Wales RL team an international career which included a tour of Australia and New Zealand in 1974-75. Originally a bricklayer, he he has been the licensee of a public house in Warrington since the mid

1970s.

WARD, William Stanford
Born Risca, 6 January 1907; died Risca, 22 November 1973
Career: Risca; Cross Keys; Pontypool

Forward in 2 matches, against: Scotland, 1934; Ireland, 1934

Bill Ward was a steelworker and was later employed in a tinplate works. A mobile second row forward and lineout specialist he captained Cross Keys in 1935-36. In later life he was a pigeon fancier.

WARLOW, Douglas John
Born Dafen, 13 February 1939
Career: Stebonheath School; Welsh Youth; Felinfoel; Llanelli

Prop in 1 match, against: Ireland, 1962

John Warlow made his first appearance for St Helens RLFC on 30 November 1963. He played in three games for the Wales RL team and in seven for Great Britain. Currently the steward of a club in Burry Port, he was previously employed in a steelworks.

WATERS, David Ralph
Born Newport, 4 June 1955
Career: Caerleon Comprehensive School; Newport Schools; Newport Youth; Magor; Newport; Barbarians; Wales B

Lock in 4 matches, against: England, 1986; Scotland, 1986; Ireland, 1986; France, 1986

In the first week of April 1991, David Waters, a lorry driver, played in his 590th game for Newport. He was a member of the Newport side which won the Schweppes Cup in 1977. He was chosen for Wales in 1985 but did not play as the match was postponed through bad weather.

WATKINS, David MBE
Born Blaina 5 March 1942
Career: Cwmcelyn School; Welsh Youth; Abertillery; Ebbw Vale; Newport; Barbarians

Stand-off in 21 matches, against: England, 1963, 1964, 1965, 1966, 1967; Scotland, 1963, 1964, 1965, 1966; Ireland, 1963, 1964, 1965, 1966, 1967; France, 1963, 1964, 1965, 1966, 1967; New Zealand, 1963; South Africa, 1964: Scored 2t 3dg - 15 points

British Isles 1966 tour Australia: 2 caps, New Zealand: 4 caps

David Watkins played for Wales Under 23 against Canada in 1962, a Wales XV against Fiji in 1964 and in the same year, played for Wales in all four games during their tour of South Africa. Two years later, he visited Australasia with the British Isles Party. In Australia he played in six games and scored sixteen points (the total including six points in the second international against Australia). He captained the tourists in the second and fourth internationals in New Zealand, scoring a drop goal in the second international match, and a try in the third. His total points tally in New Zealand was twenty seven in fourteen appearances. Before turning professional, Watkins had played in 202 games for Newport, captaining them from 1964-67, and scored 288 points (including 55 drop goals). Guaranteed to entertain with his speed and jinking ability, together with keen enthusiasm, his running ability was best seen in seven-a-side rugby, but he turned professional before modern laws would have given greater scope to his genius. On 20 October 1967, Watkins scored a try and two goals in his debut game for Salford RLFC remaining with the club until April 1979. In these years he also played at centre and full back and, when he left the club in the 1979-80 to play in twenty games for Swinton RLFC, he had scored 3,117 points in 472 matches. In the summer of 1975 he toured Australasia with a Wales RL side and was top scorer with one try and twenty six goals. He gained a total of sixteen RL caps for Wales and a further six for Great Britain. He also coached the Great Britain World Cup side in Australasia in 1977. Returning to Wales, he became managing director, and later coach, of the Cardiff City RLFC. Awarded an MBE in 1986 and granted an honorary MA by Salford University in July 1978, David Watkins is currently a finance company executive.

WATKINS, Edward
Born Neath, 27 March 1899; died Neath, 12 October 1983
Career: Neath United; Neath

Scrum-half in 4 matches, against: England, 1924; Scotland, 1924; Ireland, 1924; France, 1924: Scored 1dg - 3 points

Watkins, a council worker, served in the Royal Artillery in the First World War. He joined Halifax RLFC, making his debut on 30 August 1924. His career with Halifax was shortened by a knee injury although the club offered him a further £400 to continue playing.

WATKINS, Edward Verdun
Born Caerphilly, 2 March 1916
Career: Caerphilly Secondary School; Cardiff; Royal Air Force; Glamorgan Police; Police Union

Forward in 8 matches, against: New Zealand, 1935; Scotland, 1937, 1938, 1939; Ireland, 1937, 1938; England, 1938, 1939

Eddie Watkins, a police officer in the Glamorgan Constabulary, left the force to become a schoolmaster and taught at Surbiton Grammar School. He played as a teenager against New Zealand in December 1935 and was selected for the British Isles tour to South Africa in 1938, but had to withdraw. In March 1939, he joined Wigan RLFC, making his first appearance on 18 March. He won three caps for the Wales RL team. During the Second World War he served in the Special Investigations Branch of the Royal Air Force and played in two Services internationals

WATKINS, Emlyn
Born Blaina, 21 September 1904; died Walsall, 15 May 1978
Career: Blaina

Forward in 3 matches, against: Scotland, 1926; Ireland, 1926; France, 1926: Scored 1t - 3 points

Emlyn Watkins scored the winning try in his final game for Wales, against France. In 1926, after turning professional and joining Leeds RLFC (making his debut on 29 September), he ceased working as a collier. He took up employment with the Oldham Municipal Waterworks after joining Oldham RLFC. In later years he was prominent in rugby league administration.

WATKINS, Harry Vaughan
Born Trecastle, 10 September 1875; died Llandovery, 16 May 1945
Career: Llandovery; London Welsh; Llanelli

Forward in 6 matches, against: Scotland, 1904, 1905; Ireland, 1904, 1905; England, 1905, 1906: Scored 1t - 3 points

Harry Watkins captained Llandovery in 1898-99 and Llanelli in 1904-05. He spent a number of years in Canada and in November 1913, aged 38 years - 2 months, captained Victoria, (the British Columbia rugby club) against New Zealand. Returning to Carmarthenshire, Watkins served on the County Council and was Chief of the Fire Brigade in Llandovery. He also played cricket and hockey for Carmarthenshire.

WATKINS, Ian John
Born Ebbw Vale, 10 March 1963
Career: Pontygarreg Junior School; Glyncoed Comprehensive School; Ebbw Vale Senior Comprehensive School; Ebbw Vale Youth; Ebbw Vale; Cardiff; Barbarians; Wales B

Hooker, in 10 matches, against: England, 1988(r), 1989; Scotland, 1988, 1989; Ireland, 1988, 1989; France, 1988, 1989; New Zealand, 1988; Romania, 1988: Scored 1t - 4 points

Troubled by injuries, Ian Watkins has had little chance to challenge for the hooking spot in the Welsh team. He started his rugby career at scrum-half and centre before moving into the pack at senior school. He has had trials for Coventry AFC, and is employed with his cousin, Clive Burgess [qv], as a gas bottle distributor.

WATKINS, Leonard
Born Abergavenny, 7 December 1859; died Chajari, Entre Rios, Argentina, 7 February 1901
Career: Sherborne School; Oxford University; Llandaff

Half-back in 1 match, against: England, 1881

Leonard Watkins gained his Oxford Blue in 1879 and was a member of the first Wales XV in 1881. He emigrated to Argentina later the same year.

WATKINS, Michael John
Born Abercarn, 9 January 1952
Career: Cwmcarn School; Gwent School; South Monmouthshire Youth; Cwmcarn; Crumlin; Cardiff; Newport; Newbridge; Ebbw Vale; Barbarians; Wales B

Hooker in 4 matches, against: Ireland, 1984; France, 1984; England, 1984; Australia, 1984

'Spikey' Watkins toured Australia with Wales in 1978. In October 1980 he played for Cardiff against New Zealand, was a member of the Wales XV against Japan in 1983 and, in the following year captained Wales in all four games. He captained Newport from 1983 until 1987. Employed in engineering, he was the manager to the Cross Keys club before becoming the coach/manager of Pontypridd RFC in 1990.

WATKINS, Stuart John
Born Newport, 5 June 1941
Career: Caerleon Secondary Modern School; Cross Keys; Newport; Cardiff; Barbarians

Wing in 26 matches, against: Scotland, 1964, 1965, 1966, 1967, 1968, 1969; Ireland, 1964, 1965, 1966, 1967, 1969, 1970; France, 1964, 1965, 1966, 1967, 1969; England, 1965, 1966, 1967, 1968, 1969, 1970; Australia, 1966; New Zealand, 1967, 1969: Scored 9t - 36 points

British Isles 1966 tour Australia: 2 caps, New Zealand: 1 cap

Stuart Watkins played in one game for Wales in South Africa in 1964. In 1969, he was a member of the Wales tour party to Australasia and Fiji, making three appearances. Three years earlier he had been in Australasia with the British Lions where he had played in five games in Australia and nine in New Zealand. He appeared for the Barbarians - both games were lost - against New Zealand in 1964 and Australia in 1967. He is employed as a sales representative.

WATKINS, William Raymond
Born Newbridge, 22 March 1933
Career: Newbridge Grammar School; St Luke's College, Exeter; Cardiff College of Education; Newbridge; Pontypool; Newport; Barbarians; Devon

Scrum-half in 1 match, against: France, 1959

Billy Watkins, who taught geography at West Monmouth Grammar School from 1956-86, where he was also a deputy headmaster, played in his first game for the Newbridge 1st XV at the age of fifteen and played for the Barbarians against South Africa in 1961. He also played basketball for a Welsh team against the Royal Air Force, captained St Luke's College, Exeter City and Cardiff Training College in that sport, played cricket for Newbridge and is a keen golfer. He read for an Open University degree in geography and was, for a number of years, a commissioned officer in the Royal Air Force Volunteer Reserve.

WATTS, David
Born Maesteg, 14 March 1886; killed in action Ancre Valley, France, 14 July 1916
Career: Maesteg

Forward in 4 matches, against: England, 1914; Scotland, 1914; France, 1914; Ireland, 1914

David Watts, a collier, and the heaviest member of the 'Terrible Eight', served as a corporal in the 7th Bn King's Shropshire Light Infantry in the First World War, enlisting despite being in a reserved occupation. He fell fighting in the Ancre Valley, during the Battle of the Somme. Having no known grave, his name is recorded on the Thiepval Memorial.

WATTS, James
Born March 1878, registered in Carmarthen; died Llanelli, 2 February 1933
Career: Llanelli

Forward in 11 matches, against: England, 1907, 1908; Scotland, 1907, 1908, 1909; Ireland, 1907, 1908, 1909; France, 1908, 1909; Australia, 1908: Scored 2t - 6 points

Steelworker James Watts captained Llanelli during the 1903-04 season and was a member of the first Welsh Grand Slam side in 1908, appearing in only one losing side in eleven games.

WATTS, Wallace Howard
Born Chipping Sodbury, 25 March 1870; died Richmond, Surrey, 29 April 1950
Career: Maindee; Newport; London Welsh

Forward in 12 matches, against: England, 1892, 1893, 1894, 1895, 1896; Scotland, 1892, 1893, 1894; Ireland, 1892, 1893, 1894, 1895

Wallace Watts was in business and played rugby until he was forty-five years of age. His son David, was chairman of London Welsh RFC from 1968-75.

WATTS, William James
Born Llanelli, 16 May 1890; died Roehampton, 16 September 1950
Career: Llanelli County School; Carmarthen Training College; Llanelli Excelsiors; Llanelli; Leicester; Birkenhead Park; London Welsh

Centre in 1 match, against: England, 1914: Scored 1t - 3 points

Watts, a chartered accountant, captained Llanelli in 1913-14 and served as the president of London Welsh RFC. He was wounded while serving in the First World War.

WEAVER, David Samuel
Born Glynneath, 8 January 1942
Career: Llangattock Secondary School; Neath Technical College; Swansea Technical College; Glynneath; Neath; Swansea

Wing in 1 match, against: England, 1964

Metallurgist David Weaver played for Swansea against New Zealand in 1963 and Australia in 1966 and appeared for a Wales XV against Fiji in 1964. In 1972, he appeared for Zambia against Argentina.

WEBB, Alfred
Born Coleford, Gloucestershire, c1878; died Upper Soudley, 29 January 1955
Career: Abertillery

Forward in 20 matches, against: Scotland, 1907, 1908, 1909, 1910, 1911, 1912; England, 1908, 1909, 1910, 1911, 1912; France, 1908, 1909, 1910, 1911; Ireland, 1908, 1909, 1910, 1911; Australia, 1908: Scored 2t - 6 points

British Isles 1910 tour(r) South Africa: 3 caps

Collier Jim Webb (he was always called by this first name) was a member of three Grand Slam sides (1908, 1909 and 1911) and captained Abertillery in 1909-10. In 1910, after being called out to South Africa as a replacement for the British Isles, he appeared in ten games. He appeared in only three losing Welsh XVs. Joining St Helens RLFC he played his first game on 26 October 1912.

WEBB, James
Born Broughton Gifford, Wiltshire, 15 January 1863; died Newport, 8 March 1913
Career: Maindee School; Maindee; Newport; Caerau Albion

Full back/back in 2 matches, against: New Zealand Natives, 1888; Scotland, 1889: Scored 1con

Jim Webb, the son of a gamekeeper who had moved to live in Wales, was a painter and decorator. He played in every match for Newport for five seasons from 1885-86. When his playing career was over he became a referee, trained Newport Schoolboys, was honorary treasurer of the Newport District Rugby Junior League and was a useful cricketer.

WEBBE, Glenfield Michael Charles
Born Cardiff, 21 January 1962
Career: Herbert Thompson School, Ely; Canton High School; Welsh Youth; Canton; Bridgend; Glamorgan; Wales B

Wing in 10 matches, against: Tonga, 1986(r), [1987 World Cup]; Western Samoa, 1986; France, 1987, 1988(r); England, 1987; Scotland, 1987; United States, 1987; New Zealand, 1988; Romania, 1988: Scored 4t - 16 points

Glen Webbe's parents hail from St Kitts, in the West Indies. He appeared, aged nineteen, for Bridgend against Australia on 28 October 1981. He scored three tries against Tonga in the 1987 World Cup and, on 1 February 1991, scored a try for Bridgend against Stirling County, bringing his try total to 238 in ten years with the club, overtaking the club record previously held by Vivian Jenkins.

WEBSTER, Richard Edward
Born Swansea, 9 July 1967
Career: Cefn Hengoed Comprehensive School, Swansea; Bonymaen Youth; Welsh Youth; Swansea

Flanker in 2 matches, against: Australia, [1987 World Cup]; Barbarians, 1990

Richard Webster gained his first cap in the play-off match against Australia in the 1987 World Cup when not part of the official party. Serious injuries have hampered his progress towards claiming further international honours. He is employed as a sales representative.

WELLS, Gordon Thomas
Born Porth, Rhondda, 25 October 1928
Career: Porth County School; University College Cardiff;
St Luke's College, Exeter; Tylorstown; Penygraig; Neath;
Cardiff; Barbarians

Centre/wing in 7 matches, against: England, 1955, 1958;
Scotland, 1955, 1958; Ireland, 1957; France, 1957;
Australia, 1958: Scored 1t - 3 points

In November 1951, Gordon Wells, played for Neath and
Aberavon against South Africa. He made two tours with
the Barbarians, the first to Canada in 1957 and, in the
following year, went to South Africa. He captained Cardiff
during the 1959-60 season. A fine athlete, he represented
the Royal Air Force and Combined Services and won the
Welsh AAA triple jump title from 1949-52 and once held
the United Kingdom record in this event. He also won the
University of Wales 100 yards title in 1952. Wells, who
was previously a schoolmaster, is now employed by Shell
Chemicals.

WESTACOTT, David
Born Cardiff, 1882; killed in action France, 28 August
1917
Career: Grange National School, Cardiff; Cardiff;
Glamorgan

Forward in 1 match, against: Ireland, 1906

Dai Westacott played for Glamorgan against New Zealand
at St Helen's, Swansea, in December 1905. He was killed
in action whilst serving as a private in the Gloucestershire
Regiment during the First World War.

WETTER, John James DCM
Born Newport, 29 December 1887; died Newport, 29 July
1967
Career: Newport; Pill Harriers

Centre/stand-off in 10 matches, against: Scotland, 1914,
1920; France, 1914, 1920; Ireland, 1914, 1920, 1924;
England, 1920, 1921; New Zealand, 1924: Scored 4t 1con
- 14 points

Jack Wetter captained Newport in their invincible season
1922-23, and led Wales in three games, including the
match against New Zealand when he was one month short
of his thirty-seventh birthday. In his first season of
international rugby, in 1914, he scored four tries in three
games. It was Wetter that first suggested that the wing
should throw the ball into the lineout, rather than the
scrum-half. Initially employed as a crane driver in the
Newport docks, he later worked for the Great Western
Railway. He served in the South Wales Borderers in the
First World War when he was decorated with the
Distinguished Conduct Medal for gallantry. He also played

baseball for Wales and was the brother of W H Wetter [qv].

WETTER, William Henry
Born Battersea, 3 February 1882; died Newport, 4 Feb-
ruary 1934
Career: Newport; Pill Harriers

Forward in 2 matches, against: South Africa, 1912;
England, 1913

Harry Wetter, the brother of J J Wetter [qv], was employed
in a brick works before becoming a police officer. He also
played baseball for Wales.

WHEEL, Geoffrey Arthur
Born Swansea, 30 June 1951
Career: Danygraig School; Mumbles; Swansea; Barbar-
ians; Wales B

Lock in 32 matches, against: Ireland, 1974, 1975, 1976,
1977, 1978, 1979, 1980, 1981, 1982; England, 1974(r),
1975, 1976, 1977, 1978, 1980, 1981; France, 1975, 1976,
1978, 1980, 1981; Australia, 1975, 1978, 1978, 1981;
Scotland, 1976, 1977, 1978, 1979, 1980, 1981; New
Zealand, 1978

Geoff Wheel is employed in brewery management.
Renowned for his great strength and expertise at ripping
the ball out of mauls, his presence in the Welsh team
ensured a steady supply of good ball for the backs. He
partnered Allan Martin in the second row in twenty-seven
internationals and would have packed down with Martin
on the British Isles tour to New Zealand in 1977, but failed
to pass the necessary medical examination. He has the
dubious honour of being the first Welsh player to be sent
off in an international - in the match against Ireland, played
at Cardiff Arms Park, on 15 January 1977. He captained
Swansea in 1979-80. In his early days Geoff Wheel played
soccer for Morriston and Swansea City reserves.

WHEELER, Paul James
Born Newport, 5 February 1947
Career: Duffryn Comprehensive School; University
College, Cardiff; University of Wales Institute of Science
and Technology; Welsh Secondary Schools; Aberavon;
Swansea

Full back in 2 matches, against: New Zealand, 1967;
England, 1968

Paul Wheeler is a personnel director in Cheshire. His
father Jim made seven Football League appearances for
Newport County before the Second World War and his
uncle George won two amateur soccer caps for Wales in
1931 as well as appearing for Newport County. His sister
Anne was the Welsh women's high jump champion.

WHITEFOOT, Jeffrey
Born Bedwas, 18 April 1956
Career: Bedwas Comprehensive School; South Monmouthshire Youth; Bedwas; Cardiff; Barbarians; Wales B

Prop in 19 matches, against: Australia, 1984(r); Scotland, 1985, 1986, 1987; Ireland, 1985, 1986, 1987, {1987 World Cup]; France, 1985, 1986, 1987; England, 1985, 1986, 1987; Fiji, 1985, 1986; Tonga, 1986; Western Samoa, 1986; Canada, [1987 World Cup]

Jeff Whitefoot played for Cardiff against New Zealand in October 1980 and for a Wales XV against Japan in 1983. In 1986 he appeared for the Five Nations XV against an Overseas XV at Twickenham. He is employed as a colliery electrician.

WHITFIELD, John James
Born Newport, 23 March 1892; died Newport, 26 December 1927
Career: Pill Harriers; Newport

Forward in 12 matches, against: New Zealand Army, 1919; England, 1920, 1921, 1922; Scotland, 1920, 1922, 1924; France, 1920, 1922; Ireland, 1920, 1922, 1924: Scored 5t - 15 points

Jack Whitfield, who captained Wales in one game, was originally employed as a fitter and later became the licensee of the Globe Inn, Canal Parade, Newport. He died following an operation for a gastric ulcer. His son Tom was a schoolboy international and later played for Newport.

WHITSON, Geoffrey Keith
Born Newport, 4 December 1930; died Cwmbran, 18 May 1984
Career: St Julian's High School, Newport; Cardiff Training College; St Mark's & St John's College, London; Newport

Flanker in 3 matches, against: France, 1956; Scotland, 1960; Ireland, 1960

Geoff Whitson played in three winning Welsh teams. After a number of years in the teaching profession, he became the manager of the Cwmbran Sports Centre and the Torfaen Borough Council's leisure and recreation director. He played in 229 games for Newport.

WILLIAMS, Bleddyn
Born Taff's Well, 22 February 1923
Career: Rydal School; Welsh Schools; Taff's Well; Cardiff; Royal Air Force; Newbridge; Barbarians

Stand-off/centre in 22 matches, against: England, 1947, 1948, 1949, 1953, 1955; Scotland, 1947, 1948, 1949, 1952, 1953, 1954; France, 1947, 1948, 1953; Ireland, 1947, 1948, 1949, 1951, 1953; Australia, 1947; South Africa, 1951; New Zealand, 1953   Scored 7t - 21 points

British Isles 1950 tour New Zealand: 3 caps, Australia: 2 caps

Bleddyn Williams is the only Welsh player to score two tries against a visiting Springbok team. The first was scored for Cardiff in October 1951, and the second for Wales in December of the same year. He captained Cardiff in 1949-50 and 1953-54, and Wales in five games, all won, including the game against New Zealand in 1953. He played in three Services, and seven Victory internationals. During the tour of Australasia in 1950, he appeared in twenty games for the British Isles - fifteen games and ten tries in New Zealand (including the captaincy in the final two internationals) and five games and three tries in Australia (including scoring a try and captaining the tourists in the first international). He is one of eight brothers to play for Cardiff, including Lloyd Williams [qv], who also played for Wales. He has been the rugby correspondent of the *Sunday People*, and is the Welsh Regional Marketing Manager for Wimpey Construction, United Kingdom. Bleddyn Williams is the cousin of the late WE Tamplin [qv] and the author of *Rugger, My Life*, published in 1956.

WILLIAMS, Brian Richard
Born Penffordd, near Maenclochog, 9 July 1960
Career: Ysgol Preseli; Gelliaur Agricultural College; Narberth; Swansea; Pembrokeshire; Wales B

Prop in 5 matches, against: Scotland, 1990, 1991; Ireland, 1990; Barbarians, 1990; England, 1991

Brian Williams farms in Clynderwen, Pembrokeshire.

WILLIAMS, Brinley
Born Llanelli, 3 April 1895; died Llanelli, 5 January 1987
Career: Bryncaerau; Llanelli

Wing in 3 matches, against: Scotland, 1920; France, 1920; Ireland, 1920: Scored 4t - 12 points

Steelworker Brinley Williams scored a hat-trick of tries in his final game, against Ireland, in 1920. He was wounded on three occasions while serving in the Royal Welch Fusiliers during the First World War, and his battalion commander, Lord Howard de Walden, named a racehorse, Brynfleet, after him. He came second in the Welsh Powderhill sprint in 1919-20. On 28 August 1920, he made his debut for Batley RLFC, and later played for the Leeds and Pontypridd rugby league clubs. He won two caps for the Wales RL team in 1921-22.

WILLIAMS, Charles Derek
Born Cardiff, 28 November 1924
Career: Lansdowne Junior School; Canton High School; Cardiff Technical College; Oxford University; Penarth; Cardiff; Neath; London Welsh; Barbarians; Berkshire

Flanker in 2 matches, against: France, 1955, 1956: Scored 1t - 3 points

Derek Williams, a good all round athlete, won the Welsh AAA Youths 880 yards in 1940 and gained his Oxford Blue in 1945, ten years before winning his first cap. He also won a boxing Blue in 1948, the same year in which he carrried the Olympic Torch through Berkshire on the way to the Games at the White City. One year later he won the Berkshire mile. He played in a total of 248 games for Cardiff - including the match against the All Blacks in 1953 - and captained the club in 1958-59. He also played for Southern Counties against New Zealand in October 1953. His other sporting achievements include playing cricket for Oxford University (1946), St Fagans and Minor Counties cricket for Berkshire and Glamorgan. Now in retirement, he was previously a licensee in Cardiff following a career as assistant chief chemist in the Powell Duffryn Group. He is a distant cousin of R J David [qv].

WILLIAMS, Clifford
Born Llangennech, 20 April 1898; died Cardiff, 28 May 1930
Career: Llangennech School; Llangennech; Llanelli; Cardiff; Glamorgan Police; Royal Navy; Bargoed

Forward in 2 matches, against: New Zealand, 1924; England, 1925

Cliff Williams had been a collier before he joined the Glamorgan Constabulary. He served in the Royal Navy during the First World War. In 1924, he played for Llanelli against New Zealand. Sadly, he died very shortly after his wedding day.

WILLIAMS, Clive
Born Porthcawl, 2 November 1948
Career: Porthcawl Comprehensive School; Porthcawl; Neath; Aberavon; Swansea; Barbarians; Wales B

Prop in 8 matches, against: England, 1977, 1980, 1983; Scotland, 1977, 1980; France, 1980; Ireland, 1980; New Zealand, 1980

British Isles 1977 tour New Zealand; 1980 South Africa: 4 caps

Troubled by a ligament injury to a knee, Clive Williams played in only nine tour games for the British Isles in New Zealand in 1977. Three years later, he appeared in twelve games for the British Isles in South Africa, which was the joint highest number of appearances on this tour (shared with Graham Price, his fellow prop). In his last season of international rugby Williams made a tour of Spain with Wales B.

WILLIAMS, David Aled
Born Cardigan, 26 January 1964
Career: Llandovery College; Polytechnic of Wales, Pontypridd; Welsh Schools; Welsh Students; British Polytechnics; Llandovery; Llanelli; Swansea; Bridgend; Carmarthenshire

Wing in 1 match, against: Namibia, 1990(r)

Aled Williams, a building surveyor for Westbury Homes, played for a Wales Under 16 side in a sevens tournament in Sydney. Normally a stand-off, he came on as a replacement wing for Steve Ford in the second international against Namibia, at Windhoek. He was the leading scorer, with 120 points, for Bridgend in the 1990-91 Heineken League.

WILLIAMS, David Brynmor
Born Cardigan, 29 October 1951
Career: Cardigan Grammar School; Cardiff College of Education; Welsh Secondary Schools; Cardiff; Newport; Swansea; Barbarians; Wales B

Scrum-half in 3 matches, against: Australia, 1978; England, 1981; Scotland, 1981: Scored 1t - 4 points

British Isles 1977 tour New Zealand: 3 caps

Brynmor Williams scored a try in his debut game, against Australia in 1978. He had already played in three internationals, out of a total of twelve games, for the British Isles in New Zealand the previous year. A fine all-round athlete, he had captured the Welsh Schools high jump title and competed in a number of events in the British Youth championship. He travelled to Canada with a Barbarians party in 1976, and to the United States and Canada in 1980 with Wales B. He moved east from Swansea to Cardiff in July 1982 to join Cardiff City RLFC (making his first appearance on 29 August), and won one Wales RL cap. Previously a teacher and a building society manager, he is now the regional development executive for Heath Wales, part of C E Heath (UK) Ltd, the insurance brokers. During the winter months, he provides knowledgeable rugby commentary on Radio Cymru and Radio Wales.

WILLIAMS, Denzel
Born Trefil, 17 October 1938
Career: Welsh Youth; Tredegar; Ebbw Vale; Vichy (France); Barbarians

Prop in 36 matches, against: England, 1963, 1964, 1965,

1966, 1967, 1968, 1969, 1970, 1971; Scotland, 1963, 1964, 1965, 1966, 1969, 1970, 1971; Ireland, 1963, 1964, 1965, 1966, 1969, 1970, 1971; France, 1963, 1964, 1965, 1967, 1969, 1971; South Africa, 1964, 1970; Australia, 1966, 1969; New Zealand, 1967, 1969, 1969

British Isles 1966 tour Australia: 2 caps, New Zealand: 3 caps

Steelworker Denzel Williams made three overseas tours, the first to South Africa with Wales in 1964 (where he played in all four matches), the second to Australasia with the British Isles in 1966 (with six appearances in Australia and twelve in New Zealand), and on the final tour with Wales to Australasia and Fiji in 1969 (playing in all seven matches). He has also coached Rhymney RFC.

WILLIAMS, Edwin
Born Cwmllynfell, c1898; died Swansea, 31 January 1983
Career: Cwmllynfell; Swansea; Neath

Stand-off in 2 matches, against: New Zealand, 1924; France, 1925

Eddie Williams, a colliery fitter, 'went North' and played his first game for Huddersfield RLFC on 29 August 1925. He won one Wales RL cap.

WILLIAMS, Evan
Born Port Talbot, 18 June 1906; died Leeds, 18 November 1976
Career: Eastern School, Port Talbot; Taibach; Steel Company of Wales; Aberavon

Centre in 2 matches, against: England, 1925; Scotland, 1925

On 7 November 1925, Evan Williams scored a try in his first game for Leeds RLFC. In 425 appearances for the club he played in two winning Cup Final sides in 1932 and 1936. He served in the Royal Artillery in the Second World War. Before working as an industrial civil servant at Barnbrow Ordnance Factory, Leeds, he had been a blacksmith's striker in Port Talbot. He received the Imperial Service Medal. He is probably the youngest player to be capped by Wales this century - five months short of his nineteenth birthday.

WILLIAMS, Franklyn Lewis
Born Cardiff, 26 January 1910; died Tamworth, Staffordshire, 7 July 1959
Career: Cardiff High School; Christ College Brecon; Trinity College, Carmarthen; Cardiff; Wakefield; Headingley; Barbarians; Yorkshire

Stand-off/centre in 14 matches, against: Scotland, 1929,

1930, 1932; France, 1929, 1930, 1931; Ireland, 1929, 1930, 1931, 1932, 1933; England, 1930, 1932; South Africa, 1931: Scored 2t - 6 points

Frank Williams won his first cap, against Scotland, one week after his nineteenth birthday. He married Erith Maisie, the only daughter of E Gwyn Nicholls [qv] in August 1936 and was employed as a sports master at the Queen Elizabeth Grammar School, Wakefield. He captained Yorkshire in 1932-33. His father, Dr W G Williams, was the medical officer to Cardiff RFC.

WILLIAMS, Gareth Powell
Born Bedlinog, 6 November 1954
Career: Bridgend Grammar School; Cardiff College of Education; Welsh Secondary Schools; Bridgend; Barbarians; Glamorgan; Wales B

No 8/flanker in 5 matches, against: New Zealand, 1980; England, 1981; Scotland, 1981; Australia, 1981; Ireland, 1982

British Isles 1980 tour(r) South Africa

In the 1977-78 season Gareth Williams scored twenty-one tries, which was a club record for a forward at Bridgend. On tour with Wales B in the United States and Canada in 1980, he was called to join the British Isles party in South Africa as a replacement for Stuart Lane, where he played in six tour games. He captained Bridgend in the 1984-85 season. A former teacher, he is now a building society manager. He is the brother of O Ll Williams [qv].

WILLIAMS, Gerald
Born Swansea, 21 October 1954
Heol Gam Secondary Modern School, Bridgend; Welsh Schools; Bridgend; Newport; Pontypridd; Glamorgan Wanderers; Wales B

Scrum-half in 4 matches, against: Ireland, 1981; France, 1981; England, 1982(r); Scotland, 1982

Gerald Williams toured the United States and Canada with Wales B in 1980. He was a member of the winning Bridgend teams in the 1979 and 1980 Schweppes Cup Finals. He captained Bridgend in 1981-82 leading the club to a 12-9 victory over Australia in October 1981 and now coaches South Wales Police.

WILLIAMS, Gerwyn
Born Glyncorrwg, 22 April 1924
Career: Port Talbot Secondary School; Loughborough College; Welsh Secondary Schools; Taibach; Devonport Services; Royal Navy; London Welsh; Llanelli; Barbarians; Middlesex; Hampshire

Full back in 13 matches, against: Ireland, 1950, 1951, 1952; France, 1950, 1951, 1952; England, 1951, 1952, 1954; Scotland, 1951, 1952; South Africa, 1951; New Zealand, 1953

Gerwyn Williams played cricket for Welsh Schools. During his student days he won the Loughborough Colleges welterweight boxing title. In November 1951, he played for London Counties against South Africa and in January 1952, for the Barbarians against the same opposition. In November 1951, he appeared for London Counties against South Africa and in November 1953 for the same side against New Zealand. He was the captain of London Welsh in the 1953-54 season. A much sought after coach - he was head of PE at Whitgift School, Croydon - he coached the Cambridge University, Blackheath and London Counties sides. He was able to translate this expertise into book form, with the publication of *Tackle Rugger This Way*, published in 1957, and *Modern Rugby*, published in 1964.

WILLIAMS, Griffith Morgan
Born Pontypridd, 30 June 1907
Career: Aberavon Harlequins; Aberavon

Forward in 3 matches, against: England, 1936; Scotland, 1936; Ireland, 1936

Following a period as a labourer in the building trade and worker in a dry dock, Griff Williams was employed as a steelworker.

WILLIAMS, Henry Raymond
Born Felinfoel, 13 November 1927
Career: Llanelli Grammar School; St Luke's College, Exeter; Cardiff College of Education; Felinfoel; Llanelli

Wing in 3 matches, against: Scotland, 1954; France, 1957; Australia, 1958: Scored 1t - 3 points

Ray Williams, a schoolmaster, taught the rugby XV in Gwendraeth Grammar School. He captained Llanelli in 1955-56.

WILLIAMS, John Frederick
Born Scethrog, 18 November 1882; died Nigeria, 28 August 1911
Career: Christ College Brecon; Richmond; London Welsh; Barbarians; Glamorgan; Middlesex

Forward in 4 matches, against: Ireland, 1905; New Zealand, 1905; Scotland, 1906; South Africa, 1906

Anglo-Welsh tour 1908 Australia, New Zealand: 1 cap

'Scethrog' Williams appeared for Glamorgan against both New Zealand in 1905 and South Africa in 1906. He also played for Middlesex against South Africa in 1906. He captained London Welsh in 1907-08 and in 1908 toured Australasia with the Anglo-Welsh tourists, appearing in eight matches in New Zealand. He was in the Colonial Service in Nigeria where he died after contracting blackwater fever.

WILLIAMS, John James
Born Nantyffyllon, 1 April 1948
Career: Maesteg Grammar School; Cardiff College of Education; Welsh Secondary Schools; Maesteg; Bridgend; Llanelli; Barbarians; Wales B

Wing in 30 matches, against: France, 1973(r), 1974, 1975, 1976, 1977, 1978, 1979; Australia, 1973, 1975, 1978, 1978; Scotland, 1974, 1975, 1976, 1977, 1978, 1979; Ireland, 1974, 1975, 1976, 1977, 1978, 1979; England, 1974, 1975, 1976, 1977, 1978, 1979; New Zealand, 1978: Scored 12t - 48 points

British Isles 1974 tour South Africa: 4 caps; 1977 New Zealand: 3 caps

John Williams has scored international tries against all seven International Board countries. Except for the tries scored for the British Isles against the All Blacks and the Springboks, all the tries were scored for Wales against the other five. On the 1974 British Isles tour of South Africa, he played in twelve games, scoring two tries in the second and two tries in the third internationals. In New Zealand in 1977, he scored a try in the second international, appearing in fourteen games for the British Isles side. He was also a member of the Welsh teams that toured Canada (1973), the Far East (1975) and Australia (1978) and of the Barbarians side that toured Canada (1976). Previously a schoolmaster, he is currently a company director. He represented Wales in athletics, competing in the Commonwealth Games as a sprinter.

WILLIAMS, John L
Born Blaina, 1891; died 6 December 1965
Career: Blaina; Abertillery

Forward in 7 matches, against: England, 1920; Scotland, 1920, 1921; France, 1920, 1921; Ireland, 1920, 1921: Scored 1t - 3 points

Jack Williams, who was a colliery fireman, captained Blaina in 1912-14. In 1914, Blaina lost 0-10 to Aberavon in the South Wales Challenge Cup Final played at Bridgend. He was captain again in 1921-22 and in September 1922 moved to Abertillery which caused that club to be suspended for two weeks. The Blaina RFC history records that he was a fine singer.

WILLIAMS, John Lewis

Born Whitchurch, 3 January 1882; killed in action, Mametz Wood, France, 12 July 1916
Career: Cowbridge Grammar School; Cardiff; Newport; Whitchurch; London Welsh; Harlequins; Glamorgan

Wing in 17 matches, against: South Africa, 1906; England, 1907, 1908, 1909, 1911; Scotland, 1907, 1908, 1909, 1911; Ireland, 1907, 1908, 1909, 1910, 1911; Australia, 1908; France, 1909, 1911: Scored 17t - 51 points

Anglo-Welsh tour 1908 Australia, New Zealand: 2 caps

Averaging a try a game, Williams appeared in only two losing international matches and captained Wales against France in 1911. In 1905, he played for Glamorgan against New Zealand and in January 1907 he scored a try for Cardiff against South Africa. He scored a total of 150 tries for Cardiff and captained them in 1909-10. En route to New Zealand with the Anglo-Welsh party in 1908 (when he played in twelve tour games), he wrote reports of the voyage for the *South Wales Daily News*. A clerk in the Cardiff Coal Exchange, he served as a captain in the Welch Regiment in the First World War and was killed in the attack on Mametz Wood during the Battle of the Somme.

WILLIAMS, John Peter Rhys MBE

Born Cardiff, 2 March 1949
Career: Bridgend County School; Millfield School; St Mary's Hospital; Welsh Secondary Schools; London Welsh; Bridgend; Barbarians; Middlesex

Full back/flanker in 55 matches, against: Scotland, 1969, 1970, 1971, 1972, 1973, 1974, 1975, 1976, 1977, 1978, 1979, 1981; Ireland, 1969, 1970, 1971, 1973, 1974, 1975, 1976, 1977, 1978, 1979; France, 1969, 1970, 1971, 1972, 1973, 1974, 1975, 1976, 1977, 1978, 1979; England, 1969, 1970, 1971, 1972, 1973, 1975, 1976, 1977, 1978, 1979, 1981; New Zealand, 1969, 1969, 1972, 1978, 1980; Australia, 1969, 1973, 1975, 1978, 1978; South Africa, 1970: Scored 6t 2con 3pg - 36 points

British Isles 1971 tour Australia, New Zealand: 4 caps; 1974 South Africa: 4 caps

John 'JPR' Williams is the most capped Welsh player. Normally playing in the full back position, he played one game at flanker, against Australia in 1978. On tour with the British Isles, he appeared in one game in Australia and fourteen in New Zealand in 1971, and fifteen in South Africa in 1974. He also made five tours with Wales: to Argentina (1968), Australasia (1969), Fiji (1969), Canada (1973), the Far East (1975), and Australia (1978). 'JPR', who captained Wales in five matches, was the captain of Bridgend in 1978-79. A gifted athlete, he won the Welsh Junior tennis title, as did his three brothers, and in 1966 the Junior Wimbledon tennis title. He is an orthopaedic surgeon in Bridgend, specialising in sports injuries.

Awarded the MBE in 1977 for services to rugby, he wrote *JPR - An Autobiography* which was published in 1979 amidst charges of professionalism despite the fact that the royalties from the book were being used to further research into rugby injuries. His brother Chris won three rugby Blues at Cambridge University.

WILLIAMS, Lloyd Hugh

Born Born Taff's Well, 19 October 1933
Career: Taff's Well School; Caerphilly Secondary School; Cardiff Schoolboys; Cardiff Youth; Welsh Youth; Cardiff; Royal Air Force; Combined Services; Barbarians

Scrum-half in 13 matches, against: Scotland, 1957, 1958, 1959, 1962; Ireland, 1957, 1958, 1959; France, 1957, 1958, 1961; England, 1958, 1959, 1962

Lloyd Williams, the brother of Bleddyn Williams [*qv*], captained Cardiff between 1960 and 1962. He played with his brother Elwyn for Cardiff against the All Blacks in 1963. Another brother Gwyn played for Cardiff against the 1935 All Blacks and later went north to play for Wigan. Two uncles, Tom and Roy Roberts, also played for Cardiff. Formerly in the building industry, Lloyd Williams now runs his own wholesale meat business.

WILLIAMS, Mapson Thomas

Born Mackay, Queensland, 5 April 1891; died Wollongong, Australia, 15 July 1954
Career: St Mellons; Newport

Forward in 1 match, against: France, 1923

Regular soldier, farmer, orchardist Mapson Williams played 115 games for Newport, including thirty-one in the club's invincible 1922-23 season. His father, also named Mapson, and three uncles had played for Newport before him.

WILLIAMS, Oswald

Born Llanelli, 12 April 1921; died Risca, 23 March 1988
Career: Coleshill School, Llanelli; Furnace; Llanelli; Pontyberem; Felinfoel

Forward in 7 matches, against: England, 1947, 1948; Scotland, 1947, 1948; Australia, 1947; France, 1948; Ireland, 1948: Scored 1pg - 3 points

A steelworker, Ossie Williams captained Llanelli in 1951-52. He served in the Welsh Guards in the Second World War. He played for Llanelli against Australia in 1947 and captained the club against South Africa in 1951. He was the cousin of Stanley Williams [*qv*].

WILLIAMS, Owain Llewellyn

Born Ogmore-by-Sea, 10 October 1964

Career: Brynteg Comprehensive School, Bridgend; Welsh Schools; Welsh Students; Queensland (Australia); Glamorgan Wanderers; Bridgend

Flanker in 1 match, against: Namibia, 1990

Owain Williams, the brother of G P Williams [qv], is a television design student. He played for Queensland against England and New Zealand in 1988 and has represented Mid Glamorgan Schools in both basketball and cross-country running.

WILLIAMS, Rhys Haydn
Born Cwmllynfell, 14 July 1930
Career: Ystalyfera Grammar School; University College, Cardiff; Cwmllynfell; Llanelli; Royal Air Force; Bristol; Barbarians

Lock in 23 matches, against: Ireland, 1954, 1955, 1956, 1957, 1958, 1959; France, 1954, 1955, 1957, 1958, 1959; Scotland, 1954, 1955, 1956, 1957, 1958, 1959; England, 1956, 1957, 1958, 1959, 1960; Australia, 1958

British Isles 1955 tour South Africa: 4 caps; 1959 Australia: 2 caps, New Zealand: 4 caps

Education officer Rhys Williams played for the Combined Services against South Africa on Boxing Day 1951 and New Zealand on Boxing Day 1953. He appeared in fifteen games for the British Isles on the 1955 tour of South Africa and returned to that country in 1958 with a Barbarians team. In 1959 he played in four games in Australia and in seventeen in New Zealand for the British Isles. He captained Llanelli in 1957-58 and Wales in his final game, against England in 1960. His son Stephen is currently playing for South Wales Police.

WILLIAMS, Richard Davies Garnons
Born Llowes, Radnorshire, 15 June 1856; killed in action Loos, France, 27 September 1915
Career: Magdalen College School, Oxford; Cambridge University; Royal Military College Sandhurst; Brecon; Newport

Forward in 1 match, against: England, 1881

Richard Williams was the second son of the Rev Prebendary Garnons Williams of Abercamlais. He was killed in action during the Battle of Loos in the First World War, while serving as a lieutenant colonel in the Royal Fusiliers. His son Roger played cricket for Winchester against Eton in 1908 and saw war service in the South Wales Borderers, earning an MBE.

WILLIAMS, Robert Francis
Born 1885, registered in Pontypridd; died Cardiff, 28

October 1967
Career: Cardiff; Barbarians

Full back in 4 matches, against: South Africa, 1912; England, 1913; Scotland, 1913; Ireland, 1914

Remarkably, Bobbie Williams was able to successfully play at full back despite having fingers missing on one hand and paralysed fingers on the other. He was a clerk in the Cardiff Docks and later worked for British Railways.

WILLIAMS, Stanley
Born Llanelli, 4 November 1914; died Llanelli, 21 November 1967
Career: Felinfoel; Llanelli

Lock in 6 matches, against: England, 1947; Scotland, 1947, 1948; France, 1947, 1948; Ireland, 1947

Stanley Williams played in one Red Cross international. A cousin of Oswald Williams [qv], he worked as a steel-worker and later a council worker.

WILLIAMS, Sydney Arthur
Born Aberavon, 17 April 1918; died 28 August 1976, registered in Neath
Career: Welsh Schools; Aberavon; The Army; Barbarians

Wing in 3 matches, against: England, 1939; Scotland, 1939; Ireland, 1939

On 14 October 1939, Syd Williams scored two tries against Broughton Rangers in his first game for Salford RLFC. He was capped five times for Wales RL. He played in seven Services internationals during the Second World War. He was a café proprietor.

WILLIAMS, T
Born details unknown
Career: Swansea; London Welsh

Forward in 2 matches, against: Scotland, 1888; Ireland, 1888

Williams played for Swansea against the New Zealand Natives on Christmas Eve, 1888.

WILLIAMS, Thomas
Born Llwynypia, c1860; died Llwynypia, 4 February 1913
Career: Pontypridd; Cardiff; Llwynypia

Forward in 1 match, against: Ireland, 1882

Solicitor Tom Williams was an uncle to Willie Llewellyn [qv]. He served on the WRU committee as a vice-president and selector and was a representative on the International Board from 1901 until 1908. He refereed the match between England and Ireland in 1904 and appears in several team photographs as a touch judge.

WILLIAMS, Thomas
Born Dunvant, c1887; died Swansea, 13 August 1927
Career: Swansea

Forward in 6 matches, against: Ireland, 1912, 1914; France, 1913, 1914; England, 1914; Scotland, 1914: Scored 1t - 3 points

Tom Williams was a member of the 'Terrible Eight'. During the First World War he served as a captain in the Royal Engineers. He was a member of the Gower Rural District Council from 1925 until his death in 1927.

WILLIAMS, Trevor George
Born Aberaman, 27 May 1907; died Newbridge, 27 August 1982
Career: Cross Keys

Forward in 8 matches, against: Scotland, 1935, 1936, 1937; Ireland, 1935, 1936, 1937; New Zealand, 1935; England, 1936

'Tabber' Williams, a colliery official at North Celynnen Colliery, captained Cross Keys in 1936-37. He gave up rugby the day he married the niece of 'Docker' Winmill [qv]. His daughter Ruth won the Belgian Badminton Championship.

WILLIAMS, Tudor
Born c1899; died Gwaun-cae-gurwen, 24 July 1922
Career: Cwmllynfell; Swansea

Scrum-half in 1 match, against: France, 1921

Tudor Williams, while employed as an assistant electrician at the Blaencaegurwen Colliery, was tragically electrocuted at work, aged twenty three, the youngest Welsh cap to die.

WILLIAMS, Walter John
Born 14 December 1943, registered in Neath; died Resolven, 10 March 1985
Career: Neath

Prop in 2 matches, against: Ireland, 1974; France, 1974

Farmer Walter Williams was a member of the Neath side which defeated Llanelli in the first Schweppes Cup Final, in 1972. In 1974, he toured Argentina with Wales. He took his own life after a domestic dispute.

WILLIAMS, William Arthur
Born Crumlin, 29 December 1905; died Manchester, 4 November 1973
Career: Cross Keys; Crumlin

Forward in 4 matches, against: England, 1927; Scotland, 1927; France, 1927; Ireland, 1927

Billy Williams, the only player capped directly from Crumlin, won three Championship and one Challenge Cup winners medals with Salford RLFC, having made his debut for them on 15 October 1927. In the following year he played in twelve games for the Great Britain RL side on their tour of Australasia. He won five rugby league caps - three for Wales and two for Great Britain. A collier before moving North, he first became a dyer in a textile factory, and later, a licensee. His Wales Cap was withheld when he went north but was posthumously presented under the 1975 'amnesty'.

WILLIAMS, William Arthur
Born Talywain, 9 September 1921
Career: Talywain; Newport

Scrum-half in 3 matches, against: Ireland, 1952; France, 1952; England, 1953

Steelworker Billy Williams was a lorry driver in the Second World War.

WILLIAMS, William Edward
Born 15 December 1866; died Chepstow, 22 June 1945
Career: St John's School, Leatherhead; Cardiff; London Welsh

Forward in 5 matches, against: Scotland, 1887, 1889, 1890; Ireland, 1887; England, 1890

W E Williams, an electrical engineer, captained Cardiff in 1890-91 but was injured against Newport in November 1890 and did not play again.

WILLIAMS, William Henry
Born Pontlottyn, 1873; died Barry Dock, 9 January 1936
Career: Pontymister; London Welsh

Forward in 4 matches, against: England, 1900, 1901; Scotland, 1900; Ireland, 1900: Scored 2t - 6 points
'Buller' Williams was a monumental mason in Risca. In later years he moved to Barry where he became active in the local horticultural society and the Baptist church in Holton Road where he was a Sunday school teacher. He was also the secretary of the Barry Sunday School Union. One of his Wales caps is in the Cross Keys clubhouse.

WILLIAMS, William Leslie Thomas
Born Mynyddygarreg, 10 May 1922
Career: Cardiff Training College; Trimsaran Boys Club; Devonport Services; Royal Navy; Combined Services; Llanelli; Cardiff; Cornwall; Devon

Wing/centre in 7 matches against: England, 1947, 1949; Scotland, 1947; France, 1947; Ireland, 1947, 1948; Australia, 1947: Scored 3t - 9 points

Les Williams, who taught PE and, until his retirement in 1981, was, for twenty five years, the PE advisor to the Cornwall Education Authority, had served in the Royal Navy during the Second World War. On 22 January 1949, one week after scoring two tries against England in his final international, he made his debut for Hunslet RLFC against St Helens. He won a further fifteen Welsh caps in the professional game. In September 1983 he represented the British Athletics team in the World Veterans Championships in Puerto Rico. At the time he held the World Veterans record for the 60 and 200 metres, and the British Veterans record for the triple jump.

WILLIAMS, William Owen Gooding
Born Gower, 19 November 1929
Career: Gowerton; Swansea; Devonport Services; Royal Navy; Barbarians

Prop in 22 matches, against: France, 1951, 1952, 1953, 1954, 1955; South Africa, 1951; England, 1952, 1953, 1954, 1955, 1956; Scotland, 1952, 1953, 1954, 1955, 1956; Ireland, 1952, 1953, 1954, 1955, 1956; New Zealand, 1953: Scored 2t - 6 points

British Isles 1955 tour South Africa: 4 caps

'Stoker' Williams played for the Combined Services against South Africa on Boxing Day 1951. He toured South Africa with the 1955 British Isles, playing in sixteen games and leading the pack in the third international. A boilermaker and later a steelworker, he captained Swansea in the 1955-57 seasons. In November 1960, he played for Swansea against South Africa.

WILLIAMS-JONES, Hugh
Born Bryncethin, 10 January 1963
Career: Ynysawdre Comprehensive School; Welsh Youth; South Wales Police; Welsh Police; Combined Services; Pontypridd; Bridgend; Glamorgan; Wales B

Prop in 3 matches, against: Scotland, 1989(r); France, 1990(r); Ireland, 1990

Hugh Williams-Jones is a police officer in the South Wales Constabulary. He played cricket for Glamorgan at Under

15 level.

WILLIS, William Rex
Born Ystrad, 25 October 1924
Career: Llandaff Cathedral School; Nautical College, Pangbourne; Llandaff; Cardiff; Barbarians

Scrum-half in 21 matches, against: England, 1950, 1951, 1952, 1954, 1955; Scotland, 1950, 1951, 1952, 1953, 1954, 1955; Ireland, 1950, 1951, 1954, 1955; France, 1950, 1951, 1954, 1955; South Africa, 1951; New Zealand, 1953

British Isles 1950 tour Australia: 1 cap, New Zealand: 1 cap

Rex Willis won his first cap against England in 1950 at Twickenham in Wales' second win at this venue since 1910. At the end of that season, in which he appeared against all the championship sides, Wales had won the Triple Crown and Grand Slam. He was the biggest of the three British Isles scrum-halves in Australasia in 1950 and he played in nine games in New Zealand and three in Australia. Willis captained Cardiff in 1952-53 and Wales on two occasions. He is a cinema proprietor.

WILTSHIRE, Maxwell Lloyd
Born Milsom Point, Sydney, Australia, 16 July 1938
Career: Rhydhir Lower Comprehensive School; Vardre; Skewen; BP Llandarcy; Aberavon; Bridgend; Barbarians

Lock in 4 matches, against: New Zealand, 1967; England, 1968; Scotland, 1968; France, 1968

Max Wiltshire is a taxi driver in Aberavon following a career as an oil process worker. He captained Aberavon from 1965 until 1967. He coached BP Llandarcy RFC and is currently coaching Aberavon and the Skewen Under 16 side.

WINDSOR, Robert William
Born Newport, 31 January 1946
Career: Brynglas Secondary Modern School; Newport Saracens; Cross Keys; Cardiff; Pontypool; Barbarians; Monmouthshire; Wales B

Hooker in 28 matches, against: Australia, 1973, 1975, 1978, 1978; Scotland, 1974, 1975, 1976, 1977, 1978, 1979; Ireland, 1974, 1975, 1976, 1977, 1978, 1979; France, 1974, 1975, 1976, 1977, 1978, 1979; England, 1974, 1975, 1976, 1977, 1978, 1979: Scored 1t - 4 points

British Isles 1974 tour South Africa: 4 caps; 1977 New Zealand: 1 cap

Bobby Windsor, who captained Cross Keys in 1972-73, scored a try on his debut for Wales, against Australia, in

1973. He made three tours with Wales: Canada (1973), the Far East (1975) and Australia (1978). He also played for Wales in the following uncapped matches, Japan (1973), New Zealand (1974), Argentina (1976) and Romania (1979). On the two British Isles tours, he played in twelve games in South Africa in 1974, and in thirteen games in New Zealand in 1977. He is employed as a sales representative for an industrial products company.

WINFIELD, Herbert Ben
Born Nottingham, 1878; died Cardiff, 21 September 1919
Career: Cardiff; London Welsh

Full back in 15 matches, against: Ireland, 1903, 1904, 1906, 1907, 1908; England, 1904, 1906, 1908; Scotland, 1904, 1906, 1907, 1908; New Zealand, 1905; France, 1908; Australia, 1908: Scored 14con 6pg 1gm - 50 points

On the eve of the game against England in January 1901, Bert Winfield was called upon to play at full back for Wales instead of the chosen Billy Bancroft who was also the nominated captain. A telegram purporting to come from Bancroft, addressed to Walter E Rees, the secretary of the WRU, read: "Regret cannot play tomorrow; influenza - Bancroft". Gwyn Nicholls was made captain and the cards listing both teams, with Winfield at full back, were printed. It transpired that the telegram was a hoax; Bancroft took his place at full back, and the disappointed Winfield had to wait until February 1903 before winning his first cap. Winfield played for the Rest of England against Devon in 1902, captained Cardiff from 1901 until 1903 and Wales in one game, against Ireland in Belfast, in 1908. He kicked a conversion and a penalty for Cardiff against South Africa in January 1907. In 1912, he played in the final of the Welsh Golfing Union championships and in October of the same year played golf for Wales against the Midlands and in October 1913 for Wales against Ireland. He served in the 16th (Cardiff City) Bn, The Welch Regiment in the First World War. A partner with his brother-in-law, E G Nicholls [qv], in a laundry business in Cardiff, he died from injuries sustained after falling from his motor cycle in 1919.

WINMILL, Stanley
Born Bedwellty, 5 May 1889; died Nine Mile Point Colliery, Caerleon, 25 June 1940
Career: Cross Keys; Monmouthshire

Forward in 4 matches, against: England, 1921; Scotland, 1921; France, 1921; Ireland, 1921

'Docker' Winmill captained Cross Keys in 1912-13 and 1919-22. He was a member of the stay-down strike at the Nine Mile Point Colliery. Later employed as a policeman at the same colliery, he tripped and fell over a rail, pitching onto his head, and sustaining severe injuries which proved to be fatal. In earlier years he had lost an eye in a colliery

accident. His brother Joe played in the forwards for Abertillery and was in the team that drew with Australia in 1908. His niece (Joe's daughter) married 'Tabber' Williams [qv] - her brother Len owned the renowned Winmill School of Dancing in Risca.

WINTLE, Richard Vivian
Born Kenfig Hill, 11 December 1967
Career: Cynffig Comprehensive School, Kenfig Hill; St Mary's Hospital, London; Welsh Schools; Cornelly Youth; Kenfig Hill; Welsh Students; London Welsh; Bridgend; Wales B

Wing in 1 match, against: Western Samoa, 1988(r)

Richard Wintle, who is currently a medical student, has been capped at the following levels by Wales: Under 15 (Schools), 1983; Under 18 (Schools), 1985; Under 21, 1988. He won the Welsh men's 200 metres title in 1985 while still at school.

WOOLLER, Wilfred
Born Rhos-on-Sea, 20 November 1912
Career: Llandudno County School; Rydal School; Cambridge University; The Army; Cardiff; Sale; London Welsh; Barbarians

Centre/wing in 18 matches, against: England, 1933, 1935, 1936, 1937, 1939; Scotland, 1933, 1935, 1936, 1937, 1938, 1939; Ireland, 1933, 1935, 1936, 1937, 1938, 1939; New Zealand, 1935: Scored 6t 1con 2pg - 26 points

Wilfred Wooller, an excellent all-round sportsman, won three Cambridge rugby Blues in 1933-35, two cricket Blues in 1935 and 1936 and played centre-forward for Cardiff City in a handful of games in 1939. He played squash for Wales, and cricket for Denbighshire and Glamorgan (from 1938-62) - captaining them from 1947-60 and was the secretary from 1947 until 1977 and a Test Selector from 1955 until 1961. During the Second World War he served in the 77th Heavy Anti-Aircraft Regiment and scored three tries for the British Army in a 36-3 win over France, at the Parc des Princes, in 1940. He became a prisoner of war in Java in February 1943. An executive with a coal company and an insurance broker, he was also a correspondent for the *News Chronicle*, and an associate editor with *Welsh Rugby*. He now contributes a column to the *Sunday Telegraph* and is a cricket commentator for BBC Wales television

WYATT, Mark Anthony
Born Crickhowell, 12 February 1957
Career: Brecon Grammar School; University College Swansea; British Universities; Universities Athletics Union; Swansea; Barbarians; Breconshire; Wales B

Full back in 10 matches, against: England, 1983, 1987;

Scotland, 1983, 1985, 1987; Ireland, 1983, 1985, 1987; France, 1983; Australia, 1984: Scored 1t 7con 21pg - 81 points

Mark Wyatt is a systems officer with West Glamorgan County Council. He was a member of the Swansea VII which won the WRU National Sevens title in May 1980. He played for Wales B against Australia in October 1981 and for a Wales XV, against the Maoris (1982) and Japan (1983). His father played for Pontypool and his sister has played rugby for the Welsh Women's team.

YOUNG, David
Born Aberdare, 27 June 1967
Career: Aberdare Comprehensive School; Welsh Schools; Aberaman Youth; Welsh Youth; Swansea; Cardiff; Barbarians; Wales B

Prop in 14 matches, against: England, [1987 World Cup], 1988; New Zealand, [1987 World Cup], 1988, 1988, 1989; United States, 1987; Scotland, 1988, 1989; Ireland, 1988; France, 1988, 1990; Western Samoa, 1988; Romania, 1988: Scored 1t - 4 points

British Isles 1989 tour Australia: 3 caps

Dai Young played in eight games for the British Isles in Australia in 1985. In 1990, he signed for Leeds RLFC, making his debut against Barrow on 11 February. He transferred to Salford in April 1991.

YOUNG, George Avery
Born 1866, registered in Tynemouth; died Penarth, 21 January 1900
Career: Malvern School; Cardiff

Forward in 2 matches, against: England, 1886; Scotland, 1886

After joining Cardiff as a three-quarter, George Young captained the club in 1887-88 and in 1888-89. He also played cricket for Glamorgan in 1892-93. He was the son of shipowner Charles Octavius Young.

YOUNG, Jeffrey OBE
Born Blaengarw 16 September 1942
Career: Garw Grammar School; St Luke's College, Exeter; Welsh Secondary Schools; Blaengarw; Harrogate; Royal Air Force; London Welsh; Bridgend; Yorkshire

Hooker in 23 matches, against: Scotland, 1968, 1969, 1971, 1972, 1973; Ireland, 1968, 1969, 1970, 1971, 1973; France, 1968, 1969, 1970, 1971, 1972, 1973; England, 1969, 1970, 1971, 1972, 1973; New Zealand, 1969, 1972

British Isles 1968 tour South Africa: 1 cap

Jeff Young was a schoolmaster before joining the Royal Air Force, where he is now a wing commander. He made nine appearances for the British Isles in South Africa in 1968. He has been coach to the Welsh team and team manager at Bridgend. In December 1990, he was appointed the first technical director to the Welsh Rugby Union, a position which he took up on 1 April 1991.

ADDENDUM

Shortly after going to press it was discovered that the player's details given below had been omitted from the text due to confusion over his surname.

EVANS, Walter Rice
Born 10 September 1863, registered in Neath; died Neath, 9 June 1909
Career: Cowbridge Grammar School; Crauford College, Maidenhead; Oxford University; Swansea; Neath; London Welsh

Forward in 3 matches, against: Scotland, 1890, 1891; England, 1891

Walter Evans, a landowner at Melincrythan, Neath, gained a Blue at Oxford in 1890.

MATCH	DATE	AGAINST	SCORE			RESULT	VENUE
1	19.02.1881	England				Lost	Blackheath
2	28.01.1882	Ireland				Won	Dublin
3	16.12.1882	England				Lost	Swansea
4	08.01.1883	Scotland				Lost	Edinburgh
5	05.01.1884	England				Lost	Leeds
6	12.01.1884	Scotland				Lost	Newport
7	12.04.1884	Ireland				Won	Cardiff
8	03.01.1885	England				Lost	Swansea
9	10.01.1885	Scotland				Drawn	Glasgow
10	02.01.1886	England				Lost	Blackheath
11	09.01.1886	Scotland				Lost	Cardiff
12	08.01.1887	England				Drawn	Llanelli
13	26.02.1887	Scotland				Lost	Edinburgh
14	12.03.1887	Ireland				Won	Birkenhead
15	04.02.1888	Scotland				Won	Newport
16	03.03.1888	Ireland				Lost	Dublin
17	22.12.1888	N. Zealand Natives				Won	Swansea
18	02.02.1889	Scotland				Lost	Edinburgh
19	02.03.1889	Ireland				Lost	Swansea
20	01.02.1890	Scotland				Lost	Cardiff
21	15.02.1890	England				Won	Dewsbury
22	01.03.1890	Ireland				Drawn	Dublin
23	03.01.1891	England				Lost	Newport
24	07.02.1891	Scotland				Lost	Edinburgh
25	07.03.1892	England				Lost	Blackheath
26	07.01.1892	England				Lost	Blackheath
27	06.02.1892	Scotland				Lost	Swansea
28	05.03.1892	Ireland				Lost	Dublin
29	07.01.1893	England	12	-	11	Won	Cardiff
30	04.02.1893	Scotland	9	-	0	Won	Edinburgh
31	11.03.1893	Ireland	2	-	0	Won	Llanelli
32	06.01.1894	England	3	-	24	Lost	Birkenhead
33	03.02.1894	Scotland	7	-	0	Won	Newport
34	10.03.1894	Ireland	0	-	3	Lost	Belfast
35	05.01.1895	England	6	-	14	Lost	Swansea
36	26.01.1895	Scotland	4	-	5	Lost	Edinburgh
37	16.03.1895	Ireland	5	-	3	Won	Cardiff
38	04.01.1896	England	0	-	25	Lost	Blackheath
39	25.01.1896	Scotland	6	-	0	Won	Cardiff
40	14.03.1896	Ireland	4	-	8	Lost	Dublin
41	09.01.1897	England	11	-	0	Won	Newport
42	19.03.1898	Ireland	11	-	3	Won	Limerick
43	02.02.1898	England	7	-	14	Lost	Blackheath
44	07.01.1899	England	26	-	3	Won	Swansea
45	04.03.1899	Scotland	10	-	21	Lost	Edinburgh
46	18.03.1899	Ireland	0	-	3	Lost	Cardiff
47	06.01.1900	England	13	-	3	Won	Gloucester
48	27.01.1900	Scotland	12	-	3	Won	Swansea
49	17.03.1900	Ireland	3	-	0	Won	Belfast
50	05.01.1901	England	13	-	0	Won	Cardiff
51	09.02.1901	Scotland	8	-	18	Lost	Edinburgh

MATCH	DATE	AGAINST	SCORE			RESULT	VENUE
52	16.03.1901	Ireland	10	-	9	Won	Swansea
53	11.01.1902	England	9	-	8	Won	Blackheath
54	01.02.1902	Scotland	14	-	15	Won	Cardiff
55	08.03.1902	Ireland	15	-	0	Won	Dublin
56	10.01.1903	England	21	-	5	Won	Swansea
57	07.02.1903	Scotland	0	-	6	Lost	Edinburgh
58	14.03.1903	Ireland	18	-	0	Won	Cardiff
59	09.01.1904	England	14	-	14	Drawn	Leicester
60	06.02.1904	Scotland	21	-	3	Won	Swansea
61	12.03.1904	Ireland	12	-	14	Lost	Belfast
62	14.02.1905	England	25	-	0	Won	Cardiff
63	04.02.1905	Scotland	6	-	3	Won	Edinburgh
64	11.03.1905	Ireland	10	-	3	Won	Swansea
65	16.12.1905	New Zealand	3	-	0	Won	Cardiff
66	13.01.1906	England	16	-	3	Won	Richmond
67	03.02.1906	Scotland	9	-	3	Won	Cardiff
68	10.03.1906	Ireland	6	-	11	Lost	Belfast
69	01.12.1906	South Africa	0	-	11	Lost	Swansea
70	12.01.1907	England	22	-	0	Won	Swansea
71	02.02.1907	Scotland	3	-	6	Lost	Edinburgh
72	09.03.1907	Ireland	29	-	0	Won	Cardiff
73	18.01.1908	England	28	-	18	Won	Bristol
74	01.02.1908	Scotland	6	-	5	Won	Swansea
75	02.03.1908	France	36	-	4	Won	Cardiff
76	14.03.1908	Ireland	11	-	5	Won	Belfast
77	12.12.1908	Australia	9	-	6	Won	Cardiff
78	16.01.1909	England	8	-	0	Won	Cardiff
79	06.02.1909	Scotland	5	-	3	Won	Edinburgh
80	23.02.1909	France	47	-	5	Won	Paris
81	13.03.1909	Ireland	18	-	5	Won	Swansea
82	01.01.1910	France	49	-	14	Won	Swansea
83	15.01.1910	England	6	-	11	Lost	Twickenham
84	05.02.1910	Scotland	14	-	0	Won	Cardiff
85	12.03.1910	Ireland	19	-	3	Won	Dublin
86	21.01.1911	England	15	-	11	Won	Swansea
87	04.02.1911	Scotland	32	-	10	Won	Edinburgh
88	28.02.1911	France	15	-	0	Won	Paris
89	11.03.1911	Ireland	16	-	0	Won	Cardiff
90	20.01.1912	England	0	-	8	Lost	Twickenham
91	03.02.1912	Scotland	21	-	6	Won	Swansea
92	09.03.1912	Ireland	5	-	12	Lost	Belfast
93	25.03.1912	France	14	-	8	Won	Newport
94	14.12.1912	South Africa	0	-	3	Lost	Cardiff
95	18.01.1913	England	0	-	12	Lost	Cardiff
96	01.02.1913	Scotland	8	-	0	Won	Edinburgh
97	27.02.1913	France	11	-	8	Won	Paris
98	08.03.1913	Ireland	16	-	3	Won	Swansea
99	17.01.1914	England	9	-	10	Lost	Twickenham
100	07.02.1914	Scotland	24	-	5	Won	Cardiff
101	02.03.1914	France	31	-	0	Won	Swansea
102	14.03.1914	Ireland	11	-	3	Won	Belfast
103	21.04.1919	New Zealand Army	3	-	6	Lost	Swansea
104	17.01.1920	England	19	-	5	Won	Swansea
105	07.02.1920	Scotland	5	-	9	Lost	Edinburgh
106	17.02.1920	France	6	-	5	Won	Paris
107	13.03.1920	Ireland	29	-	4	Won	Cardiff
108	15.01.1921	England	3	-	18	Lost	Twickenham

MATCH	DATE	AGAINST	SCORE		RESULT	VENUE
109	05.02.1921	Scotland	8	- 14	Lost	Swansea
110	26.02.1921	France	12	- 4	Won	Cardiff
111	12.03.1921	Ireland	6	- 0	Won	Belfast
112	21.01.1922	England	28	- 6	Won	Cardiff
113	04.02.1922	Scotland	9	- 9	Drawn	Edinburgh
114	11.03.1922	Ireland	11	- 5	Won	Swansea
115	23.03.1922	France	11	- 3	Won	Paris
116	20.01.1923	England	3	- 7	Lost	Twickenham
117	03.02.1923	Scotland	8	- 11	Lost	Cardiff
118	24.02.1923	France	16	- 8	Won	Swansea
119	10.03.1923	Ireland	4	- 5	Lost	Dublin
120	19.01.1924	England	9	- 17	Lost	Swansea
121	02.02.1924	Scotland	10	- 35	Lost	Edinburgh
122	08.03.1924	Ireland	10	- 13	Lost	Cardiff
123	27.03.1924	France	10	- 6	Won	Paris
124	29.11.1924	New Zealand	0	- 19	Lost	Swansea
125	17.01.1925	England	6	- 12	Lost	Twickenham
126	07.02.1925	Scotland	14	- 24	Lost	Swansea
127	28.02.1925	France	11	- 5	Won	Cardiff
128	14.03.1925	Ireland	3	- 19	Lost	Belfast
129	16.01.1926	England	3	- 3	Drawn	Cardiff
130	06.02.1926	Scotland	5	- 8	Lost	Edinburgh
131	13.03.1926	Ireland	11	- 8	Won	Swansea
132	05.04.1926	France	7	- 5	Won	Paris
133	15.01.1927	England	9	- 11	Lost	Twickenham
134	05.02.1927	Scotland	0	- 5	Lost	Cardiff
135	26.02.1927	France	25	- 7	Won	Swansea
136	12.03.1927	Ireland	9	- 19	Lost	Dublin
137	26.11.1927	New South Wales	8	- 18	Lost	Cardiff
138	21.01.1928	England	8	- 10	Lost	Swansea
139	04.02.1928	Scotland	13	- 0	Won	Edinburgh
140	10.02.1928	Ireland	10	- 13	Lost	Cardiff
141	09.04.1928	France	3	- 8	Lost	Paris
142	19.01.1929	England	3	- 8	Lost	Twickenham
143	02.02.1929	Scotland	14	- 7	Won	Swansea
144	23.02.1929	France	8	- 3	Won	Cardiff
145	09.03.1929	Ireland	5	- 5	Drawn	Belfast
146	18.01.1930	England	3	- 11	Lost	Cardiff
147	01.02.1930	Scotland	9	- 12	Lost	Edinburgh
148	08.03.1930	Ireland	12	- 7	Won	Swansea
149	21.04.1930	France	11	- 0	Won	Paris
150	17.01.1931	England	11	- 11	Drawn	Twickenham
151	07.02.1931	Scotland	13	- 8	Won	Cardiff
152	28.02.1931	France	35	- 3	Won	Swansea
153	14.03.1931	Ireland	15	- 3	Won	Belfast
154	05.12.1931	South Africa	3	- 8	Lost	Swansea
155	16.01.1932	England	12	- 5	Won	Swansea
156	06.02.1932	Scotland	6	- 0	Won	Edinburgh
157	12.03.1932	Ireland	10	- 12	Lost	Cardiff
158	21.01.1933	England	7	- 3	Won	Twickenham
159	04.02.1933	Scotland	3	- 11	Lost	Swansea
160	11.03.1933	Ireland	5	- 10	Lost	Belfast
161	20.01.1934	England	0	- 9	Lost	Cardiff
162	03.02.1934	Scotland	13	- 6	Won	Edinburgh
163	10.03.1934	Ireland	13	- 0	Won	Swansea
164	19.01.1935	England	3	- 3	Drawn	Twickenham
165	02.02.1935	Scotland	10	- 6	Won	Cardiff

MATCH	DATE	AGAINST	SCORE			RESULT	VENUE
166	09.03.1935	Ireland	3	-	9	Lost	Belfast
167	21.12.1935	New Zealand	13	-	12	Won	Cardiff
168	18.01.1936	England	0	-	0	Drawn	Swansea
169	01.02.1936	Scotland	13	-	3	Won	Edinburgh
170	14.03.1936	Ireland	3	-	0	Won	Cardiff
171	16.01.1937	England	3	-	4	Lost	Twickenham
172	06.02.1937	Scotland	6	-	13	Lost	Swansea
173	03.04.1937	Ireland	3	-	5	Lost	Belfast
174	15.01.1938	England	14	-	8	Won	Cardiff
175	05.02.1938	Scotland	6	-	8	Lost	Edinburgh
176	12.03.1938	Ireland	11	-	5	Won	Swansea
177	21.01.1939	England	0	-	3	Lost	Twickenham
178	04.02.1939	Scotland	11	-	3	Won	Cardiff
179	11.03.1939	Ireland	7	-	0	Won	Belfast
180	18.01.1947	England	6	-	9	Lost	Cardiff
181	01.02.1947	Scotland	22	-	8	Won	Edinburgh
182	22.03.1947	France	3	-	0	Won	Paris
183	29.03.1947	Ireland	6	-	0	Won	Swansea
184	20.12.1947	Australia	6	-	0	Won	Cardiff
185	17.01.1948	Engalnd	3	-	3	Drawn	Twickenham
186	07.02.1948	Scotland	14	-	0	Won	Cardiff
187	21.02.1948	France	3	-	11	Lost	Swansea
188	13.03.1948	Ireland	3	-	6	Lost	Belfast
189	15.01.1949	England	9	-	3	Won	Cardiff
190	05.02.1949	Scotland	3	-	6	Lost	Edinburgh
191	12.03.1949	Ireland	0	-	5	Lost	Swansea
192	26.03.1949	France	3	-	5	Lost	Paris
193	21.01.1950	England	11	-	5	Won	Twickenham
194	04.02.1950	Scotland	12	-	0	Won	Swansea
195	11.03.1950	Ireland	6	-	3	Won	Belfast
196	25.03.1950	France	21	-	0	Won	Cardiff
197	20.01.1951	England	23	-	5	Won	Swansea
198	03.02.1951	Scotland	0	-	19	Lost	Edinburgh
199	10.03.1951	Ireland	3	-	3	Drawn	Cardiff
200	07.04.1951	France	3	-	8	Lost	Paris
201	22.12.1951	South Africa	3	-	6	Lost	Cardiff
202	19.01.1952	England	8	-	6	Won	Twickenham
203	02.02.1952	Scotland	11	-	0	Won	Cardiff
204	08.03.1952	Ireland	14	-	3	Won	Dublin
205	22.03.1952	France	9	-	5	Won	Swansea
206	17.01.1953	England	3	-	8	Lost	Cardiff
207	07.02.1953	Scotland	12	-	0	Won	Edinburgh
208	14.03.1953	Ireland	5	-	3	Won	Swansea
209	28.03.1953	France	6	-	3	Won	Paris
210	19.12.1953	New Zealand	13	-	8	Won	Cardiff
211	16.01.1954	England	6	-	9	Lost	Twickenham
212	13.03.1954	Ireland	12	-	9	Won	Dublin
213	27.03.1954	France	19	-	13	Won	Cardiff
214	10.04.1954	Scotland	15	-	3	Won	Swansea
215	22.01.1955	England	3	-	0	Won	Cardiff
216	05.02.1955	Scotland	8	-	14	Lost	Edinburgh
217	12.03.1955	Ireland	21	-	3	Won	Cardiff
218	26.03.1955	France	16	-	11	Won	Paris
219	21.01.1956	England	8	-	3	Won	Twickenham
220	04.02.1956	Scotland	9	-	3	Won	Cardiff
221	10.03.1956	Ireland	3	-	11	Lost	Dublin
222	24.03.1956	France	5	-	3	Won	Cardiff

179

MATCH	DATE	AGAINST	SCORE			RESULT	VENUE
223	19.01.1957	England	0	-	3	Lost	Cardiff
224	02.02.1957	Scotland	6	-	9	Lost	Edinburgh
225	09.03.1957	Ireland	6	-	5	Won	Cardiff
226	23.03.1957	France	19	-	13	Won	Paris
227	04.01.1958	Australia	9	-	3	Won	Cardiff
228	18.01.1958	England	3	-	3	Drawn	Twickenham
229	01.02.1958	Scotland	8	-	3	Won	Cardiff
230	15.03.1958	Ireland	9	-	6	Won	Dublin
231	29.03.1958	France	6	-	16	Lost	Cardiff
232	17.01.1959	England	5	-	0	Won	Cardiff
233	07.02.1959	Scotland	5	-	6	Lost	Edinburgh
234	14.03.1959	Ireland	8	-	6	Won	Cardiff
235	04.04.1959	France	3	-	11	Lost	Paris
236	16.01.1960	England	6	-	14	Lost	Twickenham
237	06.02.1960	Scotland	8	-	0	Won	Cardiff
238	12.03.1960	Ireland	10	-	9	Won	Dublin
239	26.03.1960	France	8	-	16	Lost	Cardiff
240	03.12.1960	South Africa	0	-	3	Lost	Cardiff
241	21.01.1961	England	6	-	3	Won	Cardiff
242	11.02.1961	Scotland	0	-	3	Lost	Edinburgh
243	11.03.1961	Ireland	9	-	0	Won	Cardiff
244	25.03.1961	France	6	-	0	Lost	Paris
245	20.01.1962	England	0	-	0	Drawn	Twickenham
246	03.02.1962	Scotland	3	-	8	Lost	Cardiff
247	24.03.1962	France	3	-	0	Won	Cardiff
248	17.11.1962	Ireland	3	-	3	Drawn	Dublin
249	19.01.1963	England	6	-	13	Lost	Cardiff
250	02.02.1963	Scotland	6	-	0	Won	Edinburgh
251	09.03.1963	Ireland	6	-	14	Lost	Cardiff
252	23.03.1963	France	3	-	5	Lost	Paris
253	21.12.1963	New Zealand	0	-	6	Lost	Cardiff
254	18.01.1964	England	6	-	6	Drawn	Twickenham
255	01.02.1964	Scotland	11	-	3	Won	Cardiff
256	07.03.1964	Ireland	15	-	6	Won	Dublin
257	21.03.1964	France	11	-	11	Drawn	Cardiff
258	23.05.1964	South Africa	3	-	24	Lost	Durban
259	16.01.1965	England	14	-	3	Won	Cardiff
260	06.02.1965	Scotland	14	-	12	Won	Edinburgh
261	13.03.1965	Ireland	14	-	8	Won	Cardiff
262	27.03.1965	France	13	-	22	Lost	Paris
263	15.01.1966	England	11	-	6	Won	Twickenham
264	05.02.1966	Scotland	8	-	3	Won	Cardiff
265	12.03.1966	Ireland	6	-	9	Lost	Dublin
266	26.03.1966	France	9	-	8	Won	Cardiff
267	03.12.1966	Australia	11	-	14	Lost	Cardiff
268	04.02.1967	Scotland	5	-	11	Lost	Edinburgh
269	11.03.1967	Ireland	0	-	3	Lost	Cardiff
270	01.04.1967	France	14	-	20	Lost	Paris
271	15.04.1967	England	34	-	21	Won	Cardiff
272	11.11.1967	New Zealand	6	-	13	Lost	Cardiff
273	20.01.1968	England	11	-	11	Drawn	Twickenham
274	03.02.1968	Scotland	5	-	0	Won	Cardiff
275	09.03.1968	Ireland	6	-	9	Lost	Dublin
276	23.03.1968	France	9	-	14	Lost	Cardiff
277	01.02.1969	Scotland	17	-	3	Won	Edinburgh
278	08.03.1969	Ireland	24	-	11	Won	Cardiff
279	22.03.1969	France	8	-	8	Drawn	Paris

MATCH	DATE	AGAINST	SCORE	RESULT	VENUE
280	12.04.1969	England	30 - 9	Won	Cardiff
281	31.05.1969	New Zealand	0 - 19	Lost	Christchurch
282	14.06.1969	New Zealand	12 - 33	Lost	Auckland
283	21.06.1969	Australia	19 - 16	Won	Sydney
284	24.01.1970	South Africa	6 - 6	Drawn	Cardiff
285	07.02.1970	Scotland	18 - 9	Won	Cardiff
286	28.02.1970	England	17 - 13	Won	Twickenham
287	14.03.1970	Ireland	0 - 14	Lost	Dublin
288	04.04.1970	France	11 - 6	Won	Cardiff
289	16.01.1971	England	22 - 6	Won	Cardiff
290	06.02.1971	Scotland	19 - 18	Won	Edinburgh
291	13.03.1971	Ireland	23 - 9	Won	Cardiff
292	27.03.1971	France	9 - 5	Won	Paris
293	15.01.1972	England	12 - 3	Won	Twickenham
294	05.02.1972	Scotland	35 - 12	Won	Cardiff
295	25.03.1972	France	20 - 6	Won	Cardiff
296	02.12.1972	New Zealand	16 - 19	Lost	Cardiff
297	20.01.1973	England	25 - 9	Won	Cardiff
298	03.02.1973	Scotland	9 - 10	Lost	Edinburgh
299	10.03.1973	Ireland	16 - 12	Won	Cardiff
300	24.03.1973	France	3 - 12	Lost	Paris
301	10.11.1973	Australia	24 - 0	Won	Cardiff
302	19.01.1974	Scotland	6 - 0	Won	Cardiff
303	02.02.1974	Ireland	9 - 9	Drawn	Dublin
304	16.02.1974	France	16 - 16	Drawn	Cardiff
305	16.03.1974	England	12 - 16	Lost	Twickenham
306	18.01.1975	France	25 - 10	Won	Paris
307	15.02.1975	England	20 - 4	Won	Cardiff
308	01.03.1975	Scotland	10 - 12	Lost	Edinburgh
309	15.03.1975	Ireland	32 - 4	Won	Cardiff
310	20.12.1975	Australia	28 - 3	Won	Cardiff
311	17.01.1976	England	21 - 9	Won	Twickenham
312	07.02.1976	Scotland	28 - 6	Won	Cardiff
313	21.02.1976	Ireland	34 - 9	Won	Dublin
314	06.03.1976	France	19 - 13	Won	Cardiff
315	15.01.1977	Ireland	25 - 9	Won	Cardiff
316	05.02.1977	France	9 - 16	Lost	Paris
317	05.03.1977	England	14 - 9	Won	Cardiff
318	19.03.1977	Scotland	18 - 9	Won	Cardiff
319	04.02.1978	England	9 - 6	Won	Twickenham
320	18.02.1978	Scotland	22 - 14	Won	Cardiff
321	04.03.1978	Ireland	20 - 16	Won	Dublin
322	18.03.1978	France	16 - 7	Won	Cardiff
323	11.06.1978	Australia	8 - 18	Lost	Brisbane
324	17.06.1978	Australia	17 - 19	Lost	Sydney
325	11.11.1978	New Zealand	12 - 13	Lost	Cardiff
326	20.01.1979	Scotland	19 - 13	Won	Edinburgh
327	03.02.1979	Ireland	24 - 21	Won	Cardiff
328	17.02.1979	France	13 - 14	Lost	Paris
329	17.03.1979	England	27 - 3	Won	Cardiff
330	19.01.1980	France	18 - 9	Won	Cardiff
331	16.02.1980	England	8 - 9	Lost	Twickenham
332	01.03.1980	Scotland	17 - 6	Won	Cardiff
333	15.03.1980	Ireland	7 - 21	Lost	Dublin
334	01.11.1980	New Zealand	3 - 23	Lost	Cardiff
335	17.01.1981	England	21 - 19	Won	Cardiff
336	07.02.1981	Scotland	6 - 15	Lost	Edinburgh

MATCH	DATE	AGAINST	SCORE			RESULT	VENUE
337	21.02.1981	Ireland	9	-	8	Won	Cardiff
338	07.03.1981	France	15	-	9	Lost	Paris
339	05.12.1981	Australia	18	-	13	Won	Cardiff
340	23.01.1982	Ireland	12	-	20	Lost	Dublin
341	06.02.1982	France	22	-	12	Won	Cardiff
342	06.03.1982	England	7	-	17	Lost	Twickenham
343	20.03.1982	Scotland	18	-	34	Lost	Cardiff
344	05.02.1983	England	13	-	13	Drawn	Cardiff
345	19.02.1983	Scotland	19	-	15	Won	Edinburgh
346	05.03.1983	Ireland	23	-	9	Won	Cardiff
347	19.03.1983	France	9	-	16	Lost	Paris
348	12.11.1983	Romania	6	-	24	Lost	Bucharest
349	21.01.1984	Scotland	9	-	15	Lost	Cardiff
350	04.02.1984	Ireland	18	-	9	Won	Dublin
351	18.02.1984	France	16	-	21	Lost	Cardiff
352	17.03.1984	England	24	-	15	Won	Twickenham
353	24.11.1984	Australia	9	-	28	Lost	Cardiff
354	02.03.1985	Scotland	25	-	21	Won	Edinburgh
355	16.03.1985	Ireland	9	-	21	Lost	Cardiff
356	30.03.1985	France	3	-	14	Lost	Paris
357	20.04.1985	England	24	-	15	Won	Cardiff
358	09.11.1985	Fiji	40	-	3	Won	Cardiff
359	17.01.1986	England	18	-	21	Lost	Twickenham
360	01.02.1986	Scotland	22	-	15	Won	Cardiff
361	15.02.1986	Ireland	19	-	12	Won	Dublin
362	01.03.1986	France	15	-	23	Lost	Cardiff
363	31.05.1986	Fiji	22	-	15	Won	Suva
364	12.06.1986	Tonga	15	-	7	Won	Nuku'alofa
365	14.06.1986	Western Samoa	32	-	14	Won	Apia
366	07.02.1987	France	9	-	16	Lost	Paris
367	07.03.1987	England	19	-	12	Won	Cardiff
368	21.03.1987	Scotland	12	-	21	Lost	Edinburgh
369	04.04.1987	Ireland	11	-	15	Lost	Cardiff
370	25.05.1987	Ireland	13	-	6	Won	Wellington
371	29.05.1987	Tonga	29	-	16	Won	Palmerston N
372	03.06.1987	Canada	40	-	9	Won	Invercargill
373	08.06.1987	England	16	-	3	Won	Brisbane
374	14.06.1987	New Zealand	6	-	49	Lost	Brisbane
375	18.06.1987	Australia	22	-	21	Won	Rotorua
376	07.11.1987	USA	46	-	0	Won	Cardiff
377	06.02.1988	England	11	-	3	Won	Twickenham
378	20.02.1988	Scotland	25	-	20	Won	Cardiff
379	05.03.1988	Ireland	12	-	9	Won	Dublin
380	19.03.1988	France	9	-	10	Lost	Cardiff
381	28.05.1988	New Zealand	3	-	52	Lost	Christchurch
382	11.06.1988	New Zealand	9	-	54	Lost	Auckland
383	12.11.1988	Western Samoa	28	-	6	Won	Cardiff
384	10.12.1988	Romania	9	-	15	Lost	Cardiff
385	21.01.1989	Scotland	7	-	23	Lost	Edinburgh
386	04.02.1989	Ireland	13	-	19	Lost	Cardiff
387	18.02.1989	France	12	-	31	Lost	Paris
388	18.03.1989	England	12	-	9	Won	Cardiff
389	04.11.1989	New Zealand	9	-	34	Lost	Cardiff
390	20.01.1990	France	19	-	29	Lost	Cardiff
391	17.02.1990	England	6	-	34	Lost	Twickenham
392	03.03.1990	Scotland	9	-	13	Lost	Cardiff
393	24.03.1990	Ireland	8	-	14	Lost	Dublin

MATCH	DATE	AGAINST	SCORE	RESULT	VENUE
394	02.06.1990	Namibia	18 - 9	Won	Windhoek
395	09.06.1990	Namibia	34 - 30	Won	Windhoek
396	06.10.1990	Barbarians	24 - 31	Lost	Cardiff
397	19.01.1991	England	6 - 25	Lost	Cardiff
398	02.02.1991	Scotland	12 - 34	Lost	Edinburgh
399	16.02.1991	Ireland	21 - 21	Drawn	Cardiff
400	02.03.1991	France	3 - 36	Lost	Paris

APPENDIX 2: Analysis of Match Results

		HOME			AWAY			NEUTRAL		TOTAL		
	P	W	L	D	W	L	D	W	L	W	L	D
England	97	30	14	4	16	24	8	1	0	47	38	12
Ireland	94	33	10	2	21	22	4	2	0	56	32	6
Scotland	95	33	14	0	19	27	2	0	0	52	41	2
France	64	22	8	2	14	17	1	0	0	36	25	3
N Zealand	15	3	7	0	0	4	0	0	1	3	12	0
Australia	12	6	2	0	1	2	0	1	0	8	4	0
South Africa	7	0	5	1	0	1	0	0	0	0	6	1
Romania	2	0	1	0	0	1	0	0	0	0	2	0
Fiji	2	1	0	0	1	0	0	0	0	2	0	0
Tonga	2	0	0	0	1	0	0	1	0	2	0	0
Western Samoa	2	1	0	0	1	0	0	0	0	2	0	0
Namibia	2	0	0	0	2	0	0	0	0	2	0	0
N Zealand Natives	1	1	0	0	0	0	0	0	0	1	0	0
N Zealand Army	1	0	1	0	0	0	0	0	0	0	1	0
New South Wales	1	0	1	0	0	0	0	0	0	0	1	0
Canada	1	0	0	0	0	0	0	1	0	1	0	0
USA	1	1	0	0	0	0	0	0	0	1	0	0
Barbarians	1	0	1	0	0	0	0	0	0	0	1	0
TOTALS	400	131	64	9	76	98	15	6	1	213	163	24

APPENDIX 3: Family Connections of Welsh Internationals

Father and son capped for Wales

	Debut Years
T B and P E R Jones	1882, 1921
H and E H Jones	1904, 1930
G and W Travers	1903, 1930
G and J R Stephens	1912, 1947
J H and W Gore	1924, 1947
W H and G W Lewis	1926, 1960
D I and D B Davies	1939, 1962
L G Blythe and W R Blyth	1951, 1974

W E Vickery played for Wales in 1938 and 1939 and his father W Vickery played for England in 1905.

Brothers (2) capped for Wales

	Debut Years
D Gwyn and W H Gwynn	1882, 1884
G F and C T Harding	1881, 1888
E and D James	1890, 1891*
D and J Samuel	1891, 1891+
C B and D W Nicholl	1891, 1894
N W and S H Biggs	1888, 1895
S H and E G Nicholls	1888, 1896
T and G A Dobson	1898, 1900
W and J Bancroft	1890, 1909
E and W L Morgan	1902, 1910
J C M and L M Dyke	1906, 1910
W H and J J Wetter	1912, 1914
W J and J Powell	1920, 1923
E T and D S Parker	1919, 1924
B G and T H Hollingdale	1912, 1927
R and R Jones	1926, 1929

J and W Roberts	1927, 1929*
B R and M J L Turnbull	1925, 1933
I G and D R Prosser	1934, 1934*
J A and A Bassett	1929, 1934
W P and T O James	1925, 1935
H W and D L Thomas	1936, 1937*
T J and L M Davies	1953, 1954
B and L H Williams	1947, 1957
R D and W P Moriarty	1981, 1986*
G O and G D Llewellyn	1989, 1990*
G P and O L Williams	1980, 1990

H M Jordan played for Wales and his brother C F Jordan played for Ireland in 1884.

F E Hancock played for Wales and his brother P F Hancock played for England.

* played together for Wales
+ made their debut together for Wales

Brothers (3) capped for Wales

	Debut
R Gould	1882
J A Gould	1885
G H Gould	1892

R and J A Gould played together for Wales.
JA and G H Gould played together for Wales.

David P Jones	1907
John P Jones	1908
James P Jones	1913

APPENDIX 4: Welsh Cap Chronology, 1881-1991, Caps 1-892

The players names are arranged in the order in which they made their first appearance for Wales. If, as was very often the case, several players received their first cap on the same day, they are all allocated the same number of precedence and are listed in alphabetical order. If however, they gained their first cap as a replacement, their name will appear after the names of those who made their debut at the start of a match. The match number refers to the game in which the player made his debut, full details of which can be found in Appendix 1.

CAP	PLAYER	MATCH	CAP	PLAYER	MATCH	CAP	PLAYER	MATCH
1	Bevan, J A	1		Staddan, W J		93	Davies, A	19
	Darbishire, G		48	Gould, J A	8		Griffiths, G	
	Girling, B E			Jordan, H M			Morgan, T	
	Harding, G F			Richards, E S		96	Bancroft, W	20
	Lewis, E J			Rowland, E M			Evans, W R	
	Mann, B B			Thomas, L C			James, E	
	Newman, C H		53	Alexander, E P	9		Lloyd, D P M	
	Peake, E			Hill, A F			Thomas, S	
	Phillips, W D			Morgan, D		101	Graham, T C	22
	Purdon, F T			Thomas, W H			Ingledew, H M	
	Rees, T A		57	Bowen, W A	10	103	Bennett, P	23
	Summers, R H B			Douglas, W			Packer, H	
	Treharne, E			Lewis, D H			Pearson, T V	
	Watkins, L			Roberts, E			Pegge, E V	
	Williams, R D G			Young, G A		107	Daniel, D J	24
16	Bridie, J	2	62	Mathews, A A	11		McCutcheon, W M	
	Clapp, T J S		63	Bland, A F	12		Escott, R B	
	Clark, S S			Evans, O J		110	Deacon, T	25
	Evans, W F			Hybart, A J			James, D	
	Gould, R			Lockwood, T W			Nicholl, C B	
	Jones, T B		67	Bowen, G E	13		Samuel, D	
	Lewis, C P			Hughes, H			Samuel, J	
	Morris, G L			Williams, W E		115	Boucher, A W	26
	Norton, W B		70	Lewis, J G	14		Mills, F M	
	Vincent, H C			Towers, W H			Phillips, H P	
	Williams, T		72	Howell, W H	15		Rowles, G A	
27	Bowen, D H	3		Kedzlie, Q D			Watts, W H	
	Cattell, A			Meredith, J		120	Rees, J C	27
	Clare, J A			Powell, R W		121	Day, H T	28
	Gwyn, D			Jenkins, T J P			Gould, G H	
	Judson, T H			Roberts, E J			Nicholls, F E	
32	Griffin, J	4		Williams, T		124	Parfitt, F C	29
	Jones, J A		79	Arthur, C S	16		Fitzgerald, D	
	Lyne, H S			Thomas, C J			Thomas, W L	
35	Allen, C P	5	81	Biggs, N W	17	127	Elliot, J	34
	Andrews, F G			Garrett, R M			Hutchinson, F O	
	Gwynn, W H			Griffiths, D			Nicholl, D W	
	Margrave, F L			Hannan, J		130	Badger, O	35
	Simpson, H J			Harding, C T			Biggs, S H	
	Smith, J S			Nicholls, S H			Davies, B	
	Taylor, C G			Thomas, G			Elsey, W J	
42	Barlow, T M	7		Webb, J			Jackson, T H	
	Goldsworthy, S J		89	Bishop, E H	18	135	George, E E	36
	Hancock, F E			Evans, D W			Lloyd, E	
	Hinton, J T			Evans, G R			Pook, T R	
	Roderick, W B			Thomas, R L		138	Jenkin, A M	37

CAP	PLAYER	MATCH	CAP	PLAYER	MATCH	CAP	PLAYER	MATCH
	Morgan, D			Pritchard, C C			Hirst, G L	
140	Bowen, C A	38		Maynard, E T			Plummer, R C S	
	Dauncey, F H			Watkins, H V		256	Hawkins, F J	92
	Ramsay, S		200	Bevan, T S	61		Hiams, H	
143	Cope, W	39		Jones, H			Jenkins, W J	
	Davies, W			Pritchard, C M			Lewis, B R	
	Evans, D		203	Jones, A W	64		Martin, W J	
	Evans, J			Williams, J F			Merry, J A	
	Morris, W		205	Bush, P F	65		Williams, T	
	Nicholls, E G		206	Maddock, H T	66	263	Thomas, H	93
149	Lloyd, G L	40	207	Gibbs, R A	67	264	Andrews, F	94
	Millar, W H		208	Evans, T H	68		Geen, W P	
151	Cornish, F H	41		Powell, J A			Hollingdale, B G	
	Hellings, D			Westacott, D			Jones, P L	
	James, D		211	Dyke, J C M	69		Morgan, J L	
	Rapps, J			Jenkins, J C			Perrett, F L	
155	Alexander, W	42		Thomas, E J			Thomas, H W	
	Booth, J			Williams, J L			Wetter, W H	
	Boots, J G		215	Brown, J A	70		Williams, R F	
	Davies, H			Davies, D		273	Davies, J A	96
	Huzzey, H V P			Dowell, W H			Jones, J P	
	Jones, W			Evans, J H			Lewis, H	
162	Blake, J	44		Watts, J			Lloyd, R	
	Brice, A		220	Webb, A	71		Richards, R	
	Hodges, J J		221	David, R J	72	278	Gething, G I	97
	Llewellyn, W			Jones, D P			Lewis, M	
	Parker, W J		223	Vile, T H	73	280	Evans, W H	99
	Scrine, F G		224	Hayward, G	74		Jones, J	
	Skrimshire, R T		225	Hopkins, P	77		Morgan, E	
169	Davies, G	47		Jones, J P			Watts, D	
	Phillips, L A			Morgan, W I			Watts, W J	
	Rees, D			Waller, P D		285	Davies, I T	100
	Thomas, R		229	Bancroft, J	78		Wetter, J J	
	Trew, W J			Blackmore, J H		287	Davies, E F	103
	Williams, W H		231	Baker, A M	79		Fowler, I J	
175	Dobson, G A	48	232	Lloyd, T J	80		Francis, D G	
176	Jones, J	50		Thomas, R			Havard, W T	
177	Gape, R T	52	234	Gronow, B	82		Jones, J	
	Jones, R			Pullman, J J			Morris, W G H	
	Jones, R H		236	Jarman, H	83		Nicholas, T J	
	Owens, R M			Pugsley, J			Parker, E T	
181	Harding, A F	53	238	Jenkins, E	84		Rees, A	
	Jones, D			Morgan W L			Rees, E B	
	Jones, J			Spiller, W			Shea, J	
	Joseph, W		241	Dyke, L M	85		Thomas, B M G	
	Morgan, E		242	Birt, F	86		Whitfield, J J	
	Osborne, W T			Coldrick, A P		300	Beynon, B	104
	Walters, N			Perry, W J			Evans, B S	
188	Jones, H	54	245	Birch, J	87		Jenkins, A E	
189	Jowett, W F	56	246	Evans, W G	89		Jones, C W	
	Travers, G		247	Davies, D E G	90		Morris, S	
191	Arnold, W R	57		Davies, H J			Oliver, G	
192	Winfield, H B	58		Lewis, J M C			Powell, W J	
193	Evans, J W	59		Stephens, G			Rees, J	
	Thomas, D J			Trump, L C			Williams, J	
195	Davies, D H	60		Uzzell, H		309	Williams, B	105
	O'Neil, W		253	Davies, W	91	310	Huxtable, R	106

CAP	PLAYER	MATCH	CAP	PLAYER	MATCH	CAP	PLAYER	MATCH
	Reeves, F C		369	Evans, T D	122		Jones, D	
312	Morgan, D E	107		Gore, J H			Jones, T I	
313	Attewell, S L	108		Hathaway, G F			Jones, W R	
	Edwards, D			Jones, W J		429	Pritchard, C C	138
	Hodder, W			Parker, D S			Skym, A	
	Johnson, T A W			Randall, R J		431	Davies, E G	141
	Jones, M D		375	Finch, E	123	432	Bassett, J A	142
	Ring, J			Jones, J			Jones, H J	
	Winmill, S			Rickards, A R			Jones, R	
320	Bowen, W	109		Stock, A			Morley, J C	
	Evans, F		379	Williams, C	124		Roberts, W	
	Jones, P E R			Williams, E		437	Barrell, R J	143
	Roberts, T		381	Hopkins, W J	125		Bowcott, H M	
324	Davies, H G	110		James, W P			Peacock, H	
	Male, B O			Jones, W I			Williams, F L	
	Williams, T			Phillips, B		441	Lemon, A W	145
327	Baker, A	111		Richards, I		442	Hickman, A	146
	Brown, A			Thomas, C R			Jones-Davies, T E	
	Davies, D H			Williams, E			Roberts, D E A	
	Prosser, F J		388	Herrera, R C	126		Thomas, W T	
331	Cummins, W	112		Lawrence, S D		446	Boon, R W	147
	Delahay, W J		390	Beynon, G E	127		Day, H C	
	Evans, H I			Lewis, W			Jones, G G	
	Hiddlestone, D D		392	Brown, J	128		Thomas, D J	
	Jones, T			Hinam, S		450	Fender, N H	148
	Palmer, F C			John, D A			Jones, E H	
	Richards, W C			Jones, D N R		452	Davey, C	149
	Stephens, J G			Turnbull, B R			Jones, E L	
339	Samuel, T F	113	397	Andrews, G E	129		Scourfield, T B	
340	Cornish, R A	116		Evans, D B		455	Day, T B	150
	Davies, D G			Hopkins, T		456	James, D R	152
	Harding, R			Jenkins, D M			Lang, J	
	Michael, G M			John, J H			Ralph, A R	
	Thomas, S G			Jones, D L		459	Davies, W	154
	Thompson, J F			Jones, R		460	Evans, B	158
346	Jenkins, J L	117		Lewis, T W			Isaacs, I	
347	John, D E	118	405	Everson, W A	130		Jenkins, V G J	
	Pascoe, D			Powell, W C			Jones, A H	
	Williams, M T			Watkins, E			Jones, R B	
350	Collins, T	119	408	Lewis, W H	131		Turnbull, M J L	
	Davies, H S			Rees, T E			Wooller, W	
	Davies, J H			Rowlands, C F		467	Bayliss, G	159
	Powell, J		411	Phillips, H T	133		Evans, D B	
	Radford, W J			Roberts, J			Morris, R R	
	Richards, T L			Thomas, W G		470	Moore, W J	160
356	Davies, D H	120		Williams, W A			Rees, L M	
	Evans, A		415	Arthur, T	134	472	Cowey, B	161
	Jones, I E			Bartlett, J D			Davies, C R	
	Morris, J I T			Jenkins, E M			Evans, D D	
	Ould, W J			Richards, E G			Evans, J R	
	Owen, A D		419	Burns, J	135		Howells, B	
	Pugh, C H			Morgan W G			Hughes, G	
	Thomas, I		421	Bowdler, F A	137		Jones, G R R	
	Watkins, E			Broughton, A S			Jones, K W J	
365	Davies, H J	121		Harris, C A			Jones, W C	
	Evans, J E			Hollingdale, T H			Prosser, I G	
	Griffiths, V M			Jenkins, D R			Rees, A M	

CAP	PLAYER	MATCH	CAP	PLAYER	MATCH	CAP	PLAYER	MATCH
	Rees, J I			Williams, O			Sparks, B A	
	Truman, W H			Williams, S			Thomas, J D	
485	Evans, I	162		Williams, W L T			Williams, R H	
	Fear, A G		543	Davies, C	181	600	Davies, L M	213
	Jones, W H			Davies, G		601	Williams, H R	214
	Prosser, D R			Evans, W J		602	Davies, N G	215
	Ward, W S			Gore, W			Edwards, A B	
490	Bassett, A	163		Tamplin, W E			Wells, G T	
491	Murphy C D	164	548	Evans, R T	183	605	Owen, G D	217
492	Rees, T J	165		Rees, P		606	Williams, C D	218
	Williams, T G		550	Davies, E P	184	607	Brace, D O	219
494	James, T O	166		Greville, H G			Davies, C L	
495	Payne, H	167		Gwilliam, J A			Morgan, H P	
	Tanner, H			James, D M		610	Prosser, T R	220
	Tarr, D J		554	Anthony, L	185	611	Richards, R C	222
	Watkins, E V			Jones, W D			Whitson, G K	
499	Long, E C	168		Trott, R F		613	Howells, W G	223
	McCall, B E W		557	Cale, W R	189		Maddocks, K	
	Thomas, H W			Coleman, E O			O'Connor, R	
	Williams, G M			Hayward, D J		616	Davies, R H	224
503	Davies, W T H	170		Meredith, A			Williams, L H	
504	Clement, W H	171	561	Cook, T	190	618	Davies, C A H	225
	Evans, E		562	Major, W C	192		Faull, J	
	Thomas, D L			Stone, P			Morgan, C H	
507	Hopkin, W H	172		Thomas, M C			Powell, G	
	Rees, H T			Thomas, R C C		622	Collins, J E	227
	Travers, W		566	Brewer, T J	193		Devereux, D B	
510	Bennett, I	173		Davies, D M			Evans, T W	
	Legge, W S G			John, E R			Evans, W R	
	Taylor, A R			Jones, B L			James, C R	
513	McCarley, A	174		Robins, J D		627	Morgan, H J	228
	Morgan F L			Willis, W R		628	Evans, J D	230
	Morgan, M E		572	Williams, G	195		Nicholls, H C W	
	Vickery, W E		573	Evans, P D	197		Priday, A J	
517	Challinor, C	177	574	Forward, A	198		Roberts, C R	
	Davies, D I		575	Edwards, B O	199	632	Ashton, C	232
	Davis, W E N			Morgan, C I			Bebb, D I E	
	Ford, F J V		577	Morris, H T	200		Davies, H J	
	Williams, S A			Williams, W O G			Ford, I R	
522	Davies, C H	178	579	Blythe, L G	201		Leleu, J	
	Davies, L		580	Thomas, A G	202		Main, D R	
	Davies, M J		581	Williams, W A	204		Price, M J	
	Jones, E L		582	Phillips, D H	205	639	Harris, D J E	234
	Manfield, L		583	Beckingham, G T	206	640	Davidge, G D	235
	Price, E R			Burnett, R			Hurrell, R J	
528	Law, V J	179		Davies, T J			Watkins, W R	
	Matthews, C M			Griffiths, G M		643	Cresswell, B R	236
530	Bevan, G W	180		Johnson, W D			Cunningham, L J	
	Blakemore, R E			Judd, S			Evans, C	
	Cleaver, W B		589	Meredith, C C	207		Lewis, G W	
	Evans, G			Robins, R J			Payne, G W	
	Jones, D C J		591	Lloyd, T	208	648	Coles, F G	237
	Jones, K J		592	Rowlands, G	210		Morgan, N H	
	Matthews, J		593	John, G	211	650	Gale, N R	238
	Parsons, G		594	Evans, V	212		Jones, B J	
	Stephens, J R			Jenkins, L H		652	Richards, T B	239
	Williams, B			Meredith, B V		653	Evans, D P	240

CAP	PLAYER	MATCH	CAP	PLAYER	MATCH	CAP	PLAYER	MATCH
	Jones, K D		711	Edwards, G O	270		Squire, J	
	Nash, D			Jones, R E		769r	Evans, G L	316
	O'Connor, A			Morris, W D		770	Williams, C	317
	Richards, K H L		714	Jarrett, K S	271	771	Davies, W G	323
	Roberts, H M		715	Hall, I	272		Williams, D B	
659	Morgan, P E J	241		Hughes, D		773r	Lane, S M	
	Rees, P M			Jeffery, J J		774	Davies, C E	324
661	Britton, G R	242		Jones, W K			Donovan, A J	
662	Price, B	243		Wheeler, P J			Holmes, T D	
	Thomas, D L			Wiltshire, M L		777r	Richardson, S J	
664	Mainwaring, H J	244	721	Gray, A J	273	778	Ringer, P	325
	Pask, A E I			James, J B		779	Rees, H E	326
	Thomas, W J			Wanbon, R		780	Clegg, B G	328
667	Coslett, T K	245	724	Rees, D	274		Richards, D S	
	Jones, D K			Young, J		782	Phillips, A J	329
	Morgan, D R R		726	Jones, I C	275	783r	Griffiths, C R	
	Rees, A			Richards, M C R		784	Butler, E T	330
671	Greenslade, D	246	728	Davies, T M	277		Keen, L	
672	Rowlands, K A	247		Williams, J P R		786r	Morgan, P J	332
673	Davies, D B	248	730r	Bennett, P	279	787	Ackerman, R A	334
	Davies, D J		731	Evans, T G	284		Williams, G P	
	Hodgson, G T R			Llewelyn, D B		789	Lewis, J R	335
	Warlow, D J			Perrins, V C			Nicholas, D L	
677	Hayward, D J	249	734	Daniel, L T D	285		Stephens, I	
	Michaelson, R C B		735r	Hopkins, R	286	792r	Evans, G	336
	Rowlands, D C T		736	Hughes, K	287	793	Pearce, P G	337
	Thomas, B		737	Gallacher, I S	288		Williams, G	
	Watkins, D			Lewis, A J L		795	Daniels, P C T	339
	Williams, D			Mathias, R			Davies, M	
683	Evans, R	250		Shanklin, J L			Moriarty, R D	
	Jones, G		741	Bevan, J C	289	798	Sutton, S	341
	Morris, W J B			Roberts, M G		799	Norster, R L	343
686	Norris, C H	252	743	Bergiers, R T E	293	800	Dacey, M	344
687	Thomas, A R F	253	744r	Quinnell, D L	295		James, W J	
	Uzzell, J		745	Shaw, G	296		Pickering, D F	
689	Bradshaw, K	254	746	Llewellyn, P D	299		Ring, M G	
	Mantle, J		747	David, T	300		Wyatt, M A	
	Weaver, D S		748r	Williams, J J		805	Eidman, I H	345
692	Prothero, G J	255	749	Martin, A J	301		Jones, S T	
	Watkins, S J			Windsor, R W			Perkins, S J	
694	Dawes, S J	256	751r	Shell, R C		808r	Donovan, R E	347
695	Price, T G	259	752	Cobner, T J	302	809	Bowen, B	348
	Waldron, R G		752	Finlayson, A A J	303		Brown, M A	
697	Morris, W J	260		Rees, C F W			Giles, R	
698	Davies, L	263		Wheel, G A			Hadley, A M	
	Lewis, R A			Williams, W J			Shaw, T W	
	Lloyd, D J		757	Robinson, I R	304		Titley, M H	
701	Braddock, K J	267	758	Blyth, W R	306	815	Davies, H	349
	Davies, T G R		759	Bevan, J D	307		Douglas, M H J	
	John, B			Evans, T P			Morgan, G R	
	Thomas, W D			Faulkner, A G		818	Watkins, M J	350
705	Hullin, W G	268		Fenwick, S P		819	Bishop, D J	353
	Mainwaring, G T			Gravell, R W R			Davies, A E	
	O'Shea, J P			Price, G			Lewis, P I	
	Raybould, W H		765r	Knill, F M D	314	822r	Whitefoot, J	
	Rees, B I		766	Burcher, D H	315	823	Morris, M S	354
	Taylor, J			Burgess, R C		824	Evans, S	356

CAP	PLAYER	MATCH	CAP	PLAYER	MATCH	CAP	PLAYER	MATCH
	Thorburn, P H		849	May, P S	377	873	Bateman, A G	392
826r	Roberts, G J		850r	Watkins, I J			Perego, M A	
827	Davies, J	357	851	Bryant, D J	381		Williams, B R	
	Davies, P T		852r	Fauvel, T J		876	Ford, S P	393
	Hopkins, K		853r	Hall, M R		877r	Edmunds, D A	
830	Devereux, J A	359	854	Davies, N G	382	878	Arnold, P	394
	Jones, R N			Griffiths, J L			Bridges, C J	
	Waters, D R			Jones, G			Knight, P	
833	Moriarty, W P	361	857r	Moseley, K			Llewellyn, G D	
834r	Webbe, G M C	364	858r	Mason, J E			Reynolds, A D	
835r	Richards, H D		859	Davies, C	383	883r	Parfitt, S A	
836	Evans, I C	366		Griffiths, M		884	Williams, O L	395
	Phillips, K H			Hall, W H		885r	Williams, D A	
838r	Collins, R G	367		Wakeford, J D M		886r	Davies, A	396
839	Francis, P W	368	863r	Wintle, R V		887	Carter, A J	397
	Jones, M A		864	Diplock, R S	384		George, G M	
841	Blackmore, S W	369	865r	Williams-Jones, H	385		Gibbs, I S	
842	Buchanan, D A	371	866	Delaney, L	386		Jenkins, N R	
843	Young, D	373	867r	Turner, P		891	Davies, J D	399
844	Webster, R E	375	868	Evans, D W	387		Lewis, E W	
845	Phillips, R D	376	869	Jones, A E	388			
	Pugh, J D		870	Llewellyn, G O	389			
	Russell, S			Pugh, P				
848r	Clement, A		872	Allen, A G	390			

SELECT BIBLIOGRAPHY

Newspapers

Cambria Daily Leader
Evening Express
Glamorgan Gazette
Monmouthshire Free Press
South Wales Argus
South Wales Daily Post
South Wales Evening Post
Sporting News
Sporting Post
Western Mail

Books

i) Reference:

Abrahams, H M and J Bruce-Kerr (compilers). *Oxford versus Cambridge. A Record of Inter-University Contests from 1827-1930*. London: Faber and Faber, 1931.
The Calendar of the University of Wales..
Carey, G V (editor). *The War List of the University of Cambridge 1914-1918*. Cambridge: The University Press, 1921.
Craig, E S (editor) and W M Gibson. *Oxford University Roll of Service*. Oxford: Clarendon Press, 1920.
Crockford's Clerical Directory.
The Dictionary of Welsh Biography. London: The Honourable Society of Cymmrodorion, 1959.
Foster, Joseph. *Alumni Oxonienses, 1715-1886*. Oxford: Parker & Co., 1888.
The Medical Register. London: General Medical Council.
Venn, John and J A Venn. *Alumni Cantabrigienses, 1752-1900*. Cambridge: The University Press, 1940-1954.

ii) Rugby:

Chester, R H and N A C McMillan. *The Visitors. The History of International Rugby Teams in New Zealand*. Auckland: MOA Publications, 1990.
de Lissa, Emile (compiler). *Barbarian Records. A complete record of the Barbarian Football Club 1890-1932*. London: Ivor Nicholson & Watson, 1933.
Gate, Robert. *Gone North*. Halifax: The Author, 1986 & 1988. Volumes I and 2.
Griffiths, John. *British Lions*. Swindon: The Crowood Press, 1990.
Griffiths, John. *The Phoenix Book of International Rugby Records*. London: Phoenix House/Dent, 1987.
James, Royston (editor). *Can Llwyddiant!* Swansea: Christopher Davies, 1981.
Marshall, Howard. *Oxford v Cambridge. The story of the University Rugby Match*. London: Clerke & Cockeran, 1951.
McLaren, John. *The History of Army Rugby*. Aldershot: The Army RFU, 1986.
McWhirter, Ross and Sir Andrew Noble. *Centenary History of the Oxford University Rugby Football Club*. Oxford: The University Rugby Football Club, 1969.
Smith, David and Gareth Williams. *Fields of Praise. The Official History of the Welsh Rugby Union. 1881-1981*. Cardiff: University of Wales Press, 1980.

iii) Annuals and Periodicals:

Playfair Rugby Annual
Rothmans Rugby [Union] Year Book
Rothmans Rugby League Year Book
Welsh Brewers Rugby Annual for Wales